International Political Economy Series

Series Editor

Timothy M. Shaw, University of Massachusetts Boston, Boston, MA, USA ;
Emeritus Professor, University of London, London, UK

The global political economy is in flux as a series of cumulative crises impacts its organization and governance. The IPE series has tracked its development in both analysis and structure over the last three decades. It has always had a concentration on the global South. Now the South increasingly challenges the North as the centre of development, also reflected in a growing number of submissions and publications on indebted Eurozone economies in Southern Europe. An indispensable resource for scholars and researchers, the series examines a variety of capitalisms and connections by focusing on emerging economies, companies and sectors, debates and policies. It informs diverse policy communities as the established trans-Atlantic North declines and 'the rest', especially the BRICS, rise.

NOW INDEXED ON SCOPUS!

Tim Zajontz

The Political Economy of China's Infrastructure Development in Africa

Capital, State Agency, Debt

palgrave
macmillan

Tim Zajontz
University of Freiburg
and Stellenbosch University
Freiburg, Germany

ISSN 2662-2483 ISSN 2662-2491 (electronic)
International Political Economy Series
ISBN 978-3-031-44448-7 ISBN 978-3-031-44449-4 (eBook)
https://doi.org/10.1007/978-3-031-44449-4

Cover credit: Rob Friedman/Stockphoto.com

This Palgrave Macmillan imprint is published by the registered company Springer Nature Switzerland AG
The registered company address is: Gewerbestrasse 11, 6330 Cham, Switzerland

This books is dedicated to
Professor Ian Taylor
who left us too early

Acknowledgements

This book is based on my Ph.D. research which I conducted between 2015 and 2020 in the School of International Relations at the University of St Andrews. I owe thanks to my supervisor Ian Taylor who sadly passed away in early 2021. I learned a lot from this incredibly knowledgeable man. Ian's authoritative and impressive body of work, his firm political beliefs as well as his humour and humility were inspiring, as the combination of these qualities is rare in our industry. I am grateful for having had the chance to get to know Ian, and I sorely miss him—as so many others do. I also want to thank Vassilios Paipais for his thoughts in the early stages of my research. Needless to say, the countless shortcomings of this study are my sole responsibility.

I am deeply indebted to my interviewees and informants for spending an hour, and sometimes much longer, to share their insights, opinions, contacts and expertise with me. Their contribution to this study is immeasurable.

Palgrave's International Political Economy series has been a great source of knowledge for me over the years. Therefore I am grateful to Timothy Shaw, Anca Pusca, Uma Vinesh and their team for publishing my work in this series. I also want to thank two anonymous reviewers for their helpful comments and suggestions.

I owe special thanks to Louise, Anna and David, Maisha and Kate as well as Patricia and Tellan for hosting me during my research stays. Thanks to Daniel Stephen from the University of Dar es Salaam for opening doors to important offices and for the quality time we spent together.

My studies would have been unthinkable without the Ph.D. scholarship I received from the Friedrich Ebert Foundation (FES). I am immensely grateful for it and for the personal support that I got from Ursula Bitzegeio and Simone Stöhr from the FES. I also appreciate the organisational assistance that I received from the FES offices in Lusaka and Dar es Salaam during my research stays. Equally, I am thankful for a Ph.D. studentship and fieldwork funding from the Economic and Social Research Council, for a mobility award from the University of St Andrew's Russell Trust as well as for a Postgraduate Research Fieldwork Bursary from the University of St Andrews and travel funds from the School of International Relations.

I am deeply grateful for the company of my fellow Ph.D. travellers. Without our conversations, lunch and cigarette breaks, coffee dates, parties, walks and pints, this journey would have been significantly less fun and certainly much lonelier. I also want to thank my other friends for bearing with me and for making me forget about my research whenever we reunited.

My gratitude for the support from my parents, Elisabeth and Peter, and my sister, Tamara, cannot be expressed in words.

Freiburg
July 2023

Tim Zajontz

Contents

1	**Introduction**	1
	The Infrastructure-Debt Nexus	4
	Chinese Capital Encounters African Infrastructure States	7
	The "African Agency Turn" in Africa–China Studies	12
	Critical Realist Research	17
	Methodology and Case Selection	22
	Research Techniques and Data Collection	24
	Positionality and Limitations of the Study	27
	Structure of the Book	28
	List of Interview	30
	References	30
2	**Chinese Capital and Its Spatio-Temporal Fix**	43
	Overaccumulation and China's Spatio-Temporal Fix	44
	The Function of Debt Finance and Accumulation by Dispossession	50
	The Chinese Infrastructural Fix in Africa	54
	The Under-Theorised Politics of the "Fix"	60
	References	65
3	**Theorising African State Agency**	71
	African State Agency in Sino-African Relations	72
	On the (Un)Usefulness of the Neopatrimonial "Moniker"	76
	Neopatrimonialism as a Mode of Accumulation	81

The Strategic-Relational Approach 85
The State as a Strategic-Relational Domain 89
Towards a Strategic-Relational Analysis of China's Infrastructure Development in Africa 93
References 101

4 The Destiny of the Freedom Railway: From Anti-imperialism to Accumulation by Dispossession? 111
The Monumental Rise and Steady Decline of the "Freedom Railway" 113
"The Uhuru Line Will Fight Imperialism": The Chinese Rescue and Its Legacy 117
The Devaluation of a Monument 120
China's Failed Attempt at a "Not so Friendly" Takeover 125
The 2016 Tripartite Negotiations 126
The Chinese Infrastructural Fix at an Impasse 131
The Path-Dependency of Railway Concession "Traumata" 133
Tanzania's Strategic Learning from a "Case of Failed Privatization" 134
Zambia's Private Railway Odyssey 138
Conclusion 140
List of Interviews 142
References 143

5 Divergent State Agency: Zambia's Debt Impasse and Magufuli's Nationalist Infrastructure State 151
TAZARA—"A Drain on Zambia's Coffers" 153
Railway Privatisation as a Potential Source of Rents? 157
From Neopatrimonialism to Autocratic Developmentalism: State Transformation under Magufuli 160
The Rise of Tanzania's Nationalist Infrastructure State 166
Scrutinising "Win–Win" Cooperation in the Freedom Railway 169
"Fixing" TAZARA on Tanzanian Terms 174
The Bagamoyo Controversy 178
The Standard Gauge Railway: From Confrontation to Pragmatism 181
Conclusion 184
List of Interviews 187
References 187

6 The Price of the Sino-Zambian "Road Bonanza" 195
Build Now, Pay Later: The Costly Ambition of a "Land-Linked Zambia" 196
Loan Financing with Chinese Characteristics 200
The Price of Chinese Road Investment 204
The Renaissance of Public–Private Partnerships 208
Accumulating by dispossessing Zambian roads 213
The Commodification of Zambia's Roads 217
Conclusion 221
List of Interviews 223
References 223

7 The Political Economy of "Not so Public" Procurement 233
Zambia's Neopatrimonial Infrastructure State 234
"Not so Public" Procurement as a Win-Win-Lose Strategy 238
Seeking rents from roads 241
In Search of "Local Content": Zambianising Chinese Circuits of Capital 241
Subcontracting as (In)formal "Trickle-Down" Strategy 244
The Lusaka-Ndola Dual Carriageway 249
A Case of "Not so Public" Procurement 251
The Fallacy of Project Finance at No Cost 254
Conclusion 257
List of Interviews 259
References 260

8 Towards a "New Era" of Sino-African Infrastructure Cooperation 267
African State Agency Matters—Yet It Matters Differentially 268
Debt and the Renaissance of PPPs 270
The "Fragility" of the "Fix" and the Regional Dimension 274
References 276

Appendix 281

List of Interviews 285

Index 329

Abbreviations and Acronyms

AfDB	African Development Bank
ANRCP	Accelerated National Roads Construction Programme
AU	African Union
BOT	Build-Operate-Transfer (contract)
BRI	Belt and Road Initiative
CARI	China Africa Research Initiative (at Johns Hopkins University)
CCECC	China Civil Engineering Construction Corporation
CCM	Chama Cha Mapinduzi (Party of the Revolution)
CEO	Chief Executive Officer
CHADEMA	Chama Cha Demokrasia na Maendeleo (Party of Democracy and Development)
CJIC	China Jiangxi Corporation for International Economic and Technical Cooperation
CMHI	China Merchants Holdings International
CR	Critical Realism
CRCC	China Railway Construction Corporation
CRET	Chinese Railway Expert Team
CTPD	Centre for Trade Policy and Development
DFBOT	Design-Finance-Build-Operate-Transfer
DRC	Democratic Republic of Congo
EPC	Engineering-Procurement-Construction (contract)
EPC+F	Engineering-Procurement-Construction + Finance (contract)
Exim Bank	Export-Import Bank
FDCOMT	Finance-Design-Construct-Operate-Maintain-Toll (contract)
FDI	Foreign Direct Investment
FOCAC	Forum on China–Africa Cooperation

G20	Group of 20
G7	Group of 7
GDP	Gross Domestic Product
GRZ	Government of the Republic of Zambia
GURT	Government of the United Republic of Tanzania
ICA	Infrastructure Consortium for Africa
ICT	Information and Communication Technology
IFI	International financial institution
IMF	International Monetary Fund
IPE	International Political Economy
IR	International Relations
MMD	Movement for Multi-Party Democracy
MTC	Ministry of Transport and Communications (Zambia)
MWTC	Ministry of Works, Transport and Communications (Tanzania)
NCC	National Construction Council
NEPAD	New Partnership for Africa's Development
NLPI	New Limpopo Bridge Projects Investments
OPP	Office of the Public Protector
PF	Patriotic Front
PPP	Public–Private Partnership
RAHCO	Reli Assets Holding Company
RDA	Road Development Agency
RITES	Rail India Technical and Economic Services
ROT	Rehabilitate-Operate-Transfer (contract)
RSZ	Railway Systems of Zambia
SGR	Standard Gauge Railway
SOB	State-Owned Bank
SOE	State-Owned Enterprise
SPV	Special Purpose Vehicle
SRA	Strategic-Relational Approach
TAZARA	Tanzania–Zambia Railway Authority
TCFPA	Tanzania China Friendship Promotion Association
TMSA	Transformational Model of Social Activity
TPA	Tanzania Ports Authority
TRC	Tanzania Railways Corporation
TRL	Tanzania Railways Limited
TSDI	Third Railway Survey and Design Institute Group Corporation
TSh	Tanzanian Shilling
UDI	Unilateral Declaration of Independence (Rhodesia)
UN	United Nations
UPND	United Party for National Development
ZCCM	Zambia Consolidated Copper Mines
ZDA	Zambian Development Agency
ZESCO	Zambia Electricity Supply Corporation
ZMK	Zambian Kwacha
ZRL	Zambia Railways Limited

List of Figures

Fig. 2.1	Chinese loan commitments to Africa by year, 2000–2020	59
Fig. 2.2	Chinese loans to Africa by sector, 2000–2020	60
Fig. 4.1	TAZARA route map	114
Fig. 4.2	Cargo conveyed by TAZARA, 1976–2019	118
Fig. 5.1	Tanzania's and Zambia's external debt (% of GDP), 2009–2019	152
Fig. 5.2	Perceived levels of public sector corruption in Zambia and Tanzania	159
Fig. 5.3	Construction phases of Tanzania's Standard Gauge Railway	183
Fig. 7.1	President Edgar Lungu at a groundbreaking ceremony for a Chinese road project in Zambia's Northern Province, 11 August 2017	234
Fig. 7.2	Route of the Lusaka-Ndola dual carriageway	250

List of Tables

Table 5.1	Projected domestic revenue in Tanzania's public budget	168
Table 6.1	Major road construction projects with Chinese participation commenced in the 2010s	199
Table 6.2	Zambia's external debt, 2015–2019	206
Table A.1	Funding commitments for African infrastructure by source (in $m)	282
Table A.2	Chinese-owned companies registered with the Zambian National Construction Council in grade 1, category R - general roads and earthworks (as at 30 June 2018)	283
Table A.3	Toll structure for Zambia-registered vehicles	284

CHAPTER 1

Introduction

In November 2021, the Chinese State Council published a White Paper on the country's relations with Africa with the title "China and Africa in the New Era: A Partnership of Equals". The document explicitly lauds "China [for having] helped African countries build more than 13,000 km of roads and railway and more than 80 large-scale power facilities" between 2000 and 2020 (State Council 2021). In the course of the 2010s, cooperation in developing infrastructures across the continent has moved to the centre of Sino-African relations and "infrastructure" and "connectivity" have become buzzwords in bilateral Sino-African relations, in the context of Beijing's engagements with African regional organisations as well as within the Forum on China–Africa Cooperation (FOCAC). Further fostered by Africa's gradual inclusion into China's Belt and Road Initiative (BRI) (see Carmody et al. 2020: 178–79; Large 2021: 27–28; Mboya 2021; van der Merwe 2019; Mthembu 2020), Sino-African cooperation in the infrastructure sector has been discursively framed as a driver of economic development that yields "mutual benefits" and "win–win results", as excerpts from the Beijing Declaration adopted by the 2018 FOCAC summit vividly exemplify:

> We applaud that, under the Belt and Road Initiative, the principle of extensive consultation, joint contribution and shared benefits is observed;

T. Zajontz, *The Political Economy of China's Infrastructure Development in Africa*, International Political Economy Series,
https://doi.org/10.1007/978-3-031-44449-4_1

> market principles and international norms are followed; openness, transparency, and win-win results are advocated and practiced; efforts are made to develop inclusive, accessible and reasonably priced infrastructure that delivers extensive benefits and are consistent with the national conditions and laws and regulations of related countries, with a view to promoting high-quality and sustainable development for all. [...] [G]reater cooperation in the planning of African infrastructure and industrial development will lend new impetus to the win-win cooperation and common development between China and Africa. [...] China supports African countries in enhancing connectivity, infrastructure development and industrialization. (FOCAC 2018: Paragraphs 4.1, 4.2, 13.2)

Overseas infrastructure development and inter-regional connectivity, epitomised by the BRI, are now central to what Breslin (2021: 113) aptly calls China's global "[a]symmetric benevolent developmentalism". As such, they are a means of overseas power projection for the Chinese state and the Communist Party (Yan 2021; Zajontz et al. 2024).

Chinese state-owned enterprises (SOEs), policy banks and private firms have gotten increasingly involved in the financing, construction, rehabilitation and, in some cases, operation of African ports, railways, highways, airports, pipelines, power plants and information and communication technology (ICT). Chinese construction firms have become market leaders in many African markets. A 2017 McKinsey report attests that Chinese firms won about half of all international Engineering-Procurement-Construction (EPC) contracts and, by value, 42 per cent of World Bank tenders in so-called Sub-Saharan Africa (Sun et al. 2017: 39). Growing Chinese interest in Africa's infrastructure sector over the past 15 years has offset the decline in infrastructure investment following the global economic crisis of 2007–2008 and has provided a major source to fill Africa's frequently invoked "infrastructure investment gap" (Nugent 2018: 25).

The African Development Bank (AfDB) estimates Africa's infrastructure financing gap at $68–108bn per annum (AfDB 2018: 63). Indeed, Africa's infrastructure still trails behind in global comparison, itself a long-term legacy of colonial spatial planning and exploitation. In 2013, Africa had a density of paved roads of 2 km per 100 sq. km of land area, compared to Latin America (3 km), Asia (25 km) and Europe (122 km) (AfDB 2018: 76). According to World Bank statistics, only 50.6 per cent of people in "Sub-Saharan Africa" had access to electricity in 2021, compared to 96.8 per cent of the population in the Middle East and

North Africa, 98.2 per cent in East Asia and the Pacific, 98.3 per cent in Latin America and the Caribbean and 100 per cent in both Europe and North America (World Bank, n.d.). Access to safely managed drinking water and sanitation services remains severely restricted in many parts of Africa (UNICEF and WHO 2019: 7–8). And Africa's ICT infrastructure also remains underdeveloped, as about 300 million Africans live more than 50 kilometres away from a fibre or cable broadband (OECD and ACET 2020: 12).

Unsurprisingly, China has been welcomed by national governments and regional organisations alike as a strategic partner in attaining long-standing development goals by improving the continent's infrastructure, not least because Western governments and international financial institutions (IFIs) have shunned state-led infrastructure development during the heyday of the Washington Consensus in the 1980s and 1990s. Scholars have pointed to synergies that may arise between China's BRI and regional infrastructure programmes which often have remained stuck at the planning stage for lack of funding (see Lisinge 2020; Vhumbunu 2016). After all, it is one of the declared goals of the Agenda 2063 of the African Union (AU) to "[c]onnect Africa with world-class infrastructure" (African Union 2015).

Notwithstanding official narratives about "win–win cooperation" (hézuò gòngyíng; 合作共赢) that Chinese projects are said to afford, China's involvement in the contemporary transformation of Africa's infrastructural spaces has also caused controversies—both in academic and political debates. Some scholars have argued that the geographical patterns of Chinese infrastructure projects in Africa resemble colonial spatial strategies and have reinforced racialised space-making in Africa, resulting in highly unequal and exclusionary effects for host country populations (see, for instance, Kimari and Ernstson 2020; Lesutis 2021; Otiso and Carmody 2024). From a macro-analytical perspective, van der Merwe asserts with respect to the BRI's impact on Africa and the Middle East that

> [t]he infrastructure plans expose the initiative [BRI] as unashamedly colonial, as it reinforces the legacy of transporting resources towards ports—and not between neighbouring states. Even in the case where transport infrastructure is created between states, the assumption is still that this would facilitate the movement of Chinese remotely manufactured goods onto markets. (2019: 210)

The distribution of costs and benefits from Chinese-funded infrastructure has remained a contentious issue. Chinese loan finance for African infrastructure projects has attracted even more public attention and academic scrutiny. At best mixed developmental impacts and significant economic risks were found with respect to infrastructure-for-resources agreements, entered, for example, by the Angolan and Congolese governments with Chinese banks and firms (see Alves 2013; Landry 2018). Mboya (2021: 71) argues that the BRI in Africa, "despite offering participant countries opportunities to bridge their infrastructure gaps and moving Africa's interregional connectivity up the agenda, the balance of gains is still heavily tilted toward China". By far the most controversies however, both in Africa and other parts of the world, have surrounded China's supposed "debt trap diplomacy" (Chellaney 2017) in relation to overseas lending from Chinese policy banks.

This introduction will proceed by outlining the main themes covered in this book, starting with said controversy around sovereign debt incurred for infrastructure. It will move on to contextualise Sino-African cooperation within the growing globalisation of Chinese capital and the emergence of the infrastructure-led development paradigm. The introduction subsequently engages with the growing body of literature on African agency in Sino-African relations and argues that a social relational ontology of the state is required to assess African state agency in Sino-African infrastructure encounters. This is followed by a brief outline of the critical realist philosophy of science which has informed my research, some methodological considerations and an outline of how the book is structured.

The Infrastructure-Debt Nexus

Chinese lending practices have been politically instrumentalised in Western capitals to discredit Chinese engagements with Africa and other regions in the "Global South" (see Bräutigam 2020). Breslin argues that the "debt trap" narrative has served to resurrect the long-standing racialised theme of a "China threat" (Breslin 2021: 229). At a press conference during a visit by British Prime Minister Rishi Sunak in June 2023, United States (US) President Joe Biden again reinforced the narrative when stating that China's "Belt and Road Initiative turns out to be a debt and confiscation program. Not going very far" (quoted in White House 2023). Amidst intensifying competition between China and "the West", Chinese-owned debt has developed into a geopolitical matter (Carmody and Wainwright 2022; Large 2021: 98; Gort and Brooks 2023).

There have been commendable research efforts to rationalise the highly politicised "debt trap" narrative by providing more reliable data on Chinese lending (see, for instance, Brautigam and Acker 2021; Gelpern et al. 2021; Horn et al. 2019). Scholars with different theoretical backgrounds agree that there is little substance to the politicised claim that China has intentionally "entrapped" countries in the "Global South" in unserviceable amounts of debt (see, for instance, Bräutigam 2020; Carmody 2020; Jones and Hameiri 2020; Zajontz 2022a). In fact, Chinese lenders have, in light of the COVID-19 pandemic, been lenient by agreeing to reschedule debt and by forgiving matured, zero-interest debt on an ad hoc basis (Brautigam 2020). Contrary to President Biden's rhetorical insinuation that China might force insolvent sovereign debtors into debt-for-equity swaps, Chinese lenders have hitherto also refrained from asset seizures, not least because such measures would further intensify the political backlash that Chinese-owned debt has caused in some countries, including in Kenya and Zambia.

The ongoing political debates around Chinese-owned debt, much of it expended on infrastructure, warrants critical examinations of structural ramifications and contradictions that sprung from China's "moving out" of surplus capital to Africa. As the Chinese leadership is still busy finding ways to deal with the country's role as the world's largest bilateral creditor, research must avoid reducing debt to the discourse about it. Debt is foremost a material relationship. One which is marked by asymmetry and which incurs obligations. A statement by Chinese Foreign Minister, Wang Yi, during his visit to Kinshasa in January 2021, during which China agreed to cancel maturing, zero-interest debt worth about $28m, is indicative of how (geo)political and financial matters intertwine, as Wang "believe[d] that the Congolese side will continue to give China understanding and support on issues involving China's core interests" (quoted in Nyabiage 2021). The statement indicates that China could have significant geopolitical leverage over countries that are heavily indebted to Chinese banks.

It is primarily the asymmetry inherent to the debt relationship and resultant power differentials—not only the politicised "debt trap" narrative, flawed and problematic as it is—that have made it increasingly difficult for the Chinese government to sustain official narratives that suggest the horizontality of relations between China and countries in the "Global South". Chinese (state) capital is now central to the global circuit of capital and, just like other capital, invests in debt in Africa and elsewhere with the intention to create a surplus. A nascent shift in the governance of Sino-African infrastructure projects from the public to the private realm is but one result of the growing debt dependency of African states vis-à-vis China (and other creditors) and leaves us wondering whether we are witnessing the history of sovereign debt crises and of ensuing privatisation waves of the 1980s and 1990s repeating itself (see Alden and Jiang 2019; Gort and Brooks 2023; van Wieringen and Zajontz 2023; Zajontz 2022a). China's new role as the world's largest bilateral creditor has affected Sino-African relations, especially with those countries that currently renegotiate their debt with a diverse set of creditors, including multilateral institutions, Paris Club creditors, the International Monetary Fund (IMF) and China, within the Common Framework set up by the Group of 20 (G20) (see Bagwandeen, Edyegu, and Otele 2023; Lippolis and Verhoeven 2022).

Not dissimilar from other foreign investments on the continent, Chinese endeavours in Africa's infrastructure sectors have been profit-seeking, even though official narratives might suggest more altruistic motives. They are the result of wider adjustments within, and a major spatial reorganisation of, the Chinese economy (Breslin 2021: Ch.4; Carmody et al. 2022a; Sum 2019; Taylor and Zajontz 2020). As such, they signify structural tendencies and contradictions inherent to capitalism and, hence, call for critical analyses as to how such tendencies have materialised in concrete political-economic contexts—something this book aspires to do. Alden and Large underscore the analytical value of contributions emanating from critical Global Political Economy which have questioned the uniqueness of Chinese investment patterns in Africa and demonstrate that China's economic engagement with the continent "reflects qualities and political relations and patterns of exploitation generally familiar to the global behaviour of capital" (Alden and Large 2019b: 11–12; see, for example, Carmody 2011; Lee 2014, 2017; Li and Farah 2013; Taylor 2014). Mohan (2013: 1260) is right in stressing that "the Chinese firms central to its internationalisation are capitalist, thus we have to acknowledge the accumulation imperative in any relationship with African actors". Therefore, Africa's Chinese-funded infrastructure boom throughout the 2010s cannot be adequately assessed without considering its main structural driver, namely chronic overaccumulation problems within China's domestic economy.

Chinese Capital Encounters African Infrastructure States

China's rise to become a powerhouse in the global economy has catalysed an immense body of literature which provides profound insights into the internal dynamics related to the country's transition towards a dirigiste market economy and into the characteristics and contradictions of what has been creatively termed "Sino-capitalism" (McNally 2012), "state neoliberalism" (Chu and So 2010), "state capitalism 3.0" (see Gu et al. 2016; Nölke 2014), "state-permeated capitalism" (Nölke et al. 2020: Ch. 2) or "party-state capitalism" (Pearson et al. 2021). The contemporary spatial reorganisation of the Chinese accumulation system and related state spatial projects, notably the BRI, has equally produced a rapidly growing body of literature (see, for instance, Cai 2018; Jones and Zeng 2019; Li 2019; Liu and Dunford 2016; Mthembu 2020; Sum 2019; Taylor and Zajontz 2020; Zhang 2017). Indeed, China's second "going out" phase has arguably constituted one of the most significant developments in the contemporary (spatial) reorganisation of global capitalism (Ayers 2013: 238; Mohan 2013: 1260).

A central argument advanced in this book is that Chinese investments in African infrastructure (and other) sectors have been driven by chronic overaccumulation crises within the Chinese economy. China's construction and infrastructure sectors had been particularly affected by dwindling domestic demand in the aftermath of the global economic crisis, leaving the country's gigantic state-owned construction conglomerates short of projects and suppliers with oversupplies of construction materials (Sum 2019: 531–32). China's contemporary attempt to geographically relocate surplus capacities within and beyond its borders has been a reaction to this mounting overaccumulation. Slumping exports, bankruptcies, growing unemployment, social unrest and deteriorating values of foreign exchange reserves challenged China's growth model and the "performance legitimacy" of the Communist Party (Sum 2019: 530–31; see Cai 2018; Hung 2022: 30; Lee 2014; Zhang 2017). As I will discuss in greater detail in Chapter 2 of this book, the Chinese government has since embarked on a major (spatial) reorganisation of its growth model to address overaccumulation in various sectors of the country's economy by globalising Chinese capital. The BRI has become the material, discursive and semiotic centrepiece of these efforts. The total value of projects with the "Belt and Road" label on them was estimated to have reached $838bn by the end of 2021 (Kynge et al. 2022). Eighty-nine per cent of contractors implementing Chinese-funded BRI projects were Chinese firms using Chinese materials, whereas only 7.6 per cent were local companies in host countries and 3.4 per cent non-Chinese foreign firms (Hung 2022: 48).

The BRI attempts to consolidate a "China-oriented infrastructural mode of growth in production, finance and security" (Sum 2019: 529; see Alden and Large 2019a; Li 2016). This is achieved by shifting overcapacities abroad by a combination of spatially expanding the Chinese accumulation system and "recycling" capital that lacks profitable outlets within existing capital circuits (Zhang 2017: 322; see Summers 2016). In *The Anti-Capitalist Chronicles*, Harvey himself describes China's contemporary spatial fix as follows:

> China becomes an aggressive net exporter of capital. Most of the export takes the form of commercial credit rather than as direct investment in production. China is supplying commercial credit to East Africa to absorb China's surplus product (e.g. steel rails). In 2000, the map of China's capital exports was essentially blank. But by 2015, Chinese surplus capital is all over the place. The whole world is being caught up in China's surplus capital. The Chinese start to orchestrate this around [...] the 'Belt and Road Initiative,' which is a geopolitical expansion plan in which surplus capital from China is allocated to rebuild the transport and communications connectivity of the Eurasian continent, with offshoots across Africa and into Latin America. (Harvey 2020: 92)

As will be elaborated on in this book, Chinese infrastructure development in Africa has been fuelled by "loan-debt investment" (Sum 2019: 539) facilitated by Chinese policy banks, especially by the Export–Import Bank of China (EXIM) and China Development Bank but also by other financial institutions. According to figures from the Infrastructure Consortium for Africa (ICA), infrastructure finance in Africa totalled $100.8bn in 2018. China contributed about a fourth thereof (ICA 2018b: 7). Between 2011 and 2017, an annual average of $13bn for African infrastructure projects originated from China (ICA 2018a: 54). Indeed, Chinese bilateral infrastructure funding for Africa has significantly dropped from a peak in 2018 ($25.7bn) to $6.5bn in 2020

(ICA 2022: 92), mostly due to debt sustainability concerns and resultant, more restrictive lending practices as well as a shift in the financial governance of the BRI towards equity investments (see Carmody et al. 2022b; van Wieringen and Zajontz 2023). Nonetheless, Beijing has remained the largest bilateral infrastructure financier by far (see Table A.1 in the Appendix). The fact that all loans and credit lines for Chinese infrastructure projects were duly signed by African state actors necessitates analytical scrutiny towards African state agencies. Even beyond the question of funding, African governments are pivotal actors in planning, negotiating, appraising and implementing infrastructure projects. Nonetheless, only recently scholars have started to question "what role elite agency in recipient states plays in shaping the outcomes" of Chinese infrastructure projects (Mohan and Tan-Mullins 2019: 1370).

There has been intriguing research which directs analytical attention towards states and societies in world regions that have received growing infrastructure investments, from China and elsewhere, in recent times. The political renaissance of large-scale infrastructure in development and spatial planning has given rise to what Schindler, DiCarlo and Paudel call the "21st-century infrastructure state" (see Schindler and DiCarlo 2022; Schindler et al. 2022). DiCarlo and Schindler (2022: 5) suggest that "contemporary infrastructure states seek to mobilise foreign capital for spatial projects that often promise to enhance transnational connectivity, with the hope that this will lead to foreign investment, industrial upgrading, and export-oriented economic growth". This points to the agency of social, political and economic forces that, collectively, make up the infrastructure state in the planning and implementation of foreign-financed infrastructure development in their countries/regions. Indeed, the growing influx of foreign capital in large-scale infrastructure and connectivity projects has boosted the "infrastructural power" of African states, viz. the "power of the state to penetrate and centrally coordinate the activities of civil society" (Mann 1984: 188). While regional economic communities (RECs) and the AU have become important interlocutors in the infrastructure realm and have set up decidedly regional infrastructure plans and programmes to coordinate cross-border and regional projects (see Zajontz 2022b), infrastructural power has remained highly concentrated in the offices of national governments which, have commonly used foreign capital for infrastructure development to bolster their own political authority and/or electoral success. There is now a growing body of literature which engages with the question as to how Chinese infrastructure projects interact with host country politics (see Chiyemura et al. 2023; Lesutis 2022; Wang 2022).

The infrastructure state has evidently existed in various "incarnations" across Africa—pre, during and post-colonially. In pre-colonial times, polities mobilised collective resources towards, for instance, consolidating regional trade routes and centres as well as connecting certain communities (usually based on kinship and/or economic ties), while shielding from others. The violent and racialised colonial infrastructure state in turn—in variegated forms—served both the occupation and control of territories and people as well as the facilitation of movements of goods, people and information. The infrastructural activities and geographies of colonial states were geared to geographically specific, trans-regional colonial economies and thoroughly integrated into the spatial logics of European empires (see Middell 2019: 38–42; Nabudere 1981; Zajontz 2022c). The fight for independence therefore also implied overcoming the colonial infrastructure state. As will be discussed in Chapter 4 of this book, the construction of the Tanzania–Zambia Railway aimed at removing extant colonial incarnations of the infrastructure state and related racialised regional political economies. The early post-independence infrastructure state was informed by state spatial strategies that aimed at climbing the (presumed modernist) ladder of economic development. Building (mostly big) "hard" infrastructure became integral to nation-building and related economic development plans (see Wethal 2019; Zajontz and Taylor 2021).

What followed after the period of early post-colonial infrastructure statism was characterised by the withdrawal of the state from large-scale infrastructure construction and provision in line with neoliberal doctrine at the time. During this period, which started in the late 1970s and lasted into the 2000s, African states, often instructed by structural adjustment programmes, remained crucial stakeholders in the infrastructure sector. The resultant "infrastructure night-watch(wo)man state" managed the commodification and privatisation of infrastructure, as will be discussed in this book with regard to Tanzania's and Zambia's failed railway privatisations. The recent rise—or better re-emergence of—the infrastructure state in Africa has occurred in another historically specific global politico-economic context. Major (spatial) transformations in the global economy, not least China's ascent to become an economic (and geopolitical) powerhouse, have challenged previous neoliberal orthodoxies regarding the state's role in the economy.

Framed by hypermodern imaginations and discourses that emphasise the potential of large-scale infrastructure to reap Africa's economic potential, the 2000s have heralded gradual, though profound, political shifts resulting in a more proactive role of African states in developing and providing infrastructure. Nugent (2018: 22) points out that "African governments, corporate investors and the international agencies [...] are [now] fixated upon the transformative potentialities of infrastructure". As part of broader adaptations to neoliberal economic policy consensus and practice, orthodox development economists, multilateral and bilateral donors, private investors and African governments rediscovered the importance of sound economic infrastructure for economic growth, with infrastructure having become the "magic bullet" in global development discourse and practice (Wethal 2019: 474; see Collier 2006; Sachs et al. 2004). This trend was expedited in the aftermath of the global financial crisis when capital, not least Chinese capital, was in need of new frontiers (Schindler et al. 2023). This is when a "global growth coalition" consisting of multilateral development banks, IFIs, multinational corporations, consultancies, and governments of powerful states, including the USA and China, increasingly promoted a global "infrastructure-led development regime" to "get the territories" right in less connected world regions for their seamless integration into global value chains. Under this regime, "financing and financializing infrastructure" has rapidly accelerated (Schindler and Kanai 2021: 41).

The institutional counterpart to said global growth coalition has been the current incarnation of the infrastructure state which is keen to attract foreign capital for infrastructure development. As DiCarlo and Schindler (2022: 4) point out, the concrete form and practices of the infrastructure state vary over time and across regions. This book aspires to provide further empirical insights into concrete manifestations of the infrastructure state, while simultaneously contributing to further theorising the internal and external relations of infrastructure states. Hence, in order to explain the influence of African actors in co-determining infrastructure projects with Chinese participation, it seems essential to unpack "the" African infrastructure state. To do so, a decidedly non-reductionist strategic-relational ontology of the (African) state is proposed in Chapter 3 which addresses some of the shortcomings in the extant literature on African agency in Sino-African relations.

The "African Agency Turn" in Africa–China Studies

Considering mounting public controversies about the questionable economic viability of some Chinese-funded infrastructure projects, the issue of (infrastructure) debt dependency and allegations of corruption in tender processes, Mohan and Tan-Mullins have rightly drawn attention to the role of political elites in brokering infrastructure deals with Chinese banks and contractors. They argue that "[t]he interaction between Chinese state-backed actors and the agency of Southern political elites shapes how infrastructure is financed, funded and utilised, which are ultimately questions of 'who benefits?'" (Mohan and Tan-Mullins 2019: 1370). The authors' research agenda follows a general "upsurge of interest in the role of African agency in shaping the relationship with China" (Carmody and Kragelund 2016: 4). A growing number of scholars have directed analytical attention to the varied ways in which African agency—exerted by state, non-state or hybrid actors—has shaped engagements with China (see, for instance, Carmody and Kragelund 2016; Chiyemura et al. 2023; Corkin 2013; Gadzala 2015; Hodzi 2018; Lampert and Mohan 2015: 109; Links 2021; Lopes 2016; Soulé 2020; Zajontz 2022e). This scholarship has helped to balance a long-standing weakness in some of the China–Africa literature which presented a biased picture of Sino-African relations as heavily tilted in favour of China which left limited room for a thorough engagement with African agency, as identified by various scholars who have made the case for more analytical sensitivity towards African agency. As Carmody and Kragelund argue, "previous writing on the subject of Sino-African relations presented an unbalanced picture in which an all-powerful China subjugated weak African states, thereby replicating previous Orientalist tropes about Africa" (2016: 1; see Alden and Large 2019a: 330–31; Gadzala 2015: xviii; Power et al. 2012: 17).

The growing body of work on African agency has provided valuable insights as to how a myriad of African actors within and beyond state institutions, at various levels of governance and through formal and informal channels engage with Chinese state actors and businesses. Cheru takes the position

> that the rise of emerging powers in Africa neither necessarily produces a new colonial-type relationship nor automatically guarantees policy space for

> African countries. Transforming the new relationship into a win-win partnership will ultimately depend on African agency: in particular the nature of the state in each African country, whether it has a long-term national development vision, the necessary institutional capacity, and strong and committed political leadership capable of engaging all external partners strategically. (2016: 594)

This suggests that the scope and nature of African (state) agency depends not least on prevalent state forms and on political, institutional and economic determinants in particular country contexts. Mohan and Lampert (2013: 93) similarly underline that "the ability of African actors to exercise such agency is highly uneven and can have as much to do with African politics as it does with the politics of China–Africa relations". Therefore, some authors have underscored the value of case studies to account for the polymorphy of African agency and to assess its scope, limits and effectiveness (Alden and Large 2019a: 337; Lampert and Mohan 2015: 110). Empirically rich analyses can help to advance conceptualisations of African agency and to transcend prevalent "theorizing from supposition" (Mohan and Lampert 2013: 95). Alden and Large (2019b: 13) conjecture that the African "agency turn" could "perhaps [become] the main possible exception to the general lack of systematic treatment of theory and method in China–Africa studies". This, however, requires us to take stock of theoretical shortcomings, some of which this book aspires to help remedy.

Much of the research that has heralded the "African agency turn" in China–Africa studies has remained preoccupied with the agency of political elites (Carmody and Kragelund 2016: 5; Mohan and Lampert 2013: 94–95; Ziso 2018: 39). While political elites and state officials, by means of their access to state institutions and resources, are certainly key actors in shaping their countries relations with China, they are not autonomous from the societies they represent. The analytical preoccupation with the role of top officials in much of the literature can ultimately be traced back to reductionist, especially anthropomorphic and monolithic, ontologies of the state as well as voluntarist readings of state agency that have long afflicted much of International Relations (IR) and International Political Economy (IPE) theory (see Ayers 2013: 228; Koivisto 2010: 69–70; Niemann 2000: 67–68, 90; Onuf 1998: 207; Rosenberg 2013: 569–70; Watson 2005: 179–81; Wight 1999: 126, 2004, 2006: 177–78). Mohan correctly argues that research on "China in Africa" often falls into "methodological statism that ignores wider structural forces" (2013: 1256; see Ayers 2013: 227–28; Ziso 2018: 9). This points to the need for a theoretical reconsideration of "the" (African) state, in order to account for the embeddedness of the state, its institutions and its personnel in social structures that span across and beyond particular national territories.

In his study on the impact of Chinese capital on Ethiopian state-society relations, Ziso (2018: 39) rightly warns against assuming Africa's political elite as "the only agency in explaining state behaviour". African political elites do not exercise state powers in isolation from, but in constant relation with, social forces within and beyond their polities (Mohan and Lampert 2013: 95; Ziso 2018: 35). This, of course, is also the case in the context of Chinese-funded and/or built infrastructure projects across the continent where African (state) agency is exerted in different "spheres" through, with and sometimes against the state. Thereby, as we have argued elsewhere (Chiyemura et al. 2023: 105), "the extent and forms of state agency exerted are inherently interrelated with and, thus, highly contingent upon concrete institutional, economic, political, and bureaucratic contexts in which African state actors are firmly embedded". The question is therefore not whether we incorporate African state agency into our theoretical frameworks of "China in Africa" (of course we should), theoretical reconsideration must rather focus on how we do so.

A closely related theoretical challenge emanates from the fact that, thus far, research on African agency has largely abstained from theoretically engaging with the concept of agency and how it ontologically relates to social structures (Carmody and Kragelund 2016: 5; Mohan and Lampert 2013: 95). Most attempts to counter crudely structuralist narratives of an all-powerful China, which supposedly sets the "rules of the game" and deprives African actors of their agency, have largely remained confined to a methodological move towards analysing African actors and practices. While we now have empirically rich accounts documenting the variety of "African agency", theory-informed analyses of how the latter interrelates with structural contexts over time and in particular spatio-temporal conjunctures are rare (for a notable exception, see Lampert and Mohan 2015). Hodzi (2018: 192) argues that "[t]he delimitation of what African agency is, its limits, effect, and impact on China's engagement with Africa is still largely missing".

Most of the literature on African agency in Sino-African relations fails to thoroughly theorise agency and instead employs a "rather static and one-dimensional concept of agency" (Carmody and Kragelund 2016: 5). This is due to reductionist conceptualisations of the structure-agency conundrum. In this book, I propose a more nuanced understanding of African (state) agency by dialectically relating causal powers that arise from structural configurations to efficient causality that emanates from human conduct (see Lewis 2002: 20–21). As Joseph (2008: 102) puts it, "[u]nless we have a structurally grounded approach, there is little basis for understanding the powers and possibilities that agents may possess". I will argue that the Strategic-Relational Approach (SRA), developed by Bob Jessop and Colin Hay (see Hay 1996, 2002; Hay and Lister 2006; Jessop 1990, 2007, 2016), adds significant analytical value. Theoretically, situating African agency within particular structural contexts is paramount for an investigation of Sino-African cooperation in the infrastructure sector and how it is shaped by African state actors.

This book aspires to identify structural drivers that underlie the increase in Chinese-funded infrastructure development in Africa and to shed light on the degree to and the ways in which the latter is co-determined and conditioned by African state agency. The book focuses on two main "case studies", namely Chinese involvement in Zambia's road sector and the planned rehabilitation of the Tanzania–Zambia Railway Authority (TAZARA). Other sub-case studies include the Lusaka-Ndola dual carriageway, the Bagamoyo port project and Tanzania's Standard Gauge Railway (SGR). While the book provides necessary historical contextualisations for the analysis of Chinese engagement in both countries' infrastructure sector, the main period of analysis has been the terms of presidency of Edgar Chagwa Lungu in Zambia (2015–2021) and John Pombe Magufuli in Tanzania (2015–2021). Both presidencies, so I argue, have engendered distinct forms of the infrastructure state, themselves reflections of historically specific state-society relations in the two countries leading up to and during their terms. Guided by a critical realist philosophy of science, the empirical investigation has been paralleled by theorisation at several levels of abstraction, with the aim of shedding light on structural and agential determinants as well as their dialectical interaction in the concrete cases under scrutiny.

The study aspires to make a contribution to the existing literature in at least two regards. Firstly, rooting the study in a critical realist depth ontology allows for an integration of structural and agential factors into the analysis of China–Africa relations. The proposed strategic-relational approach to the structure-agency relation enriches the growing scholarly debate on African agency in Sino-African engagements, as it provides a sufficiently rich conceptual repertoire for analysing specific strategic actions within particular, differentially constraining/enabling, structural contexts (see Hay 2002: 126–34; Jessop 2005, 2006b). It thereby transcends the common practice to analytically bracket African agency from its structural context or vice versa, which ensues from reductionist ontologies of the structure-agency dialectics (see Jessop 2001: 1223). The strategic-relational "resolution" of the structure-agency conundrum proposed in this study transcends both structuralist readings of a neo-colonial/-imperial China which dictates the terms of engagement to passive African recipients and shallowly theorised accounts of African agency that skip over constraining/enabling effects of structural contexts. The theoretical framework presented in this book aspires to what Wight describes as "a structurally aware, although non-structuralist theory of IR" (2004: 270; also cited in Lampert and Mohan 2015: 111). By extension, the study provides a decidedly non-reductionist reading of African state agency in Sino-African relations by conceptually locating African state actors and institutions firmly within a mutable balance of political forces and social relations that constitute the state (see Jessop 2016: 54; Koivisto 2010: 79–80). This addresses questions as to why the scope of African (state) agency in Sino-African relations is wider in some cases than in others, and whose interests it serves in the concrete cases under investigation.

Secondly, the employment of David Harvey's theory of spatio-temporal fixes and related concepts, such as accumulation by dispossession (2003: 115–27, 137–52, 2004), provides for a neo-Marxian analysis of the contemporary production and reorganisation of African infrastructural spaces by Chinese (state) capital, thereby complementing problem-solving research on the topic. Harvey's concepts explain dynamics related to the overaccumulation of Chinese capital and the resultant functions of infrastructure, debt and privatisation in the contemporary process of shifting Chinese surplus capacities to Africa (and elsewhere). This analytical focus appears timely considering the high relevance of matters related to debt sustainability/management, the economic feasibility of infrastructure projects and public–private partnerships (PPPs) in both Chinese and African policy circles. Drawing on "general abstract theories" (see Danermark et al. 2002: 116; Sayer 1992: 138), like Harvey's, allows for conclusions about the extent to which Chinese-financed infrastructure development features tendencies common to capitalist accumulation as well as insights into concrete, historically specific manifestations of such tendencies. What is more, the study complements Harvey's theory of the spatio-temporal fix by bringing the African state into the theoretical equation. The case studies reveal that African state and non-state actors play a significant role in co-determining the spatio-temporal fix, for which Harvey's theory however lacks adequate conceptualisations. Complementing Harvey's concepts with state-theoretical considerations offers crucial insights into the extra-economic dimensions and contradictions of China's contemporary spatio-temporal fix (see Jessop 2004: 491, 2006a: 163). The proposed theoretical "synthesis" allows for an analysis of the politics that affect, mediate, facilitate and potentially disrupt the Chinese "infrastructural fix" in Africa. In the remainder of this introduction, I explain how I have reached the findings and conclusions presented in this book and provide a brief outline of how the book is structured.

Critical Realist Research

Critical realist thought has served as the philosophical "under-labourer" for this study (Bhaskar 2008 [1975]: xxxi). As a philosophy of science, critical realism (CR) posits a stratified social ontology that cannot be reduced to the realm of the empirical. Fundamentally, CR assumes that there is an objective world that exists independently of our perceptions of it. At the same time, it acknowledges that mind-dependent social forms, such as our ideas, theories and concepts, affect how we relate to the world (O'Mahoney and Vincent 2014: 2–3; Patomäki and Wight 2000: 217; Wight and Joseph 2010: 9–10). Hence, CR guards against two forms of reductionism. It avoids reducing reality to socially constructed, (inter)subjective conceptions and/or linguistic conventions, which is common to strictly idealist philosophical ontologies (Danermark et al. 2002: 22; Jessop 2010: 187; Patomäki and Wight 2000: 223; Wight and Joseph 2010: 10). Equally, it avoids the neopositivist reduction of reality to the empirical domain by recognising that the latter "forms an important core to our understanding of the world around us, but it does not exhaust it" (Wight and Joseph 2010: 10).

CR counters the reductionist conflation of the empirical with the real with a "depth ontology" that is best illustrated in Bhaskar's famous distinction of three domains of reality: The empirical, the actual and the real or non-actual (Bhaskar 1978: 56–62; Elder-Vass 2010: 44; Fletcher

2017: 183; Jessop 2005: 41; Wight 2006: 34–35; Wight and Joseph 2010: 10). The "empirical" is the ontological domain of events as we observe or experience them. It entails objects and events that are susceptible to our sensory perceptions and/or detectable through measurement and observation. The empirical constitutes a crucial part of reality and, thus, an important element in any epistemology (Wight 2006: 34–35; Wight and Joseph 2010: 10).

However, as Marx writes in the third volume of *Das Kapital*, "all science would be superfluous if the outward appearances and essences of things directly coincided" (Marx 1971: Vol.3: 871). In other words, the empirical does not exhaust reality. Bhaskar's level of the "actual" refers to "actual objects of *potential* direct experience", those events and "states-of-affairs" that result from real tendencies and counter-tendencies (Wight and Joseph 2010: 10, italics added). They occur whether we observe them or not and often differ from what is empirically experienced (Fletcher 2017: 183; see also Danermark et al. 2002: 20). Last but not least, the domain of the "real" is where Bhaskar's "intransitive objects" of science are to be found. These are non-observable properties, structures and generative mechanisms which hold the potential to cause events and phenomena to actually manifest. Following this, the criterion for an entity to be ontologically real is not its phenomenological perceptibility but its potential causal efficacy (Wagner 2016: 33, 41; Yalvaç 2010: 170).

The "function" of theorisation in CR-informed research therefore differs from empiricist epistemologies. Instead of regarding theories as "ordering frameworks" for the "causal" relations between observable events and/or variables, critical realists employ theories to conceptualise the interrelations among central concepts "in a rigorous and reasoned fashion" (Danermark et al. 2002: 120; see also Sayer 1992: 50; Wagner 2016: 59). Theories are flexibly employed throughout the research process as tools to break down the research theme, to reinterpret empirical phenomena in a different or broader, read more general, way or as conceptual resources to draw on in order to identify and explain the basic conditions and characteristics of generative mechanisms in concrete empirical settings (Wagner 2016: 59).

With the help of abstractions, research informed by CR seeks to "decompose" the concrete object and bring into analytical focus those structures, properties and mechanisms that are considered necessary to produce a particular phenomenon, while temporarily bracketing out all the others, thus "distinguish[ing] the more essential aspects of the phenomenon examined from the more circumstantial ones" (Wagner 2016: 47; see Danermark et al. 2002: 47–48). Thereby, abstractions serve as a tool to deal with, not to cover, the complexity of the social world. Conceptual abstraction separates or isolates in thought "one particular aspect of a concrete object or phenomenon; and what we abstract from is all the other aspects possessed by concrete phenomena" (Danermark et al. 2002: 42; see also Sayer 1992: 87; Wagner 2016: 46–47). The complexity and variation of concrete phenomena that we try to grasp might require us to draw on or "synthesise" several abstractions and to iteratively refine the latter to better account for the interplay of mechanisms that we consider necessary for their generation (Danermark et al. 2002: 49–50; see also Jäger et al. 2016: 109; Sayer 1992: 87).

Abstractions, per definition, do not attempt to represent their concrete referent in all its complexity and variation, since, in Marx's words, the "concrete is concrete because it is the concentration of many determinations, hence unity of the diverse" (1973: 101). Methodologically, this implies that abstractions constitute necessary, but not sufficient, tools in critical realist research. They must be complemented by empirical investigations of concrete conditions and circumstances that determine whether posited causal mechanisms actually operate or not (Danermark et al. 2002: 48; see Wagner 2016: 47; see Yeung 2010: 332).

However, owing to CR's depth ontology, abstractions cannot be applied to particular concrete phenomena by means of direct empirical "testing" (Jackson 2016: 116). A dialectical methodology is required, whereby the concrete phenomenon under study necessarily serves as both the starting point of the abstraction process and the concrete referent for our abstract concepts in what has been described as a "double movement" from the concrete to the abstract and, ultimately, back to the concrete (Sayer 1992: 87; see also Danermark et al. 2002: 51; Jessop 2010: 188; Wagner 2016: 47). In research practice, the double movement is rather a "continual and incomplete spiral movement" (Jessop 2004: 482, see also 2010: 188) or a "ladder of abstraction" (Jäger et al. 2016: 110) which the researcher repeatedly climbs up and down. Jessop's description of critical realist explanation as a methodological move between "abstract-simple" to more "concrete-complex" planes of analysis therefore seems apt and I will make occasional use of it in the remainder of this book (Jessop 2010: 188; Jessop and Sum 2017: 345; Jones and Jessop 2010: 1125, 1127; see also Jessop 2002).

This brings me to a central methodological concern, namely how to relate the abstract and the concrete in the practice of theoretically informed empirical research. For the research summarised in this book, I did employ two "thought operations" (Danermark et al. 2002: 79) that are typical for CR-informed research, namely abduction and retroduction. Both infer from the particular to the general by means of abstraction (Wagner 2016: 56). Abduction is a way of redescribing and recontextualising a concrete phenomenon with the help of conceptual/theoretical frameworks that we borrow from other contexts (Danermark et al. 2002: 91; see Jensen 1995: 148; Wagner 2016: 56). Thereby, the "starting point" for abductive reasoning is existing general theories which serve as "frame[s] of interpretation" for a particular empirical explanandum (Danermark et al. 2002: 89, 90). By reinterpreting a concrete phenomenon in the light of plausible general theories and concepts, abduction "adds" insights to our understanding of the concrete object of study (Danermark et al. 2002: 90). In this research, abductive reasoning has resulted in a thorough reinterpretation of Chinese engagements in African infrastructure sectors with the help of David Harvey's theory of spatio-temporal fixes.

I "applied" the spatio-temporal fix, an abstraction positing a generative mechanism at the level of the real, to the cases of the TAZARA railway and Zambia's road sector. For reasons discussed below, these two cases crystallised as particularly valuable concrete-complex objects of enquiry. The stage of application was driven by the analytical questions as to whether and how the spatio-temporal fix actualises in concrete historical conjunctures. It also aimed at establishing what contextual conditions and other mechanisms facilitate or hinder its actualisation. Answering these questions necessitated further engagement with empirical data from primary, secondary and media sources as well as several research stays in Tanzania and Zambia. It resulted in an examination of yet more concrete "sub-cases", notably the 2016 negotiations about TAZARA's privatisation, the Lusaka-Ndola dual carriageway as well as Tanzania's Standard Gauge Railway and the Bagamoyo mega-port project. During this second move to the concrete-complex plane of analysis, I identified contextual conditions that affected the actualisation of the spatio-temporal fix. These empirical findings made plain that theoretical elaboration and complementation were required.

As Jäger and colleagues (2016: 109) rightly underline, the dialectical nature of research with critical realist underpinnings makes it "necessary to use additional abstractions at a more concrete level". For this purpose, retroduction served as a second "moment of abstraction" in my research. It sheds light on the basic conditions and characteristics of general structures that are identified by means of abduction (Danermark et al. 2002: 97).[1] It asks the question as to what properties and conditions must exist for a posited mechanism to come into existence (Ackroyd and Karlsson 2014: 24; see Danermark et al. 2002: 97, 100). The conceptual "modelling" that is at the heart of retroduction suggests a pragmatic and potentially trans-disciplinary engagement with theories and, as O'Mahoney and Vincent (2014: 18, original italics) underscore, "implies a commitment to *theoretical pluralism* [...]. Multiple theoretical lenses can be considered for what they tell us about the various and stratified influences that are affecting the things we observe".

From the primary data gathered, it became clear that the actualisation of the spatio-temporal fix is dependent on a myriad of political parametres and actors. Harvey's theory, as I shall critique in Chapter 2, provided little to account for African (state) agency in the unfolding of the spatio-temporal fix in the cases of Zambia's road sector and TAZARA. I drew on Jessop's SRA to the structure-agency conundrum to complement Harvey's theory with a state-theoretical framework (see Jessop 2006a: 160). The SRA allows us to "examine structure in relation to action and action in relation to structure, rather than bracketing one of them" (Jessop 2001: 1223). The SRA provided the conceptual richness to do justice to the dialectical interaction between structural tendencies and agential strategies in the context of the Chinese infrastructural fix in Africa. Resultingly, Chapter 3 offers a strategic-relational conceptualisation of "the" African (infrastructure) state in order to account for political-economic and institutional dynamics that condition the actualisation of the Chinese infrastructural fix in concrete conjunctures.

[1] In research practice, the two explanatory logics of abduction and retroduction cannot be kept apart (Danermark et al. 2002: 147), as we necessarily practice a reiterative, cognitive pendular movement between abductive and retroductive reasoning. Yet, the swing from abduction to retroduction implies a move from higher levels of abstraction to more concrete conceptualisations.

Methodology and Case Selection

The empirical part of this study relied on a case study design. Case studies are often considered "archetypical" research designs for CR-informed research. Whereas positivists mistrust them for their incapacity to allow for formal empirical generalisation, critical realist research frequently draws on case studies, since they allow for the in-depth analysis of social phenomena (Ackroyd and Karlsson 2014; Easton 2010; Flyvbjerg 2010). Case studies are suitable for the examination of "sequences of causation or causal mechanisms at work [...], with successful designs identifying a context in which a specific causal mechanism is identified and explored" (Ackroyd and Karlsson 2014: 24). "Successful" in this context means that the in-depth analysis of a particular case allows us to identify "the operation of a mechanism or a process in whole or in part" from which we can then abstract its general characteristics and conceive it in its totality (by means of abduction). Case studies also provide rich contextualisation, a methodological necessity for retroductive reasoning (Ackroyd and Karlsson 2014: 24). Last but not least, case studies allow for generalising knowledge claims which, in critical realist terms, do not aim "for formal empirical generalization" but at advancing concepts of structural properties and generative mechanisms that are considered general (Wagner 2016: 45).

The cases for the present study were theoretically sampled. In theoretical sampling "cases are selected specifically because the analysis is intended to shed light on some aspect of theory that you are interested in" (Henn et al. 2009: 71; see also Swanborn 2010: 62; Flick 2018: 179). The cases were considered "critical" to examine the ways in which China's spatio-temporal fix actualises in concrete-complex conjunctures (see Henn et al. 2009: 71; Swanborn 2010: 62). Zambia had become a main destination for Chinese trade and investment since the 2000s. Bilateral trade between the two countries exceeded \$5bn in 2018 (Ministry of Finance 2019), a steep rise from \$300m in 2005 (Mutesa 2010: 170). In the beginning, mostly concentrated in the extractive industries, Chinese businesses have since managed to increase their presence in Zambia's retail, wholesale and service sectors, in agribusiness and forestry as well as in the construction sector (Carmody 2011: 165–69; Kragelund 2010: 211–13; Muneku 2009: 212–14; Schoneveld et al. 2014: 11–31). As I shall discuss in Chapter 6, Chinese companies, both state-owned and private, have secured an overwhelming market share in road construction in Zambia.

The provision of concessional loans by Chinese state-owned banks has spurred this development and allows for a more concrete-complex analysis of the role of debt in the unfolding of the spatio-temporal fix (see Brautigam 2022; Zajontz 2022d). The gradual commodification and privatisation of Zambia's trunk roads as well as the combination of formal and informal modes of governance in the procurement and negotiations of road projects point to political contradictions related to the inflow of Chinese capital into Zambia's road sector. Hence, Zambia's road sector has offered an insightful case to assess the role of the African state and non-state actors in the actualisation of the Chinese infrastructural fix.

The political significance and the sheer magnitude of the TAZARA construction in the 1970s heralded a new era of Sino-African social, cultural, political and economic relations (see Liu 2024; Monson 2009). To this day, TAZARA serves as the symbol of Sino-African friendship and anti-colonial solidarity and is frequently portrayed, in official discourses, as a role model for the mutual benefits that arise from Sino-African cooperation in the infrastructure sector (see Baregu 2006: 212–14; Bwayla 2013: 195; Carmody 2013: 29; Kahama 2018: Ch. 2; Leslie 2016: 91; Mutesa 2010: 67; Taylor 2006: 26–31). TAZARA allows for an assessment as to whether and how the decades-long cooperation among the Chinese, Tanzanian and Zambian governments has been altered by the generative mechanism of China's contemporary spatio-temporal fix. TAZARA furthermore constitutes a prime case of a largely devalued state-owned corporation, which is instructive in theoretical terms. What is more, TAZARA's corporate constitution as a binational SOE provides insights as to how respective structural contexts in Tanzania and Zambia condition African agency and, in turn, the actualisation of the "fix". Crucially, the case studies represent two dissimilar cases in the sense that in Zambia's road sector, the Chinese infrastructural fix has been in full swing for years, while its actualisation is pending with respect to TAZARA—another crucial reason for the case selection made.

The case studies in the present work are stratified in the sense that the broader cases, viz. Zambia's road sector and TAZARA, led me to investigate more confined "sub-cases", namely the Lusaka-Ndola dual carriageway in the former case and the 2016 privatisation negotiations in the latter. This design implies a move from concrete-complex to even more concrete-complex, in order to better understand particular contextual conditions and the workings of co-acting mechanisms. In the following section, the research methods that were employed to gather data will be discussed.

Research Techniques and Data Collection

CR's depth ontology and the methodological pendular movement between theory and empirical contingencies require flexibility and adaptability regarding both the process and the methods of data gathering (Ackroyd and Karlsson 2014: 22). During several field work stays in Zambia and Tanzania in 2017 and 2019, passive and participatory observations and informal conversations with key informants served as crucial sources of background information. The field work also comprised extensive travels across Zambia, Tanzania and along the TAZARA corridor. Travels along Zambia's road network included the road from Sesheke at the Zambian border with Namibia to Livingstone, the southern route from Livingstone to Lusaka, the northern route from Lusaka to Kapiri Mposhi, Ndola, Kitwe, Chingola and Kasumbalesa at the Congolese border, the T5 between Chingola and Solwezi in Zambia's "New Copperbelt" as well as the Great North Road from Lusaka to Nakonde at the Tanzanian border. Along the TAZARA line, I visited, in some cases several times, the stations in Kapiri Mposhi, Kasama, Nakonde, Makambako, Mbeya and Dar es Salaam as well as the company's headquarters in Mpika and Dar es Salaam. Observational data was a valuable source of background information both on ongoing or recently finished road projects as well as on the state of TAZARA's infrastructure and assets. Moreover, many informal conversations with people from all walks of life during my stays in various parts of Zambia and Tanzania further broadened my understanding of socio-economic, cultural and political contextualities. The information obtained was fed into semi-structured, in-depth interviews, the main method for the collection of qualitative primary data.

For the initial research, 68 interviews were conducted.[2] Interviewees were selected through a combination of snowball sampling and theoretical sampling (see Arber 1993: 74; Henn et al. 2009: 183). The sample of interviewees comprised government officials and politicians (15), academics (6) as well as representatives from the private sector

[2] All but two interviews from the initial sample were conducted in person in Zambia and Tanzania. One was interviewed in person in the United Kingdom. Further interviews followed in the context of other research on related topics.

and SOEs (31) and from non-governmental or civil society organisations (16). Most interviewees agreed to be tape-recorded. Interviewees were anonymised or named according to their preferences.[3] In order not to impair the reading flow, I refrained from indicating grammatical errors in direct interview quotes.

The role of the researcher in CR-informed empirical research is a very active one, as she moulds explanations that relate conceptual abstractions with empirical data. This translates into the way critical realists conduct interviews. According to Smith and Elger, interviewing in social research is characterised by the "active, investigative, and analytically informed orientation of the CR interviewer" (2014: 130). Scrutiny was exercised through "probing questions", "leading questions", careful persistence to overcome vagueness or by respectfully confronting the interviewee with alternative interpretations and accounts. Moreover, a thorough comparison of information across interviews but also between interviews and other data sources has helped to "develop a more adequate understanding of social structures and processes" (Smith and Elger 2014: 115, 116; see Hammersley and Atkinson 1995: Ch.5).

During interviews, with the necessary respect, I questioned interviewees on some of their responses and confronted them with divergent or contradictory information I had obtained from media sources, official documents, governmental statements or other interviewees. This was particularly necessary when interviewing senior-level officials and executives who, not uncommon for elite interviews, had "more or less prepared 'talk tracks' to promote the viewpoints they wanted to communicate by means of the interview, which requires considerable skill from the interviewer to get beyond" (Kvale 2007: 70). This active and critical engagement with interviewees' accounts not only served the purpose to establish the actual course of specific events, which in a few cases proved impossible after all. More importantly, it allowed me to better locate interviewees' responses within their "positioned-practice-places" (Wight 1999: 133) as well as to correlate their interpretations with accounts from

[3] In a few cases, because of the sensitivity of the information provided, I anonymised interviews, although research participants had not asked me to do so. For the same reason, I decided not to mention the location and/or date of some interviews. In three cases, I did not further specify the interviewees' professional position, in order to rule out any potential negative repercussions for my research participants. Where quoted, these interviewees are referred to as "key informants".

those at different levels of seniority, in different sectors (public, business, civil society, academia) or of different nationalities (Zambian, Tanzanian, Chinese).

My interviews were also theory-led, though to varying degrees. Particularly in interviews with academics, theoretical concepts and some of my explanatory conjectures played a central role. These interviews resembled Pawson's "theory-driven interview" in that they allowed me to discuss the applicability and usefulness of concepts, not least the spatio-temporal fix as a posited generative mechanism, with theoretically informed research participants (1996: 303; see Smith and Elger 2014: 116–18). What Pawson called the "'I'll show-you-my-theory-if-you'll-show-me-yours' strategy" ultimately contributed to the iterative refinement and complementation of my theoretical "model" (1996: 307).

Interviews and other primary data were analysed through a combination of what Kvale calls "bricolage approach" and "theoretical reading" (2007: 115–19). The former, "a free interplay of techniques", was employed at an early stage of the research. Among the techniques employed were: Noting patterns and themes, seeing plausibility and making metaphors in order to integrate the diverse set of data (Kvale 2007: 116). Such flexible analysis provided for the necessary analytical space to interpret interview data through various conceptual lenses, applying abductive and retroductive reasoning. In later stages of the research, interview data was iteratively analysed by means of "theoretical reading", whereby the researcher "read[s] through his or her interviews again and again, reflect[s] theoretically on specific themes of interest, [and] writes[s] out interpretation" in a non-systematic way (Kvale 2007: 117). When and where possible, interview data was triangulated "within the method" by speaking to different people in different places at different times (Flick 2018: 191; see Denzin 1989: 237–41). It was also triangulated with data gained from other, particularly textual, sources. Since 2016, I closely monitored the major English-language newspapers in both Zambia and Tanzania and other relevant media outlets for information relevant to my research focus. Official documents and governmental statements were another major textual source.

Positionality and Limitations of the Study

Some reflection is indicated on my own role in the research that led to this book. It is worthwhile recalling Mohan's observation, namely that "Africa is spoken *of* or spoken *for*" in much of the literature on China in Africa (2013: 1257, original italics). While it is one of the objectives of this study to bring into focus African perspectives and strategies in the context of Chinese-sponsored infrastructure projects, the attainment of this aim is limited by my own positionality. As a white, male scholar from Germany, enrolled at a British institution at the time, I have become complicit in the continuation of the above representation.

Naturally, this research has been informed and affected by personal predispositions, by my background, my sex, my skin colour, the books I have read, the experiences I have made, the theories I have consulted, etc.—in short, my positionality. The latter has had an impact on how I engaged with research participants and vice versa. An obvious example to underline my point is the usage of a former colonial language as the language of conduct. While English is an official language in Zambia, it is not in Tanzania. More profoundly, as James Mittelman argues:

> [I]it is right to listen to subjects, but listening is not a neutral exercise. Interlocutors exercise power in expressing the views of their subjects. An interviewer's own voice is present. Although some analysts may deny, or seek to minimize, their own role in this process of translation, the best that a researcher can do is be honest about the difficulties of representation, possible misrepresentation, and one's own commitments. (2014: 117)

Researchers are never beyond misrepresenting viewpoints expressed by research participants. This point, together with other aspects related to research ethics, I communicated in the interaction with my interviewees. As one Tanzanian top official aptly stated after giving his view on Tanzania's current approach vis-à-vis China: "The interpretation, we cannot control it" (Interview Tanzanian top official).

This study has limitations beyond the ones owed to my subjectivity. For one, access to information on Chinese-run infrastructure projects has proven extremely difficult. One reason being that negotiations of projects happen "in camera" and information on the same is usually classified. Equally, the content of contracts and finance agreements for infrastructure projects are subject to the principle of contractual confidentiality. Moreover, the political sensitivity of issues related to Chinese economic engagement in both countries further impeded the access to information on China's role in the infrastructure sector.[4] Officials in Tanzania treaded particularly warily, a circumstance locals and expatriates in Dar es Salaam, in our conversations, linked to President Magufuli's stringent dealing with civil servants (see Andreoni 2017: 36; Polus and Tycholiz 2019: 67). I tried to remedy this limitation by triangulating data from a broad spectrum of sources, ranging from official documents, media sources to interviews and observations. Nonetheless, some aspects could not be revealed to the intended extent.

Another limitation of the study arises from the fact that developments in the context of both case studies have unfolded in real time. I tried to stay "up to date" as much as possible by constantly monitoring the Tanzanian and Zambian media landscape as well as by following-up on current developments with key informants and interviewees. Yet, I cannot rule out that I missed some crucial information.

Structure of the Book

This book is structured into three main parts. The first part (Chapters 2 and 3) presents theoretical abstractions that are considered instructive to better understand structural economic drivers behind Chinese investments in Africa's infrastructure markets and how these are conditioned by African state agency. Chapter 2 outlines David Harvey's theory of spatio-temporal fixes and the concept of accumulation by dispossession. The concepts are then used for an analysis of the Chinese infrastructural fix in Africa. The chapter concludes by problematising the relative under-theorisation of the politics of the "fix", setting the stage for a "theoretical synthesis" with state-theoretical concepts. Chapter 3 brings the African state into the "explanatory equation". It first problematises contributions that have reduced African state agency to elite agency in China–Africa relations. This leads to a thorough reconsideration of the concept of neopatrimonialism and the suggestion that the coexistence and interpenetration of legal-bureaucratic and patrimonial types of domination must be analysed in conjunction with (global) capital accumulation. Following Jessop (see 1990, 2007, 2016), the SRA is applied to the state, which culminates in reading the state as a strategic-relational domain. Finally,

[4] Corkin (2012: 476) reports similar experiences.

Chapter 3 conceptually "merges" the spatio-temporal fix with the SRA, positing that the Chinese infrastructural fix in Africa must be understood as a strategic-relational process.

The first case study, the TAZARA, is discussed in Chapters 4 and 5. The former opens by providing a brief history of the "monumental" railway and by problematising its steady devaluation. It then scrutinises the 2016 intergovernmental negotiations between China, Tanzania and Zambia and, specifically, the Chinese proposal to rehabilitate and operate TAZARA for 30 years. Lastly, the chapter examines how experiences of failed railway privatisations have shaped Tanzania's and Zambia's strategies in the negotiations with China. Chapter 5 examines how the two governments are differentially constrained in rehabilitating TAZARA. It is shown that Zambia's indebtedness has adversely affected the government's strategic scope with regard to the rehabilitation of the railway. The emergence of a nationalist infrastructure state under the late President Magufuli in Tanzania has hindered the privatisation and has obstructed Chinese investments in Tanzanian infrastructure generally.

Chapters 6 and 7 comprise the second case study, namely Chinese involvement in Zambia's road sector. Chapter 6 is concerned with the financial governance of what I call the Sino-African "road bonanza". It outlines Zambia's ambitious "development-through-infrastructure" agenda which came along with an expansive fiscal policy and which was fuelled by the inflow of Chinese capital and particular characteristics of Chinese loan finance. The chapter documents the financial repercussions of the "road bonanza" and problematises the commodification and privatisation of Zambian roads which has been accelerated by Zambia's rapidly deteriorating financial situation. Chapter 5 sheds light on the interplay between formal and informal modes of governance in the negotiation and procurement of road projects. It first historicises the neopatrimonial state in Zambia, before discussing how the informality of Sino-Zambian intergovernmental relations has fostered "not so public" procurement processes. The chapter also analyses Zambia's underregulated "local content" policy and how it has been exploited by particular African and Chinese actors. Chapter 7 completes the analysis of Zambia's road sector by illustrating both the trend towards private project finance and "not so public" procurement in the concrete case of the Lusaka-Ndola dual carriageway.

In the concluding chapter, I extrapolate empirical and theoretical findings that speak to broader themes and potential avenues for future research on Sino-African cooperation in the infrastructure sector.

List of Interview

Tanzanian top official (anonymised), 15 November 2019

References

Ackroyd, Stephen, and Jan Ch. Karlsson. 2014. "Critical Realism, Research Techniques, and Research Designs." Pp. 21–45 in *Studying Organizations Using Critical Realism: A Practical Guide*, edited by P. K. Edwards, J. O'Mahoney, and S. Vincent. Oxford: Oxford University Press.

AfDB. 2018. *African Economic Outlook 2018*. Abidjan: African Development Bank.

African Union. 2015. *Agenda 2063: The Africa We Want*. Addis Ababa: African Union Commission.

Alden, Chris, and Lu Jiang. 2019. "Brave New World: Debt, Industrialization and Security in China–Africa Relations." *International Affairs* 95(3):641–57. https://doi.org/10.1093/ia/iiz083.

Alden, Chris, and Daniel Large. 2019a. "Conclusion." Pp. 329–42 in *New Directions in Africa-China Studies*, edited by C. Alden and D. Large. Abingdon: Routledge.

Alden, Chris, and Daniel Large. 2019b. "Studying Africa and China." Pp. 3–35 in *New Directions in Africa-China Studies*, edited by C. Alden and D. Large. Abingdon: Routledge.

Alves, Ana Cristina. 2013. "China's 'Win-Win' Cooperation: Unpacking the Impact of Infrastructure for-Resources Deals in Africa." *South African Journal of International Affairs* 20(2):207–26. https://doi.org/10.1080/10220461.2013.811337.

Andreoni, Antonio. 2017. *Anti-Corruption in Tanzania: A Political Settlements Analysis*. AEC Working Paper 1. London: Anti-Corruption Evidence Research Consortium.

Arber, Sara. 1993. "Designing Samples." Pp. 68–93 in *Researching Social Life*, edited by N. Gilbert. London: Sage.

Ayers, Alison J. 2013. "Beyond Myths, Lies and Stereotypes: The Political Economy of a 'New Scramble for Africa.'" *New Political Economy* 18(2):227–57. https://doi.org/10.1080/13563467.2012.678821.

Bagwandeen, Mandira, Christopher Edyegu, and Oscar M. Otele. 2023. "African Agency, COVID-19 and Debt Renegotiations with China." *South African Journal of International Affairs* 30(1):1–27. https://doi.org/10.1080/10220461.2023.2180083.

Baregu, Mwesiga. 2006. "Tanzania-China Relations in Historical Perspective." Pp. 209–16 in *China in Africa: Mercantilist Predator, or Partner in Development*, edited by G. le Pere. Braamfontein: The Institute of Global Dialogue and The South African Institute of International Affairs.

Bhaskar, Roy. 1978. *A Realist Theory of Science*. Hemel Hempstead: Harvester.

Bhaskar, Roy. 2008 [1975]. *A Realist Theory of Science*. Abingdon: Routledge.

Bräutigam, Deborah. 2020. "A Critical Look at Chinese 'Debt-Trap Diplomacy': The Rise of a Meme." *Area Development and Policy* 5(1):1–14. https://doi.org/10.1080/23792949.2019.1689828.

Brautigam, Deborah. 2022. "China and Zambia: Creating a Sovereign Debt Crisis." *International Affairs* 98(4):1347–65. https://doi.org/10.1093/ia/iiac109.

Brautigam, Deborah, and Kevin Acker. 2021. "Chinese Lending to Africa in the Pandemic Era." Pp. 165–77 in *Shaping Africa's Post-Covid Recovery*, edited by R. Arezki, S. Djankov, and U. Panizza. London: Centre for Economic Policy Research.

Breslin, Shaun. 2021. *China Risen? Studying Chinese Global Power*. Bristol: Bristol University Press.

Bwayla, Edgar. 2013. "China-Zambia Relations." Pp. 189–213 in *China's Diplomacy in Eastern and Southern Africa*, edited by S. Adem. Farnham: Ashgate.

Cai, Kevin G. 2018. "The One Belt One Road and the Asian Infrastructure Investment Bank: Beijing's New Strategy of Geoeconomics and Geopolitics." *Journal of Contemporary China* 27(114):831–47. https://doi.org/10.1080/10670564.2018.1488101.

Carmody, Pádraig. 2011. *The New Scramble for Africa*. Cambridge: Polity Press.

Carmody, Pádraig. 2013. *The Rise of the BRICS in Africa: The Geopolitics of South-South Relations*. London: Zed Books.

Carmody, Pádraig. 2020. "Dependence Not Debt-Trap Diplomacy." *Area Development and Policy* 5(1):23–31. https://doi.org/10.1080/23792949.2019.1702471.

Carmody, Pádraig, and Joel Wainwright. 2022. "Contradiction and Restructuring in the Belt and Road Initiative: Reflections on China's Pause in the 'Go World.'" *Third World Quarterly* 43(12):2830–51. https://doi.org/10.1080/01436597.2022.2110058.

Carmody, Pádraig, and Peter Kragelund. 2016. "Who Is in Charge? State Power and Agency in Sino-African Relations." *Cornell International Law Journal* 49(1):1–24. https://doi.org/10.1038/nmeth.2841.

Carmody, Pádraig, Peter Kragelund, and Ricardo Reboredo. 2020. *Africa's Shadow Rise: China and the Mirage of African Economic Development*. London: Zed Books.

Carmody, Pádraig, Ian Taylor, and Tim Zajontz. 2022a. "China's Spatial Fix and 'Debt Diplomacy' in Africa: Constraining Belt or Road to Economic Transformation?" *Canadian Journal of African Studies* 56(1):57–77. https://doi.org/10.1080/00083968.2020.1868014.

Carmody, Pádraig, Tim Zajontz, and Ricardo Reboredo. 2022b. "From 'Debt Diplomacy' to Donorship? China's Changing Role in Global Development." *Global Political Economy* 1(2):198–217. https://doi.org/10.1332/uzhw7185.

Chellaney, Brahma. 2017. "China's Debt-Trap Diplomacy." *Project Syndicate*. Retrieved May 19, 2019 (https://www.project-syndicate.org/commentary/china-one-belt-one-road-loans-debt-by-brahma-chellaney-2017-01?barrier=accesspaylog).

Cheru, Fantu. 2016. "Emerging Southern Powers and New Forms of South–South Cooperation: Ethiopia's Strategic Engagement with China and India." *Third World Quarterly* 37(4):592–610. https://doi.org/10.1080/01436597.2015.1116368.

Chiyemura, Frangton, Elisa Gambino, and Tim Zajontz. 2023. "Infrastructure and the Politics of African State Agency: Shaping the Belt and Road Initiative in East Africa." *Chinese Political Science Review* 8(1):105–31. https://doi.org/10.1007/s41111-022-00214-8.

Chu, Yin-wah, and Alvin Y. So. 2010. "State Neoliberalism: The Chinese Road to Capitalism." Pp. 46–72 in *Chinese Capitalisms: Historical Emergence and Political Implications*, edited by Y. Chu. Basingstoke: Palgrave Macmillan.

Collier, Paul. 2006. "African Growth: Why a 'Big Push'?" *Journal of African Economies* 15(suppl_2):188–211.

Corkin, Lucy. 2012. "Chinese Construction Companies in Angola: A Local Linkages Perspective." *Resources Policy* 37(4):475–83. https://doi.org/10.1016/j.resourpol.2012.06.002.

Corkin, Lucy. 2013. *Uncovering African Agency: Angola's Management of China's Credit Lines*. Farnham: Ashgate.

Danermark, Berth, Mats Ekström, Liselotte Jakobsen, and Jan Ch. Karlsson. 2002. *Explaining Society: Critical Realism in the Social Sciences*. London: Routledge.

Denzin, Norman K. 1989. *The Research Act: A Theoretical Introduction to Sociological Methods*. 3rd edition. Englewood Cliffs: Prentice Hall.

DiCarlo, Jessica, and Seth Schindler. 2022. "Introduction: Geopolitics, Infrastructure, and the Emergent Geographies of US-China Competition." Pp. 1–10 in *The Rise of the Infrastructure State: How US–China Rivalry Shapes*

Politics and Place Worldwide, edited by S. Schindler and J. DiCarlo. Bristol: Bristol University Press.

Easton, Geoff. 2010. "Critical Realism in Case Study Research." *Industrial Marketing Management* 39(1):118–28. https://doi.org/10.1016/j.indmarman.2008.06.004.

Elder-Vass, Dave. 2010. *The Causal Power of Social Structures: Emergence, Structure and Agency*. Cambridge: Cambridge University Press.

Fletcher, Amber J. 2017. "Applying Critical Realism in Qualitative Research: Methodology Meets Method." *International Journal of Social Research Methodology* 20(2):181–94. https://doi.org/10.1080/13645579.2016.1144401.

Flick, Uwe. 2018. *An Introduction to Qualitative Research*. 6th edition. London: Sage.

Flyvbjerg, Bent. 2010. "Five Misunderstandings About Case-Study Research." Pp. 133–56 in *Realist Methodology Volume II: Realist Methods*, edited by W. Olsen. London: Sage.

FOCAC. 2018. "Beijing Action Plan (2019–2021)." *Forum on China–Africa Cooperation*. Retrieved June 1, 2019 (https://www.focac.org/eng/zywx_1/zywj/t1594297.htm).

Gadzala, Aleksandra W. 2015. "Introduction." Pp. xv–xxix in *Africa and China: How Africans and Their Governments Are Shaping Relations with China*, edited by A. W. Gadzala. Lanham: Rowman & Littlefield.

Gelpern, Anna, Sebastian Horn, Scott Morris, Brad Parks, and Christoph Trebesch. 2021. *How China Lends: A Rare Look into 100 Debt Contracts with Foreign Government*. Peterson Institute for International Economics, Kiel Institute for the World Economy, Center for Global Development and AidData at William & Mary.

Gort, Joris, and Andrew Brooks. 2023. "Africa's Next Debt Crisis: A Relational Comparison of Chinese and Western Lending to Zambia." *Antipode* 55(3):830–52. https://doi.org/10.1111/anti.12921.

Gu, Jing, Chuanhong Zhang, Alcides Vaz, and Langton Mukwereza. 2016. "Chinese State Capitalism? Rethinking the Role of the State and Business in Chinese Development Cooperation in Africa." *World Development* 81:24–34. https://doi.org/10.1016/j.worlddev.2016.01.001.

Hammersley, Martyn, and Paul Atkinson. 1995. *Ethnography: Principles in Practice*. 2nd edition. London: Routledge.

Harvey, David. 2003. *The New Imperialism*. Oxford: Oxford University Press.

Harvey, David. 2004. "The 'New' Imperialism: Accumulation by Dispossession." *Socialist Register* 40:63–87.

Harvey, David. 2020. *The Anti-Capitalist Chronicles*. London: Pluto Press.

Hay, Colin. 1996. *Re-Stating Social and Political Change*. Milton Keynes: Open University Press.

Hay, Colin. 2002. *Political Analysis: A Critical Introduction*. London: Red Globe Press.

Hay, Colin, and Michael Lister. 2006. "Introduction: Theories of the State." Pp. 1–20 in *The State: Theories and Issues*, edited by C. Hay, M. Lister, and D. Marsh. London: Red Globe Press.

Henn, Matt, Mark Weinstein, and Nick Foard. 2009. *A Critical Introduction to Social Research*. London: Sage.

Hodzi, Obert. 2018. "China and Africa: Economic Growth and a Non-Transformative Political Elite." *Journal of Contemporary African Studies* 36(2):191–206. https://doi.org/10.1080/02589001.2017.1406191.

Horn, Sebastian, Carmen Reinhart, and Christoph Trebesch. 2019. *China's Overseas Lending*. Kiel Working Paper No. 2132. Kiel Institute for the World Economy.

Hung, Ho-fung. 2022. *Clash of Empires: From "Chimerica" to the "New Cold War."* Cambridge: Cambridge University Press.

ICA. 2018a. *Infrastructure Financing Trends in Africa—2017*. Abidjan: Infrastructure Consortium for Africa.

ICA. 2018b. *Infrastructure Financing Trends in Africa—2018*. Abidjan: Infrastructure Consortium for Africa.

ICA. 2022. *Infrastructure Financing Trends in Africa: 2019–2020*. Abidjan: Infrastructure Consortium for Africa.

Jackson, Patrick Thaddeus. 2016. *The Conduct of Inquiry in International Relations: Philosophy of Science and Its Implications for the Study of World Politics*. 2nd edition. Abingdon: Routledge.

Jäger, Johannes, Laura Horn, and Joachim Becker. 2016. "Critical International Political Economy and Method." Pp. 101–18 in *The Palgrave Handbook of Critical International Political Economy*, edited by A. Cafruny, L. S. Talani, and G. P. Martin. London: Palgrave Macmillan.

Jensen, Klaus Bruhn. 1995. *The Social Semiotics of Mass Communication*. London: Sage.

Jessop, Bob. 1990. *State Theory: Putting the Capitalist State in Its Place*. Cambridge: Polity Press.

Jessop, Bob. 2001. "Institutional Re(Turns) and the Strategic-Relational Approach." *Environment and Planning A* 33(7):1213–35. https://doi.org/10.1068/a32183.

Jessop, Bob. 2002. "Capitalism, the Regulation Approach, and Critical Realism." Pp. 88–115 in *Critical Realism and Marxism*, edited by A. Brown, S. Fleetwood, and J. M. Roberts. London: Routledge.

Jessop, Bob. 2004. "On the Limits of the Limits to Capital." *Antipode* 36(3):480–96. https://doi.org/10.1111/j.1467-8330.2004.00427.x.

Jessop, Bob. 2005. "Critical Realism and the Strategic-Relational Approach." *New Formations: A Journal of Culture, Theory and Politics* (56):40–53.

Jessop, Bob. 2006a. "Spatial Fixes, Temporal Fixes and Spatio-Temporal Fixes." Pp. 142–66 in *David Harvey: A Critical Reader*, edited by N. Castree and D. Gregory. Malden: Blackwell.

Jessop, Bob. 2006b. "The Strategic-Relational Approach: An Interview with Bob Jessop (by Joo-Hyoung Ji and Sandra Kytir)." Retrieved January 14, 2020 (https://bobjessop.wordpress.com/2014/12/02/the-strategic-relational-approach-an-interview-with-bob-jessop/).

Jessop, Bob. 2007. *State Power: A Strategic-Relational Approach.* Cambridge: Polity Press.

Jessop, Bob. 2010. "World Market, World State, World Society: Marxian Insights and Scientific Realist Interrogations." Pp. 186–202 in *Scientific Realism and International Relations*, edited by J. Joseph and C. Wight. Basingstoke: Palgrave Macmillan.

Jessop, Bob. 2016b. *The State: Past, Present, Future.* Cambridge: Polity Press.

Jessop, Bob, and Ngai-Ling Sum. 2017. "Putting the 'Amsterdam School' in Its Rightful Place: A Reply to Juan Ignacio Staricco's Critique of Cultural Political Economy." *New Political Economy* 22(3):342–54. https://doi.org/10.1080/13563467.2017.1286639.

Jones, Lee, and Shahar Hameiri. 2020. *Debunking the Myth of "Debt-Trap Diplomacy": How Recipient Countries Shape China's Belt and Road Initiative.* Asia-Pacific Programme Research Paper. London: Chatham House.

Jones, Lee, and Jinghan Zeng. 2019. "Understanding China's 'Belt and Road Initiative': Beyond 'Grand Strategy' to a State Transformation Analysis." *Third World Quarterly* 40(8):1415–39. https://doi.org/10.1080/01436597.2018.1559046.

Jones, Martin, and Bob Jessop. 2010. "Thinking State/Space Incompossibly." *Antipode* 42(5):1119–49. https://doi.org/10.1111/j.1467-8330.2010.00796.x.

Joseph, Jonathan. 2008. "On the Limits of Neo-Gramscian International Relations: A Scientific Realist Account of Hegemony." Pp. 101–24 in *Gramsci, Political Economy, and International Relations Theory: Modern Princes and Naked Emperors*, edited by A. J. Ayers. Basingstoke: Palgrave Macmillan.

Kahama, Joseph K. 2018. *The Challenge to China–Tanzania Relationship: To Enhance Cooperation and Mutual Benefits.* Dar es Salaam: Tema Publishers.

Kimari, Wangui, and Henrik Ernstson. 2020. "Imperial Remains and Imperial Invitations: Centering Race Within the Contemporary Large-Scale Infrastructures of East Africa." *Antipode* 52(3):825–46. https://doi.org/10.1111/anti.12623.

Koivisto, Marjo. 2010. "State Theory in International Relations: Why Realism Matters." Pp. 69–87 in *Scientific Realism and International Relations*, edited by J. Joseph and C. Wight. Basingstoke: Palgrave Macmillan.

Kragelund, Peter. 2010. "The Price of 'Openness': Towards Chinese Economic Control in Zambia." Pp. 208–17 in *The Rise of China and India in Africa*, edited by F. Cheru and C. Obi. London: Zed Books.

Kvale, Steinar. 2007. *Doing Interviews*. London: Sage Publications.

Kynge, James, Kathrin Hille, Benjamin Parkin, and Jonathan Wheatley. 2022. "China Reckons with Its First Overseas Debt Crisis." Retrieved July 16, 2023 (https://www.ft.com/content/ccbe2b80-0c3e-4d58-a182-8728b443df9a).

Lampert, Ben, and Giles Mohan. 2015. "Making Space for African Agency in China–Africa Engagements: Ghanaian and Nigerian Patrons Shaping Chinese Enterprise." Pp. 109–26 in *Africa and China: How Africans and Their Governments are Shaping Relations with China*, edited by A. W. Gadzala. Lanham: Rowman & Littlefield.

Landry, David. 2018. "The Risks and Rewards of Resource-for-Infrastructure Deals: Lessons from the Congo's Sicomines Agreement." *Resources Policy* 58(October):165–74. https://doi.org/10.1016/j.resourpol.2018.04.014.

Large, Daniel. 2021. *China and Africa: The New Era*. Cambridge: Policy Press.

Lee, Ching Kwan. 2014. "The Spectre of Global China." *New Left Review* September(89):29–66.

Lee, Ching Kwan. 2017. *The Specter of Global China: Politics, Labor, and Foreign Investment in Africa*. Chicago: University of Chicago Press.

Leslie, Agnes Ngoma. 2016. "Zambia and China: Workers' Protest, Civil Society and the Role of Opposition Politics in Elevating State Engagement." *African Studies Quarterly* 16(3–4):89–106.

Lesutis, Gediminas. 2021. "Infrastructure as Techno-Politics of Differentiation: Socio-Political Effects of Mega-Infrastructures in Kenya." *Transactions of the Institute of British Geographers* (April 2020):1–13. https://doi.org/10.1111/tran.12474.

Lesutis, Gediminas. 2022. "Disquieting Ambivalence of Mega-Infrastructures: Kenya's Standard Gauge Railway as Spectacle and Ruination." *Environment and Planning D: Society and Space* 026377582211254. https://doi.org/10.1177/02637758221125475.

Lewis, Paul A. 2002. "Agency, Structure and Causality in Political Science: A Comment on Sibeon." *Politics* 22(1):17–23. https://doi.org/10.1111/1467-9256.00154.

Li, Xing, ed. 2019. *Mapping China's "One Belt One Road" Initiative*. Cham: Palgrave Macmillan.

Li, Xing, and Abdulkadir Osman Farah, eds. 2013. *China-Africa Relations in an Era of Great Transfromations*. Farnham: Ashgate.

Links, Stacey. 2021. "Ascertaining Agency Africa and the Belt and Road Initiative." Pp. 113–39 in *Global Perspectives on China's Belt and Road Initiative: Asserting Agency through Regional Connectivity*, edited by F. Schneider. Amsterdam: Amsterdam University Press.

Lippolis, Nicolas, and Harry Verhoeven. 2022. "Politics by Default: China and the Global Governance of African Debt." *Survival* 64(3):153–78. https://doi.org/10.1080/00396338.2022.2078054.
Lisinge, Robert Tama. 2020. "The Belt and Road Initiative and Africa's Regional Infrastructure Development: Implications and Lessons." *Transnational Corporations Review* 12(4):425–38. https://doi.org/10.1080/19186444.2020.1795527.
Liu, Haifang. 2024. "The Freedom Railway Now and Then: The Enduring Relevance of the 'TAZARA Spirit' for South-South Cooperation." Pp. 68–88 in *Africa's Railway Renaissance: The Role and Impact of China*, edited by T. Zajontz, P. Carmody, M. Bagwandeen, and A. Leysens. Abingdon: Routledge.
Liu, Weidong, and Michael Dunford. 2016. "Inclusive Globalization: Unpacking China's Belt and Road Initiative." *Area Development and Policy* 1(3):323–40. https://doi.org/10.1080/23792949.2016.1232598.
Lopes, Carlos. 2016. "Reinserting African Agency into Sino-Africa Relations." *Strategic Review for Southern Africa* 38(1):50–68.
Mann, Michael. 1984. "The Autonomous Power of the State: Its Origins, Mechanisms and Results." *European Journal of Sociology* 25(2):185–213.
Marx, Karl. 1971. *Capital: A Critique of Political Economy*. 3 Volumes. Moscow: Progress.
Marx, Karl. 1973 [1939]. *Grundrisse*. New York: Random House.
Mboya, Cliff. 2021. "The Maritime Silk Road Initiative: Connecting Africa." Pp. 53–80 in *China's Maritime Silk Road Initiative, Africa, and the Middle East Feats, Freezes, and Failures*, edited by J.-M. F. Blanchard. Singapore: Palgrave Macmillan.
McNally, Christopher A. 2012. "Sino-Capitalism: China's Reemergence and the International Political Economy." *World Politics* 64(4):741–76. https://doi.org/10.1017/s0043887112000202.
van der Merwe, Justin. 2019. "The One Belt One Road Initiative: Reintegrating Africa and the Middle East into China's System of Accumulation." Pp. 197–217 in *Mapping China's "One Belt One Road" Initiative*, edited by X. Li. Cham: Palgrave Macmillan.
Middell, Matthias. 2019. "Category of Spatial Formats: To What End?" Pp. 15–47 in *Spatial Formats under the Global Condition: Dialectics of the Global*, Vol. 1, edited by M. Middell. Berlin: De Gruyter.
Ministry of Finance. 2019. "Increase in China-Zambia Trade Projected." *Ministry of Finance*. Retrieved January 16, 2020 (https://www.mof.gov.zm/6114-2/).
Mittelman, James H. 2014. "A Global Perspective on International Regulation and Governance in Africa." *Global Change, Peace & Security* 26(1):113–20. https://doi.org/10.1080/14781158.2013.814628.

Mohan, Giles. 2013. "Beyond the Enclave: Towards a Critical Political Economy of China and Africa." *Development and Change* 44(6):1255–72. https://doi.org/10.1111/dech.12061.

Mohan, Giles, and Ben Lampert. 2013. "Negotiating China: Reinserting African Agency into China–Africa Relations." *African Affairs* 112(446):92–110. https://doi.org/10.1093/afraf/ads065.

Mohan, Giles, and May Tan-Mullins. 2019. "The Geopolitics of South–South Infrastructure Development: Chinese-Financed Energy Projects in the Global South." *Urban Studies* 56(7):1368–85. https://doi.org/10.1177/0042098018794351.

Monson, Jamie. 2009. *Africa's Freedom Railway: How a Chinese Development Project Changed Lives and Livelihoods in Tanzania*. Bloomington: Indiana University Press.

Mthembu, Philani. 2020. "China's Belt & Road Initiative: How Can Africa Advance Its Strategic Priorities?" Pp. 134–158 in *Africa and the World: Navigating Shifting Geopolitics*, edited by F. Kornegay and P. Mthembu. Johannesburg: Mapungubwe Institute for Strategic Reflection and Jacana Publishers.

Muneku, Austin. 2009. "Chinese Investments in Zambia." Pp. 199–254 in *Chinese Investments in Africa: A Labour Perspective*, edited by A. Y. Baah and H. Jauch. Harare: African Labour Research Network.

Mutesa, Fredrick. 2010. "China and Zambia: Between Development and Politics." Pp. 67–78 in *The Rise of China and India in Africa*, edited by F. Cheru and C. Obi. London: Zed Books.

Nabudere, Dan. 1981. *Imperialism in East Africa Volume 1: Imperialism and Exploitation*. London: Zed Press.

Niemann, Michael. 2000. *A Spatial Approach to Regionalisms in the Global Economy*. Basingstoke: Macmillan Press.

Nölke, Andreas. 2014. "Introduction: Toward State Capitalism 3.0." Pp. 1–14 in *Multinational Corporations from Emerging Markets: State Capitalism 3.0*, edited by A. Nölke. Basingstoke: Palgrave Macmillan.

Nölke, Andreas, Tobias ten Brink, Christian May, and Simone Claar. 2020. *State-Permeated Capitalism in Large Emerging Economies*. Abingdon: Routledge.

Nugent, Paul. 2018. "Africa's Re-Enchantment with Big Infrastructure: White Elephants Dancing in Virtuous Circles?" Pp. 22–40 in *Extractive Industries and Changing State Dynamics in Africa*, edited by J. Schubert, U. Engel, and M. Elisio. Abingdon: Routledge.

Nyabiage, Jevans. 2021. "China cancels Democratic Republic of Congo loans as it joins Belt and Road." *South China Morning Post*. Retrieved February 22, 2022 (https://www.scmp.com/news/china/diplomacy/article/3116837/china-cancels-democratic-republic-congo-loans-itjoins-belt).

OECD and ACET. 2020. *Quality Infrastructure in 21st Century Africa: Prioritising, Accelerating and Scaling Up in the Context of PIDA (2021–30)*. Paris: Organisation for Economic Cooperation and Development, African Center for Economic Transformation.

O'Mahoney, Joe, and Steve Vincent. 2014. "Critical Realism as an Empirical Project: A Beginner's Guide." Pp. 1–20 in *Studying Organizations Using Critical Realism: A Practical Guide*, edited by P. K. Edwards, J. O'Mahoney, and S. Vincent. Oxford: Oxford University Press.

Onuf, Nicholas Greenwood. 1998. *The Republican Legacy in International Thought*. Cambridge: Cambridge University Press.

Otiso, Kefa M., and Pádraig Carmody. 2024. "Powering African Transport or Transporting Chinese Power? The Spatial Political Economy of Chinese Railways in Africa." Pp. 49–67 in *Africa's Railway Renaissance: The role and impact of China*, edited by T. Zajontz, P. Carmody, M. Bagwandeen, and A. Leysens. Abingdon: Routledge.

Patomäki, Heikki, and Colin Wight. 2000. "After Postpositivism? The Promises of Critical Realism." *International Studies Quarterly* 44(2):213–37. https://doi.org/10.1111/0020-8833.00156.

Pawson, Ray. 1996. "Theorizing the Interview." *The British Journal of Sociology* 47(2):295. https://doi.org/10.2307/591728.

Pearson, Margaret, Meg Rithmire, and Kellee S. Tsai. 2021. "Party-State Capitalism in China." *Current History* 120(827):207–13.

Polus, Andrzej, and Wojciech Tycholiz. 2019. "David versus Goliath: Tanzania's Efforts to Stand up to Foreign Gas Corporations." *Africa Spectrum* 54(1):61–72. https://doi.org/10.1177/0002039719848507.

Power, Marcus, Giles Mohan, and May Tan-Mullins. 2012. *China's Resource Diplomacy in Africa: Powering Development?* Basingstoke: Palgrave Macmillan.

Rosenberg, Justin. 2013. "The 'Philosophical Premises' of Uneven and Combined Development." *Review of International Studies* 39(3):569–97. https://doi.org/10.1017/S0260210512000381.

Sachs, Jeffrey D., John W. Mcarthur, Guido Schmidt-Traub, Margaret Kruk, Chandrika Bahadur, Michael Faye, and Gordon McCord. 2004. "Ending Africa's Poverty Trap." *Brookings Papers on Economic Activity* (1):117–240. https://doi.org/10.1353/eca.2004.0018.

Sayer, Andrew. 1992. *Method in Social Science: A Realist Approach*. London: Routledge.

Schindler, Seth, Ilias Alami, and Nicholas Jepson. 2023. "Goodbye Washington Confusion, Hello Wall Street Consensus: Contemporary State Capitalism and the Spatialisation of Industrial Strategy." *New Political Economy* 28(2):223–40. https://doi.org/10.1080/13563467.2022.2091534.

Schindler, Seth, and Jessica DiCarlo, eds. 2022. *The Rise of the Infrastructure State: How US–China Rivalry Shapes Politics and Place Worldwide*. Bristol: Bristol University Press.

Schindler, Seth, Jessica DiCarlo, and Dinesh Paudel. 2022. "The New Cold War and the Rise of the 21st-Century Infrastructure State." *Transactions of the Institute of British Geographers* 47(2):331–46. https://doi.org/10.1111/tran.12480.

Schindler, Seth, and J. Miguel Kanai. 2021. "Getting the Territory Right: Infrastructure-Led Development and the Re-Emergence of Spatial Planning Strategies." *Regional Studies* 55(1):40–51. https://doi.org/10.1080/00343404.2019.1661984.

Schoneveld, George, Laura German, and Davison Gumbo. 2014. *The Developmental Implications of Sino-African Economic and Political Relations: A Preliminary Assessment for the Case of Zambia*. CIFOR Working Paper 133. Bogor: Center for International Forestry Research.

Smith, Chris, and Tony Elger. 2014. "Critical Realism and Interviewing Subjects." Pp. 109–31 in *Studying Organizations Using Critical Realism: A Practical Guide*, edited by P. K. Edwards, J. O'Mahoney, and S. Vincent. Oxford: Oxford University Press.

Soulé, Folashadé. 2020. "'Africa+1' Summit Diplomacy and the 'New Scramble' Narrative: Recentering African Agency." *African Affairs* 119(477):633–46. https://doi.org/10.1093/afraf/adaa015.

State Council. 2021. "China and Africa in the New Era: A Partnership of Equals." *Ministry of Foreign Affairs of the People's Republic of China*. Retrieved March 2, 2022 (https://www.fmprc.gov.cn/mfa_eng/wjdt_665385/2649_665393/202111/t20211126_10453904.html).

Sum, Ngai-Ling. 2019. "The Intertwined Geopolitics and Geoeconomics of Hopes/ Fears: China's Triple Economic Bubbles and the 'One Belt One Road' Imaginary." *Territory, Politics, Governance* 7(4):528–52. https://doi.org/10.1080/21622671.2018.1523746.

Summers, Tim. 2016. "China's 'New Silk Roads': Sub-National Regions and Networks of Global Political Economy." *Third World Quarterly* 37(9):1628–43. https://doi.org/10.1080/01436597.2016.1153415.

Sun, Irene Yuan, Kartik Jayaram, and Omid Kassiri. 2017. *Dance of the Lions and Dragons: How Are Africa and China Engaging, and How Will the Partnership Evolve?* New York: McKinsey & Company.

Swanborn, Peter G. 2010. *Case Study Research: What, Why and How?* London: Sage Publications.

Taylor, Ian. 2006. *China and Africa: Engagement and Compromise*. Abingdon: Routledge.

Taylor, Ian. 2014. *Africa Rising? BRICS—Diversifying Dependency*. Woodbridge: James Currey.

Taylor, Ian, and Tim Zajontz. 2020. "In a Fix: Africa's Place in the Belt and Road Initiative and the Reproduction of Dependency." *South African Journal of International Affairs* 27(3):277–295. https://doi.org/10.1080/10220461.2020.1830165.

UNICEF and WHO. 2019. *Progress on Household Drinking Water, Sanitation and Hygiene: 2000–2017*. New York: United Nations Children's Fund and World Health Organization.

Vhumbunu, Clayton Hazvinei. 2016. "Enabling African Regional Infrastructure Renaissance through the China-Africa Partnership: A Trans-Continental Appraisal." *International Journal of China Studies* 7(3):271–300.

Wagner, Maren. 2016. *Social Emergence in International Relations*. Palgrave Macmillan.

Wang, Yuan. 2022. "Executive Agency and State Capacity in Development: Comparing Sino-African Railways in Kenya and Ethiopia." *Comparative Politics* 54(2):349–73. https://doi.org/10.5129/001041522x16225661565091.

Watson, Matthew. 2005. *Foundations of International Political Economy*. Basingstoke: Palgrave Macmillan.

Wethal, Ulrikke. 2019. "Building Africa's Infrastructure: Reinstating History in Infrastructure Debates." *Forum for Development Studies* 46(3):473–99. https://doi.org/10.1080/08039410.2019.1616609.

White House. 2023. "Remarks by President Biden and Prime Minister Rishi Sunak of the United Kingdom in Joint Press Conference." Retrieved July 16, 2023 (https://www.whitehouse.gov/briefing-room/speeches-remarks/2023/06/08/remarks-by-president-biden-and-prime-minister-rishi-sunak-of-the-united-kingdom-in-joint-press-conference/).

van Wieringen, Kjeld, and Tim Zajontz. 2023. "From Loan-Financed to Privatised Infrastructure? Tracing China's Turn towards Public-Private Partnerships in Africa." *Journal of Current Chinese Affairs*, online first. https://doi.org/10.1177/18681026231188140.

Wight, Colin. 1999. "They Shoot Dead Horses Don't They? Locating Agency in the Agent-Structure Problematique." *European Journal of International Relations* 5(1):109–42. 0803973233.

Wight, Colin. 2004. "State Agency: Social Action without Human Activity?" *Review of International Studies* 30(2):269–80. https://doi.org/10.1017/S0260210504006060.

Wight, Colin. 2006. *Agents, Structures and International Relations: Politics as Ontology*. 2nd edition. Cambridge: Cambridge University Press.

Wight, Colin, and Jonathan Joseph. 2010. "Scientific Realism and International Relations." in *Scientific Realism and International Relations*, edited by J. Joseph and C. Wight. Basingstoke: Palgrave Macmillan.

World Bank. n.d.-a. "Access to Electricity (% of Population)." Retrieved July 15, 2023 (https://data.worldbank.org/indicator/EG.ELC.ACCS.ZS).

Yalvaç, Faruk. 2010. "Critical Realism, International Relations Theory and Marxism." in *Scientific Realism and International Relations*, edited by J. Joseph and C. Wight. Basingstoke: Palgrave Macmillan.

Yan, Karl. 2021. "The Railroad Economic Belt: Grand Strategy, Economic Statecraft, and a New Type of International Relations." *British Journal of Politics and International Relations* 23(2):262–79. https://doi.org/10.1177/1369148120940938.

Yeung, Henry Wai-chung. 2010. "Critical Realism and Realist Research in Human Geography: A Method or a Philosophy in Search of a Method?" Pp. 325–54 in *Realist Methodology Volume I: Practical Realist Ontology*, edited by W. Olsen. London: Sage.

Zajontz, Tim. 2022a. "Debt, Distress, Dispossession: Towards a Critical Political Economy of Africa's Financial Dependency." *Review of African Political Economy* 49(171):173–83. https://doi.org/10.1080/03056244.2021.1950669.

Zajontz, Tim. 2022b. "Infrastructure." Pp. 120–38 in *Yearbook on the African Union*. Vol. 2. Leiden: Brill.

Zajontz, Tim. 2022c. "Railway Imperialisms in East Africa: Laying the Tracks for Exploitation." Pp. 515–34 in *Oxford Handbook of Economic Imperialism*, edited by Z. Cope and I. Ness. Oxford: Oxford University Press.

Zajontz, Tim. 2022d. "The Chinese Infrastructural Fix in Africa: Lessons from the Sino-Zambian 'Road Bonanza.'" *Oxford Development Studies* 50(1):14–29. https://doi.org/10.1080/13600818.2020.1861230.

Zajontz, Tim. 2022e. "'Win-Win' Contested: Negotiating the Privatisation of Africa's Freedom Railway with the 'Chinese of Today.'" *Journal of Modern African Studies* 60(1):111–34. https://doi.org/10.1017/S0022278X21000446.

Zajontz, Tim, Pádraig Carmody, Mandira Bagwandeen, and Anthony Leysens. 2024. "Introduction: China's Role in Africa's Railway Renaissance." Pp. 1–25 in *Africa's Railway Renaissance: The Role and Impact of China*, edited by T. Zajontz, P. Carmody, M. Bagwandeen, and A. Leysens. Abingdon: Routledge.

Zajontz, Tim, and Ian Taylor. 2021. "Capitalism and Africa's (Infra)Structural Dependency: A Story of Spatial Fixes and Accumulation by Dispossession." Pp. 190–213 in *Africa and the Global System of Capital Accumulation*, edited by A. D. Cooper and E. Oritsejafor. Abingdon: Routledge.

Zhang, Xin. 2017. "Chinese Capitalism and the Maritime Silk Road: A World-Systems Perspective." *Geopolitics* 22(2):310–31. https://doi.org/10.1080/14650045.2017.1289371.

Ziso, Edson. 2018. *A Post State-Centric Analysis of China-Africa Relations: Internationalisation of Chinese Capital and State-Society Relations in Ethiopia*. Cham: Palgrave Macmillan.

CHAPTER 2

Chinese Capital and Its Spatio-Temporal Fix

> Capital by its nature drives beyond every spatial barrier. Thus the creation of the physical conditions of exchange—of the means of communication and transport—the annihilation of space by time—becomes an extraordinary necessity for it. (Marx 1973 [1939]: 524)

Marx famous dictum from the *Grundrisse* points to the centrality of infrastructure for capital accumulation. This chapter advances the argument that infrastructure development in Africa (and elsewhere) has indeed become necessary for Chinese capital. Africa's recent infrastructure boom has been fuelled by the outer transformation of the Chinese accumulation system, i.e. "its transformation through the export of surplus capital or labour beyond the boundaries of the space or region in which it was generated" (Jessop 2006: 147). This book posits David Harvey's spatio-temporal fix as a key generative mechanism that explains growing Chinese (loan-debt) investments in African infrastructure markets throughout the 2010s. A growing number of studies on China's contemporary geo-economic strategy have drawn on David Harvey's concept of the spatio-temporal fix to conceptualise the spatial reorganisation of China's growth model (see, for instance, Hung 2008; Lim 2010; van der Merwe 2016, 2019; Ovadia 2013: 236; Sum 2019; Zhang 2017). However,

T. Zajontz, *The Political Economy of China's Infrastructure Development in Africa*, International Political Economy Series,
https://doi.org/10.1007/978-3-031-44449-4_2

less effort has been made to analyse the unfolding of China's contemporary spatio-temporal fix at more concrete-complex levels of inquiry in the African context—a research gap this book aspires to fill.

To do so, theorisation is required at various levels of abstraction and with regard to both economic and political determinants that affect the materialisation of a spatio-temporal fix in specific territorial and historical contexts. This chapter commences this theoretical task by first recounting Harvey's theory of spatio-temporal fixes and the function of debt and processes of accumulation by dispossession in the recurrent spatial reorganisation of capital accumulation. The chapter then discusses China's contemporary spatial fix and its "convenient conjuncture" with Africa's so-called infrastructure gap which has culminated in the present Chinese infrastructural fix across Africa (Zajontz 2022b: 16). The chapter concludes with a critique of the relative under-theorisation of the politics of the spatio-temporal fix and suggests a state-theoretical complementation which is offered in Chapter 3.

Overaccumulation and China's Spatio-Temporal Fix

In a series of influential publications, most importantly *The Limits to Capital* of 1982, David Harvey developed what he calls an "exegesis and extension of Marx's political economy onto the terrain of geography" (Harvey 2004a: 544).[1] Harvey further develops the idea that capital incessantly reverts to the production, destruction and reorganisation of space in order to counter its endemic vulnerability to crisis. Building on Marx's law of value and the falling rate of profit, Harvey derives a "pervasive tendency of capitalism to produce crises of overaccumulation" (2003:

[1] Some segments in this and in the next section were previously published in Zajontz and Taylor (2021).

108; see also 1982: Chs. 6, 7; 2004b).[2] He suggests that overaccumulation crises within a given territory can be temporarily averted by what he calls the "spatio-temporal fix" (Harvey 2003: 115).[3] Harvey's abstraction of the spatio-temporal fix is considered an apt "model" of a generative causal mechanism that underlies the production and transformation of infrastructural spaces across Africa by Chinese capital.

The term "fix" has a double meaning for Harvey: a literal one and a metaphorical one. The former implies that a share of capital is "literally fixed in and on the land for a relatively long period of time (depending on its economic and physical lifetime)" (Harvey 2003: 115). The capitalist imperative to accumulate implies a constant drive to overcome spatial barriers (Arrighi 2005: 35–36; Harvey 2001: 243–47). Marx famously argued that

> while capital must on one side strive to tear down every spatial barrier to intercourse, i.e. to exchange, and conquer the whole earth for its market,

[2] In *The Limits to Capital*, Harvey undertakes three "cuts" at a theory of capitalist crisis. Akin to Marx's original analysis, Harvey's "first cut" entails the cyclical alternation of booms and busts. Productivity gains are made by remunerating workers below the value of their labour and/or by replacing them with machinery and technology. This, in turn, leads to under-consumption. Overproduction, paired with under-consumption, results in overaccumulation and substantiates the "tendency towards a falling rate of profit, as a consequence of the operation of the law of value" (Sheppard 2004: 471). The economic boom is followed by a bust, characterised by devalued fixed capital which again provides for the next boom. Harvey's "second cut" problematises the role of financial institutions and the credit system in "bridging" the time lags between capitalist investment in production and the realisation of surpluses by means of credit and "ficticious capital", such as derivatives or securities. By smoothening capital flows within the economy, finance and the credit system can provide for a "temporal fix". However, they cannot do away with contradictions inherent to capitalist accumulation. New technologies and competition can result in rapidly devaluing fixed capital, just as loss in investors' confidence in ficticious capital can cause new forms of economic busts. Spatial fixes, as a form of crisis management, are featured in Harvey's "third cut" at crisis theory (Sheppard 2004: 471, 472; see Harvey 1982, 2001: Ch. 12; Jessop 2006). In later works, Harvey (2004b: 63) emphasises that spatial fixes "cannot be divorced from temporal fixes [...], since geographical expansion often entails investment in long-lived physical and social infrastructures".

[3] Harvey only starts employing the composite adjective "spatio-temporal" in *The New Imperialism* to do terminological justice to the dialectics of space–time. However, the latter is already established in *The Limits to Capital*, despite him formally distinguishing "temporal" and "spatial" fixes. For discussions of Harvey's conceptualisation of the spatio-temporality of capitalism, see Castree (2009) and Sheppard (2006).

it strives on the other hand to annihilate this space with time, i.e. to reduce to a minimum the time spent in motion from one place to another (1973: 539).

As spatial barriers delay and diminish the realisation of profits, infrastructural facilities help reduce the circulation time between places of production and places of consumption (Sheppard 2004: 472).[4] Or, in Marx's words, the costs of circulation "can be reduced by improved, cheaper and more rapid transportation" (1967: Vol. 2: 142; also cited in Harvey 2001: 243).

The literal meaning of Harvey's "fix" underscores the dependence of capital accumulation on particular spatial structures which are comprised of capital that is embedded in the landscape and which allow for the circulation of other physically mobile capitals in search of maximum surplus (Arrighi 2005: 35; Jessop 2006: 147). Examples include transport, communication or other physical infrastructures as well as territorialised and thus geographically fixed social expenditures, such as education or health-care systems (Arrighi 2005: 35; Harvey 2003: 115, see also 2004b: 65). As Harvey puts it, "[f]luid movement *over* space can be achieved only by fixing certain physical infrastructure *in* space" (2003: 99; original italics). However, the incessant tendency to reduce spatial barriers by "fixing" certain capital in the landscape "unwittingly undermin[es] the monopolistic privileges attached to specific locations through the intensification of competition across geographical space" (Arrighi 2005: 36). The necessary result is overproduction and overaccumulation, i.e. capital and/or labour can no longer be invested within a particular territory at the average rate of profit or, worse, at no profit at all (Jessop 2006: 149). Commodities pile up, as they lack profitable markets, while productive capital lies idle and financial capital is deficient of investment goods (Arrighi 2005: 36; Harvey 2003: 109). This brings us to the second meaning of the spatio-temporal fix, as overaccumulated capital which cannot be reinvested profitably (enough) within a given territory can be

[4] Marx defines the turnover time of a given capital as the sum of its production time and its circulation time. More distant markets "eat up" profits by increasing the time lag between investment and profit realisation. Hence, "any reduction in circulation time increases surplus production and enhances the accumulation process" (Harvey 2001: 244; see Marx 1967: Vol. 2: 248).

absorbed through "temporal" or "spatial displacements" or a combination of the two (Harvey 2003: 109, see also 2004b: 64; Jessop 2006: 149).

The metaphorical meaning stands for "a particular solution to capitalist crises through temporal deferral and geographical expansion" (Harvey 2003: 115, see also 2004b: 65). Harvey uses the terms "temporal displacement" and "temporal deferral", on the one hand, and "spatial displacement" and "geographical expansion", on the other, synonymously. The concepts refer to two analytically distinct, yet empirically intricately interrelated, "moments" of the spatio-temporal fix. First, temporal displacement ties up surplus capital in long-term, geographically "fixed" capital projects ("secondary circuit" of capital) or long-term investments in social infrastructures ("tertiary circuit"), thereby deferring its re-entry into the "primary circuit" of capital, viz. the one of immediate production and consumption (Castree 2009: 47; Harvey 2003: 109–10; Jessop 2006: 147–48). Investments in infrastructures, be they physical or social, generally absorb large amounts of capital and are characterised by a "long gestation and turnover time" (Jessop 2006: 151; see Castree 2009; Schoenberger 2004). Consequently, they provide for a *temporal* "solution" to overaccumulation, because they "absorb *current* surplus capital and increase its *future* productivity and profitability" (Jessop 2006: 148, original italics; see Harvey 2003: 109). In other words, temporal deferral buys time, in anticipation of profit realisation in the future.

Second, spatial displacement refers to the utilisation of surplus capital by extending the spatial reach of an existing system of accumulation. This implies tapping into new markets, new production capacities or new sources of commodities, including labour (Harvey 2003: 109). The two "moments" of the spatio-temporal fix are usually interdependent. Temporal deferral constitutes the production and reorganisation of space that is necessary for opening up new markets for consumption (of surplus commodities) and investment (for surplus finance and productive capital). Even if the two tendencies do not necessarily occur in neat temporal sequences, temporal deferral prepares the ground for the geographical expansion of an accumulation system, whereby other, geographically mobile, forms of capital are absorbed in spatially expanded circuits of capital (Arrighi 2005: 36, 2007: 217).

Harvey's theory points to a central contradiction of capitalist accumulation: its "inherent tension between the 'fixity' and 'mobility' of capital at any given moment and over time" (Jessop 2006: 148). Synchronically, the tension becomes evident within the categories of "fixed" capital (railways depend on rolling stock for their operation) and "mobile" capital (raw materials need to be "unlocked", certain products to be "finished" before they can be circulated) as well as between the two (Harvey 2001: 332; Jessop 2004: 489, 2006: 148, 147). As "transportation is simultaneously produced and consumed at the moment of its use" (Harvey 2001: 243), it depends on circulating capital to realise its value, whereas mobile capitals depend on fixed infrastructure for their circulation. Equally, geographically mobile commodities are generally traded at spatially "fixed" commercial centres and so on (Jessop 2004: 489, 2006: 148). Diachronically, "fixed", capital-intensive infrastructure, be they developed by the state, private investors or a combination of the two, are dependent on mobile capitals to "circulate[s] down spatial paths and over a timespan consistent with the geographical pattern and duration of such commitments" (Harvey 2001: 332; also cited in Jessop 2006: 148). This theoretical assumption is empirically highly relevant in the context of Chinese-funded projects across Africa. If and where insufficient mobile capital, for instance, in the form of commodities or manufactured goods, circulates down the spatial path of a specific infrastructure investment, so-called "white elephants" are born. While it seems too early to come to definite and comprehensive economic assessments of recent large-scale infrastructure projects, there have been doubts about the economic viability of, for instance, Kenya's and Ethiopia's Chinese-funded Standard Gauge Railways (SGRs) (Carmody et al. 2022a; Taylor 2020).

Over time, "fixed" capital that is embedded in the landscape in terms of the built environment acts as a barrier to further accumulation (Harvey 2001: 247). Innovation and improvements in the transport and communication sectors, for their part, facilitate new "fixes" (Harvey 2001: 243; Jessop 2006: 148). Spatial restructuring and geographical expansions therefore threaten the value of capital that is already "fixed" in the landscape (Harvey 2003: 116). As a consequence, recurrent rounds of spatio-temporal fixes constitute a "geographical variant" of the Schumpeterian dynamic of "creative destruction" (Arrighi 2005: 36; see Brenner 2009: 34; Harvey 2003: 101, 2004b: 66; Schumpeter 1943). Harvey describes this central contradiction of capitalist accumulation as follows:

> [C]apital has to build a fixed space (or "landscape") necessary for its own functioning at a certain point in its history only to have to destroy that space (and devalue much of the capital invested therein) at a later point in order to make way for a new "spatial fix" (openings for fresh accumulation in new spaces and territories). (2001: 25; see Brenner 1999: 43; Jessop 2006: 148)

The periodic drive towards the production, destruction and renewed production of space has highly unequal economic impacts across space and time. As investments in the built environment and in physical infrastructure tend to be geographically concentrated in locations profitable for other capital investment, i.e. centres of production, extraction, commerce and finance, they reinforce patterns of uneven spatial development (Harvey 2006: 101). Therefore, a direct result of any spatio-temporal fix is "an internal as well as an external differentiation of winners and losers from a particular fix, linked to the uneven social and spatial distribution of benefits from a given fix and to its associated uneven development" (Jessop 2003: 183, 2006: 162–63). This notion appears highly relevant in the context of Chinese infrastructure projects some of which have been strongly contested by segments within host country populations.

Profit realisation of surplus capital that is geographically shifted into other territories depends on the availability of tradable commodities or (financial) resources in these territories. In case of a shortage of the same, credit and aid provide for a "solution", as they ensure that territories that do not possess (enough) commodities or reserves in return can still serve as spatial destinations for foreign surplus capital (Harvey 2003: 117–18). Financial capital temporarily ameliorates overaccumulation by expanding the credit system, since debt makes possible the absorption of overcapacities in the present, based on the agreement that future surpluses are used to recover the price (Bond 2015: 20–21). This is not least the case in the context of capital-intensive, long-term infrastructure development and engenders contradictions which I will discuss next.

The Function of Debt Finance and Accumulation by Dispossession

Inequality in capital distribution between territories in which surplus capital accumulates and territories that offer opportunities for investing such surpluses reveals structural contradictions in the unfolding of spatio-temporal fixes (see Harvey 2003: 113–14, 117–18, 2004b: 64–65). In *The New Imperialism*, Harvey expands his conceptual repertoire by the notion of accumulation by dispossession, which he considers a central aspect of the new imperialism. The concept is a terminological modernisation of Marx's notion of "primitive" or "original accumulation", as Harvey argues for a "general re-evaluation of […] [the latter's] continuous role and persistence" (Harvey 2003: 144, see also 2004b: 74; Ashman and Callinicos 2006: 116; Perelman 2000). Marx considered "primitive accumulation" a historical prerequisite for capitalist accumulation. He describes it as the "process which takes away from the labourer the possession of his means of production; a process that transforms, on the one hand, the social means of subsistence and of production into capital, on the other, the immediate producers into wage-labourers". For Marx, primitive accumulation formed the "pre-historic stage of capital", which set the conditions for capital accumulation under expanded reproduction (2013: 502). As Amin knew, "[t]he characteristic feature of primitive accumulation, in contrast to normal expanded reproduction, is unequal exchange, that is, the exchange of products whose prices of production, in the Marxist sense, are unequal" (1976: 187; also cited in Bieler and Morton 2014: 38).

Harvey posits that the predatory practice of dispossession is not historically confined to the transition from pre-capitalist to capitalist societies but a continual aspect of advanced capitalisms (2003: 144; see Ashman and Callinicos 2006: 116; Levien 2018: 12, 15, 16; Shivji 2017: 10). He follows Luxemburg who suggested that the "historical career of capitalism" is characterised by an "organic link" between surplus creation by means of commodity-based exchange of equivalents between the capitalist and the wage labourer, i.e. expanded reproduction, and predatory practices that are aimed at bringing non-capitalist modes of production under the logic of capitalist accumulation, or primitive accumulation in Marx's terminology (Luxemburg 2003 [1913]: 433; see Harvey 2003: 137–38, 141, 2004a: 549, 2010: 306, 311–12; Shivji 2009: 34).

The "organic link" between expanded reproduction and accumulation by dispossession is reflected in the operation of spatio-temporal fixes, as the spatial reorganisation of accumulation systems can be based on equal and/or unequal exchange. As discussed, spatio-temporal fixes have stabilising effects on capital accumulation by opening up new spaces for investment and consumer goods. Even in cases where effective demand is not readily available in foreign territories, geographical expansion and reorganisation may serve the quest for lower costs of inputs, such as labour, raw materials, land or intermediate inputs (Harvey 2003: 139). Schoenberger (2004: 431) describes this as "another face of the spatial fix insofar as significant resources are acquired cheaply in one part of the globe to sustain the general process of accumulation centred elsewhere". This is accomplished by bringing non-commodified goods, raw materials, land or labour under the logic of capitalist accumulation by means of dispossession.

Accumulation by dispossession takes on many guises and Harvey describes its "*modus operandi*" as "both contingent and haphazard" (2003: 149; original italics, see also 2004a: 549). Harvey lists, among others, the commodification and privatisation of land and related expulsions of peasant populations, the conversion of communal or public into exclusive private property rights, the restraint of access to commons or the privatisation of the same and "colonial, neo-colonial, and imperial processes of appropriation of assets (including natural resources)" (2003: 145, see 2004a: 547; Levien 2018: 16). In cases of accumulation by dispossession, "resources are expropriated once and for all from a 'commons' that has been built up over many years and/or where the rate of economic exploitation of a given resource exceeds its natural rate of renewal or the absorptive capacity of the environment" (Jessop 2006: 151). Gaining access to natural resources allows for particularly "rapid surplus production" (Harvey 2006: 91).

Harvey, here akin to Marx, Lenin, Hilferding and Luxemburg, emphasises the crucial role of the credit system and finance capital in the process of accumulation by dispossession (2003: 145, 152, 2006: 94; see also Arrighi 2007: 224, 233; Luxemburg 2003 [1913]: 432). Backed by state power, finance capital and credit institutions provide for the "umbilical cord" which ties together expanded reproduction and accumulation by dispossession (Harvey 2003: 152). By promoting "levels of debt incumbency that reduce whole populations [...] to debt peonage" imperial states, international financial institutions (IFIs) as well as private and state-owned banks ensure that territories that do not possess (enough) commodities or reserves in return can still serve as spatial destinations for overaccumulated capital (Harvey 2003: 147). The "infrastructure-led development" paradigm, which has crystallised in the sequel of the global financial crisis of 2007–2008 appears to be a case in point (Schindler and Kanai 2021: 45; see Zajontz 2022a).

What Harvey conceptualises in his earlier writings on the theorisation of capitalist crises as the "temporal fix" (see footnote 1) refers to the facilitation of investments with long gestation and turnover time by means of credit (Jessop 2006: 151). In order to finance the built environment and infrastructure that facilitate the expanded circulation of other capitals, "temporal barriers" need to be overcome, namely the time lag between investment and profit realisation of such investments (Sheppard 2004: 472). For this purpose, "fictitious capital", in the form of credit or securities, is directed towards "future-oriented projects", such as highway or railway constructions. However, the redemption of "fictitious values" is dependent on the future productivity of related investments, i.e. the facilitation of more productive forms of accumulation. They must create sufficient returns, either directly or indirectly in the form of higher tax revenues, to service the debt. If they fail to do so, spatio-temporal fixes result in the devaluation of assets and/or sovereign debt crises (Harvey 2003: 113–14, 2004b: 64–65; see Castree 2009: 47).

In this context, "the question perpetually hovers: what happens when, for whatever reason, the 'spatial fix' is stymied and the debts incurred by temporal displacement fall due?" (Harvey 2001: 338). In the context of the BRI, Sum (2019: 545) has warned against possible long-term effects of "loan-debt obligations [which] allow China to renegotiate the terms, collateralise the debt and claim assets/resources by converting debt into equity". Harvey's rhetorical question has become a highly politicised point of contention in the concrete context of Chinese infrastructure projects in Africa, as governments in Addis Ababa, Djibouti, Lusaka, Nairobi and elsewhere have struggled to service infrastructure loans from Beijing's policy banks (see Brautigam 2022; Carmody et al. 2022a; Gort and Brooks 2023). While financial flows, such as loans for large-scale infrastructure projects, potentially boost economic growth in recipient economies, they can also increase their vulnerability vis-à-vis fictitious, speculative forms of capital and can "be used to impose savage devaluations" upon debtor societies (Harvey 2004b: 67; see Jessop 2006: 151). Harvey argues that "[f]inancial control through indebtedness is now the chief means for imposing the devaluation of capital elsewhere" (2006: 94). The current, renewed round of sovereign debt crises across Africa, in some cases not least caused by loan finance from Chinese and non-Chinese creditors, is a relevant case in point (see Carmody and Wainwright 2022; Gort and Brooks 2023; Zajontz 2022a). The empirical chapters of this book will document how particularly Zambia's growing indebtedness to Chinese and other creditors has structurally constrained the agency of the Zambian state. In contrast, President Magufuli's economic nationalism entailed a rather restrictive use of foreign loan finance, as will be discussed in Chapter 5.

The intricate relationship between accumulation by dispossession and spatio-temporal fixes cannot be overemphasised, as the former provides yet another avenue for the latter to materialise. The devaluation of particular "fixed" capital offers potential investment objects for new rounds of surplus generation:

> Devalued capital assets can be bought up at fire-sale prices and profitably recycled back into the circulation of capital by overaccumulated capital. [...] Valuable assets are thrown out of circulation and devalued. They lie fallow and dormant until surplus capital seizes upon them to breath [sic!] new life into capital accumulation. [...] One of the prime functions of state interventions and of international institutions is to orchestrate devaluations in ways that permit accumulation by dispossession to occur without sparking a general collapse. (Harvey 2003: 150–51)

By means of devaluation, expropriation, commodification or privatisation, accumulation by dispossession "release[s] a set of assets (including labour power) at very low (and in some instances zero) cost" which, in turn, serve as profitable outlets for surplus capital (Harvey 2003: 149; see Arrighi 2007: 224; Ashman and Callinicos 2006: 116; Levien 2018: 16). Accumulation by dispossession creates demand for surplus capital where there was none or not enough before (Harvey 2003: 139).

Privatisation has been a predominant form of accumulation by dispossession in the era of neoliberal capitalism since the 1970s, as it subjected hitherto unavailable goods and assets to market forces. The transfer of devalued assets from public into private ownership, not least in lower-income countries, at negligible costs has provided profitable ventures for chronically overaccumulated capital in the global economic centres (Arrighi 2007: 224–25; Ashman and Callinicos 2006: 116–17; Harvey

2003: 149–50). Hence, privatisation of elements of the built environment that traditionally were under state tutelages, such as transport infrastructure, telecommunications, energy, water and waste management, has become a "new incarnation" of the spatio-temporal fix (Schoenberger 2004: 431).

As many African governments again face debt distress or outright debt crises, following a decade and a half of expansive borrowing from multilateral institutions, sovereign creditors and private capital markets, the inflow of foreign surplus capital in the form of loans is much lower in the post-pandemic era. Accumulation by dispossession by means of privatisation currently becomes the renewed order of the day. Both the planned privatisation of Africa's devalued "Freedom Railway" and the commodification and gradual privatisation of Zambia's road network as a result of unsustainable sovereign debt underline the intricate link between the spatio-temporal fix and patterns of accumulation by dispossession. Harvey's concepts have significant explanatory power for the Chinese infrastructural fix in Africa.

The Chinese Infrastructural Fix in Africa

Harvey's theory helps us to understand the value-theoretical drivers underlying the rapid growth of Chinese finance and firms in African infrastructure markets over the past two decades. In *The New Imperialism*, Harvey describes how China itself has, for the longest time, served as the spatial destination for surplus capital mostly from Western economies. In the course of the 1990, China had been "an obvious candidate to absorb surplus capital" with net foreign direct investment (FDI) having increased tenfold. Moreover, since 1998, the Chinese state has embarked upon major debt-financed infrastructure programmes to absorb growing labour surpluses (Harvey 2003: 122, 123; see also Arrighi 2007: 219). In hindsight Harvey foresaw that China's accumulation system, focused on attracting FDI, growing both export-oriented industries and domestic markets as well as boosting country-wide infrastructure development, could only be a temporary solution to global overaccumulation dynamics. He noted that China's massive domestic infrastructure upgrading is "deficit-financed, and that entails high risks since if the investments do not return their value to the accumulation process in due course, then a fiscal crisis of the state will quickly engulf China with serious consequences for economic development and social stability" (Harvey 2003: 123). In

Adam Smith in Beijing, Arrighi (2007: 359) observed the "constant over-accumulation of capital and downward pressure on rates of profits" within the Chinese economy and anticipates what little later would result in problems of systemic magnitude. The meltdown of the global economy in the late 2000s following the global financial crisis of 2007–2008 caused a major accumulation crisis in China, as global demand for Chinese exports dwindled (Hung 2022: 27; Sum 2019; Taylor and Zajontz 2020).

The Chinese government tried to counteract this by means of a massive stimulus package (擴大內需十項措施) worth some $586bn most of which went into infrastructure (Liu et al. 2018; Sum 2019). Besides further driving up public debt, China's domestic infrastructure funding spree aggravated overcapacities in the infrastructure and construction sectors and related industries which had chronically experienced overaccumulation problems even before the crisis (Hung 2022: 27). Surplus capacities exceeded 30 per cent in the early 2010s in industries such as steel, iron, aluminium, glass, cement and power generation, while many SOEs in the infrastructure sector faced major profitability crises (Jones and Zeng 2019). Revenue growth of construction machine manufacturers, such as Xuzhou Construction Machinery Group (XCMG), Sany and Zoomlion, plunged again after a short-lived recovery following the 2009–2010 stimulus (Hung 2022: 49). Sum (2019: 531–32) describes how post-crisis stimulus funding, which allowed for vast investments in real estate and infrastructure within China, resulted in "[t]ripple bubbles" in property markets, the infrastructure and construction sectors and the finance and credit industry. Then Premier Li Keqiang's later attempts to inject liquidity and lower public debt by issuing sovereign bonds and publicly listing SOEs, a policy that was termed "Likonomics", proved unsustainable to boost domestic demand, while it further aggravated overcapacities and financial instability through stock market bubbles (Sum 2019: 532). Li's 2016 Report on the Work of the Government acknowledged that "overcapacity is a serious problem in certain industries" and committed the government to "focus on addressing the overcapacity in the steel, coal, and other industries facing difficulties" (quoted in Lu 2017).

Since 2013 under the leadership of Xi Jinping, the Chinese state has sought a new model that decreases China's reliance on exports and domestic investment and addresses the "twin constraints caused by chronic overcapacity (particularly in construction related industries) and 'excessive' foreign exchange reserves" (Breslin 2021: 101; see Gonzalez-Vicente 2019). The Chinese government embarked on a major transformation of the Chinese accumulation system, both discursively and materially. The "New Normal" narrative promises "slower but higher quality growth" (Sum 2019: 533). Spatially, there has been "a significant transformation from 'bringing in' to 'going global'" with the aim of addressing industrial overcapacity by linking Chinese firms with international markets (Yan 2021: 268–69). It is worth citing China's former Deputy Foreign Minister, He Yafei, at some length, since he aptly described the rationale behind the outer transformation and the geographical reorganisation of the Chinese economy:

> With the ensuing knock-on effects of the global financial crisis manifesting in the economic stagnation of advanced nations, coupled with the slowdown in China's domestic demand, industrial overcapacity, accumulated over several decades, has been brought into sharp relief [...]. This has resulted in a steep drop in profits, the accumulation of debt and near bankruptcy for many companies. If left unchecked, it could lead to bad loans piling up for banks, harming the ecosystem, and bankruptcy for whole sectors of industries that would, in turn, affect the transformation of the [Chinese] growth model and the improvement of people's livelihoods. It could even destabilise society. The Chinese government [...] has put forward guidelines for its resolution. The most important thing is to turn the challenge into an opportunity by 'moving out' this overcapacity on the basis of its development strategy abroad and foreign policy. (He 2014)

Overseas infrastructure markets were identified as particularly suitable "surplus valves" by the Chinese government, as a report by the China Investment Promotion Agency underlines: "China's overcapacity problem is becoming increasingly severe, and 'infrastructure export' could significantly ease the demand pressure of China's construction and manufacturing industries" (quoted in Freeman 2020). The BRI has become the material, institutional and semiotic vehicle for the global expansion of Sino-centric value and supply chains by establishing trans-regional connectivity networks (Gonzalez-Vicente 2019; Mayer and Zhang 2021; Schindler and Kanai 2021; Sum 2019; Taylor and Zajontz 2020).

The "moving out" of surplus capital and supplies in China's infrastructure and construction sectors and related industries has been strongly facilitated by Chinese financial institutions. The latter had been piling up foreign exchange reserves to more than \$3tn, while the post-crisis environment continuously curtailed them of secure lending opportunities within China (Jones and Zeng 2019: 1422). The Chinese move into overseas infrastructure markets, since 2013 under the BRI brand, has therefore been fuelled by "another round of stimulus package based on loan-debt investment"—this time on a global scale (Sum 2019: 539; see Alden and Large 2019: 338). To boost demand for Chinese infrastructure firms, the Chinese government has drawn on a host of financial instruments, such as the extensive disbursement of concessional and commercial loans from SOBs, export and supplier credits, sovereign guarantees and insurance schemes for both state-owned and private companies that invest abroad as well as the promotion of equity investment in infrastructure projects (Alden and Jiang 2019: 642–43; Lee 2014: 41–44; Sum 2019: 541–43).

Gonzalez-Vicente (2019: 491) describes Chinese efforts to facilitate overseas (infrastructure) projects as "state-coordinated investment partnerships" in which at least three sets of Chinese actors are commonly involved: Chinese state diplomacy to facilitate project negotiations with other governments, Chinese banks to provide loan finance and Chinese firms that actually implement a project. Moreover, new financial institutions, such as the Silk Road Fund, the BRICS New Development Bank and the Asian Infrastructure Investment Bank were established in the 2010s to raise further liquidity for Chinese infrastructure projects all across the world (Sum 2019: 542–43). Once again, former Deputy Foreign Minister He's explanations are instructive since they describe how the Chinese state has facilitated China's spatio-temporal fix. According to He, China's SOBs were instructed to "smooth the transfer of overcapacity overseas":

> The China Banking Regulatory Commission has issued directives for Chinese banks to assist in addressing overcapacity in a number of ways, including by expanding green credit, supporting efficient expansion of demand, and supporting the "go out" strategy and overseas M&As [mergers and acquisitions]. Banks have been asked to provide such companies with domestic insurance and overseas credit, more credit both in renminbi and foreign exchange, trade finance and international insurance, as appropriate, thus also facilitating the export of Chinese equipment, products and services, together with Chinese standards. (He 2014)

Harvey supposes that market and credit transactions that are aimed at resolving overaccumulation crises "function very well under conditions of uneven geographical development in which surpluses available in one territory are matched by lack of supply elsewhere" (2004b: 67). In the case of the Chinese infrastructural fix in Africa, this has manifested in the "convenient conjuncture" of Chinese surplus capital in search of profitable investment and Africa's often invoked infrastructure investment gap (Zajontz 2022b). Indeed, as noted in the introduction, the state of infrastructure across Africa trails behind in global comparison and the capacity to mobilise capital internally is commonly considered insufficient capital has been mobilised internally to address infrastructural needs (see Zajontz 2021). Driven by Beijing's policies to "move out" Chinese excess capital, Chinese state-owned banks have stepped in to fill Africa's so-called infrastructure funding gap. China became by far Africa's largest bilateral infrastructure financier in the course of the 2010s (ICA 2018: 8; Zajontz and Taylor 2021; see also Table A.1 in the Appendix).

According to data collected by the Boston University Global Development Policy Center, Chinese loan commitments to African countries amounted to $159.9bn between 2000 and 2020 (Boston University Global Development Policy Center 2022), although definite numbers remain difficult to obtain because of the opacity of Chinese loan finance and the lack of official Chinese publications on its overseas lending. Figure 2.1 shows the Chinese loan commitments to African countries from 2000 until 2020. As Fig. 2.2 shows, Chinese loan finance over the past two decades went primarily into infrastructure sectors, with transport ($48.8bn) receiving the most, followed by power ($40.5bn) in second place and ICT in fourth ($13.5bn) (Boston University Global Development Policy Center 2022). China's overseas loan-debt investments have afforded Chinese firms dominant market shares in African infrastructure and construction sectors (Carmody et al. 2022a; Taylor and Zajontz 2020; Zajontz 2022b; Zajontz and Taylor 2021). According to one report, Chinese firms constructed 41.9 per cent of all infrastructure projects in East Africa and 17.6 per cent in Southern Africa by 2016 (Deloitte 2016: 21, 25).[5]

[5] Deloitte's definition of East Africa: Burundi, Comoros, Djibouti, Eritrea, Ethiopia, Kenya, Rwanda, Seychelles, Somalia, Tanzania, Uganda. Southern Africa: Angola, Botswana, Lesotho, Madagascar, Malawi, Mauritius, Mozambique, Namibia, South Africa, Swaziland, Zambia, Zimbabwe (Deloitte 2016: 19, 23).

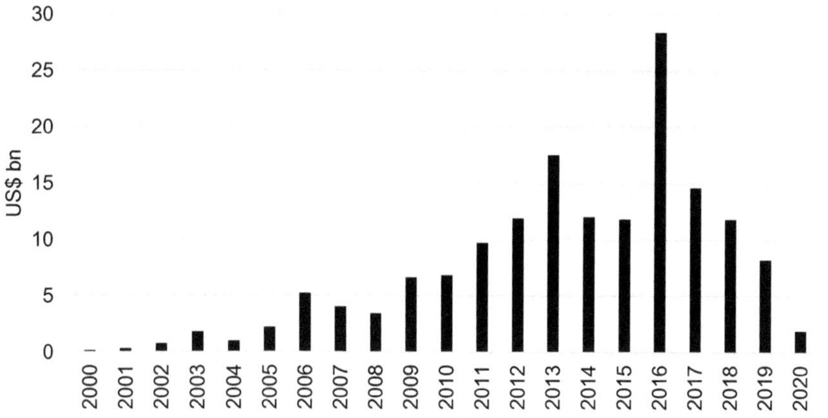

Fig. 2.1 Chinese loan commitments to Africa by year, 2000–2020 (*Source* Author's depiction, based on data from the Chinese Loans to Africa Database, Boston University Global Development Policy Center, https://www.bu.edu/gdp/chinese-loans-to-africa-database/ [accessed 28 May 2023])

Chinese loan finance for infrastructure has contributed to rapid debt accumulation in several African countries including Djibouti, Ethiopia, Kenya and Zambia. Following mounting public controversies in Africa and beyond over China's alleged "debt trap diplomacy" (see Bräutigam 2020; Carmody 2020; Zajontz 2022a), debt sustainability became a major concern for Chinese policymakers who intervened by putting in place stricter lending policies for the country's policy banks. As a consequence, China's overseas lending has slowed down significantly in recent years, with reports suggesting that total loan financing from China Exim Bank and China Development Bank fell from $75bn in 2016 to just $4bn in 2019 (Wheatley and Kynge 2020). New loan commitments to Africa fell by 93 per cent between 2016 and 2020 (Carmody et al. 2022b: 206; see Fig. 2.1). To uphold the demand for Chinese firms which are mobilised globally and across Africa, there has been a gradual shift in the financial governance of the BRI from sovereign debt finance towards private project finance, as Chapter 6 will reveal in the case of Zambia's road sector.

Harvey's theory is instructive to identify the structural and economic drivers behind the "going global" of Chinese infrastructure and construction firms, flanked by the country's policy banks. Yet, while Chinese

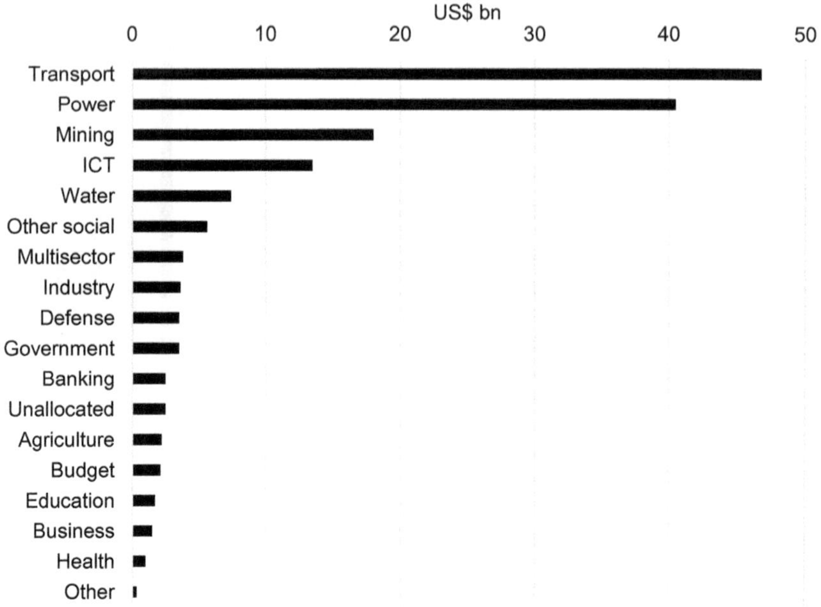

Fig. 2.2 Chinese loans to Africa by sector, 2000–2020 (*Source* Author's depiction, based on data from the Chinese Loans to Africa Database, Boston University Global Development Policy Centre, https://www.bu.edu/gdp/chinese-loans-to-africa-database/ [accessed 26 June 2023])

investments in Africa can be generally explained by the structural logics of the spatio-temporal fix, the manifestation of a "fix" in a particular country context is necessarily contingent upon specific political, economic and institutional factors and the agency of (state) actors in that country. This is where Harvey's theory does not provide a sufficiently rich conceptual arsenal.

The Under-Theorised Politics of the "Fix"

For Harvey, "capitalist imperialism" is a "contradictory fusion" of the "'territorial' and the 'capitalist' logics of power". He borrows this distinction from Arrighi's *The Long Twentieth Century* (see Arrighi 1994: 33–34, 2005: 28 n 15; Harvey 2003: 26, 27). Theoretically rooted in an over-accumulation theory of capitalist crisis, spatio-temporal fixes are driven by the capitalist logic of power. Yet, Harvey emphasises that they depend on political power as well as on territorialised forms of governance and administration for their materialisation (2003: 89, 93). He argues that "[w]hat happens with respect to internal dynamics and external relations depends on the class structure that arises and the forms of class alliance that form in and around issues of governance" (Harvey 2003: 102).

Despite some attempts to move beyond value-theoretical considerations (see, for instance, Harvey 2001: 328–33, 2003: 101–3, 2006: 102–7), Harvey does not problematise the extra-economic dimensions of capitalism at the same high levels of abstraction as the value-theoretical ones (Jessop 2004: 491, 2006: 163). Indeed, Harvey (2003: 30) insists on the dialectics between the capitalist and territorial logics of power inherent to the spatio-temporality of capitalist imperialism and emphasises that "concrete analyses of actual situations" require "to keep the two sides of this dialectic simultaneously in motion and not to lapse into either a solely political or a predominantly economic mode of argumentation". Yet, his accounts of the territorial logic of power remain largely descriptive, "pre-theoretical" and "overdetermined by the logic of capital" (Jessop 2006: 157, 156). With regard to spatio-temporal fixes, the role of territorial power is largely reduced to "ensur[ing] open spaces within which surplus capitals in particular can move" (Harvey 2006: 108). Contrary to his own aspiration (see Harvey 2003: 29), Harvey presupposes a capitalist state which, in its inner and outer relations, is ultimately subservient to the primacy of the capitalist logic, as he does not theoretically engage with the relative autonomy of territorial power which, at least potentially, restricts the "tendential ecological dominance" of the capitalist logic (Jessop 2006: 160). As a consequence, Harvey ultimately underrates the profoundly political dimension of the capital relation (Jessop 2004: 491, 2006: 162–63; see Ashman and Callinicos 2006).

In Harvey's work, whether and how social struggles and politics affect and condition spatio-temporal fixes as well as how state and non-state actors facilitate, contest or even forestall the materialisation of a "fix" are mostly treated as empirical questions. Jessop, in contrast, proposes a more comprehensive conceptualisation of the spatio-temporal fix which integrates economic and extra-economic dimensions of the capital relation and does justice to the constant "fragility" of the "fix" (2013: 312–15, see 2004: 493, 2006: 162; Sum and Jessop 2013: 243). In so far as "extra-economic mechanisms also reproduce the contradictions and dilemmas inherent in the economic mechanisms of the capital relation, they further expand the scope of agency, strategies and tactics to shape the course of accumulation and the manner in which these contradictions and dilemmas are expressed" (Sum and Jessop 2013: 242–43).

This reading provides the theoretical room for the causal efficacy of African state agency in the unfolding of the Chinese infrastructural fix. Social, political and cultural contestations that arise from spatio-temporal fixes require institutional and politico-juridical mediation. Therefore, the spatio-temporal fix is "necessarily social and typically also institutional and/or organizational", as structured coherence within a given spatio-temporal framework depends on a range of institutionalised compromises about the social and spatial distributions of costs and benefits of a particular "fix" (Sum and Jessop 2013: 248). In turn, social and political contestations over the regularisation and governance of spatio-temporal fixes imply their necessarily provisional nature (Jessop 2004: 493, 2006: 162, 2013: 312–15; Sum and Jessop 2013: 243, 248). Spatio-temporal fixes must therefore be understood not only as economic but also as highly political processes. They "emerge, in so far as they do, in a contested, trial-and-error process, involving different economic, political and social forces and diverse strategies and projects; and they typically rest on an institutionalized, unstable equilibrium of compromise" (Sum and Jessop 2013: 247). Hence, the actualisation of any particular spatio-temporal fix is dependent on the strategic-relational interactions between a myriad of social forces and their particular structural contexts—both within and without the region the "fix" emanates from.

This brings us to a second shortfall in Harvey's theory of spatio-temporal fixes, namely its "theoretical silence" vis-à-vis territories that "host" spatio-temporal fixes as a result of overaccumulation elsewhere. One analytical focus of this study lies on the role of African state agents in the context of Chinese-funded infrastructure projects. Unfortunately, Harvey offers little theorisation on the politics of the "fix" from the perspective of territories which get spatially drawn into spatio-temporal fixes. Harvey remains theoretically preoccupied with imperial formations—first and foremost with the power of imperial capital, then, as discussed to a much lesser extent, with the territorial power of capitalist states and empires. Where he engages with the territorial logic of power, he one-sidedly focuses on the politics of the imperial state or power bloc, whereas the relationship between the latter and territories that are subjected to capitalist imperialism remains theoretically unexplored.

Indeed, in his descriptive-empirical analyses of historical imperialisms, Harvey points to contradictions and conflicts between imperial states and territories that are subjugated to imperialism, for instance, in the case of US imperialism in Latin America or Iraq (2003: 8–25, 74–81, 2006: 9–25). Elsewhere, he argues that such territories "may be prized open by military force, colonization or commercial pressure, or they may voluntarily open themselves up to take advantage of surplus capitals from elsewhere" (Harvey 2006: 108). However, while stating that "[i]nternal unrest, disruptions in the class alliance of governance and belligerence towards external powers may result" (Harvey 2006: 109), his theory does not provide a more concrete-complex conceptualisation of the interrelations between endogenous and exogenous actors in regions which are drawn into spatio-temporal fixes.

This critique can be extended to the concept of accumulation by dispossession. I concur with Sheppard that Harvey's concept of accumulation by dispossession "describes well the continuities between old-style colonialism and contemporary empire, but its spatiality is not unpacked". In fact, in *The New Imperialism* Harvey pays scant attention to concrete forms of spatio-temporal fixes and dynamics of accumulation by dispossession that take shape in post-colonial world regions (Sheppard 2006: 138). Levien's critique takes a similar direction. For him, Harvey's conceptualisation of accumulation by dispossession remains too abstract and all-encompassing, as it "include[s] so many forms of theft and fraud" (Levien 2018: 16). As a result, it proves rather inapt to grasp the specificity of contemporary forms of dispossession—in Levien's own study land dispossessions in India. Moreover, while Harvey argues that spatio-temporal fixes can follow the logic of accumulation by dispossession, specifically when and where there is a shortage of demand for overaccumulated capital or lack of resources to "pay" for surplus commodities or services, he does not attempt to conceptualise the politics that co-determine as to whether "fixes" translate into forms of expanded reproduction or accumulation by dispossession. Levien (2018: 16; original italics) points out that "[b]y reading every instance of dispossession as a result of the global impulses of capital, Harvey fails to answer why and how impulses of capital translate into *dispossession* rather than merely commodification". Levien (2018: 16) rightly emphasises that accumulation by dispossession can be driven "by domestic capitalists in alliance with the state". Harvey does acknowledge that "state power […] [is] always a major player in accumulation by dispossession" (2003: 156). Yet, he conceptualises state powers insufficiently.

All the above points to a pivotal role played by state actors, social forces and factions of capital in the unfolding of spatio-temporal fixes and related patterns of accumulation by dispossession. Put differently, social forces—both within and beyond the territory in which overaccumulation occurs—are not mere bystanders but actively involved in the spatial reorganisation of capital accumulation. When capital moves into "new" territories and common goods are commodified and/or privatised, state actors generally act as legislating and regulating facilitators for either expanded reproduction or accumulation by dispossession. It is instructive to quote Shivji at some length, as he describes the analytical quest the study of capital accumulation in a peripheral context implies:

> The relationship between the two tendencies, that is, accumulation by dispossession and accumulation by expanded reproduction, and the territorial terrain (national or international) on which they operate, determines the *character of accumulation in the periphery*. In *investigating the political economy of accumulation in the periphery*, therefore, one must identify the two tendencies, their relationship and their specific forms as well as the terrain of their operation and the contradictions thus generated. The contradiction between the capitalist and the territorial logic presents itself in the periphery as the contradiction between accumulation by dispossession and accumulation by expanded reproduction on the one hand (capitalist logic), and the contradiction between nation and imperialism (territorial logic), on the other. (2009: 57, italics added)

The contradiction between accumulation by dispossession and accumulation by expanded reproduction calls for an analysis of specific forms of accumulation the "fix" takes in concrete-complex conjunctures. Regarding the contradiction between nation and imperialism, an investigation must recalibrate analytical focus towards the inner and outer relations of states that receive foreign surplus capital.

In summary, spatio-temporal fixes are contingent upon historically specific social, political and economic conjunctures for their materialisation. Grasping the politico-economic dynamics in the context of the Chinese infrastructural fix necessitates conceptual elaboration with regard to the African and Sino-African politics that co-condition the specific forms that Chinese investments in African infrastructure markets take on.

The need to do so arose in the process of gathering more empirical data which pointed to the central role played by African state actors in strategically influencing whether and how the Chinese-oriented infrastructural fix materialises in specific contexts. Without unpacking how various social and political forces affect and shape actual manifestations of the spatio-temporal fix and, thus, co-determine the distribution of related costs and benefits, studying spatio-temporal fixes runs the risk to "degenerate into a reified and largely economistic analysis of the logic of capital" (Jessop 2006: 163). To avoid this, I complemented Harvey's theory of spatio-temporal fixes with state-theoretical considerations which I introduce in the following chapter.

References

Alden, Chris, and Lu Jiang. 2019. "Brave New World: Debt, Industrialization and Security in China–Africa Relations." *International Affairs* 95(3):641–57. https://doi.org/10.1093/ia/iiz083.

Alden, Chris, and Daniel Large. 2019. "Conclusion." Pp. 329–42 in *New Directions in Africa-China Studies*, edited by C. Alden and D. Large. Abingdon: Routledge.

Amin, Samir. 1976. *Unequal Development: An Essay on the Social Formations of Peripheral Capitalism*. Sussex: The Harvester Press.

Arrighi, Giovanni. 1994. *The Long Twentieth Century: Money, Power and the Origin of Our Times*. London: Verso.

Arrighi, Giovanni. 2005. "Hegemony Unravelling 1." *New Left Review* 32:23–80.

Arrighi, Giovanni. 2007. *Adam Smith in Beijing: Lineages of the Twenty-First Century*. London: Verso.

Ashman, Sam, and Alex Callinicos. 2006. "Capital Accumulation and the State System: Assessing David Harvey's The New Imperialism." *Historical Materialism* 14(4):107–31.

Bieler, Andreas, and Adam David Morton. 2014. "Uneven and Combined Development and Unequal Exchange: The Second Wind of Neoliberal 'Free Trade'?" *Globalizations* 11(1):35–45. https://doi.org/10.1080/14747731.2014.860334.

Bond, Patrick. 2015. "BRICS and the Sub-Imperial Location." Pp. 15–26 in *BRICS: An Anti-Capitalist Critique*, edited by A. Garcia and P. Bond. London: Pluto Press.

Boston University Global Development Policy Center. 2022. "Chinese Loans to Africa Database." Retrieved July 15, 2023 (http://bu.edu/gdp/chinese-loans-to-africa-database).

Bräutigam, Deborah. 2020. "A Critical Look at Chinese 'Debt-Trap Diplomacy': The Rise of a Meme." *Area Development and Policy* 5(1):1–14. https://doi.org/10.1080/23792949.2019.1689828.

Brautigam, Deborah. 2022. "China and Zambia: Creating a Sovereign Debt Crisis." *International Affairs* 98(4):1347–65. https://doi.org/10.1093/ia/iiac109.

Brenner, Neil. 1999. "Beyond State-Centrism? Space, Territoriality, and Geographical Scale in Globalization Studies." *Theory and Society* 28(1):39–78. https://doi.org/10.1023/A:1006996806674.

Brenner, Neil. 2009. "A Thousand Leaves: Notes on the Geographies of Uneven Spatial Development." Pp. 27–49 in *Leviathan Undone? Towards a Political Economy of Scale*. Vancouver: University of British Columbia Press.

Breslin, Shaun. 2021. *China Risen? Studying Chinese Global Power*. Bristol: Bristol University Press.

Carmody, Pádraig. 2020. "Dependence Not Debt-Trap Diplomacy." *Area Development and Policy* 5(1):23–31. https://doi.org/10.1080/23792949.2019.1702471.

Carmody, Pádraig, and Joel Wainwright. 2022. "Contradiction and Restructuring in the Belt and Road Initiative: Reflections on China's Pause in the 'Go World.'" *Third World Quarterly* 43(12):2830–51. https://doi.org/10.1080/01436597.2022.2110058.

Carmody, Pádraig, Ian Taylor, and Tim Zajontz. 2022a. "China's Spatial Fix and 'Debt Diplomacy' in Africa: Constraining Belt or Road to Economic Transformation?" *Canadian Journal of African Studies* 56(1):57–77. https://doi.org/10.1080/00083968.2020.1868014.

Carmody, Pádraig, Tim Zajontz, and Ricardo Reboredo. 2022b. "From 'Debt Diplomacy' to Donorship? China's Changing Role in Global Development." *Global Political Economy* 1(2):198–217. https://doi.org/10.1332/uzhw7185.

Castree, Noel. 2009. "The Spatio-Temporality of Capitalism." *Time & Society* 18(1):26–61. https://doi.org/10.1177/0961463X08099942.

Deloitte. 2016. *Africa's Changing Infrastructure Landscape: Africa Construction Trends Report*. Diegem: Deloitte University.

Freeman, Duncan. 2020. "The Belt and Road Initiative and the Overcapacity Connection." Pp. 120–138 in *The Belt and Road Initiative and Global Governance*, edited by M. A. Carrai, J.-C. Defraigne, and J. Wouters. Cheltenham: Edward Elgar.

Gonzalez-Vicente, Ruben. 2019. "Make Development Great Again? Accumulation Regimes, Spaces of Sovereign Exception and the Elite Development Paradigm of China's Belt and Road Initiative." *Business and Politics* 21(4):487–513. https://doi.org/10.1017/bap.2019.20.

Gort, Joris, and Andrew Brooks. 2023. “Africa’s Next Debt Crisis: A Relational Comparison of Chinese and Western Lending to Zambia.” *Antipode* 55(3):830–52. https://doi.org/10.1111/anti.12921.

Harvey, David. 1982. *The Limits to Capital*. Oxford: Basil Blackwell.

Harvey, David. 2001. *Spaces of Capital: Towards a Critical Geography*. Edinburgh: Edinburgh University Press.

Harvey, David. 2003. *The New Imperialism*. Oxford: Oxford University Press.

Harvey, David. 2004a. “Retrospect on the Limits to Capital.” *Antipode* 36(3):544–49. http://doi.org/papers2://publication/uuid/97396CC0-28E6-4674-9D45-0BDAA3110F4D.

Harvey, David. 2004b. “The ‘New’ Imperialism: Accumulation by Dispossession.” *Socialist Register* 40:63–87.

Harvey, David. 2006. *Spaces of Global Capitalism: Towards a Theory of Uneven Geographical Development*. London: Verso.

Harvey, David. 2010. *A Companion to Marx’s Capital*. London: Verso.

He, Yafei. 2014. “China’s Overcapacity Crisis Can Spur Growth through Overseas Expansion.” *South China Morning Post*. Retrieved May 25, 2019 (https://www.scmp.com/comment/insight-opinion/article/1399681/chinas-overcapacity-crisis-can-spur-growth-through-overseas).

Hung, Ho Fung. 2008. “Rise of China and the Global Overaccumulation Crisis.” *Review of International Political Economy* 15(2):149–79. https://doi.org/10.1080/09692290701869654.

Hung, Ho-fung. 2022. *Clash of Empires: From “Chimerica” to the “New Cold War.”* Cambridge: Cambridge University Press.

ICA. 2018. *Infrastructure Financing Trends in Africa—2018*. Abidjan: The Infrastructure Consortium for Africa.

Jessop, Bob. 2003. “The Political Economy of Scale and the Construction of Cross-Border Micro-Regions.” Pp. 179–96 in *Theories of New Regionalism: A Palgrave Reader*, edited by F. Söderbaum and T. M. Shaw. Basingstoke: Palgrave Macmillan.

Jessop, Bob. 2004. “On the Limits of the Limits to Capital.” *Antipode* 36(3):480–96. https://doi.org/10.1111/j.1467-8330.2004.00427.x.

Jessop, Bob. 2006. “Spatial Fixes, Temporal Fixes and Spatio-Temporal Fixes.” Pp. 142–66 in *David Harvey: A Critical Reader*, edited by N. Castree and D. Gregory. Malden: Blackwell.

Jessop, Bob. 2013. “Finance-Dominated Accumulation and the Limits to Institutional and Spatio-Temporal Fixes in Capitalism.” Pp. 303–28 in *Fragile Stabilität – stabile Fragilität*, edited by S. A. Jansen, E. S. Schröter, and N. Stehr. Wiesbaden: Springer VS.

Jones, Lee, and Jinghan Zeng. 2019. “Understanding China’s ‘Belt and Road Initiative’: Beyond ‘Grand Strategy’ to a State Transformation Analysis.” *Third*

World Quarterly 40(8):1415–39. https://doi.org/10.1080/01436597.2018.1559046.
Lee, Ching Kwan. 2014. "The Spectre of Global China." *New Left Review* September 89:29–66.
Levien, Michael. 2018. *Dispossession Without Development: Land Grabs in Neoliberal India*. Oxford: Oxford University Press.
Li, Xing. 2016. "Conceptualising the Dialectics of China's Presence in Africa." Pp. 77–106 in *Emerging Powers in Africa: A New Wave in the Relationship?*, edited by J. Van der Merwe, I. Taylor, and A. Arkhangelskaya. Basingstoke: Palgrave Macmillan.
Lim, Kean Fan. 2010. "On China's Growing Geo-Economic Influence and the Evolution of Variegated Capitalism." *Geoforum* 41(5):677–88. https://doi.org/10.1016/j.geoforum.2010.04.003.
Liu, Weidong, Michael Dunford, and Boyang Gao. 2018. "A Discursive Construction of the Belt and Road Initiative: From Neo-Liberal to Inclusive Globalization." *Journal of Geographical Sciences* 28:1199–1214.
Lu, Zhiyao. 2017. "China's Excess Capacity in Steel: A Fresh Look." *Peterson Institute for International Economics*. Retrieved February 26, 2022 (https://www.piie.com/blogs/china-economic-watch/chinas-excess-capacity-steel-fresh-look).
Luxemburg, Rosa. 2003 [1913]. *The Accumulation of Capital*. London: Routledge.
Marx, Karl. 1967. *Capital: A Critique of Political Economy*. 3 Volumes. New York: International Publishers.
Marx, Karl. 1973 [1939]. *Grundrisse*. New York: Random House.
Marx, Karl. 2013. *Capital: A Critical Analysis of Capitalist Production*. Volumes 1 and 2, edited by M. G. Spencer. Ware: Wordsworth Editions.
Mayer, Maximilian, and Xin Zhang. 2021. "Theorizing China-World Integration: Sociospatial Reconfigurations and the Modern Silk Roads." *Review of International Political Economy* 28(4):974–1003. https://doi.org/10.1080/09692290.2020.1741424.
van der Merwe, Justin. 2016. "Theorising Emerging Powers in Africa within the Western-Led System of Accumulation." Pp. 17–38 in *Emerging Powers in Africa: A New Wave in the Relationship?*, edited by J. Van der Merwe, I. Taylor, and A. Arkhangelskaya. Basingstoke: Palgrave Macmillan.
van der Merwe, Justin. 2019. "The One Belt One Road Initiative: Reintegrating Africa and the Middle East into China's System of Accumulation." Pp. 197–217 in *Mapping China's "One Belt One Road" Initiative*, edited by X. Li. Cham: Palgrave Macmillan.
Ovadia, Jesse Salah. 2013. "Accumulation with or Without Dispossession? A 'Both/And' Approach to China in Africa with Reference to Angola." *Review*

of African Political Economy 40(136):233–50. https://doi.org/10.1080/03056244.2013.794724.

Perelman, Michael. 2000. *The Invention of Capitalism: Classical Political Economy and the Secret History of Primitive Accumulation*. Durham, NC: Duke University Press.

Schindler, Seth, and J. Miguel Kanai. 2021. "Getting the Territory Right: Infrastructure-Led Development and the Re-Emergence of Spatial Planning Strategies." *Regional Studies* 55(1):40–51. https://doi.org/10.1080/00343404.2019.1661984.

Schoenberger, Erica. 2004. "The Spatial Fix Revisited." *Antipode* 36(3):427–33. https://doi.org/10.1111/j.1467-8330.2004.00422.x.

Schumpeter, Joseph A. 1943. *Capitalism, Socialism and Democracy*. London: George Allen & Unwin.

Sheppard, Eric. 2004. "The Spatiality of the Limits to Capital." *Antipode* 36(3):470–79. https://doi.org/10.1111/j.1467-8330.2004.00426.x.

Sheppard, Eric. 2006. "David Harvey and Dialectical Space-Time." Pp. 121–41 in *David Harvey: A Critical Reader*, edited by N. Castree and D. Gregory. Malden: Blackwell.

Shivji, Issa G. 2009. *Accumulation in an African Periphery: A Theoretical Framework*. Dar es Salaam: Mkuki na Nyota Publishers.

Shivji, Issa G. 2017. "The Concept of 'Working People.'" *Agrarian South: Journal of Political Economy* 6(1):1–13. https://doi.org/10.1177/2277976017721318.

Sum, Ngai-Ling. 2019. "The Intertwined Geopolitics and Geoeconomics of Hopes/Fears: China's Triple Economic Bubbles and the 'One Belt One Road' Imaginary." *Territory, Politics, Governance* 7(4):528–52. https://doi.org/10.1080/21622671.2018.1523746.

Sum, Ngai-Ling, and Bob Jessop. 2013. *Towards a Cultural Political Economy: Putting Culture in Its Place*. Cheltenham: Edward Elgar.

Taylor, Ian. 2020. "Kenya's New Lunatic Express: The Standard Gauge Railway." *African Studies Quarterly* 19(3–4):29–52.

Taylor, Ian, and Tim Zajontz. 2020. "In a Fix: Africa's Place in the Belt and Road Initiative and the Reproduction of Dependency." *South African Journal of International Affairs* 27(3):277–295. https://doi.org/10.1080/10220461.2020.1830165.

Wheatley, Jonathan, and James Kynge. 2020. "China Curtails Overseas Lending in Face of Geopolitical Backlash." *Financial Times*. Retrieved December 18, 2020 (https://www.ft.com/edinburgh?ft-content-uuid=1cb3e33b-e2c2-4743-ae41-d3fffffa4259).

Yan, Karl. 2021. "The Railroad Economic Belt: Grand Strategy, Economic Statecraft, and a New Type of International Relations." *British Journal of Politics and International Relations* 23(2):262–79. https://doi.org/10.1177/1369148120940938.

Zajontz, Tim. 2021. "Infrastructure." Pp. 127–47 in *Yearbook on the African Union: Volume 1*, edited by U. Engel. Leiden: Brill.

Zajontz, Tim. 2022a. "Debt, Distress, Dispossession: Towards a Critical Political Economy of Africa's Financial Dependency." *Review of African Political Economy* 49(171):173–83. https://doi.org/10.1080/03056244.2021.1950669.

Zajontz, Tim. 2022b. "The Chinese Infrastructural Fix in Africa: Lessons from the Sino-Zambian 'Road Bonanza.'" *Oxford Development Studies* 50(1):14–29. https://doi.org/10.1080/13600818.2020.1861230.

Zajontz, Tim, and Ian Taylor. 2021. "Capitalism and Africa's (Infra)Structural Dependency: A Story of Spatial Fixes and Accumulation by Dispossession." Pp. 190–213 in *Africa and the Global System of Capital Accumulation*, edited by A. D. Cooper and E. Oritsejafor. Abingdon: Routledge.

Zhang, Xin. 2017. "Chinese Capitalism and the Maritime Silk Road: A World-Systems Perspective." *Geopolitics* 22(2):310–31. https://doi.org/10.1080/14650045.2017.1289371.

CHAPTER 3

Theorising African State Agency

> Understanding how the state in Africa really functions and its attributes has critical implications for China's initiatives on the continent. (Taylor 2006b: 956)

This assessment from the late Ian Taylor remains apt almost twenty years after its publication. The success of China's BRI and its countless infrastructure projects across the African continent are crucially dependent on interactions with the states they occur in. Generally, the state owns much of the hard infrastructure, such as roads and railways, and its agencies are responsible for questions related to the provision, construction, maintenance, operation, financing or privatisation of public infrastructure. The notion of the "infrastructure state" (DiCarlo and Schindler 2022: 5), discussed in the introduction, suggests that state institutions play a central role when foreign capital flows into a country's infrastructure sector. As established in the previous chapter, the extent to and the ways in which the Chinese infrastructural fix in Africa materialises is crucially contingent upon state strategies pursued by African governments.

This chapter therefore provides a state-theoretical complementation to Harvey's largely value-theoretical theory of spatio-temporal fixes which culminates in a "theoretical synthesis" that allows for a strategic-relational analysis of the Chinese infrastructural fix in Africa. The chapter first

T. Zajontz, *The Political Economy of China's Infrastructure Development in Africa*, International Political Economy Series,
https://doi.org/10.1007/978-3-031-44449-4_3

engages with existing literature on African state agency in Africa–China relations and problematises that it commonly equates state agency with the agency of political elites due to reductionist ontologies of the state. In the second part, the literature on neopatrimonialism is engaged. Yet, instead of understanding neopatrimonialism as an internal pathology of African statehood, the chapter suggests that the coexistence and interpenetration of legal-bureaucratic and patrimonial types of domination must be analysed in conjunction with modes of capital accumulation.

In a last step, this chapter introduces the Strategic-Relational Approach (SRA) and its social relational state ontology. Understanding the state as a strategic-relational domain helps us to relate strategies pursued by African state actors to the strategically selective structural context they find themselves in. The SRA provides theoretical room to incorporate merits of both the neopatrimonialism concept and neo-Marxian accounts but, at the same time, transcends their respective limitations. The chapter concludes by integrating the spatio-temporal fix with the SRA and argues that the latter offers the necessary state-theoretical supplement to understand the concrete-complex manifestation of the former in specific African territories.

African State Agency in Sino-African Relations

A prominent theme in the existing literature on Sino-African relations has been the interplay of "formal" and "informal" institutions and practices in intergovernmental relations between China and Africa. Accordingly, neopatrimonialism and related concepts, such as patronage, rent-seeking and corruption, have experienced somewhat of an epistemic renaissance and have been frequently deployed to account for the personalised and informalised conduct among African political elites and Chinese state and non-state actors. Taylor suggests a degree of politico-cultural and institutional congruence between the Chinese and African polities, arguing

> that, in China, the party is the government and the government is the state, just as is the case in much of Africa. Thus the concept of politics in China is very similar to that in many African countries, and the Chinese have been accused of personalizing their political engagement with African leaders, hence reifying the extant neopatrimonial regimes (2009: 11; see also 2007).

Personalised relations among Chinese and African elites are seen by many as reinforcing highly exclusive, opaque and patrimonial governance modalities. Carmody and colleagues (2012: 220) argue that Sino-Zambian geogovernance is based on an "(il)liberal bargain between domestic and Chinese political elites", whereby African governments refrain from imposing regulations on Chinese investments and the Chinese government from political conditionalities. Generally, Beijing's nominal foreign policy principle of non-interference in the domestic affairs of its "partners" is claimed to consolidate neopatrimonial governance in Africa, as political elites are presented a preferable alternative to Western "good governance" conditionalities (Hodzi 2018: 196, 198; Taylor 2007: 142). The developmental impact of the Sino-African liaison has been claimed to be compromised and biased in favour of a small African elite which uses its access to political power for personal enrichment (Carmody et al. 2012; Hodzi 2018; Large 2021: 33; Taylor 2010: 81). Mohan and Lampert assert that "the sections of the state that benefit from (and so fight for) Chinese investment are often part of a highly select elite" (2013: 97).

Such assessments are reflected in numerous case studies. Taylor, for instance, demonstrates how Nigerians within, or with close connections into, government offices exert "agency-as-corruption" in their engagement with Chinese investors. Exposed to corrupt practices, the latter develop corresponding counter-agencies to adapt to the inner workings and behavioural norms prevalent in Nigeria's shadow state/economy. As Taylor argues: "Where the state is the major source of wealth and fortune, agency for self-advancement is necessarily focused on capturing power within the state" (2015: 31–32). Makundi and colleagues examine the capacity of the Tanzanian government to extract knowledge and technology transfers from Chinese investments. While they record gradual improvement as a result of President Magufuli's anti-corruption campaign, they conclude that

> official Chinese engagement in Tanzania has persistently remained vulnerable to corruption and rent-seeking behaviour among the local and Chinese agents, leading to new challenges such as higher project costs and the biased allocation of some projects in favour of the ruling elites. (Makundi et al. 2017: 346)

Undeniably, the “African agency turn” in the literature has helped to challenge the prevailing myth, not least in popular discourses, of powerless African states that are degraded to passive bystanders in the continent’s engagement with China. Especially the case studies provide valuable and rich empirical insights into the interaction between African governments (and the societies they represent) and Chinese state, non-state and hybrid actors. Moreover, the research interest in African elite agency and the deployment of neopatrimonialism and related concepts as analytical categories has helped to balance the long-standing Sino-centrism in the literature and has revealed important insights into institutional and politico-economic dynamics that co-determine the nature, and ultimately the developmental outcome, of Sino-African relations in particular spatio-temporal conjunctures.

However, I agree with Carmody and Kragelund (2016: 5; see Wai 2012: 40) that the “recent emphasis on African agency risks unwittingly reinforcing ‘internalist’ explanations of African underdevelopment”. The analytical preoccupation with the role of African political elites in the continent’s engagement with China, in many cases, neglects the structural context in which elite agency is exerted. Carmody and Kragelund rightly caution that

> [p]ositing African elites as largely being in the driving seat in relations with China risks implying that they have the power to reshape fundamentally the nature of their state-societies. This is patently untrue. [...] [W]e have raised reservations about how agency is conceptualized in African studies and cautioned that it needs to be, if not discarded, at least situated in the context of massive power differentials between states in the international system and the continuing and arguably deepening power of transnational capital [...]. While it is certainly accurate and salutary to highlight the power of African state elites and other actors on the continent, there is a need to temper this through recognition of the ongoing realities and structural conditions of the functioning of the global political economy. (2016: 23, italics added)

The two authors are not alone in their attempt to go beyond reductionist readings of African agency. In his case study on Sino-Ethiopian relations, Ziso cautions against reducing African agency to elite agency (2018: 39). He counters the tendency to essentialise African state forms and insists that “informal institutions and the relationship between the formal and the informal are not merely part of political culture or the continuity of African traditions" (Ziso 2018: 50). Drawing on Migdal's "state-in-society" approach (see Migdal 1994), which cautions against treating the state as a unitary actor that reacts to outside forces independently of domestic social forces, Ziso shifts attention to the alteration of formal and informal institutions as a result of the influx of Chinese capital into the Ethiopian economy. He finds that

> the increasing role of informal institutions in Ethiopia reflects, in part, the emergence of new social forces that are emerging out of the effects of Chinese capital. Hence, the growing informalisation of institutions is reflective of the new dynamics of the Chinese capital. For example, corruption, policy networks, patrimonialism, norms and cultures are some of the informal institutions that have either emerged or been reinforced by various forms of Chinese capital in Ethiopia. (Ziso 2018: 50)

Other contributions have complemented arguments about neopatrimonial governance with considerations about wider structural parameters that condition Sino-African relations (see Alves and Chichava 2019; Carmody and Kragelund 2016; Zajontz 2022b). Scrutinising China's impact on political-economic structures underlying Angola's and Mozambique's external relations, Alves and Chichava (2019) undertake the theoretical attempt to relate neopatrimonial practices with Bayart's theory of extraversion, which posits that African elites appropriate material resources through their relations with foreign actors in order to bolster their political power domestically and accumulate personal wealth. The authors conclude that, in the Angolan case, "ruling elite agency remains largely subservient to the logic of extraversion". Accordingly, instead of strengthening Africa's structural position in international relations, African extraversion strategies vis-à-vis China deepen the continent's dependency on external powers, while, at the same time, sustaining highly personalised rule in neopatrimonial political contexts (Alves and Chichava 2019: 255; see also Carmody and Kragelund 2016: 7, 17–21; Corkin 2013: 14–17, 2015: 65, 77–79). Carmody (2013: 140) argues in a similar vein that "the broad structure of African political economy—economic extraversion coupled with often authoritarian governance—is likely to remain largely intact in the medium term at least".

Notwithstanding these attempts to situate African state agents within broader structural configurations, the bulk of other research on African (state) agency has mostly relied on uncritical ad hoc applications of a myriad of concepts, such as neoptrimonialism, and on static and reductionist conceptions of agency (Carmody and Kragelund 2016; Mohan and Lampert 2013). In this instance, we can discern a continuity in Africa–China studies with much of the research on the neopatrimonial state, which is characterised by reductionist state ontologies (Zhuawu 2013: 8). Next, I shall therefore engage with the concept of neopatrimonialism and related concepts, before embedding "the" African state within the broader structures of capitalism.

On the (Un)Usefulness of the Neopatrimonial "Moniker"

Neopatrimonialism has long served as a "catch-all concept" (Theobald 1982: 555) to describe all kinds of governmental practices and state-society relations in Africa that do not fit Eurocentric, modernist conceptualisations of the rational-bureaucratic state and of a neat separation between the public and the private spheres (Bach 2012: 221; Erdmann and Engel 2006; Pitcher et al., 2009). There has been little consensus regarding a definition of neopatrimonialism. Despite the "conceptual muddle" (deGrassi 2008: 112) that surrounds the term, there has been a "mute culture of acceptance of the concept" (Erdmann and Engel 2006: 5). The term has served as the "common denominator" for a wide range of disparate practices, such as "despotism, clannish behaviour, so-called 'tribalism,' regionalism, patronage, 'cronyism,' 'prebendalism,' corruption, predation, factionalism, etc." (Bach 2012: 221; originally in French by Médard 1991: 330). Moreover, Pitcher and colleagues (2009: 126) observe that the concept is frequently incurred without reference to particular spatio-temporalities. Consequently, "neopatrimonialism has become the convenient, all-purpose, and ubiquitous moniker for African governance" (Mkandawire 2015: 563).

Meanwhile, Africanist scholarship has received profound critique for its tendency to essentialise the neopatrimonial form of "the" African state (see, for instance, deGrassi 2008: 112; Erdmann 2013: 59; Hodzi 2018: 192–93; Mkandawire 2015: 569; Wai 2012: 38–40). Bratton and van de Walle (1997: 62; original italics) have, for instance, suggested that neopatrimonial rule are the "*core* feature of politics in Africa" and that personal relationships "constitute the foundation and superstructure of political institutions" on the continent. For Hyden (2000: 19), neopatrimonialism is the "institutionalised curse" that has afflicted Africa.

Both in academic and policy circles neopatrimonialism has been misused as a convenient scapegoat for Africa's developmental impasse, thereby locating its root causes firmly in the realm of African domestic politics and eliding wider structural parameters (Mkandawire 2015: 563; Pitcher et al. 2009: 134; Wai 2012: 40; Zhuawu 2012b: 131–32; Ziso 2018: 37–39). Reductionist claims about the prevalence of a particular form of state and mode of domination in Africa commonly ignore social, cultural and political differences across African societies and neglecting the complexity, dynamism and mutability of African state-society relations (Ziso 2018: 38–39). Zhuawu (2012b: 132) is right in that "neopatrimonialism is created contingently by political actors in social, political and economic conditions in which they are situated". Instead of essentialising the neopatrimonial nature of the state, its conjunctural and intricate interrelations with external social, economic and political forces must be accounted for theoretically (see Alves and Chichava 2019; Ziso 2018).

Notwithstanding such justified critique of underdefined, ahistorical, reductionist and arguably neocolonial applications of the neopatrimonialism "moniker", it would be equally reductionist to altogether neglect the causal significance of the interplay of personal and impersonal rule, as well as of formal and informal institutions, when analysing African political economies. I agree with Erdmann and Engel (2006: 6; original italics) that neopatrimonialism "is a concept that *does make sense* if it is properly defined". Their definition of neopatrimonialism is worth citing at length:

> Neopatrimonialism is a mixture of two co-existing, partly interwoven, types of domination: namely, patrimonial and legal-rational-bureaucratic domination. Under patrimonialism, all power relations between ruler and ruled, political as well as administrative relations, are personal relations; there is no differentiation between the private and the public realm. However, under neopatrimonialism the distinction between the private and the public, at least formally, exists and is accepted, and public reference can be made to this distinction. Neopatrimonial rule takes place within the framework of, and with the claim to, legal-rational bureaucracy or "modern" stateness. Formal structures and rules do exist, although in practice the separation of the private and public sphere is not always observed. (Erdmann and Engel 2007: 105)[1]

[1] Originally, the term neopatrimonialism has derived from the reception of Max Weber's political sociology and his conceptualisation of patrimonialism (Erdmann and Engel 2006: 7–17; see Eisenstadt 1973; Médard 1982). The theoretical novelty of Erdmann and

The defining characteristic of neopatrimonialism is thus the coexistence and interpenetration of patrimonial and legal-rational-bureaucratic logics and institutions (Erdmann and Engel 2006: 17–18; see also Bratton and van de Walle 1997: 62). The definition provides for the "hybrid structure" of neopatrimonialism and an "equal treatment" of both types of domination, thus shielding against the common tendency in the literature to minimise the significance of legal-rational bureaucracy in neopatrimonial states (Erdmann and Engel 2007: 104). It is correct to assume that in most states that are characterised by neopatrimonial governance "there is more than a legal-rational façade" (Erdmann and Engel 2006: 17). Ideas of "modern" statehood and the rational-bureaucratic state have found entrance into constitutions and political systems all across Africa. The fact that this has been partly the result of (neo)colonial imposition does not belie the centrality of the bureaucratic state in African politics, which is formally based on legal-rational principles.

Erdmann and Engel's definition is useful for another reason. Acknowledging that legal-bureaucratic and patrimonial norms and procedures permeate one another transcends binary dichotomisations of formal versus informal institutions as well as of the public and the private spheres (Erdmann 2013; Erdmann and Engel 2007). Informality and formality are intricately linked in various ways and to varying degrees (Erdmann

Engel's definition is the combination of two types of Weber's "three pure types of legitimate domination" (legal-rational, traditional and charismatic), namely legal-rational bureaucracy and patrimonialism (Erdmann and Engel 2006: 17–18, 2007: 104–5; see also Bratton and van de Walle 1997). Legal-rational bureaucracy claims its legitimacy from a "legally established impersonal order", which is characterised by a "continuous rule-bound conduct of official business", a "specific specified sphere of competence (jurisdiction)" and an "organization of offices [which] follows the principle of hierarchy" (Weber 1978 [1922]: 215–18; also cited in Erdmann 2013: 61). Under patrimonialism, in turn, which falls into Weber's category of traditional domination, "obedience is owed to the person [...] who occupies the traditionally sanctioned position of authority". The legitimacy of this type of domination thus flows from "[p]ersonal loyalty, not the official's impersonal duty" (Weber 1978 [1922]: 227; also cited in Erdmann 2013: 60). Importantly, as Pitcher and colleagues (2009: 125–26) point out, Weber's conceptualisation of patrimonialism does not provide for its equation with malgovernance, typical for much of the literature on neopatrimonialism. It is conceptualised as an ideal type of legitimate domination, marked by "reciprocity and voluntary compliance between rulers and the ruled". Wai (2012: 35) is right in that Weber's ideal–typical abstractions have all too often been misappropriated as blueprints to assess the degree of modern statehood in Africa. For detailed discussions of the conceptual genesis of neopatrimonialism, see Erdmann and Engel (2006, 2007) and Pitcher et al. (2009).

and Engel 2006: 18). Hence, neopatrimonialism is characterised by a continuum, as opposed to a dichotomy, of formal and informal institutions, norms and practices. The relative significance of formal and informal institutions and procedures, as well as the specific ways in which they are combined, then become subject to concrete analyses of particular politico-historical conjunctures.

Other concepts, which are frequently invoked in the discourse about neopatrimonialism and, at times, are employed without clear definitional delineation, are relevant in the context of this study, namely clientelism and patronage. I follow Erdmann and Engel (2007: 106) in subsuming clientelism and patronage as "integral" to neopatrimonialism. However, they are not the same as neopatrimonialism but rather a subset of institutions and practices typical for the patrimonial end of the continuum. Both practices refer to the brokerage or distribution of specific resources or services, aimed at securing political support from the recipient (Erdmann and Engel 2006: 20–21). The latter is, in the case of clientelism, an individual, and in the case of patronage a social, political, ethnic or religious group. Even though the benefits of patronage are generally collective goods, for instance, roads or schools, its redistributive effect can be limited, as patronage serves foremost politically motivated, symbolic purposes (Erdmann and Engel 2006: 21). Both clientelism and patronage must be understood as "specific features of late capitalist transformation relating to the challenge of consolidating power within formal institutions that are supported neither by a significant capitalist surplus nor by traditional sources of authority" (Gray 2015: 385).

Crucially, patrimonial institutions and practices are not necessarily unlawful. Corruption, however, is per definition. As Fatton (1988: 259; see also Taylor 2007: 141) famously argues, corruption can become the "rampant and pervasive cement" between patrons and their clientele. Yet, Scott Taylor (2006c: 282) rightly criticises that "[t]he neopatrimonial model, which has been applied to virtually all sub-Saharan countries, assumes a virtually intractable culture of clientelism and corruption". Just as neopatrimonialism, corruption is not endemic to Africa. It constitutes an illicit practice that can be more or less institutionalised, depending on path-dependencies and contingencies in the social, politico-juridical and economic realms within specific time–space frameworks.

This study draws on another concept that frequently features in the literature on neopatrimonialism, namely rent-seeking. Rentier activities elucidate, at a yet more concrete-complex level, the intermediary role of state actors, by means of formal and informal procedures and strategies, in cycles of capital accumulation. In neoclassical economics, rents are a "premium above opportunity costs for a given set of resources" (Lewis 1994: 440; also cited in Erdmann and Engel 2006: 26; see Krueger 1974). Rents occur when the price-setting mechanisms of the market are distorted by non-market forces (Erdmann and Engel 2006: 26). We speak of political rents when such non-market forces arise from government interventions in markets. Rentier activities then refer to "politically mediated opportunities for obtaining wealth through non-productive economic activity" (Boone 1990: 427; see Erdmann and Engel 2006: 26). The inflow of capital for infrastructure projects offers manifold opportunities for rent-seeking, especially in neopatrimonial governance contexts (Gil et al. 2019: 7). Rent-seeking is also a relevant analytical category when scrutinising state actors involvement in economic decision-making that determines whether accumulation takes on the form of expanded reproduction or of accumulation by dispossession. As discussed in Chapter 2, privatisation releases public assets into cycles of private capital accumulation. Thereby, state actors can provide economic opportunities for both domestic and external fractions of capital to accumulate through non-productive means. Furthermore, state actors can appropriate rents through state interventions in the form of public contracts and procurements (Erdmann and Engel 2006: 26–27). This has been prevalent in the Sino-Zambian "road bonanza", as discussed in Chapter 7.

Politically mediated rentier activities allude to the patrimonial entanglement of political elites and domestic capital, as the profiteers from such particularistic state interventions usually stand in close, personal relationship with political elites. Broader redistributive effects of such activities are generally not to be expected, since

> [t]he short-term horizon of these entrepreneurs […] means that their "investments" are geared to making quick profits such as entering into one-sided contracts, on utterly unequal terms, with the state or state companies […]; using state positions or contracts to obtain lucrative tenders; colluding with dubious "local and foreign investors" to establish front banks, exchange bureaus, or housing condominiums. (Shivji 2009: 72)

The informal alliances between state managers and aligned fractions of capital, be they internal or foreign to a particular state, casts into doubt a common misconception about the incompatibility of neopatrimonialism and capitalist accumulation which has been prevalent in mainstream discourses, as Mkandawire has convincingly critiqued (see Mkandawire 2015: 575–78). This demands theoretical reflection on the relationship between (foreign) capital and the African state. This is where the discourse on neopatrimonialism can profit from neo-Marxian state theory and vice versa.

Neopatrimonialism as a Mode of Accumulation

The bulk of literature on neopatrimonialism has remained preoccupied with the agency of corrupt and nepotistic political elites and has reified "the" (African) state into a singular, autonomous power apparatus which is conceived as largely detached from societal dynamics and external influences (Ziso 2018: 38–39; see also Zhuawu 2012b: 132, 2013: 6). But "Africa's leaders are neither autonomous nor robots; they reflect diverse class and fractional interests" (Shaw 1985: 5; see Taylor 2014: 5; Taylor and Williams 2008: 147). Neopatrimonial governance does not occur in a structural vacuum and in isolation from social forces within and beyond a given polity. As noted, scholars have pointed to the "external relations" of neopatrimonial regimes and their entanglement with foreign capital (see, for instance, Alves and Chichava 2019; Ziso 2018). The inflow of foreign capital provides opportunities for rentier activities, clientelism, patronage and corruption. Thus, it affects the class structure and the balance of social forces within a given state. As Carmody (2009: 1202) points out, increased FDI in specific sectors or industries is associated with "domestic capitalist class (re)formation [...], as some niches are opened up for a domestic rentier class". Ziso's study (2018: 30, 50) on the effects of the influx of Chinese capital in Ethiopia documents how the interaction of foreign capital with local social forces has transformed the Ethiopian state and affected the relative significance of formal and informal institutions that govern state-society relations. It follows that solely focusing on political elites and state institutions narrowly conceived fails to do justice to the complex structural embeddedness of the state in processes of capital accumulation.

This is why neo-Marxian scholarship, which has a long tradition in shedding analytical attention to the role of the state within capitalism, adds theoretical value (for overviews, see Jessop 1982, 1990: Ch. 1, 2016b: Chs. 2–5). Power and colleagues are right in that Africa–China studies can benefit from neo-Marxian theorisation of the relationship between transnational capital and peripheral states and of the latter's degree of autonomy from the former (Power et al. 2012: 162; see Lampert and Mohan 2015: 110). Some authors have conceptualised the intermediary role of peripheral states in globalised processes of capital accumulation with conceptual reference to the historical role of compradors (see, for instance, Amin 1990; Frank 1972). Etymologically, the term comprador was used for native servants in European households in Asia. The comprador was responsible for the purchase and stewardship of provisions and necessities for the colonialists. He was an agent for the foreigners. The Chinese term to describe this position, mâi-pan, which predates European colonisation, translates into purveyor (Simpson and Weiner 1989: Vol. 3, p. 630).

By analogy, central to the role of the comprador class within African states is its intermediary function between foreign capital and local social forces (Shivji 2009: 70). As such, this class is dependent on foreign capital, as it lacks a productive base of their own (Taylor 2017: 29). Shivji points to the historical role of "*compradorial* capitals (merchant, state, petty bourgeois, etc.)" in mediating between local (peasant) labour and foreign capital (2009: 70, original italics). Compradorial capital "may take different forms, including state or private, depending on the state of class struggles and the nature of global political economy, but its logic is grounded in accumulation by dispossession, that is, non-equivalent exchange" (Shivji 2009: 70). Crucial for the purpose of this study which is inter alia concerned with the privatisation of infrastructure, Shivji describes the pivotal role of state managers in processes of accumulation by dispossession as follows:

> In this expropriation, the state as the ultimate custodian of public domain is closely involved. The political-bureaucratic class thus reaps political rents (corruption, bribes) by alienating the commons. They are compradors in the original Chinese sense of the word. [...] State positions, including its coercive powers, become the means of extracting surplus from producers, or expropriating values from weaker capitals. (2009: 71, original italics)

Implicitly, Shivji's deliberations allude to the coexistence and interpenetration of patrimonial and legal-bureaucratic logics of domination. The political-bureaucratic class owes parts of its power to authority that is derived from legal-rational norms and institutions. At the same time, this authority is used to further particularistic economic interests by means of political rents, thereby consolidating authority through patrimonial means. Shivji argues that "[i]n an African periphery, monopoly capital is able to extract even greater concessions and super profits given the weakness of internal forces and the state" (2009: 68). While there is, without a doubt, ample historical evidence for this, the "weakness of internal forces and the state" must be conceptually unpacked to provide for concrete-complex analyses of the contradictions between the capitalist and territorial logics of power in a peripheral context (see Shivji 2009: 57). It is indeed unfortunate that most radical political economists categorically reject the notion of neopatrimonialism on the grounds that it has served neoliberals as an ideological justification for slashing the interventionist role of the state in the developing world (Erdmann and Engel 2006: 6; see Beckmann 1993: 21–22; Mustapha 2002; Olukoshi 1998: 14). I argue that re-conceptualising neopatrimonial modes of governance as dialectically related to globalised capital accumulation can provide valuable state-theoretical insights into the contradictions between the capitalist and political logics of power in post-colonial world regions.

Neo-Marxian scrutiny towards the class character of the state reveals that particular forms of state incorporate specific social relations between dominant and subaltern classes, be they situated within or beyond the boundaries of a given state. As a consequence, they embody contradictions that accrue from historically specific class struggles (Ziso 2018: 35; see Bryan 1987). While the degree of autonomy of the political sphere from the economic base has remained a point of intra-Marxian contention (see Jessop 2016b: 100–101), there is overall consensus that the state internalises, mediates and reproduces contradictions inherent to capitalism. Bieler and Morton argue that

> capital is not simply represented as an autonomous force beyond the power of the state but is embodied by classes or fractions of classes *within* the very constitution of the state. There are contradictory and heterogeneous relations internal to the state, which are induced by class antagonisms between different fractions of (nationally or transnationally based) capital. (2018: 127, original italics)

Reinterpreted in this light, the neopatrimonial state, characterised by the combination of legal-rational and patrimonial norms and principles in the conduct of political domination, is a politico-institutional reflection of class relations in particular capitalist social formations, which are conditioned by domestic *and* external structures and social forces.

Hence, it appears indicated to reconsider the interdependence between neopatrimonialism and capitalist accumulation. Mkandawire recounts three common arguments in the literature on neoptarimonialism about the supposed "anticapitalist posture of neopatrimonial states". Firstly, it has been argued that neopatrimonial regimes fear the development of an economically independent capitalist class, as this would undermine their political power which is based on the exclusive and patrimonial, as opposed to open and competitive, distribution of economic means (Mkandawire 2015: 575, 576; see Konings 2007; Lewis 1994; Sandbrook and Oelbaum 1997; Tangri 1998). Closely related, the second argument suggests that the mutual dependency inherent to patron-client relationships obstructs the "social differentiation essential to capitalist development", thus the development of relatively independent classes (Mkandawire 2015: 576; see Chabal and Daloz 1999; Hyden 1983).

Thirdly, neopatrimonialism is considered by some to be incompatible with capital accumulation, because it compromises the legal-bureaucratic institutional framework, not least the guarantee of property rights, which capital is portrayed to depend on (Mkandawire 2015: 577; see Callaghy 1988; Sandbrook and Oelbaum 1997). While all three arguments point to contradictions between neopatrimonial economic governance and capital accumulation, by far do they suggest that the two are antithetical. Mkandawire rightly argues that

> [c]apitalist development does not always originate in a full-blown capitalist class. It often takes place within a range of class coalitions, cultural expressions, and logics. Many of the practices associated within neopatrimonialism are at the core of primitive accumulation. (2015: 578)

As discussed in Chapter 2, capitalism does not solely rely on the logic of expanded reproduction. Primitive means of accumulation, characterised by unequal exchange, are a constant feature of capitalism (Ashman and Callinicos 2006: 116; Harvey 2003: 144; Shivji 2017: 10). Thus, neopatrimonial governance constitutes one possible politico-institutional environment that mediates and reproduces contradictions that arise from the "organic link" between expanded reproduction and accumulation by dispossession as well as from the relations between imperial capital and African social forces (see Harvey 2003: 137–38, 141, 2004a: 549, 2010: 306, 311–12; Luxemburg 2003: 433; Shivji 2009: 34). As the late Thandika Mkandawire (2015: 578) asserted, "[n]eopatrimonialization of the bourgeoisie can be quite compatible with capitalist accumulation".

Shivji rightly points out that "[t]he configuration of internal classes and their alliance with foreign capital is evidently a concrete question requiring concrete investigation" (2009: 68). Such investigation necessitates nuanced conceptualisations that locate African states firmly within their structural contexts which co-determine not only the configuration of social forces within the state but also their differential strategic capacities to reproduce or transform existing structures. Here, the SRA provides conceptual redress. It provides conceptual room to incorporate the theoretical added value of both the neopatrimonialism concept and neo-Marxian accounts but, at the same time, transcends their respective limitations, namely the common theoretical decoupling of the state apparatus from wider societal dynamics in the former case and the epiphenomenalisation of the state to an instrument of class domination in the case of the latter (see Kelly 1999: 110; MacKinnon, Shaw, and Docherty 2008: 15; Zhuawu 2012b: 134).

The Strategic-Relational Approach

The SRA helps us to transcend "rather static and one-dimensional concept[s] of agency" (Carmody and Kragelund 2016: 5) which have characterised the African "agency turn" (Alden and Large 2019: 13) in Africa–China studies. The bulk of research in the subfield has remained surprisingly unconcerned with structure-agency dialectics and has relied on voluntarist conceptions of agency which ultimately fail to explain how agents are differentially affected by their structural contexts. Structural constraints are occasionally mentioned but seldomly integrated into conceptualisations of African agency. Structuralist reductionism has been countered by accounts of agency that are void of structure. Links (2021: 115–16) recognises this when referring to agency as "both the act of holding specific interests and goals as well as the capacity that actors possess to set agendas, negotiate, and act in accordance with their specific interests and goals. Power then, is not a focal or defining characteristic of agency but is closely related to structure". Hence the apposite call for a "contextual approach [...] that considers the contours and specificities of African agency" (Links 2021: 124). Such an approach must transcend the conceptual structure-agency dualism that is inherent to much of the literature associated with the African "agency turn".

The SRA to the structure-agency conundrum, as developed by Bob Jessop and Colin Hay (see, for instance, Hay 1996, 2002; Jessop 1990, 2001, 2005, 2007), provides useful conceptual tools for an examination of the interplay between differentially efficacious causal properties of structures and differential strategic capacities of agents, both in specific conjunctures and over time (Jessop 2006b: n.n.). As Jessop puts it:

> structure consists in differential constraints and opportunities that vary by agent; agency in turn depends on strategic capacities that vary by structure as well as according to the actors involved. (2016b: 55)

Strategy thus serves as the conceptual connector which relates structures and agents dialectically, thereby overcoming dualist ontologies of structure and agency (Hay 2002: 128–29; Koivisto 2012: 45–46). Strategy is understood as "intentional conduct oriented towards the environment in which it is to occur", motivated by specific objectives and intended outcomes (Hay 2002: 129). Crucially, strategies are not only oriented towards particular structural contexts but also conditioned by them (Hay 2002: 129).

According to the SRA, structures have "strategically-selective" properties which "may privilege some actors, some identities, some strategies, some spatial and temporal horizons, some actions over others" (Jessop 2005: 48). Central to the notion of "strategic selectivity" is that the extent to and the ways in which structures constrain or enable actors differ from actor to actor (Jessop 2006b: n.n., 2016b: 55). As Hay has it, "[s]ocial, political and economic contexts are densely structured and highly contoured. As such, they present an unevenly distributed configuration of opportunity and constraint to actors" (2014: 38). This implies differential chances of particular strategies being selected or rejected by specific actors (Jessop 2006b: n.n.). Yet, structures are not "*absolutely constraining*". There is scope to "overwhelm, circumvent, or subvert structural constraints" (Jessop 2016b: 55, original italics; see Wylde 2017: 74). In critical realist terms, the "strategic selectivity" of structures is a "causal property at the level of the real". Structures only tendentially impose biases towards the selection or rejection of some strategies (and not others). The actuation of strategic selectivities however depends on the interplay of a particular strategic selectivity with other (counter-)

tendencies at the level of the actual and on differential agential capacities (Jessop 2006b: n.n.).

The SRA posits that agents act (or retain to act) upon "structurally-oriented strategic calculation" which is aimed at either stabilising or transforming particular structures and their selectivities (Jessop 2005: 48). Importantly, strategic calculation must not necessarily be explicit or utilitarian. Actions can flow from routines, intuition or habit and thus their strategic articulation might be less explicit. Yet, even unreflexive actions are "based upon perceptions (accurate or otherwise) of the strategic context and the likely consequences of specific actions" (Hay 2002: 133, see also 2014: 38). In addition, agents choose their strategies and actions on the basis of differential capacities to reflect, learn and act (Jessop 2001: 1223, 2005: 49). The reproduction or modification of particular structures and their strategic selectivity therefore depends on how reflective specific actors are of particular structural contexts, what capacities they have at their disposal to follow through with a preferred strategy and if oppositional agential strategies are pursued by other actors (Jessop 2005: 51). As Jessop puts it, "because subjects are never unitary, never fully aware of the conditions that affect (their) strategic action, never fully equipped to engage in strategic reflection and learning, there are no guarantees that they will largely realize their strategic goals" (2016b: 55). In the recursive interaction between structures and agents, "*[s]trategic learning*" becomes essential to agents' strategic calculation, as actors try to enhance their awareness of structural constraints and opportunities and adjust their strategies in order to maximise the chances to modify specific structural contexts in the intended way (Hay 2002: 133, original italics).

The SRA invokes a "double dialectic". The first-order dialectic arises from the interplay between the "structurally-inscribed strategic selectivity of structures" and the capacity of agents to carry out "strategic-context analysis" in any particular conjuncture (Jessop 2006b: n.n., see also 2016a: 55). This first-order dialectic implies that strategic selectivity is not located purely within structures, which would amount to reifying them. Differential constraints and opportunities of structures ever only materialise in relation to specific agents with specific strategic capacities (Jessop 2006b: n.n., 2016b: 55; Zhuawu 2013: 7). The second-order dialectic is concerned with the reflexive-recursive dimension of the structure-agency relation. It takes into consideration how the succession of conjunctures stabilises or modifies the strategic selectivities of structures. Thus, it dialectically relates the "selective retention of strategies" that are favoured by selectivities within a given structural configuration and the "capacity of strategically reflexive agents" to transform particular structural constraints and opportunities "through shifts in strategy, tactics, alliances, spatio-temporal horizons, scale-jumping, etc." (Jessop 2006b: n.n., see also 2005: 49–50; Wylde 2017: 74). This second dialectic underscores the "processual" and "evolutionary" nature of the structure-agency relationship, as it incorporates the logic of path-dependency, in terms of "inherited structures and strategic capacities", as well as the logic of path-shaping, in terms of the "modification of structures and capacities" (Jessop 2005: 52, 2006b: n.n.). Hay summarises the two dialectical moments of the SRA neatly:

> Jessop seeks to bring agency into structure—producing a structured context (an action setting)—and to bring structure into agency—producing a contextualised actor (a situated agent). [...] A repeat move—bringing the situated actor back into the structured context and the structural context to the situated actor—yields a new conceptual pairing in which the dualism of structure and agency has been dissolved. Jessop now identifies a *strategic actor* within a *strategically selective context*. (2002: 128, original italics; see also Koivisto 2012: 45)

The SRA lends itself well for a process-oriented analysis of strategies of African states actors in their densely structured context. To my knowledge, thus far only Zhuawu has employed the SRA to analyse African state strategies (see 2012a, 2012b, 2013).[2] In his research on Mauritius' role within the World Trade Organization, he critiques essentialist and reductionist tendencies in much of the literature on African statehood and argues that the "SRA allows for an examination of different African states by providing contexts within which political actors are situated analytically, and the institutional landscape which political actors must negotiate" (Zhuawu 2013: 7, see also 2012b: 134). It is therefore insightful to engage with some of the state-theoretical assumptions of the SRA.

[2] Soulé-Kohndou (2019: 189) refers to the SRA in her work on bureaucratic agency in Benin-China relations but neither further engages with nor applies its concepts. The same is true for Lampert and Mohan (2015: 111).

The State as a Strategic-Relational Domain

The SRA avoids the reification of a highly complex entity, the state, into a monolithic actor with a presumed "pre-given national interest" (Watson 2005: 179; also cited in Zhuawu 2013: 8; see Brenner et al. 2003: 2; Taylor and Williams 2008: 147). The "'state-as-agent' thesis" has arguably been the single most impactful and insistent theoretical reductionism in IR and IPE theory (Wight 2006: 177–78; see also 1999: 126; Koivisto 2010: 69–70; Niemann 2000: 68, 90; Onuf 1998: 207; Watson 2005: 179–81). As Agnew underlines, both liberal and realist IR theories conventionally treat states "as if they are the ontological and moral equivalents to individual persons" (1998: 3, see also 2010; Söderbaum 2016: 55).

Contrasting reified conceptions of the state, the SRA disentangles state agency by emphasising that the state itself does not act. State power is exerted by altering sets of politicians and officials who (temporarily) occupy particular state institutions and organisations (Jessop 1990: 367, 2007: 37; Koivisto 2010: 80). This does not imply that the state can be reduced to its personnel or the state apparatus narrowly defined. The SRA shields from the common "tendency to reify the state-society distinction" (Jessop 2007: 79; see also 1990: 2; Hay and Lister 2006). Neo-Weberian state-theoretical accounts, including the bulk of the literature on neopatrimonialism, have rightly drawn critique for their analytical preoccupation with state managers and their portrayal of state institutions as quasi-autonomous entities that hover above society (Hay and Lister 2006: 9; Lampert and Mohan 2015: 110; Zhuawu 2012b: 132, 134; Ziso 2018: 37–39).

The SRA locates politicians, state officials, governments and bureaucracies firmly within the structural context of the state (Jessop 2007: 6). Jessop notes that "[a]lthough these 'insiders' are key players in the exercise of state powers, they always act in relation to a wider balance of forces within and beyond a given state" (2016b: 56). This relational ontology of the state guards against voluntarist conceptions of state agency and the reduction of the latter to elite agency (Zhuawu 2013: 8). As an "institutional ensemble", the state provides "a set of institutional capacities and liabilities" necessary to exert state power. Yet, "the power of the state is the power of the social forces acting in and through the state" (Jessop 1990: 269–270 n. 13, see also 2007: 37; Brenner 2004: 89; see Koivisto 2010: 79–80).

Jessop takes inspiration from, among others, Gramsci's concept of the integral state[3] and Poulantzas' notion of the state as a social relation to theorise the "interdependence of state and society" (Kelly 1999: 110; see Jessop 2007: 23–24, Chs. 4, 5; Gramsci 1971; Poulantzas 1978). Rejecting static conceptions of the state, Poulantzas famously argues that "like 'capital'", the state is "a relationship of forces, or more precisely the material condensation of such a relationship among classes and class fractions, such as this is expressed within the State in a necessarily specific form" (1978: 128–29; also cited in Jessop 2016b: 54). The SRA, however, transcends those strands of neo-Marxian state theory that reduce the state to an "epipheomenon of an ultimately determining economic base" and, hence, equate state power and class power (Kelly 1999: 110; see Jessop 1990: 85–94, 354, 2007: 56). In an attempt to de-essentialise the capitalist state, the SRA acknowledges that "many other political strategies, besides economic or class interests, determine state policy" (Kelly 1999: 111). Jessop argues that

> state power is capitalist to the extent that it creates, maintains or restores the conditions necessary for capital accumulation in a given situation. It is non-capitalist to the extent that these conditions are not realised. This view radically displaces our theoretical focus from the search for guarantees that the state apparatus and its functions are necessarily capitalist in all aspects to a concern with the many and varied contingent effects of state power on accumulation in specific conjunctures. (1990: 354)

Accordingly, the SRA explicitly refrains from "captur[ing] the 'essence' of the state" and focuses instead on conceptualising "its changing forms, functions and effects" (Hay 1996: 7; see also Jessop 1990: 10, 2016b: 54).

This is accomplished by theorising the state as a strategic-relational domain that is characterised by the interaction between strategic selectivities inherent to the relations that constitute the state and strategic agents who orient their strategies towards, against and/or through the state (Jessop 2016b: 54; Koivisto 2010: 79–80). Again following in Poulantzas' footsteps, the SRA considers the state not only as relational

[3] Gramsci (1971: 263) famously set up the equation "State = political society + civil society, in other words hegemony protected by the armour of coercion" (1971: 263). His "integral" conception of the state suggests an "interconnection and dialectical unity of the state and civil society" (Humphrys 2018: 30; see Jessop 2007: 24).

but also as strategically selective (Kelly 1999: 110; see Jessop 2016b: 54). In any given historical conjuncture, the organisation of the state apparatus as well as the capacities and resources of the state present an uneven strategic terrain that differentially privileges certain actors, strategies and interests over others (Jessop 2006b: n.n.; Zhuawu 2012b: 134–35, 2013: 7). As Hay describes it, the state's "structures, practices and *modus operandi* are more amenable to some types of political strategy and certain types of intervention than others" (1996: 7, original italics; see Jessop 1990: 260).

Conceptualising the state as a strategic-relational domain allows for a reevaluation of the neopatrimonial state form as a product of the recurrent interaction between the state's strategic selectivity and actors' strategies oriented towards constraints and opportunities that arise from this selectivity. Viewed through the SRA lens, the neopatrimonial state constitutes a particular institutional ensemble with specific structural biases which are contingently reproduced—or potentially transformed—by strategic actors within and beyond a given state. As Jessop has it, "[p]articular forms of state privilege some strategies over others, privilege the access of some forces over others, some interests over others, some time horizons over others, some coalition possibilities over others" (1990: 10, see also 2016b: 56; Brenner 2004: 90). As a result of its specific set of structural constraints and opportunities, the neopatrimonial state form privileges certain strategies, tactics, interests and policies over others. Concretely, it enables political actors to draw on patrimonial strategies within a formally legal-bureaucratic institutional set-up to exert certain state powers (see Erdmann and Engel 2007: 105). Its particular institutional ensemble provides uneven access to state resources and, by extension, to broader economic means. Crucially, the neopatrimonial state is not autonomous from society, but firmly embedded in societal relations that constitute it (see Jessop 2016b: 54). The reproduction of its strategic selectivities depends on a particular balance of forces as well as on the retention of agential strategies that allow for its sustenance. By implication, any given state form can be transformed through changes in the balance of forces as a result of political struggle and concurrent strategic actions of agents within and beyond state institutions (Jessop 2016b: 56).

Whether, how and to what extent structural biases of a given state (form) actualise in specific historical conjunctures depends on the contingent balance of forces and the strategic capacities of political actors (Jessop 2016b: 54). As noted above, actors' strategic capacities differ according to their differential awareness and reflexivity about specific structural constraints and opportunities (Jessop 2001: 1223, 2005: 49, 51). The success of strategies to transform structural biases of the state is not least contingent on the occurrence of oppositional strategic action (see Jessop 2005: 51). Recalling the second-order dialectic discussed above, current structural biases of the state are the result of interactions between past strategic selectivities and strategic actions aimed at transforming the same (Brenner 2004: 88; Jessop 1990: 263, 2016b: 56; Koivisto 2010: 81). This indicates a "spiral of path dependency and path shaping" that marks the recursive-reflexive retention or modification of strategies oriented towards or articulated through the state (Jessop 2016b: 56).

Understanding the state as "the site, the generator and the product of strategies" (Jessop 1990: 260; see Brenner 2004: 87) allows us to analyse how state managers employ specific "state strategies" in particular historical conjunctures to modify particular structural constraints. State strategies can be understood as

> initiatives to mobilize state institutions in order to promote particular forms of socioeconomic intervention: they focus upon the articulation of the state to non-state institutions and attempt to instrumentalize the state in order to regulate the circuit of capital and to modify the balance of forces within civil society. (Brenner 2004: 88; see Jessop 1990: 260–61)

Again, state strategies result from the strategic interplay and political contestation among various social forces within and beyond the institutional ensemble of the state and are subject to a state's inherent strategic selectivity, as some social and political forces have privileged access to state capacities and resources (Brenner 2004: 88).

Overall, the state constitutes a site of political contestation among social forces for (access to) state power*s* (Koivisto 2010: 80; Ziso 2018: 35). Jessop suggests to speak of "*various potential* structural power*s* (or state capacities), in the plural". While they are inscribed in the "institutional ensemble" of the state, their actuation depends on the "agency of definite political forces in specific conjunctures" (Jessop 2007: 37, italics added; see 1990: 366; Koivisto 2010: 86). This way, the SRA captures not only the state's orginisational structure but draws attention to the ways in which state powers are contingently exercised by specific political actors (Jessop 2016b: 54). Thus, it allows for an *analytical* differentiation between the more structural and the more strategic, i.e. contingent, dimensions of the state (Jessop 2006b: n.n; see Heigl 2011: 83; Koivisto 2010: 80). Jessop underlines that "by virtue of its [the state's] structural selectivity and always specific strategic capacities, state powers are always conditional and relational". Their effectiveness depends on a state's structural links to and interdependencies with social and political forces within and beyond its territory (2007: 78–79; see also Jessop 1990: 269 n. 13).

This observation seems highly relevant with respect to African (state) agency in Sino-African relations. Understanding the state as a strategic-relational domain helps us to relate strategies pursued by African state actors in relation to the strategically selective structural context they find themselves in.

Towards a Strategic-Relational Analysis of China's Infrastructure Development in Africa

To conclude the theoretical part of this book, I now integrate the main concepts discussed in this and in Chapter 2 into a theoretical framework that is the result of an iterative movement between the discussed concepts and the concrete case studies. In the following empirical chapters, there will be references to the theoretical arguments that were developed in Chapters 2 and 3. To briefly recapitulate: I identified the spatio-temporal fix as a generative mechanism that has driven Chinese-funded infrastructure development in Africa (and elsewhere). A generative mechanism is a posited structural process that is involved in the generation of a particular social phenomenon (Wagner 2016: 52; Wight 2004: 288). It is situated at the level of the "real" in Bhaskar's stratified conception of reality (see 1978: 56–62). For its actuation it depends on human agency (Danermark et al. 2002: 55–56; Jessop 2005: 42). The realisation and outcomes of a spatio-temporal fix are therefore historically contingent and specific, according to the interplay of the posited generative mechanism with other structural and agential forces in concrete-complex conjunctures (see Danermark et al. 2002: 55; Wagner 2016: 68; Yeung 2010: 332).

As a result of retroductive reasoning, the SRA (to state power) provided complementary abstractions to account for the "necessary contextual conditions" (Fletcher 2017: 189) for the actuation of the spatio-temporal fix in specific African infrastructure states. In its concrete-complex manifestation, the spatio-temporal fix is to be understood as a strategic-relational process in which a myriad of strategic actors facilitate, oppose or mediate its inherent structural tendencies through strategic action. Jessop underlines that the SRA's

> assumptions, concepts, and arguments [can be used] to theorize spatio-temporal fixes, their relative coherence and stability, and, provided that we also integrate a materialist analysis of the inevitable, incompressible, and unsurpassable contradictions and dilemmas of the capital relation, the necessary crisis-tendencies and eventual weakening of any given spatio-temporal fix. (2004a: n.n.)

Combining the concept of the spatio-temporal fix with the SRA adds theoretical value in several regards. First, as established in Chapter 2, spatio-temporal fixes require a combination of social, cultural, political, regulatory and institutional compromises that guarantee their (always temporary) "success" (Jessop 2006a: 162). The SRA offers the theoretical "toolkit" to assess whether, to what extent and how such compromises are fabricated in specific spatio-temporal environments. Thereby, it is analytically sensitive to economic and extra-economic, not least political and institutional, relations among social forces which differentially affect strategic action in concrete conjunctures. Concretely, the SRA conceptually accounts for the historically, politically and economically specific contextualities of particular infrastructure states into which Chinese surplus capital and materials have flowed.

A second advantage of the proposed theoretical "synthesis" stems from the possibility to analyse specific strategic action within particular strategically selective structural contexts (see Hay 2002: 128; Jessop 2001: 1223; Zhuawu 2013: 7). This provides for a differentiated and process-oriented examination of African (state) agency in the context of Chinese infrastructure projects. For its materialisation, a spatio-temporal fix is not only dependent on compromises among social forces within polities in which overaccumulation originates (in our concrete case China) but between foreign actors and social forces within territories that are drawn into a particular "fix". Lastly, strategic alliances must be forged within recipient territories for a spatio-temporal fix to "succeed". A central institutional "mediator" in the facilitation of such alliances is the state in recipient regions. As primi inter pares in "a complex, heterogenous, and multilevel network" of governance (Jessop 2016b: 185), African states—or rather their political representatives—facilitate, mediate or alter the actual forms of the spatio-temporal fix and the ways in which its inherent contradictions manifest. Thereby, state strategies in the infrastructure sector are contingent upon the structural selectivity inscribed into the institutional ensemble of a given state, on state actors' strategic capacities as well as on the relative effectiveness of competing strategies, viz. the existing balance of social and political forces within a state or region (see Jessop 2005: 50–51, 2016b: 56).

Thirdly, owing to the dialectical relationship between "structurally-inscribed strategic selectivity" and "structurally-oriented" strategic action (Jessop 2005: 50, 51, see also 2006b), the SRA guards against bracketing out the "material causality" (Lewis 2002: 21) of structures in our assessment of African (state) agency. As discussed, this has been a flaw in much of the existing literature of the "African agency turn" (see Carmody and Kragelund 2016: 23). The particular structural constraints and opportunities that African state actors are confronted with in the context of infrastructure projects condition the strategic scope for African agency and ultimately the contingent form of the infrastructure state. Furthermore, the relational tendencies inherent to the spatio-temporal fix present new structural constraints and opportunities for African states, while they reproduce others and transform yet others. Hence, they differentially affect (but do not determine) African state strategies in the infrastructure sector. The scope of African agency in the unfolding of the Chinese infrastructural fix is therefore dependent on the reflective capacity of state actors to engage in "'strategic context' analysis" and corresponding adjustments of goals, strategies, tactics and policies (Jessop 2016b: 55). This includes political actors' awareness and reflective assessment of the ways in, and the extent to, which Chinese participation in infrastructure development will affect existing structural constraints and opportunities.

The reflexive-recursive selection of strategies is furthermore dependent on the learning capacities of relevant individuals, groups or organisations, which, for their part, are informed by the success (or lack thereof) of previously selected strategies (Jessop 2004: n.n.). Strategic learning in the concrete cases under investigation also includes reflection about previous experiences with (Chinese-funded) infrastructure projects or investments in a particular state and potentially also in other countries. Moreover, a state's strategic capacity in the infrastructure sector is influenced by its institutional and organisational means, such as necessary technocratic expertise as well as human and technological resources to engage with

Chinese actors in the planning, negotiation and implementation stages of infrastructure projects.

Analysing the actualisation of the Chinese infrastructural fix through strategic-relational lenses adds a fourth theoretical advantage. The SRA's theoretical sensitivity towards the path-dependency and path-shaping logics of the interaction between structures and agents provides for an analysis of how the actualisation of the spatio-temporal fix contingently affects "inherited structures and strategic capacities" of African states (Jessop 2006b: n.n.; see 2005: 52, 2016b: 55). It has been argued that Sino-African engagements have reinforced Africa's dependent integration into the global economy (see, for instance, Carmody 2020; Cowaloosur 2015; Taylor 2014; Taylor and Zajontz 2020). Carmody and Kragelund (2016: 22) argue that, thus far, African states "have been unable to alter fundamentally the nature of the dependency that characterises their relations with China and other foreign powers and companies". Dependency, as a structural relation of difference, also characterises China's engagement in Africa's infrastructure sector. The dependence on foreign capital to develop or maintain infrastructure constitutes a crucial strategically selective structural constraint for African governments (see Alden and Jiang 2019: 642–643). It is strategically selective in the sense that it might affect some states more or differently than others. While the availability of Chinese (financial) capital for African infrastructure projects has diversified and increased the sources of infrastructure finance for African governments and regional organisations, it has not fundamentally altered but rather reproduced this particular structural constraint (see Brautigam 2022; Carmody and Wainwright 2022; Zajontz 2022a).

Closely related to this, sovereign debt obligations make for another structural constraint for African strategic action. The crucial function of credit and debt in the unfolding of spatio-temporal fixes tendentially reinforces sovereign indebtedness (see Bond 2015: 20–21; Castree 2009: 47; Harvey 2003: 113–14, 117, 147, 2004b: 64–67; Jessop 2006a: 151). Where African state managers recursively take on Chinese loans unreflective of structural constraints that arise from debt dependency, growing sovereign debt further narrows their strategic scope in the infrastructure sector and other policy realms. The Zambian case is unfortunately emblematic of this, as the country's extensive borrowing from Chinese and other creditors throughout the 2010 has increasingly constrained the government's policy space and ultimately rendered the country dependent on the goodwill of the IMF and a diverse group of creditors in a strenuous debt restructuring process under the so-called Common Framework (see Bagwandeen et al. 2023; Brautigam 2022). Analytical focus must therefore be placed upon African governments' capacity and willingness (or lack thereof) to modify the strategic selectivity of foreign capital dependency and debt structures, for instance, through domestic capital mobilisation or debt restraint.

Debt dependency vis-à-vis particular creditors, be they sovereign creditors, multilateral institutions or private investors, co-conditions the relative probability of accumulation strategies and resultant governance modalities of infrastructure projects in the unfolding of the Chinese infrastructural fix. Where governments lack sufficient financial resources to construct or rehabilitate infrastructure and where loan financing has become politically and economically too costly, the commodification of public infrastructure or its privatisation by means of PPPs often serve as "last resort" strategies (see van Wieringen and Zajontz 2023). Changing structural constraints/opportunities in financial terms are therefore crucial to understand whether the Chinese infrastructural fix materialises by means of expanded reproduction or accumulation by dispossession. In this instance, governments' fiscal space as well as state actors' reflective capacity about previous experiences of infrastructure privatisation affect a given state's strategic capacity regarding preferred governance schemes for Chinese infrastructure projects. The conceptual considerations have become highly relevant in both the context of TAZARA's planned rehabilitation and the growing commodification of Zambian roads.

Further structural constraints for African state actors arise from the fact that the Chinese infrastructural fix is multi-scalar in its form and articulations. As a result, it necessitates territorialised systems of governance on various spatial scales for its materialisation (see Harvey 2003: 93). The multi-scalar governance of China's spatio-temporal fix becomes most apparent in the context of the BRI which "envisages a new (trans-) regional scale to manage over-accumulation problems" (Sum 2019: 533). Tendentially, capital strives to overcome spatial boundaries and to ensure the seamless flow of other capital in search of new profitable outlets (Jessop 2006a: 155–160). To facilitate the same, the Chinese state, in alliance with both state and private fractions of Chinese capital, sets rules and conditions under which Chinese-centred accumulation is to be spatially reorganised—think, for instance, of loan and investment conditions. Chinese accumulation strategies leave differential room for African agency in negotiating Chinese investments and loans, depending not least on structural constraints and opportunities prevalent in a given state at a specific time. As Wylde points out, "[s]tructural constraints can be imposed by the agency of the more powerful, setting the context for the less powerful (or powerless)" (2017: 54). This becomes, for example, evident in the context of "commercial conditions", such as the coupling of Chinese loan financing to the selection of particular contractors (Mohan and Tan-Mullins 2019: 1373; see Alden and Jiang 2019: 641; Corkin 2012: 476).

However, Chinese and African agential powers do not necessarily stand in opposition but are "inter-constitutive" and hence variable, as Carmody and Kragelund correctly point out (2016: 9). In the Angolan case, they demonstrate, for example, that the power of African states which heavily rely on rents from sales of natural resources is highly dependent on commodity prices. The higher the prices at the international markets, the larger the power of African states in Sino-Angolan economic relations (Carmody and Kragelund 2016: 5). They rightly underscore that power "not only exits in the nation-state, but also [...] in numerous interstate structures, in non-state actors, in structures, and in actors" (Carmody and Kragelund 2016: 9). Their argument is very much in line with the strategic-relational conception of state power as "always conditional and relational" (Jessop 2007: 78–79, see also 1990: 269 n. 13). Yet, the SRA provides a more elaborate conceptual repertoire than their assemblage approach (see Carmody and Kragelund 2016: 8–10).

The state powers African actors can exert in the context of Chinese infrastructure projects is a function of the interaction between various structural constraints and state actors' capacity to strategically influence their structural environment against competing or oppositional agential strategies. This implies that Sino-African cooperation in the infrastructure sector must not necessarily be biased in favour of presumably more powerful Chinese actors. The discussed dependency on foreign capital for infrastructure development is not the only structural relationship that conditions the unfolding of the infrastructural fix. Since the "fix" is driven by overaccumulation, Chinese (state) capital is in search of markets to dispose of overcapacities in the infrastructure and construction sectors (see Jones and Zeng 2019; Sum 2019). Africa offers untapped infrastructure and construction markets. African agency in the infrastructural fix is therefore conjectured to increase with increasing competition for African infrastructure projects, not least among Chinese companies, both state-owned and private (see Burke 2007: 332; Sun et al. 2017: 31). Again, depending on the strategic capacities of African state actors, China's dependency on foreign markets can open up structural opportunities for strategic action on the part of African governments and social forces that try to influence the circuits of Chinese capital in their favour.

This brings us to a fifth explanatory merit which crystallised by analysing the Chinese infrastructural fix through strategic-relational state-theoretical lenses. The retention or adjustment of African state strategies in the context of Africa's contemporary Chinese-sponsored infrastructure boom necessarily stabilises or transforms the structural biases of a given state. Thus, the causal tendencies of the Chinese infrastructural fix, to the extent they are realised, are interrelated with the structural selectivity inscribed in the neopatrimonial state form. Globalisation generally and, in particular, the inflow of foreign capital (and/or labour) into sovereign territories necessarily affects the prevalent balance of social forces and thus "exert[s] pressure on—or indeed strengthen[s]—particular forms of state with particular state capacities and liabilities" (Wylde 2017: 75; see Jessop 2016b: 197). As established in this chapter, neopatrimonial states are not autonomous from but very much integrated into global circuits of capital. Therefore, as Ziso convincingly argues in his case study on Ethiopia, "Chinese globalisation, just like any other globalisation, does have state transformation consequences in those countries where its international capital interacts with local social forces through the state" (2018: 30). This includes the relative importance and specific interplay of formal and informal institutions as well as the emergence of new informal institutions in African state-society relations (Ziso 2018: 50).

The case studies consider whether neopatrimonial modes of governance are routinely or habitually reproduced by using Chinese investments in infrastructure to channel resources towards patron-client networks linked to the infrastructure state. This provides insights as to how the "institutional ensembles" of the Tanzanian and Zambian state with their respective structural biases towards certain actors, certain strategies and certain interests co-condition the concrete materialisation of the infrastructural fix. In turn, it is instructive to see how both Chinese and African states, non-state and hybrid actors retain or modify their strategies to reproduce or transform the strategic selectivity of the neopatrimonial state. This concerns the extent to which actors informalise procurement procedures, draw on clientelistic/patronage-based networks to redistribute shares of inflowing Chinese capital, as well as whether and how public contracts are exploited by rentiers or corrupt individuals. Informal strategic alliances between Chinese fractions of capital and African elites are expected to facilitate particular patterns of accumulation by dispossession, such as rent-seeking or corruption, in the unfolding of the infrastructural fix.

Yet, despite empirical evidence of informal governance patterns in Sino-African relations, some of which I discussed above, the influx of Chinese capital into African economies does not necessarily result in the (further) neopatrimonialisation of African states. On the contrary, changes in interests, resources or goals of particular social forces may provide strategic scope for political actors to transform certain structural biases inscribed in the neopatrimonial state form (see Jessop 2016b: 55). This can result in the containment of informal/patrimonial practices in public contracting and procurement as well as in strengthening the regulatory environment and legal enforcement to ensure competitive public tendering and curb corruption. Changes in state strategies with regard to "inherited" structural constraints of the neopatrimonial state appear particularly relevant in the Tanzanian case, as will be discussed in Chapter 5.

Last but not least, particularly in Zambia and Tanzania, comprehensive social, political, cultural and economic ties with China date back sixty years—so does their international cooperation in the infrastructure sector, with the TAZARA railway as its cornerstone (see, for instance, Kahama 2018: Ch. 2; Kamata 2013: 90–93; Kopinski and Polus 2011: 183–184; Taylor 2006a: Ch. 9). China's support for the construction of the railway evidently increased the strategic scope of the then newly independent African states in a structural context characterised by far-reaching politico-economic constraints of colonialism and white-minority rule in southern Africa. Framed by official discourses around mutually beneficial "win–win" cooperation (see Alves 2013; Lumumba-Kasongo 2011: 238), Chinese and African elites frequently emphasise that current Sino-African collaboration in the infrastructure sector signifies the continuation of solidarity-based engagements among "all-weather friends". Yet, China's recent rise to become an "infrastructure giant" across Africa has taken place in a vastly different global political economy. The structural tendencies inherent to the spatio-temporal fix suggest that Chinese strategies in Africa's infrastructure sector (and beyond) are driven by the profit-seeking logic of capitalist accumulation. In this context, the SRA allows us to scrutinise whether concrete Chinese involvements in African infrastructure projects result from historico-political path dependencies. In turn, changes in the strategies of African state actors towards more critical appraisals of Chinese loans, proposals and bids could signal the emergence of more pragmatic political and economic relationships between China and African states.

References

Agnew, John. 1998. "Political Power and Geographical Scale." Paper presented at the Third Pan-European IR Conference and Joint Meeting with ISA, 16–19 September, Vienna.

Agnew, John. 2010. "Still Trapped in Territory?" *Geopolitics* 15(4):779–84. https://doi.org/10.1080/14650041003717558.

Alden, Chris, and Daniel Large. 2019. "Studying Africa and China." Pp. 3–35 in *New Directions in Africa-China Studies*, edited by C. Alden and D. Large. Abingdon: Routledge.

Alden, Chris, and Lu Jiang. 2019. "Brave New World: Debt, Industrialization and Security in China–Africa Relations." *International Affairs* 95(3):641–57.https://doi.org/10.1093/ia/iiz083.

Alves, Ana Cristina. 2013. "China's 'Win-Win' Cooperation: Unpacking the Impact of Infrastructure for-Resources Deals in Africa." *South African Journal of International Affairs* 20(2):207–26. https://doi.org/10.1080/10220461.2013.811337.

Alves, Cristina, and Sérgio Chichava. 2019. "Neo-Patrimonialism and Extraversion in China's Relations with Angola and Mozambique: Is Beijing Making a Difference?" Pp. 243–59 in *New Directions in Africa-China Studies*, edited by C. Alden and D. Large. Abingdon: Routledge.

Amin, Samir. 1990. *Maldevelopment: Anatomy of a Global Failure*. Tokyo: United Nations University Press.

Ashman, Sam, and Alex Callinicos. 2006. "Capital Accumulation and the State System: Assessing David Harvey's The New Imperialism." *Historical Materialism* 14(4):107–31.

Bach, Daniel C. 2012. "Conclusion: Neopatrimonialism and Developmental—The Emerging States' Syndrome." Pp. 221–24 in *Neopatrimonialism in Africa and Beyond*, edited by D. C. Bach and M. Gazibo. Abingdon: Routledge.

Bagwandeen, Mandira, Christopher Edyegu, and Oscar M. Otele. 2023. "African Agency, COVID-19 and Debt Renegotiations with China." *South African*

Journal of International Affairs 30(1):1–27. https://doi.org/10.1080/10220461.2023.2180083.
Beckmann, Björn. 1993. "The Liberation of Civil Society: Neo-Liberal Ideology and Political Theory." *Review of African Political Economy* 20(58):20–33.
Bhaskar, Roy. 1978. *A Realist Theory of Science*. Hemel Hempstead: Harvester.
Bieler, Andreas, and Adam David Morton. 2018. *Global Capitalism, Global War, Global Crisis*. Cambridge: Cambridge University Press.
Bond, Patrick. 2015. "BRICS and the Sub-Imperial Location." Pp. 15–26 in *BRICS: An Anti-Capitalist Critique*, edited by A. Garcia and P. Bond. London: Pluto Press.
Boone, Catherine. 1990. "The Making of a Rentier Class: Wealth Accumulation and Political Control in Senegal." *The Journal of Development Studies* 26(3):425–49.
Bratton, Michael, and Nicolas van de Walle. 1997. *Democratic Experiments in Africa: Regime Transitions in Comparative Perspective*. Cambridge: Cambridge University Press.
Brautigam, Deborah. 2022. "China and Zambia: Creating a Sovereign Debt Crisis." *International Affairs* 98(4):1347–65. https://doi.org/10.1093/ia/iiac109.
Brenner, Neil. 2004. *New State Spaces: Urban Governance and the Rescaling of Statehood*. Oxford: Oxford University Press.
Brenner, Neil, Bob Jessop, Martin Jones, and Gordon MacLeod. 2003. "Introduction: State Space in Question." Pp. 1–26 in *State/Space: A Reader*, edited by N. Brenner, B. Jessop, M. Jones, and G. MacLeod. Malden: Blackwell Publishing.
Bryan, Richard. 1987. "The State and the Internationalisation of Capital: An Approach to Analysis." *Journal of Contemporary Asia* 17(3):253–75.
Burke, Christopher. 2007. "China's Entry into Construction Industries in Africa: Tanzania and Zambia as Case Studies." *China Report* 43(3):323–36. https://doi.org/10.1177/000944550704300304.
Callaghy, Thomas M. 1988. "The State and the Development of Capitalism in Africa: Theoretitorical, Historical, and Comparative Reflections." Pp. 67–99 in *The Precarious Balance: State and Society in Africa*, edited by D. Rothchild and N. Chazan. Boulder: Westview Press.
Carmody, Pádraig. 2009. "An Asian-Driven Economic Recovery in Africa? The Zambian Case." *World Development* 37(7):1197–1207. https://doi.org/10.1016/j.worlddev.2008.12.002.
Carmody, Pádraig. 2013. *The Rise of the BRICS in Africa: The Geopolitics of South-South Relations*. London: Zed Books.
Carmody, Pádraig. 2020. "Dependence Not Debt-Trap Diplomacy." *Area Development and Policy* 5(1):23–31. https://doi.org/10.1080/23792949.2019.1702471.

Carmody, Pádraig, Godfrey Hampwaye, and Enock Sakala. 2012. "Globalisation and the Rise of the State? Chinese Geogovernance in Zambia." *New Political Economy* 17(2):209–29. https://doi.org/10.1080/13563467.2011.552107.

Carmody, Pádraig, and Peter Kragelund. 2016. "Who Is in Charge? State Power and Agency in Sino-African Relations." *Cornell International Law Journal* 49(1):1–24. https://doi.org/10.1038/nmeth.2841.

Carmody, Pádraig, and Joel Wainwright. 2022. "Contradiction and Restructuring in the Belt and Road Initiative: Reflections on China's Pause in the 'Go World.'" *Third World Quarterly* 43(12):2830–51. https://doi.org/10.1080/01436597.2022.2110058.

Castree, Noel. 2009. "The Spatio-Temporality of Capitalism." *Time & Society* 18(1):26–61. https://doi.org/10.1177/0961463X08099942.

Chabal, Patrick, and Jean-Pascal Daloz. 1999. *Africa Works: Disorder as Political Instrument*. London: James Currey.

Corkin, Lucy. 2012. "Chinese Construction Companies in Angola: A Local Linkages Perspective." *Resources Policy* 37(4):475–83. https://doi.org/10.1016/j.resourpol.2012.06.002.

Corkin, Lucy. 2013. *Uncovering African Agency: Angola's Management of China's Credit Lines*. Farnham: Ashgate.

Corkin, Lucy. 2015. "Understanding Angolan Agency: The Luanda-Beijing Face-Off." Pp. 61–84 in *Africa and China: How Africans and their Governments are Shaping Relations with China*, edited by A. W. Gadzala. Lanham: Rowman & Littlefield.

Cowaloosur, Honita. 2015. *Re-Inscribing Dependency: The Political Economy of Mauritius Jinfei Economic and Trade Cooperation Zone Co. Ltd.* PhD dissertation, University of St Andrews.

Danermark, Berth, Mats Ekström, Liselotte Jakobsen, and Jan Ch. Karlsson. 2002. *Explaining Society: Critical Realism in the Social Sciences*. London: Routledge.

deGrassi, Aaron. 2008. "'Neopatrimonialism' and Agricultural Development in Africa: Contributions and Limitations of a Contested Concept." *African Studies Review* 51(3):107–33. https://doi.org/10.1353/arw.0.0087.

DiCarlo, Jessica, and Seth Schindler. 2022. "Introduction: Geopolitics, Infrastructure, and the Emergent Geographies of US-China Competition." Pp. 1–10 in *The Rise of the Infrastructure State: How US-China Rivalry Shapes Politics and Place Worldwide*, edited by S. Schindler and J. DiCarlo. Bristol: Bristol University Press.

Eisenstadt, Samuel N. 1973. *Traditional Patrimonialism and Modern Neopatrominialism*. London: Sage Publications.

Erdmann, Gero. 2013. "Neopatrimonialism and Political Regimes." Pp. 59–69 in *Routledge Handbook of African Politics*, edited by N. Cheeseman, D. M. Anderson, and A. Scheibler. Abingdon: Routledge.

Erdmann, Gero, and Ulf Engel. 2006. *Neopatrimonialism Revisited: Beyond a Catch-All Concept*. GIGA Working Paper No. 16. Hamburg: German Institute of Global and Area Studies.

Erdmann, Gero, and Ulf Engel. 2007. "Neopatrimonialism Reconsidered: Critical Review and Elaboration of an Elusive Concept." *Commonwealth and Comparative Politics* 45(1):95–119. https://doi.org/10.1080/14662040601135813.

Fatton, Robert. 1988. "Bringing the Ruling Class Back in: Class, State, and Hegemony in Africa." *Comparative Politics* 20(3):253–64.

Fletcher, Amber J. 2017. "Applying Critical Realism in Qualitative Research: Methodology Meets Method." *International Journal of Social Research Methodology* 20(2):181–94. https://doi.org/10.1080/13645579.2016.1144401.

Frank, André Gunder. 1972. *Lumpenbourgeoisie and Lumpendevelopment: Dependency, Class and Politics in Latin America*. New York: Monthly Review Press.

Gil, Nuno, Anne Stafford, and Innocent Musonda. 2019. "Duality by Design: The Global Race to Build Africa's Infrastructure." Pp. 1–30 in *Duality by Design: The Global Race to Build Africa's Infrastructure*, edited by N. Gil, A. Stafford, and I. Musonda. Cambridge: Cambridge University Press.

Gramsci, Antonio. 1971. *Selections from the Prison Notebooks*. London: Lawrence and Wishart.

Gray, Hazel S. 2015. "The Political Economy of Grand Corruption in Tanzania." *African Affairs* 114(456):382–403. https://doi.org/10.1093/afraf/adv017.

Harvey, David. 2003. *The New Imperialism*. Oxford: Oxford University Press.

Harvey, David. 2004a. "Retrospect on the Limits to Capital." *Antipode* 36(3):544–49. https://doi.org/papers2://publication/uuid/97396CC0-28E6-4674-9D45-0BDAA3110F4D.

Harvey, David. 2004b. "The 'New' Imperialism: Accumulation by Dispossession." *Socialist Register* 40:63–87.

Harvey, David. 2010. *A Companion to Marx's Capital*. London: Verso.

Hay, Colin. 1996. *Re-Stating Social and Political Change*. Milton Keynes: Open University Press.

Hay, Colin. 2002. *Political Analysis: A Critical Introduction*. London: Red Globe Press.

Hay, Colin. 2014. "Levels of Governance and Their Interaction." Pp. 32–47 in *Handbook of the International Political Economy of Governance*, edited by A. Payne and N. Phillips. Cheltenham: Edward Elgar.

Hay, Colin, and Michael Lister. 2006. "Introduction: Theories of the State." Pp. 1–20 in *The State: Theories and Issues*, edited by C. Hay, M. Lister, and D. Marsh. London: Red Globe Press.

Heigl, Miriam C. 2011. "An Operationalization of the Strategic-Relational Approach: The Contested Privatization of the Mexican Oil Sector (1982–2006)." *Globalizations* 8(1):81–96. https://doi.org/10.1080/14747731.2011.545663.

Hodzi, Obert. 2018. "China and Africa: Economic Growth and a Non-Transformative Political Elite." *Journal of Contemporary African Studies* 36(2):191–206. https://doi.org/10.1080/02589001.2017.1406191.

Humphrys, Elizabeth. 2018. "Anti-Politics, the Early Marx and Gramsci's 'Integral State.'" *Thesis Eleven* 147(1):29–44. https://doi.org/10.1177/0725513618787638.

Hyden, Göran. 1983. *No Shortcuts to Progress: African Development Management in Perspective*. Berkeley: University of California Press.

Hyden, Göran. 2000. "The Governance Challenge in Africa." Pp. 5–32 in *African Perspectives on Governance*, edited by G. Hyden, D. Olowu, and H. W. O. Okoth Ogendo. Trenton: African World Press.

Jessop, Bob. 1982. *The Capitalist State: Marxist Theories and Methods*. Oxford: Blackwell.

Jessop, Bob. 1990. *State Theory: Putting the Capitalist State in Its Place*. Cambridge: Polity Press.

Jessop, Bob. 2001. "Institutional Re(Turns) and the Strategic-Relational Approach." *Environment and Planning A* 33(7):1213–35. https://doi.org/10.1068/a32183.

Jessop, Bob. 2004. *From Localities via the Spatial Turn to Spatial-Temporal Fixes: A Strategic-Relational Odyssey*. SECONS Discussion Forum Contribution No. 6. Socio-Economics of Space, University of Bonn.

Jessop, Bob. 2005. "Critical Realism and the Strategic-Relational Approach." *New Formations: A Journal of Culture, Theory and Politics* (56):40–53.

Jessop, Bob. 2006a. "Spatial Fixes, Temporal Fixes and Spatio-Temporal Fixes." Pp. 142–66 in *David Harvey: A Critical Reader*, edited by N. Castree and D. Gregory. Malden: Blackwell Publishing.

Jessop, Bob. 2006b. "The Strategic-Relational Approach: An Interview with Bob Jessop (by Joo-Hyoung Ji and Sandra Kytir)." Retrieved January 14, 2020 (https://bobjessop.wordpress.com/2014/12/02/the-strategic-relational-approach-an-interview-with-bob-jessop/).

Jessop, Bob. 2007. *State Power: A Strategic-Relational Approach*. Cambridge: Polity Press.

Jessop, Bob. 2016a. "Territory, Politics, Governance and Multispatial Metagovernance." *Territory, Politics, Governance* 4(1):8–32. https://doi.org/10.1080/21622671.2015.1123173.

Jessop, Bob. 2016b. *The State: Past, Present, Future*. Cambridge: Polity Press.

Jones, Lee, and Jinghan Zeng. 2019. "Understanding China's 'Belt and Road Initiative': Beyond 'Grand Strategy' to a State Transformation Analysis." *Third*

World Quarterly 40(8):1415–39. https://doi.org/10.1080/01436597.2018.1559046.

Kahama, Joseph K. 2018. *The Challenge to China-Tanzania Relationship: To Enhance Cooperation and Mutual Benefits*. Dar es Salaam: Tema Publishers.

Kamata, Ng'wanza. 2013. "Perspectives on Sino-Tanzanian Relations." Pp. 87–106 in *China's Diplomacy in Eastern and Southern Africa*, edited by S. Adem. Farnham: Ashgate.

Kelly, Duncan. 1999. "The Strategic-Relational View of the State." *Politics* 19(2):109–15. https://doi.org/10.1111/1467-9256.00093.

Koivisto, Marjo. 2010. "State Theory in International Relations: Why Realism Matters." Pp. 69–87 in *Scientific Realism and International Relations*, edited by J. Joseph and C. Wight. Basingstoke: Palgrave Macmillan.

Koivisto, Marjo. 2012. *Normative State Power in International Relations*. Oxford: Oxford University Press.

Konings, Piet. 2007. "The Neoliberalising African State and Private Capital Accumulation: The Case of Cameroon." Pp. 251–73 in *Big Business and Economic Development: Conglomerates and Economic Groups in Developing Countries and Transition Economies under Globalisation*, edited by A. E. Fernández Jilberto and B. Hogenboom. Abingdon: Routledge.

Kopinski, Dominik, and Andrzej Polus. 2011. "Sino-Zambian Relations: 'An All-Weather Friendship' Weathering the Storm." *Journal of Contemporary African Studies* 29(2):181–92. https://doi.org/10.1080/02589001.2011.555193.

Krueger, Anne O. 1974. "The Political Economy of the Rent-Seeking Society." *The American Economic Review* 64(3):291–303.

Lampert, Ben, and Giles Mohan. 2015. "Making Space for African Agency in China-Africa Engagements: Ghanaian and Nigerian Patrons Shaping Chinese Enterprise." Pp. 109–26 in *Africa and China: How Africans and Their Governments are Shaping Relations with China*, edited by A. W. Gadzala. Lanham: Rowman & Littlefield.

Large, Daniel. 2021. *China and Africa: The New Era*. Cambridge: Policy Press.

Lewis, Paul A. 2002. "Agency, Structure and Causality in Political Science: A Comment on Sibeon." *Politics* 22(1):17–23. https://doi.org/10.1111/1467-9256.00154.

Lewis, Peter M. 1994. "Economic Statism, Private Capital, and the Dilemmas of Accumulation in Nigeria." *World Development* 22(3):437–51.

Links, Stacey. 2021. "Ascertaining Agency Africa and the Belt and Road Initiative." Pp. 113–39 in *Global Perspectives on China's Belt and Road Initiative: Asserting Agency through Regional Connectivity*, edited by F. Schneider. Amsterdam: Amsterdam University Press.

Lumumba-Kasongo, Tukumbi. 2011. "China-Africa Relations: A Neo-Imperialism or a Neo-Colonialism? A Reflection." *African and Asian Studies* 10(2):234–66. https://doi.org/10.1163/156921011X587040.

Luxemburg, Rosa. 2003 [1913]. *The Accumulation of Capital*. London: Routledge.
MacKinnon, Danny, Jon Shaw, and Iain Docherty. 2008. *Diverging Mobilities? Devolution, Transport and Policy Innovation*. Amsterdam: Elsevier.
Makundi, Hezron, Huib Huyse, and Patrick Develtere. 2017. "Negotiating the Technological Capacity in Chinese Engagements: Is the Tanzanian Government in the Driving Seat?" *South African Journal of International Affairs* 24(3):331–53. https://doi.org/10.1080/10220461.2017.1391116.
Médard, Jean François. 1982. "The Underdeveloped State in Africa: Political Clientelism or Neo-Patrimonialism?" Pp. 162–89 in *Private Patronage and Public Power: Political Clientelism and the Modern State*, edited by C. Clapham. London: Frances Pinter.
Médard, Jean François. 1991. "L'État Néo-Patrimonial En Afrique Noire." Pp. 323–53 in *États d'Afrique Noire. Formations, Mécanismes et Crise*, edited by J. F. Médard. Paris: Karthala.
Migdal, Joel S. 1994. "Introduction: Developing a State-in-Society Perspective." Pp. 1–4 in *State Power and Social Forces: Domination and Transformation in the Third World*, edited by J. S. Migdal, A. Kohli, and V. Shue. Cambridge: Cambridge University Press.
Mkandawire, Thandika. 2015. "Neopatrimonialism and the Political Economy of Economic Performance in Africa: Critical Reflections." *World Politics* 67(3):563–612. https://doi.org/10.1017/s004388711500009x.
Mohan, Giles, and Ben Lampert. 2013. "Negotiating China: Reinserting African Agency into China-Africa Relations." *African Affairs* 112(446):92–110. https://doi.org/10.1093/afraf/ads065.
Mohan, Giles, and May Tan-Mullins. 2019. "The Geopolitics of South–South Infrastructure Development: Chinese-Financed Energy Projects in the Global South." *Urban Studies* 56(7):1368–85. https://doi.org/10.1177/0042098018794351.
Mustapha, Abdul Raufu. 2002. "States, Predation and Violence: Reconceptualizing Political Action and Political Community in Africa." Paper presented at the 10th General Assembly of CODESIRA, Kampala, Uganda, 8–12 December.
Niemann, Michael. 2000. *A Spatial Approach to Regionalisms in the Global Economy*. Basingstoke: Macmillan Press.
Olukoshi, Adebayo O. 1998. *The Elusive Prince of Denmark. Structural Adjustment and the Crisis of Governance in Africa*. Research Report No. 104. Uppsala: Nordiska Afrikainstitutet.
Onuf, Nicholas Greenwood. 1998. *The Republican Legacy in International Thought*. Cambridge: Cambridge University Press.

Pitcher, Anne, Mary H. Moran, and Michael Johnston. 2009. "Rethinking Patrimonialism and Neopatrimonialism in Africa." *African Studies Review* 52(1):125–56. https://doi.org/10.1353/arw.0.0163.

Poulantzas, Nicos. 1978. *State, Power, Socialism*. London: Verso.

Power, Marcus, Giles Mohan, and May Tan-Mullins. 2012. *China's Resource Diplomacy in Africa: Powering Development?* Basingstoke: Palgrave Macmillan.

Sandbrook, Richard, and Jay Oelbaum. 1997. "Reforming Dysfunctional Institutions through Democratisation? Reflections on Ghana." *Journal of Modern African* 35(4):603–46.

Shaw, Timothy M. 1985. *Towards a Political Economy for Africa: The Dialectics of Dependence*. London: Macmillan Press.

Shivji, Issa G. 2009. *Accumulation in an African Periphery: A Theoretical Framework*. Dar es Salaam: Mkuki na Nyota Publishers.

Shivji, Issa G. 2017. "The Concept of 'Working People.'" *Agrarian South: Journal of Political Economy* 6(1):1–13. https://doi.org/10.1177/2277976017721318.

Simpson, John A., and Edmund S. C. Weiner, eds. 1989. *The Oxford English Dictionary*. 2nd edition. Oxford: Oxford University Press.

Söderbaum, Fredrik. 2016. *Rethinking Regionalism*. London: Palgrave.

Soulé-Kohndou, Folashadé. 2019. "Bureaucratic Agency and Power Asymmetry in Benin-China Relations." Pp. 189–204 in *New Directions in Africa-China Studies*. Abingdon: Routledge.

Sum, Ngai-Ling. 2019. "The Intertwined Geopolitics and Geoeconomics of Hopes/ Fears: China's Triple Economic Bubbles and the 'One Belt One Road' Imaginary." *Territory, Politics, Governance* 7(4):528–52. https://doi.org/10.1080/21622671.2018.1523746.

Sun, Irene Yuan, Kartik Jayaram, and Omid Kassiri. 2017. *Dance of the Lions and Dragons: How Are Africa and China Engaging, and How Will the Partnership Evolve?* New York: McKinsey & Company.

Tangri, Roger. 1998. "Politics, Capital and the State in Sub-Saharan Africa." *Commonwealth & Comparative Politics* 36(2):108–22.

Taylor, Ian. 2006a. *China and Africa: Engagement and Compromise*. Abingdon: Routledge.

Taylor, Ian. 2006b. "China's Oil Diplomacy in Africa." *International Affairs* 82(5):937–59. https://doi.org/10.1111/j.1468-2346.2006.00579.x.

Taylor, Scott D. 2006c. "Divergent Politico-legal Responses to Past Presidential Corruption in Zambia and Kenya: Catching the 'big fish' or Letting Him Off the Hook?" *Third World Quarterly* 27(2):281–301. https://doi.org/10.1080/01436590500432325.

Taylor, Ian. 2007. "Governance in Africa and Sino-African Relations: Contradictions or Confluence?" *Politics* 27(3):139–46. https://doi.org/10.1111/j.1467-9256.2007.00293.x.

Taylor, Ian. 2009. *China's New Role in Africa*. Boulder: Lynne Rienner Publishers.

Taylor, Ian. 2010. *The International Relations of Sub-Saharan Africa*. New York: Continuum International.

Taylor, Ian. 2014. *Africa Rising? BRICS—Diversifying Dependency*. Woodbridge: James Currey.

Taylor, Ian. 2015. "The Good, the Bad, and the Ugly: Agency-as-Corruption and the Sino-Nigerian Relationship." Pp. 27–44 in *Africa and China: How Africans and their Governments are Shaping Relations with China*, edited by A. W. Gadzala. Lanham: Rowman & Littlefield.

Taylor, Ian. 2017. "Transnationalizing Capitalist Hegemony: A Poulantzian Reading." *Alternatives: Global, Local, Political* 42(1):26–40. https://doi.org/10.1177/0304375417732849.

Taylor, Ian, and Paul D. Williams. 2008. "Political Culture, State Elites and Regional Security in West Africa." *Journal of Contemporary African Studies* 26(2):137–49. https://doi.org/10.1080/02589000802124797.

Taylor, Ian, and Tim Zajontz. 2020. "In a Fix: Africa's Place in the Belt and Road Initiative and the Reproduction of Dependency." *South African Journal of International Affairs* 27(3):277–295. https://doi.org/10.1080/10220461.2020.1830165.

Theobald, Robin. 1982. "Patrimonialism." *World Politics* 34(4):548–59.

Wagner, Maren. 2016. *Social Emergence in International Relations*. Palgrave Macmillan.

Wai, Zubairu. 2012. "Neo-Patrimonialism and the Discourse of State Failure in Africa." *Review of African Political Economy* 39(131):27–43. https://doi.org/10.1080/03056244.2012.658719.

Watson, Matthew. 2005. *Foundations of International Political Economy*. Basingstoke: Palgrave Macmillan.

Weber, Max. 1978 [1922]. *Economy and Society: An Outline of Interpretative Sociology*, edited by G. Roth and C. Wittich. Berkley: University of California Press.

van Wieringen, Kjeld, and Tim Zajontz. 2023. "From Loan-Financed to Privatised Infrastructure? Tracing China's Turn towards Public-Private Partnerships in Africa." *Journal of Current Chinese Affairs*. https://doi.org/10.1177/18681026231188140.

Wight, Colin. 1999. "They Shoot Dead Horses Don't They? Locating Agency in the Agent-Structure Problematique." *European Journal of International Relations* 5(1):109–42. https://doi.org/10.1177/1354066199005001005.

Wight, Colin. 2004. "Theorizing the Mechanisms of Conceptual and Semiotic Space." *Philosophy of the Social Sciences* 34(2):283–99.

Wight, Colin. 2006. *Agents, Structures and International Relations: Politics as Ontology*. 2nd edition. Cambridge: Cambridge University Press.

Wylde, Christopher. 2017. *Emerging Markets and the State: Developmentalism in the 21st Century*. London: Palgrave Macmillan.

Yeung, Henry Wai-chung. 2010. "Critical Realism and Realist Research in Human Geography: A Method or a Philosophy in Search of a Method?" Pp. 325–54 in *Realist Methodology Volume I: Practical Realist Ontology*, edited by W. Olsen. London: Sage Publications.

Zajontz, Tim. 2022a. "Debt, Distress, Dispossession: Towards a Critical Political Economy of Africa's Financial Dependency." *Review of African Political Economy* 49(171):173–83. https://doi.org/10.1080/03056244.2021.1950669.

Zajontz, Tim. 2022b. "'Win-Win' Contested: Negotiating the Privatisation of Africa's Freedom Railway with the 'Chinese of Today.'" *Journal of Modern African Studies* 60(1):111–34. https://doi.org/10.1017/S0022278X21000446.

Zhuawu, Collin. 2012a. *Engaging Africa in a Changing International Political Economy: Mauritius' Activism and Co-Operation in the World Trade Organisation (WTO)*. PhD dissertation, University of Birmingham.

Zhuawu, Collin. 2012b. "Reconceptualising the African State in the Strategic Relational Approach: A Case of Mauritius State and Trade Policy-Making." *African Journal of Political Science and International Relations* 6(7):130–41. https://doi.org/10.5897/ajpsir11.134.

Zhuawu, Collin. 2013. *Applying the Strategic Relational Approach to African States: A Case of Mauritius and Trade Policymaking*. South African Institute of International Affairs Occasional Paper No. 147.

Ziso, Edson. 2018. *A Post State-Centric Analysis of China-Africa Relations: Internationalisation of Chinese Capital and State-Society Relations in Ethiopia*. Cham: Palgrave Macmillan.

CHAPTER 4

The Destiny of the Freedom Railway: From Anti-imperialism to Accumulation by Dispossession?

> From what Mwalimu [late President Nyerere] told me, Mao Zedong asked them [referring to presidents Nyerere and Kaunda] one question: "Would that [construction of a railway] assist the liberation of Africa?" And the answer was "yes". And the reaction was: "It will be built". Just like that. (Interview Lusinde)

In an interview in his home in Dodoma in November 2019 the late Job Lusinde, a member of Tanganyika's first cabinet after independence in 1961, recalled a conversation with President Julius Nyerere in which Tanzania's first president described Mao Zedong's resolute support for the construction of the Tanzania–Zambia Railway during a state visit to Beijing. China's role in the construction of the Tanzania–Zambia Railway is commonly considered as the historical cornerstone of the Sino-African "all-weather friendship".[1] The efforts undertaken by China under Mao Zedong to support newly independent African nations in their struggle against white-minority rule in southern Africa are frequently

[1] Some sections in this chapter and in Chapter 5 were previously published under the title "'Win–win' contested: negotiating the privatisation of Africa's Freedom Railway with the 'Chinese of today'" in the *Journal of Modern African Studies* (Creative Commons CC BY licence).

T. Zajontz, *The Political Economy of China's Infrastructure Development in Africa*, International Political Economy Series,
https://doi.org/10.1007/978-3-031-44449-4_4

remembered—both in Africa and in China. Chinese decision-makers, representatives of SOEs as well as the media often refer to the railway to emphasise Sino-African solidarity and mutual benefits that are said to result from Chinese infrastructure development in Africa (see, for instance, Chen and Morangi 2019; Chinese Ministry of Foreign Affairs 2015; Guo 2019). Liu underlines the enduring relevance of the "Tazara spirit" (坦赞铁路精神) which she describes as

> an intersubjective assemblage of meaning-making surrounding the railway's history, [which] is characterised by the shared motif of seeking and maintaining sovereignty through self-reliance and the willingness to make sacrifices out of the sentiments of solidarity and friendship among the three nations that are involved in the so-called Freedom Railway. (2024: 69)

But China's participation in the planned rehabilitation of the cross-border railway does not only bear symbolic and ideational significance. The highly indebted, undercapitalised binational parastatal with its dilapidated infrastructural assets has also become a potential investment outlet for Chinese surplus capital. In 2016, intergovernmental negotiations about a Chinese participation in TAZARA resumed. The negotiations were characterised by irreconcilable differences between the shareholding governments and a Chinese consortium regarding the terms and conditions under which TAZARA should be privatised. This makes TAZARA's planned rehabilitation an ideal case to assess how African (state) actors co-determine whether as well as how Chinese capital is invested in African infrastructure.

This chapter and Chapter 5 offer insights as to how the Chinese infrastructural fix has been mediated, shaped and obstructed by politico-economic contexts and reflective agential strategies in the case of TAZARA. The protracted (and hitherto unsuccessful) negotiations about TAZARA's privatisation provide for a valuable in-depth analysis of the processual, trial-and-error character of spatio-temporal fixes as well as into the contentious politics related to the institutionalisation of "fixes" in particular spatio-temporal conjunctures (see Sum and Jessop 2013: 247). Moreover, this chapter and the next shed light on differential degrees of African state agency oriented towards structural configurations against which the Chinese infrastructural fix unfolds. The present chapter first recounts TAZARA's history as well as its steady devaluation over time. It then sheds light on the 2016 tripartite negotiations among China,

Tanzania and Zambia about a Chinese participation in TAZARA and on the ultimately irreconcilable differences in the positions of the negotiating parties. Lastly, it documents how previous, unsuccessful railway concessions in both Tanzania and Zambia have shaped the negotiating strategies of the shareholding governments, underlining the impact of strategic learning and, hence, the path-dependent and path-shaping logics inherent to the structure-agency dialectics (see Jessop 2005: 52, 2016: 55).

The Monumental Rise and Steady Decline of the "Freedom Railway"

> We will not abandon TAZARA; it is the realization of the thoughts of our founders [...] aided by China; this is in their memory. TAZARA will never die in our hands. (the late Tanzanian President John Magufuli, quoted in Lusaka Times 2019)

To this day, the 1860 km railway that connects Kapiri Mposhi in Zambia's Central Province with Dar es Salaam at the Indian Ocean remains China's largest foreign aid project. China's decision to get involved had lasting path-shaping effects for Sino-African relations. Figure 4.1 depicts the TAZARA route. The railway construction was significantly influenced by geopolitical and geoeconomic developments in the region. TAZARA became the single most important infrastructure project aimed at decolonising southern Africa's transport infrastructure. As the late Kenneth Kaunda who became Zambia's first president in 1964 put it: "All we want to see is the railway line being built, so that we are never again dependent on the route from the south" (quoted in Essack 1970: 937).

For over a century, Zambia had been fully integrated into the political economy of colonial southern Africa and its regionalised networks of trade, (labour) migration and infrastructure. This closely tied Zambia's economy and society to South Africa, Rhodesia and Mozambique for the import and export of commodities as well as for the provision of labour (Essack 1970; Niemann 2000: 102–6; Rettman 1973; Söderbaum 2002: 62). At independence, Zambia's transport infrastructure was overwhelmingly oriented towards the south, a legacy of Cecil Rhodes' Cape-to-Cairo

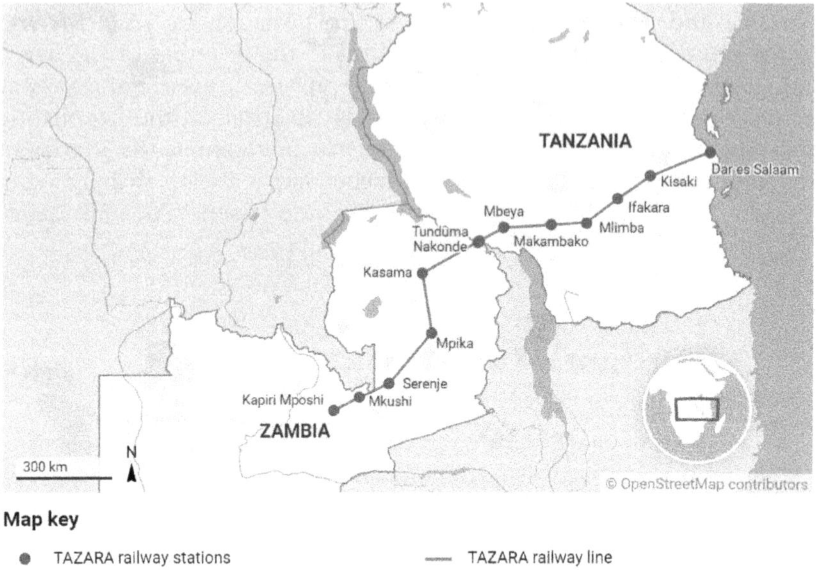

Fig. 4.1 TAZARA route map (*Source* Usifo Omozokpea, The Conversation, https://theconversation.com/tanzania-and-zambia-want-to-upgrade-the-uhuru-railway-but-can-they-190659 [Creative commons licence, reprinted with permission])

plan and pursuant infrastructure development in British colonial territories. Geoeconomically, Zambia's railways and roads primarily served the purpose to connect the mines of the Central African Copper Belt with South African and Mozambican ports. The country's rail line, until independence an integral part of Rhodesia Railways, was fully integrated into the "Cape gauge" (1.067m width) rail network. As a 1976 report published by the United Nations Development Programme asserts, "[t]he territory [colonial Northern Rhodesia] was, in a very real sense, the northern-most extremity of white minority-ruled southern Africa". The report lists among major "characteristics of the Zambian economy at independence which tend to be recurring themes of the post-independence period [...] [a]n infrastructure geared solely to the needs of the mining and European agricultural sectors and oriented southwards" (UNDP 1976: 2, 3).

Zambia's economic vulnerability became blatant upon Rhodesia's unilateral declaration of independence (UDI) under Ian Smith in November 1965 which provoked British-imposed sanctions, including an oil embargo (Gleave 1992: 251; see Monson 2009: 33; Yu 1971: 1105). It caused a "transportation emergency for landlocked Zambia" during which oil and other essential goods needed to be airlifted into Zambia (Monson 2009: 23). Zambia's refusal to recognise the Smith regime resulted in "systematic sabotage" (Essack 1970: 937), such as the withholding of crucial goods and supplies and frequent border closures between 1966 and 1979 (Gleave 1992: 251). Newly independent Zambia was almost exclusively dependent on the export of copper, which amounted to 97 per cent of its foreign exchange earnings in 1969. Its major export route went through Rhodesia for which the transit of Zambian copper "has been a major source of foreign exchange" (Rettman 1973: 240, 257 n. 21; see Sklar 1974: 346). Pre-independence agreements between British, American and South African mining houses and Rhodesia Railways ensured that, even after Zambia's political liberation, most of its copper was exported via Rhodesia to the ports of Beira and Lourenço Marques (now Maputo) (Mwase 1987: 196; Rettman 1973: 241, 257 n. 25).[2]

Only a minor share of Zambian copper travelled on the Benguela Railway to the Angolan port of Lobito via Katanga. Even after the UDI, when Zambia actively sought alternative transport routes, the Benguela Railway did not meet Zambian needs, as it faced severe capacity constraints and was controlled by an increasingly hostile Portuguese colonial regime. Ultimately, the Lobito corridor ceased to provide an alternative route to the sea as of 1975, after the Benguela line had been subjected to attacks and acts of sabotage in Angola's civil war (Duarte et al. 2014: 2; Gleave 1992: 252; Monson 2009: 23; Mwase 1987: 197). The road infrastructure of the mid-1960s also failed to provide a viable alternative. Whereas the southbound trunk roads were tarred, the sole road corridor to the sea that did not transit colonial territories, namely the one to Dar es Salaam, was unsurfaced and had earned itself the nickname "the hell run" due to its dangerous bends and

[2] Nkrumah (1965: 156, 160, 185) strikingly outlines the intricate entanglement of British and South African mining interests and Rhodesia Railways, prior to Zambian independence.

steep gradients, particularly on the Tanzanian side (Gleave 1992: 250, 253; also interviews senior official Zambian MTC; Lusinde).

The construction of a railway linking Zambia with the Indian Ocean via Tanzania had become the top priority for Kenneth Kaunda's government. Kaunda found a like-minded leader in Tanzania's President Julius Nyerere whose country had become the hub for the region's anti-colonial struggle. Both leaders "envisioned a post-colonial transportation infrastructure that would be based upon regional cooperation rather than colonial dependency" (Monson 2009: 15). The TAZARA project "was thus removed from the sphere of purely economic-financial considerations and coated with political and ideological significance" (Rettman 1973: 235). An alternative railroad to the sea was expected to emancipate Zambia vis-à-vis foreign interests that controlled its economy and to make it less vulnerable to economic sabotage by its southern neighbours. Not least, it would provide infrastructural support for anti-colonial struggles in Mozambique, Rhodesia and South Africa (Monson 2009: 22; Rettman 1973: 248–49). As Monson (2009: 4) underlines, "TAZARA represented the concrete realization of pan-African development cooperation", an "anti-hegemonic project" through which "the boundaries of colonial-era transport infrastructures" could be dismantled.

The Tanzanian and Zambian governments sought support for the railway construction from the United Kingdom, the USA, West Germany, France, Japan, the Soviet Union, the World Bank, the AfDB and the multinational corporation Lonhro—without success (Gleave 1992: 253–54; Guo 2019: 24; Mwase 1987: 193; Shangwe 2017: 82; interview Lusinde). In 1964, two surveys undertaken by the World Bank and the United Nations (UN) came to the conclusion that the project was neither economically feasible nor necessary (Gleave 1992: 254; Rettman 1973: 241–42). However, a later study, the so-called Stamp Report from 1966, attested to the economic viability of the rail line and pointed to the "safeguard afforded the Zambia[n] economy by an alternative route able both to carry all its traffic, and at competitive rates" (cited in Rettman 1973: 244; see Monson 2009: 24). The Western reluctance to finance the project served the purpose to protect British and American economic interests that were vested in Zambia's mineral sector and threatened by the degree of economic independence that an alternative railroad to the sea promised for Zambia (Rettman 1973: 248–49). For Tanzania and Zambia, the UDI had become the decisive factor to proceed with the project, even without Western support.

"The Uhuru Line Will Fight Imperialism"[3]*: The Chinese Rescue and Its Legacy*

China offered its support for the construction of the railway during Nyerere's China visit in February 1965. Nyerere left no doubt about his firm commitment to the railway: "I don't care whether I get Communist or Western money. [...] I want this railway line and I'm not going to be stopped" (quoted in Rettman 1973: 243; see Friedman 2021: 135–36). A tripartite agreement among the Chinese, Tanzanian and Zambian governments was signed in Beijing in September 1967, followed by a survey and agreements on the exact route in 1968 (Guo 2019; Monson 2009: 24; Rettman 1973). In July 1969, the governments signed a finance agreement over estimated costs of ¥988m (about $415m at the time). The amount was provided by a combination of an interest-free loan (about $328m), which initially foresaw repayment within thirty years after a grace period of five years, and commodity credit arrangements (Gleave 1992; Monson 2009: 30; Mwase 1987; Rettman 1973). Construction of the railway commenced in the latter half of 1970. Tracklaying was completed in mid-1975 and operations were taken up in October 1975. The railway was officially handed over to the Tanzanian and Zambian governments at a ceremony in Kapiri Mposhi in July 1976 (Gleave 1992; Guo 2019). TAZARA's design capacity was 2.5m tons per annum and direction and its initial operating capacity was 2.16m tons (Gleave 1992). However, as Fig. 4.2 shows, its actual performance remained far below its capacity. Its peak performance in haulage was recorded in the financial year of 1977/78 when 1.27m tons were transported.

China's involvement in financing and constructing the "Freedom Railway"—Reli ya Uhuru in Swahili—was heavily coated in an anti-imperialist narrative promoted by the Chinese government which emphasised the solidarity-based "friendship" character of Sino-African relations as well as the shared histories of colonial subjugation and anti-imperial struggles (Liu 2024; Monson 2009: 3, 6, 26–27). As Zambia's former Vice-President Guy Scott (2019: 182) remembers in his memoirs, TAZARA's "justification from the Chinese point of view was strongly political—a 'monumental' construct representing the determination on

[3] Slogans like this one or "Socialists rejoice while imperialists weep" could be read on placards which were carried by youths during the ground-breaking ceremony in Dar es Salaam in October 1970 (Hall and Peyman 1976: 124).

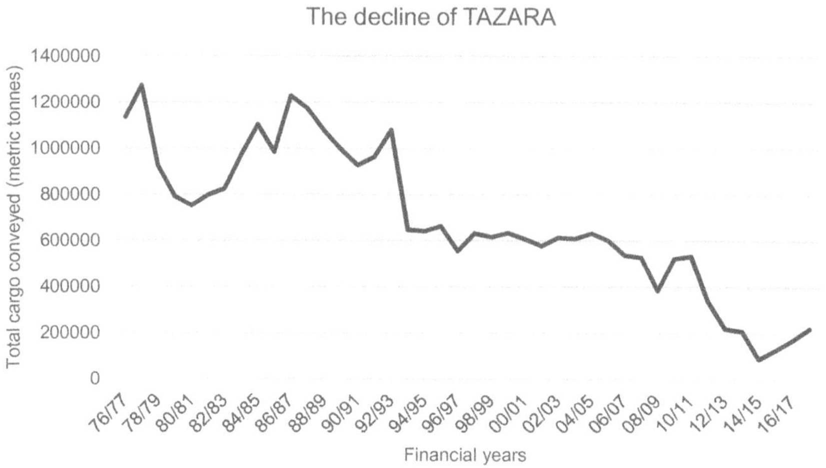

Fig. 4.2 Cargo conveyed by TAZARA, 1976–2019 (*Source* Author's compilation, based on TAZARA data; previously published in Zajontz (2022c: 117) under a CC BY 4.0 creative commons licence)

the world's largest and poorest countries' refusal to be dominated by capitalism, imperialism, and so forth". Strategically, China's support for the railway construction served the objectives to establish diplomatic relations with newly independent African states and to secure support for the Chinese bid for UN membership (Guo 2019; Rettman 1973).

The finance arrangement to construct TAZARA was strongly guided by China's Eight Principles for Economic Aid and Technical Assistance to Other Countries, which were announced by Chinese Premier Zhou Enlai in 1964 (Guo 2019; Monson 2009: 30). The Principles stipulated "equality and mutual benefit" as well as non-interference and non-conditionality as the basis for Chinese aid (GPRC 1964). Principle 3 reads as follows:

> China provides economic aid in the form of interest-free or low-interest loans and extends the time limit for the repayment when necessary so as to lighten the burden of the recipient countries as far as possible. (GPRC 1964; also cited in Monson 2009: 30)

Since TAZARA's construction, China has lived up to the principle by having repeatedly postponed loan repayments, both for loans from the construction period and debt incurred under technical cooperation protocols. Most importantly, in December 2009, the Chinese government announced the cancellation of half of the outstanding construction loan (Guo 2019).[4] The Eight Principles also stipulated that China's aid policy should not make recipient countries dependent on the PRC but instead strengthen their "self-reliance" (GPRC 1964). China's approach to development aid was openly cherished by President Nyerere at TAZARA's official inauguration:

> Africa was, and is still, not used to getting assistance on such terms. Yet, there has been no hidden cost, and no concealed string, to this aid. We can say this now out of experience, not out of trust. Not once has the Chinese Government attempted to interfere with the political or economic policies of Tanzania or Zambia. There have been important differences of opinion on international affairs between our countries, but there has never been any suggestion that we are indebted to China, and should act accordingly. (Nyerere 2015: 65)

The construction of TAZARA fostered comprehensive political, economic and cultural ties among China, Tanzania and Zambia and facilitated what is often called an "all-weather friendship" among the three nations (see Baregu 2006; Bwayla 2013: 195; Carmody 2013: 29; Kahama 2018: Ch. 2; Leslie 2016; Mutesa 2010; Taylor 2006: 26–31). The railway has remained a major discursive reference point in Sino-African relations, not least in the context of contemporary Chinese investments in Africa's railway sector (Zajontz et al. 2024). In China, Ethiopia's new SGR, which was jointly constructed by China Railway Construction Corporation (CRCC) and China Railway Engineering Corporation (CREC), is commonly referred to as "Tanzania Zambia Railway of the New Era" (新时代的"新坦赞铁路"; xin shidai de "xin tan zan tielu") (see, for instance, Wang 2018). The Chinese government unflaggingly invokes TAZARA as a symbol of Sino-African solidarity and describes it as a "[m]onument to China-Africa Friendship" (Chinese Ministry of Foreign Affairs 2015).

[4] The debt relief of about $150m was effectuated by a tripartite protocol signed in Lusaka in February 2011 (Liu and Monson 2011: 299 n. 2).

Since the construction period, China has supported TAZARA by means of hitherto 15 Protocols of Economic and Technical Cooperation. The regular trilateral protocols are implemented by a team of staff from China Civil Engineering Construction Corporation (CCECC)[5] that has been seconded to TAZARA on a permanent basis since the time of construction, the so-called Chinese Railway Expert Team (CRET) (Interviews key informant 1; key informant 2; executive CCECC).[6] Recent protocols have primarily aimed at ameliorating TAZARA's shortage in rolling stock, locomotives, spare parts and equipment (Interview key informant 2). However, despite continual Chinese support, TAZARA has experienced a steady decline.

The Devaluation of a Monument

The economic decline of TAZARA has obviously various political and economic reasons, which lie beyond the scope of this study. Nonetheless, it is instructive to raise some of them briefly to contextualise the company's devaluation, which has made the historic railway a potential capital investment object in the contemporary Chinese infrastructural fix. TAZARA's performance took a first hit following the partial re-opening of southern transport routes in October 1978, which caused a significant drop in the share of Zambia's foreign trade that travelled along the Dar es Salaam corridor (Gleave 1992; Mwase 1987). Yet, the liberalisation of African economies in general and the transport industry in particular which accelerated in the 1980s proved more detrimental for TAZARA. As Mwase underlines, "[e]conomic liberalisation has entailed a shift from away [sic!] subsidies and towards a cost-based tariff, virtually doing away with the railway's traditional 'public service' obligations" (2003: ii180; see also Zajontz et al. 2024). This led to fierce competition from a rapidly growing road transport industry, as a railway executive explained:

[5] CCECC was established in 1979. It grew out of the Foreign Aid Office of the Ministry of Railways which was specifically set up for the construction of TAZARA. The company's long-time CEO, Liu Zhiming, describes the bond between TAZARA and CCECC as "indeed indissoluble", as "[w]ithout the TAZARA, there would be no CCECC" (Chinese Ministry of Foreign Affairs 2015: 38, 39). An interviewee reiterated that "TAZARA spirit is CCECC spirit" (Interview executive CCECC).

[6] For a detailed review of the technical cooperation since construction, see Liu and Monson (2011).

> When the whole economy was privatised, it also gave opportunity for individuals to go into investment. The easiest which everybody thinks about is transport. [...] So, there was an influx of private investment. And who are the people with private investment? People who are in a specific class. So, of course, transport attracted a lot of interest at all levels and these interests need to protect themselves. So, they become a lobby group to increase the tonnage. (Interview Musonda, C.)

As funding for large public infrastructure had started to dry up as of the late-1970, the competitiveness of the rail sector continuously decreased and African railways became subject to a "steady process of attrition" (Nugent 2018: 22). Consequently, "[t]he decline of Africa's railways systems is merely the most striking example of a technology that had come to be regarded as too expensive and unsuited to African requirements" (Nugent 2018: 22).

In the Zambian and Tanzanian contexts, the conjuncture of economic stagnation, rising sovereign debt and resultant policy straightjackets imposed by structural adjustment programmes further limited the shareholding governments' capacity to maintain TAZARA's infrastructure and rolling stock (see Baregu 2006; Kaiser 1996: 231–32; Kamata 2013: 93; Kragelund 2010; Simutanyi 1996). A senior TAZARA manager explained that one "aspect of the liberalisation in the transport sector" was that "over the years, the investments in the railway infrastructure hasn't been as much as in the road sector" (Interview senior TAZARA manager). As an exception to the general lack of reinvestment, TAZARA, in 1985, received capital injections totalling $150m as part of donor-funded projects following Tanzania's eventual adoption of conditionalities set out by the World Bank and the IMF. The aid projects aimed at increasing the efficiency of the binational railway and included the purchase of 17 locomotives and spare parts, the establishment of a new locomotive workshop in Mbeya and technical training (Liu and Monson 2011). The capacity increase in rolling stock, alongside the involvement of a team of Chinese experts in the "cooperative management" of TAZARA, led to recovering freight volumes and passenger numbers in the late 1980s (Liu and Monson 2011: 240; see Fig. 4.2).

However, TAZARA's recovery was of short duration. The devaluation continued in the 1990s against the background of the successive privatisation of Zambia's mining sector between 1992 and 2000 (see Craig 2001; Larmer 2005). The latter entailed the end of the longstanding "symbiosis" between Zambia Consolidated Copper Mines (ZCCM) and TAZARA. Henceforth, an increasing share of copper exports was transported on the road, both along refurbished southern routes but also along the TANZAM Highway (Interviews Chilumbu; senior official Zambian MTC; Musonda, C.; Mwila). TAZARA had become increasingly uncompetitive against road transporters. Contributing factors have been inefficiencies, capacity constraints, long dwell times and high port fees (in regional comparison) at Dar es Salaam port (Scholvin 2016: 138; World Bank 2013: x, 27, 31; interview senior official Zambian MTC). Moreover, clientelistic networks of Tanzanian politicians and business people involved in road haulage along the Dar es Salaam corridor have greatly profited from TAZARA's degradation and, hence, have had little interest in reversing it—an issue that I shall pick up in Chapter 5 (Scott 2019: 183; interviews Kamata; Mtonga; Musonda, C.; Mwila; Shone).

Besides external political and economic factors, the company has faced challenges that arise from its institutional set-up. The late Job Lusinde, the Tanzanian cabinet minister continuously in charge of transport and works between 1965 and 1975, explained that "our structure, our administration, I think was wrong from the beginning and it was never changed. The management that was built up was mainly political, it was not technical" (Interview Lusinde). An interviewee with in-depth knowledge of the procedures at the state-owned company confirmed that political "interference" has been the order of the day, stating that TAZARA

> is a parastatal, owned by two governments. So, there are quite some politics involved, because there are two countries involved. But I'm sure you understand the politics of parastatals. Especially parastatals in Africa – state-owned enterprises. There are quite some politics. You cannot distance yourself from the government or from the politicians. So, it's always a problem. So, what makes it particularly challenging is that we have two governments with two different interests at any given time. (Interview key informant 1)

In line with this assessment, the AfDB asserts that "public railway agencies are usually crippled with bureaucracy, legacy interests and political interference" (2015: 124). One interviewee traced long-standing management inefficiencies within the company back to the way the company's top management has been selected in the past. Accordingly, managing directors have been "political appointees" without the necessary qualifications to steer the company, as political decision-makers "would actually even choose somebody who is a relative" or a "supporter of a party" (Interview TAZARA manager). This assessment was shared by a trade union leader who asserted that "TAZARA is run by a board [which] comprises of political appointees". In the past, even the managing directors and their deputies "were purely babies of politicians", which "meant that TAZARA had serious political inclination[s] on how it operated". Accordingly, "when we were operating, we were not of a full business sense. It was too much politics per se" (Interview TAZARA labour union executive). Yet, an interviewee argued that the current managing directors and deputies were "picked on merit" and "looked at critically" (Interview TAZARA manager). Another interviewee described the senior management that came into office in 2016 as "seriously committed" (Interview TAZARA labour union executive). The fact that the managing director appointed in 2016, Bruno Ching'andu, was still in office in mid-2023 is at least proof of a certain degree of continuity in TAZARA's top management.

However, reminiscent of Harvey's (2003: 150) notion of the devaluation of labour power, previous mismanagement and lack of planning has also affected skills development and training within the company. TAZARA has experienced "massive retirements" among highly skilled employees from the company's founding generation with "no succession plan" in place to adequately replace the workers who "retired with their experience and expertise" (Interview TAZARA trade union executive). An interviewee remembered that a tamping machine could no longer be operated, as the entire team who used to operate it had retired. He also emphasised difficulties to recruit qualified staff which "aris[e] from the poor salaries" (Interview TAZARA trade union executive).

TAZARA's decade-long devaluation has been reflected in its economic performance. The company reached a new all-time low, in terms of haulage, in the financial year 2014/15 when it transported a mere 87,860 metric tonnes (TAZARA data that was shared with the author). To put the number into perspective: In 2015, an amount of 2.5m tonnes of cargo left Dar es Salaam port destined for Zambia (Domasa 2016). According to the Zambia Chamber of Mines, Zambia produced 711,515 tonnes in copper alone in the same year (Hill 2016). TAZARA's performance gradually improved in the second half of the 2010s. The yearly cargo volumes averaged 174,000 tonnes in the four financial years following the negative record (TAZARA data). The transit time between the two termini has also improved, not least as a result of maintenance works at "speed restricted zones" which decreased the amount of the latter from more than 50 to less than 20 (Interview key informant 1). While cargo trains occasionally needed up to 21 days in 2006, which "scared a lot of clients, they ran away" (Interview key informant 1), the transit time between the two termini could be brought down to an average of 6.6 days in the financial year 2017/18 (TAZARA 2018: 7). According to one source, it averaged four days in February 2019 (Interview key informant 1).

Notwithstanding recent improvements, TAZARA still faces serious infrastructural and operational challenges. TAZARA's signalling system, for instance, is outdated and, as a result of copper theft along the line, practically inoperative. Hence, in 2019 there was no single system of communication among TAZARA trains, stations and signal boxes (Interview key informant 1; Interview TAZARA trade union executive). In 2021, services were severely impacted for several months because of damages of the Chambeshi rail bridge (Liu 2024). Significant limitations in rolling stock pose a major challenge to meet market demand. In February 2019, the company "on a daily basis" was operating "with just about 12 locomotives". In order to reach its estimated break-even point of 600,000 tonnes in cargo, the enterprise would need no less than twenty locomotives. Moreover, the company is highly indebted, with outstanding liabilities amounting to \$800m (Interview key informant 1). TAZARA has remained chronically undercapitalised, as a senior Zambian official acknowledged:

> TAZARA hasn't had as much a good share of investment. Most of the investment that has gone into TAZARA over the years have been the Chinese protocols on one side, which largely focused on the Chinese providing equipment or selling us spare parts – to TAZARA. The financing from the government, from both governments – Tanzania and Zambia – has largely been focused on paying salaries and that is because – basically it's a way of quieting up the workers. But then the investments that required to be able to make the company viable and vibrant was not being looked at. (Interview senior official Zambian MTC)

With its ailing infrastructure, large corporate debts, an inefficient corporate structure and a severe shortage in rolling stock, TAZARA represents largely devalued capital assets in dire need of recapitalisation (see Harvey 2003: 150). While talks among the Chinese, Tanzanian and Zambian governments about TAZARA's privatisation have been recurring since the late 1990s (Africa-Asia Confidential 2010; Liu and Monson 2011; Monson 2006, 2009: 153), a Chinese participation in the company has never materialised "in part because of concerns raised by China" (Monson 2006: 113 n. 1).

Earlier reservations to invest in TAZARA were dispelled in the context of China's current spatio-temporal fix and, more concretely, Beijing's strategy to "move out" surplus capacities in China's infrastructure and construction sectors, which were exacerbated by stimulus packages following the 2007–2008 global financial crisis (Taylor and Zajontz 2020; Zajontz 2022b). To borrow Harvey's wording (2003: 151), Chinese surplus capital stands ready to "breath [sic!] new life" into the devalued railway. Thereby, as will be established in the remainder of this chapter, the profitability of a Chinese investment in TAZARA has been paramount for the Chinese SOEs involved in the negotiations about "revitalising" the railway.

China's Failed Attempt at a "Not so Friendly" Takeover

> TAZARA is the monument of the China-Africa friendship. Revitalisation of the project [...] signals a new era of cooperation. It means developing the railway of freedom and friendship to the railway of development and prosperity. (Then Chinese Ambassador to Tanzania, Lu Youqing, quoted in The Citizen 2017)

The "new era of cooperation", which then Chinese Ambassador to Tanzania, Lu Youqing, referred to, is not least characterised by Chinese interests in long-term investments in infrastructural assets across Africa and, where possible, the operation and management of the same. Unsurprisingly, TAZARA's rehabilitation is considered a BRI priority project (Interview senior official Tanzanian MWTC). But negotiations about a Chinese equity investment in TAZARA predate the BRI. As a result of TAZARA's ailing condition, the shareholding governments, in 2012, approached their Chinese counterpart to determine options to rehabilitate TAZARA. In the light of its critical role in the history of the railway, China has been considered as the logical partner for a private-sector participation in TAZARA (Interviews key informant 1; Kamata; Chinese journalist). In this section, I first recapitulate the 2016 intergovernmental negotiations and discuss some of the terms and conditions that have caused controversies. In a second step, I set the stage for the subsequent strategic-relational analysis as to why the Chinese infrastructural fix has, thus far, failed to materialise in the case of TAZARA.

The 2016 Tripartite Negotiations

> The China that we are dealing with today is not the same China that we were dealing with forty years ago. It's a different China. These are capitalist-oriented Chinese. They want to make money. The way they are driving this thing [negotiations about a Chinese participation in TAZARA] is to make sure they maximise their benefits. They are not saying: "We are just helping TAZARA […]." No, they want to make money. […] What they've been proposing is way too much. What they've been asking for is way too much. (Interview key informant 1)

In March 2012, the three governments signed a protocol which provided for a feasibility study for the "Renovation Project of Tanzania–Zambia Railway". Subsequently, the study was assigned to the Chinese state-owned Third Railway Survey and Design Institute Group Corporation (TSDI) and released in May 2016 (TSDI 2016: 2).[7] The study formed the basis for tripartite negotiations among the three governments. It inter alia recommended "that the government [sic!] of Tanzania and Zambia enact appropriate laws and create an agreeable commercial environment for the future development of [the] Tanzania-Zambia Railway so as to attract investment and improve the management level". Total investment required is estimated at \$370m (TSDI 2016: 230). The study recommended the closure of nine of TAZARA's remaining 57 active stations, five in Tanzania (Gwata, Kangaga, Malamba, Lumba, Mbalizi) and four in Zambia (Msanza, Kawila, Chimba, Finkuli) (TSDI 2016: 31 interview senior TAZARA manager).

[7] Curiously, the "feasibility study report (official version) was finalized in June 2013" already (TSDI 2016: 9). Yet, the English version was released to the shareholding governments only in 2016 when tripartite negotiations about a Chinese participation resumed in 2016 (Interview official Tanzanian MWTC).

Intergovernmental negotiations resumed in May 2016 when a technical committee met to explore options for a Chinese participation in TAZARA on the basis of the TSDI study. The Chinese delegation was headed by Liu Junfeng, Deputy Director General of the Ministry of Commerce, while Zambia was represented by Secretary to the Cabinet, Roland Msiska, and Tanzania by Chief Secretary at the State House, Ambassador John Kijazi. According to a post-meeting working document which is quoted in the The Citizen, "[t]he Chinese, Tanzania[n] and Zambian sides all agree that the current form of management and operation shall be changed and *commercial operation* shall be introduced to realise the revitalisation and sustainable development of Tazara". Furthermore, "Tanzania and Zambia will do their best to ensure Tazara is provided with preferential policies and legal instruments to make it commercially viable". The document reportedly also adumbrates the downsizing of the TAZARA workforce (The Citizen 2016; italics added).

Based on the TSDI feasibility study, in the words of a Tanzanian top official, three options to rehabilitate TAZARA were "on the table": "Concession, management contract or complete rehabilitation by the shareholding governments". The interviewee claimed that, while the Tanzanian government "left all the three options open", for their Zambian counterparts rehabilitation by means of own resources was financially unfeasible (Interview Tanzanian top official). Consequently, the two shareholding governments "had both agreed that what would be best for TAZARA is a management contract" (Interview key informant 1; also interview senior official Zambian MTC). Management contracts are generally short-term (3–5 years) arrangements between a public authority and a private corporation. Ownership and capital expenditure remain with the public authority, whereas operation and maintenance are handled by the private contractor. The latter is compensated through set management fees (Farquharson et al. 2011: 10; World Bank, n.d.).

The Chinese side however declined a management contract and proposed a long-term Rehabilitate-Operate-Transfer (ROT) PPP instead (Interviews senior official Zambian MTC; official Tanzanian MWTC; key informant 1; key informant 2).[8] A CCECC executive explained that the "key question" had been whether to invest in rebuilding or in mere

[8] Some terminological clarification is indicated, as the terms "ROT contract" and "concession" are often used interchangeably, including by some of my interviewees. Generally, both refer to long-term contractual arrangements, usually of 20–30 years duration. A ROT

maintenance, with either "big money" or "little money" being spent. The Chinese government preferred a major, long-term investment over a timespan of 30 years, which would aim at "refresh[ing]" and "rebuilding TAZARA only once", over short-term capital injections towards the maintenance of the railway (Interview executive CCECC). The Chinese preference towards a ROT contract was also reflected in the institutional set-up for the intergovernmental negotiations. The Chinese government set up an advisory working group which was steered by China Railway. As a Chinese interviewee reasoned, China Railway "ha[s] the experience of running railways. That's why they were chosen [...] by the Chinese government to be the leading company in that joint working group". Other members are CCECC (on behalf of CRCC), TSDI and China Railway Rolling Stock Corporation (CRRC) (Interview key informant 2).

The Chinese proposal of 2016 foresaw a contract duration of 30 years and provided for the injection of $380m into the railway's debilitated infrastructure and rolling stock (Interview key informant 1). As a precondition for an investment, the Chinese consortium expected the shareholding governments to assume TAZARA's outstanding debts, which amount to "no less than 800 million dollars" (Interview key informant 1; also interviews TAZARA labour union executive; Tanzanian top official; senior official Tanzanian MWTC; official Tanzanian MWTC). As one interviewee put it, the Chinese side expected that "the books must be cleaned completely. The two governments must receive those debts—must clean the books of TAZARA" (Interview key informant 1). This was confirmed by a Tanzanian top official who was involved in the negotiations: "One of the terms was to clear out the balance sheet of TAZARA". The interviewee underscored that, for the Tanzanian government, the offer made little economic sense. "If you have the capacity of doing that, why do you find someone else? [...] If you were to pay all the debt before someone thinks of [a] concession, then you can as well do

PPP is a variant of a Build-Operate-Transfer (BOT) contract. It includes the rehabilitation of a facility/asset as well as the ownership and the right to operate and manage the same for a specified period of time. The contractor is paid either by the public authority or through user fees. Concessions transfer the operation and management of an asset to the concessionaire. Concession agreements can equally contain contractual obligations to rehabilitate and/or extend an infrastructural asset. Ownership of the asset however remains with the contracting authority and remuneration is generally based on the "user-pays" principle (Farquharson et al. 2011: 11–12; World Bank 2020, n.d.; Yescombe and Farquharson 2018: 11–14).

it yourself". The Tanzanian official stated that the Zambian government equally considered it impossible to clear TAZARA's outstanding debt (Interview Tanzanian top official). While the Chinese forgave parts of the debt from the initial construction loans in 2010 (Erdmann 2011: 530), one interviewee suggested that the Chinese side used TAZARA's debts and other financial liabilities towards suppliers and (former) employees as a "negotiation tool" (Interview key informant 1).

Not only did the question as to who would guarantee for TAZARA's outstanding debt cause controversies among the three governments. The Chinese side also requested tax concessions to make an investment economically feasible. In its financial appraisal section, the TSDI study comes to the sobering conclusion that

> [t]he financial internal rate of returns of project investment is below 0 and the financial benefit of the project is poor. The government of the three countries should provide certain support, so as to provide [a] powerful guarantee for the financial viability of the project. (TSDI 2016: 257)

Most importantly, the feasibility study presupposes the continuation of tax abatements after privatisation: "In view that Tanzania-Zambia Railway is the project aided by China, and it shall be [a] tax-exempt[ed] project. In this study, it is considered that Tanzania-Zambia Railway still has income tax immunity rights" (TSDI 2016: 255). The Chinese negotiators asked for tax holidays until TAZARA could be run profitably, which according to their projections could take 15–20 years. The Chinese calculated that TAZARA would reach the break-even point only when it transported 1m metric tonnes of cargo per annum, whereas TAZARA's own estimates project the same with an annual cargo volume of 600,000 tonnes (Interview key informant 1). A Tanzanian official confirmed that the Chinese set the break-even point at 1.05m tonnes and argued that the Chinese consortium expected the shareholding governments to subsidise TAZARA until this threshold was met (Interview official MWTC). According to a Tanzanian top official, the differing bases of calculation were "the gist of the matter". The interviewee recalled that "the numbers were very, very different what they had and what we had. So, we said: 'No, we cannot discuss on these particular terms. When we are saying that on this basis we break even at 600,000 tonnes and then you [referring to the Chinese] are saying 1.2 [million tonnes]" (Interview Tanzanian top official).

The demand for tax holidays effectively constituted an investment conditionality. Indeed, tax exemptions and state subsidies are a common instrument to ensure profitability of investments in transport infrastructure and are clearly not confined to Chinese investments (see Hildyard 2016). Nonetheless, the Chinese demands were considered disproportionate by the shareholding governments. One interviewee described the Chinese request for tax holidays "as a trick or rather as a tactic to evade tax". The interviewee also argued that it was the Tanzanian government which deemed the far-reaching tax exemptions unacceptable, stating that "if you are a nationalist [referring to President Magufuli] [...] you ask the question: So, why should I bring this company from China? Why should they come? They are saying, they don't want to pay tax. They will not pay tax after 15, 20 years" (Interview key informant 1). As I shall discuss further in Chapter 5, fiscal concessions of such kind would appear antithetical to developmentalist policies pursued by the Tanzanian government under Magufuli.

Besides the discordance over financial terms and conditions, another condition of the Chinese concession proposal was highly controversial. According to one interviewee, the Chinese consortium planned to retrench the entire TAZARA workforce and re-employ parts of it under new contracts. The official stated that the investor expected the shareholding governments to defray costs related to the retrenchment of TAZARA employees. The interviewee underscored the political sensitivity of questions related to the workforce of TAZARA, stating that: "If you touch someone, retrench workers, you have political chaos" (Interview official Tanzanian MWTC; also interview key informant 1). Political veteran Job Lusinde, who supervised TAZARA's construction as Minister of Transport, underlined this assessment, stating a central question in the context of the planned TAZARA restructuring is necessarily: "What will happen to the African workforce? Are you going to remove all the managers and bring in Chinese? You are looking for trouble" (Interview Lusinde). As past rounds of retrenchments have shown, the TAZARA workforce has traditionally been strongly identified with the company and proven ready to defend their jobs (Liu and Monson 2011; Monson 2013: 56–57; interview Shivji).

The terms and conditions put forward by the Chinese negotiators were considered "not workable" by the shareholding governments (Interview Tanzanian top official; also interviews senior official Tanzanian MWTC; official Tanzanian MWTC; key informant 1). For one interviewee, the Chinese proposal "does not make economic sense, unless somebody is just desperate to get involved" (Interview key informant 1). In disagreement with the Chinese side over the terms, conditions and model of privatisation, the two shareholding governments rejected the 2016 concession proposal. They asked the Chinese negotiators to update the feasibility study, in order to account for the increase in cargo volumes in recent years as well as for recent revenues created from an access agreement with the South African company Calabash Freight Limited, and to present a revised concession proposal (Interviews Tanzanian top official; key informant 1). According to one interviewee, the Chinese consortium submitted an updated feasibility study in late 2017. However, the only major alteration concerned the number of TAZARA stations recommended for closure. The controversial terms regarding the operational model, the company's outstanding debts, financial concessions and subsidies and major layoffs remained unaltered (Interview official Tanzanian MWTC). As a result, formal negotiations were put on hold for several years (Interviews official Tanzanian MWTC; key informant 2). It took until 2022 for the two governments—now under the leadership of Hakainde Hichilema and Samia Suluhu Hassan—to publicly announce that they would jointly approach the Chinese side for renewed negotiations over an investment in the company (Liu 2024; Zajontz 2022a).

The Chinese Infrastructural Fix at an Impasse

The Chinese ROT proposal of 2016 is exemplary for a nascent shift in the financial governance of Chinese overseas infrastructure projects, especially in countries where debt sustainability has become an issue. Since the mid-2010s the Chinese government has actively promoted PPPs as a financially more sustainable alternative to sovereign debt-funded infrastructure projects (van Wieringen and Zajontz 2023). In 2017, the government further restricted the lending practices of its policy banks (Carmody et al. 2022). Correspondingly, Chinese companies have started to adapt their engagements in African infrastructures markets by no longer acting only as contractors in EPC projects but increasingly also as investors and operators of infrastructural assets (Alden and Jiang 2019; Brautigam 2022; Gonzalez-Vicente 2019; Zajontz 2022b). The 2016 proposal reveals the concrete institutional form the Chinese infrastructural fix is inclined to take on in the case of TAZARA. In theoretical terms, a long-term contractual arrangement, be it in the form of a ROT contract, would provide for the "temporal displacement" of large amounts of surplus capital by means of investment in a project with a long gestation time. At the same time, the rehabilitation of the railway as well as its operation and management would facilitate (and accelerate) the circulation of other (Chinese) capitals in the region (Harvey 2003: 109; see Jessop 2006).

Moreover, the privatisation of TAZARA, especially if it was to involve a transfer of the company's outstanding debts to the Zambian and Tanzanian treasuries, far-reaching fiscal and tax concessions and labour rationalisations, amounts to accumulation by dispossession and its logic of unequal exchange. As Harvey (2003: 150) suggests, particularly devalued assets, of which TAZARA is a prime example, "can be bought up at fire-sale prices and profitably recycled back into the circulation of capital by overaccumulated capital". However, this particular manifestation of the Chinese infrastructural fix has not materialised because of counteracting strategies on the part of the shareholding governments. It remains to be seen whether the shareholding governments' positions on the conditions of a PPP are going to be reversed in the light of Zambia's debt crisis and the recent recourse to more liberal economic policies under President Hassan in Tanzania. The new political leadership in Dodoma and Lusaka announced in August 2022 that they would re-enter into negotiations with the Chinese side (Liu 2024). At the time of writing, an agreement about a Chinese investment had not been reached.

The disagreement over the terms of the 2016 ROT contract proposal was strongly informed by previous negative experiences with railway privatisations both in Tanzanias and Zambia. Both states unsuccessfully privatised their national railway companies in the 2000. An interviewee emphasised the importance to avoid mistakes made in the context of previous railway concessions through which "both countries got burnt" (Interview senior official Zambian MTC). The relatively recent instances of early terminated railway concessions have not only affected the strategic calculations of the shareholding governments, as I will discuss below, but also of the Chinese investor, considering that "the two expropriated concessions Tanzania (Rites) and Zambia (Transnet) had a rather stable shareholding involving experienced railways operators but it was the conflicting interests between the sponsors and the government that led to termination" (AfDB 2015: 64). The terms of the Chinese ROT proposal underscore that the Chinese investor has tried to achieve a maximum of investment security and profitability. A Chinese interviewee argued that the disagreement about the actual mode of privatisation was "the biggest challenge for the negotiation" and the reason why the "three governments are stuck". At the same time, the Chinese side was very aware of the political sensitivity of railway privatisations in both national contexts:

> The Tanzanian and Zambian governments had experiences of concession of a railway. For Tanzania, they had a concession of the Central Line and Zambia Railway was also concessioned. Both governments are claiming that according to their experience, concession for a railway is not going to work. Because the concessionaire – I mean the company who's coming – is always focusing on its own profits. It will not be interested in invest[ing] in the railway itself. That's the major barriers for the two governments. (Interview key informant 2)

Interestingly, the Chinese interviewee mentioned that: "For [the] Chinese side, it seems we don't want to call it concession. We call it – it's like a – how to say? It's like a kind of BOT [contract] – I mean we do the rehabilitation, we operate for some time and then transfer – kind of like that" (interview key informant 2). Such terminological reframing can reasonably be assumed to aim at tactically distinguishing the Chinese proposal from previous unsuccessful railway concessions. However, both concessions and BOT/ROT contracts imply the long-term transfer of operation and management of an asset to the contractor. In fact, ROT arrangements are generally more comprehensive than concessions, as they usually transfer the ownership of an asset to a private entity (see footnote 8 in this chapter for a definitional distinction). In the following, I elaborate on path-dependencies that have arisen from Zambia's and Tanzania's previous experiences with railway concessions and how they shaped the governments' strategies in the context of the planned rehabilitation of TAZARA.

The Path-Dependency of Railway Concession "Traumata"

> The Tanzanian government does not believe in concessioning [TAZARA]. Because they are equally coming from an experience where they had concessioned Tanzania Railways – to the Indians – which failed. They again grabbed it back to themselves and they're running it now themselves. Again, on the Zambian side, we're coming from an experience, we've

> concessioned ZRL [Zambia Railways Limited] to Rail Systems. Again, it was a failed project. (Interview TAZARA labour union executive)

As this introductory quote exemplifies, the failed railway privatisations of the 2000s were a prominent theme in my interviews and were considered as decisive factors for the positions of the shareholding governments in the negotiations about the TAZARA rehabilitation (Interview senior official Zambian MTC; interview Tanzanian top official; interview senior official Tanzanian MWTC; interview key informant 1; interview key informant 2). Indeed, Tanzania's and Zambia's World Bank-sponsored railway restructuring projects have become cautionary tales even within IFIs. As a 2015 report on rail infrastructure finance in Africa, compiled by the AfDB, finds, "[i]n most [African] countries, the introduction of concessions has proved rather unsettling to the point that two of them [referring to the Tanzanian and Zambian cases] [have] been terminated after a very short time" (AfDB 2015: xiv). In theoretical terms, I posit that these unsuccessful experiences constitute a strategic selectivity for both governments that have conditioned the unfolding of the Chinese infrastructural fix in the concrete case of TAZARA. This section first addresses Tanzania's, then Zambia's, experiences with privatising their national railway systems and respective strategic reflection on the part of the governments.

Tanzania's Strategic Learning from a "Case of Failed Privatization"

Tanzania's Railway Act No. 4 of 2002 restructured the Tanzania Railways Corporation (TRC) by transferring the ownership of rail assets to the newly established state-owned Reli Assets Holding Company (RAHCO) and mandating the same to delegate the provision of freight and passenger transport services by means of a vertically integrated concession. The latter, in 2007, was awarded for 25 years to Tanzania Railways Limited (TRL), a consortium in which Rail India Technical and Economic Services (RITES) held a majority share of 51 per cent and the Tanzanian government the remaining 49 per cent. The concessionaire was entitled to use movable and immovable assets but, in turn, was responsible for their management, maintenance and development and had to pay regular concession fees (World Bank 2005: 109, 2014: 5). The PPP was facilitated by the World Bank and its International Finance Corporation which "acted in close coordination to pursue the agenda of putting the state-owned enterprises on the commercial track" (Shlyk 2009: 34–35). However, soon after the concession had started, disputes between grantor and concessionaire about the condition and maintenance of assets, demands for wage increases and the underperformance of TRL resulted in the cancellation of the concession by the government in 2010 and an "amicable" transfer of RITES' shares in 2011 (AfDB 2015: 181, 184; Shlyk 2009: 37–41; World Bank 2014: 5). As a Tanzanian top official reflected:

> It didn't work well. Because the privatised company, which took over the services, did not do it to the expectation of the government. [...] That company neglected the maintenance part which was required by the contract and that led to the deterioration of services and finally to collapse. (Interview Tanzanian Top official)

In an implementation report, even the World Bank ascertains that TRL has been a "case of failed privatization". Despite "a decade of Bank-assisted effort to prepare the firm for private participation [...], [t]he private operator has not succeeded in meeting any of the major performance targets" (World Bank 2010: 12). The restructuring of Tanzania's railway sector was conclusively rolled back under President Magufuli in 2017, when the 2002 Railway Act was repealed. This regulatory revision aimed at improving efficiency in service delivery by merging the two SOEs RAHCO and TRL, which, since 2011, had remained responsible for infrastructure and operation respectively. Since March 2018, the infrastructure and operation of Tanzania's 2605 km metre-gauge rail lines are again under the organisational roof of the reinstated TRC. The latter also oversees the construction of the new SGR Central Line (Kandoya 2018; Railway Gazette 2018).

It is crucial to consider that, as Minister of Works, Transport and Communication (2000–2005, 2010–2015), Magufuli first oversaw the legislation for the restructuration of TRL and, in the same capacity, the re-nationalisation of TRL in 2011. Hence, his experience with the previous state strategy of concessioning railway services and maintenance was immediate and very personal and can be assumed to have shaped his state interventionist approach towards the development and management of infrastructure which I further discuss in Chapter 5. One interviewee argued that, in light of the failed TRC concession, open access agreements with private operators were currently the only conceivable public–private cooperation model, while operating concessions were politically "untenable" under the Magufuli government. More generally, the official appraised that decision-makers in Tanzania "have learned a lot" and were reflective about previous PPP experiences: "Even if you tell the decision-makers about PPP, they tell you of the past mistakes" (Interview official Tanzanian MWTC). A Tanzanian academic argued in a similar vein, when he suggested that "this government [referring to the Magufuli administration] is not very much keen on PPP, private–public partnership, because it has been a major source of ripping off government money" (Interview Kamata).

However, a Tanzanian top official insisted that there has not been a general policy shift under Magufuli against concessions but rather that the government's strategy and capacity to evaluate and negotiate PPPs has changed:

> Now we are more equipped with the information during negotiations than we previously were. And we are determined to discuss these concessions and everything to be a win-win situation. So, there is no paradigm shift of saying "no more concessions", no. (Interview Tanzanian top official)

This assessment is in line with policy documents. Tanzania's 2016 Five Year Development Plan calls for the "promotion of public–private partnerships nationally and regionally". Moreover, the plan states that

> [t]he public sector, through public-private partnerships, is encouraged to maximize synergies between the public and private sectors in mobilizing and deploying resources. PPP approach has been widely used in other countries to finance infrastructure and other long-term investment projects. PPP is a way to amalgamate public and private capital and expertise for public projects in which the private sector has interest in sharing ownership. (GURT 2016: 82, 95–96)

At the same time, the document identifies key challenges in the planning, negotiation and implementation of PPPs, such as insufficient "legal and institutional frameworks, guidelines and procedures", the "[l]ack of realistic and comprehensive technical, socio-economic and commercial feasibility analysis which leads to poor project design" and "[i]nsufficient capacity for negotiations, procurement, implementation and management of PPPs" (GURT 2016: 96). By centralising control and oversight in the presidency, Magufuli tried to address the governance problems, as discussed in Chapter 5.

The unsuccessful TRL concession has had a crucial impact on the strategic calculation of the Tanzanian government in the negotiations about a Chinese participation in TAZARA. It is instructive to quote a senior Tanzanian official at some length, since the statement vividly reveals organisational reflection and learning as well as the resulting strategic calculation regarding the privatisation of TAZARA. The official acknowledged that the experience of the TRC concession

> has played a role, because it was not a very good lesson that we had when we concessioned TRC. And we don't want to repeat the mistakes that have been done. So, we keep on improving – even the quality of negotiation is not the same. We look into other parameters which maybe were not considered previously. But the bottom line is the national interest is primary now to our negotiations. That should come first. What are we going to gain in whatever arrangement that we are going to enter? That is the bottom line. […] We learned a lot in terms of concession arrangements. So, we don't want to go back into that bad experience we have had. But again, our keen interest is to make sure the national interest prevails. The national interest should prevail. That whatever arrangement that we are going to agree on – what are going to be the benefits? Are we going to gain much more compared to the situation we have now? Or are we going to enter into huge debts that again will come back for the government to service? Because that is what happened when we concessioned TRC. So, we are a bit hesitant because we are conscious of the bad experience that we had. And we are saying better late than never. So maybe – on [the] Tanzanian side – that is what is haunting us. But we are not saying [that] we are not going to concession, but we want to be pretty sure of whatever decision that we are going – we need to make an informed kind of decision. […] We should not regret whatever decision that we take. So, we want it, but we are doing it maybe gradually and cautiously. And that's what we are doing. So, an outsider might say that we are dragging our feet, but actually we want to do it correctly. (Interview senior official Tanzanian MWTC)

In conceptual terms, the statement underlines how the strategic calculation of the Tanzanian government in the TAZARA negotiations was affected by previous strategic-relational interactions between structural constraints and strategic action regarding railway governance modalities. Moreover, it reveals how the government tried to avoid the retention of previously unsuccessful strategies by improving its negotiation capacities and defining and evaluating economic parameters that are considered necessary for the government to profit from a concession. As I discuss in Chapter 5, Tanzania's strategy during and after the negotiations was informed by President Magufuli's economic nationalism and autocratic developmental state which in turn resulted from a changing balance of political forces in Tanzania. First, however, Zambia's railway privatisation experience will be recapitulated.

Zambia's Private Railway Odyssey

Zambia's railway PPP interlude was promoted by a Railway Restructuring Project, agreed between the World Bank and Zambia in 2000 (World Bank 2000). According to the Managing Director of Zambia Railways Limited (ZRL), the concession to a private company was motivated by an urgent need of recapitalisation and "deferred maintenance which this company suffered" (Interview Musonda, C.). In the run-up to the privatisation of ZRL, a World Bank loan was granted to upgrade the track with concrete sleepers and repair some of the rolling stock in order to make the company "fit" for private investment (Bullock 2005: 22). The loan also covered advisory and legal services related to the privatisation as well as $20.5m in retrenchment costs arising from staff rationalisation. According to the Bank's Independent Evaluation Group the labour force "was downsized from 3,300 to 800 staff by the concessioning date" (IEG 2006: n.n.). In 2003, following an international tender process, the Zambian government awarded a twenty-year concession for freight transport and a seven-year concession for passenger transport to Railway Systems of Zambia (RSZ), a newly established consortium which was controlled by the Mauritius-registered investment holding New Limpopo Bridge Projects Investments (NLPI), while Spoornet, the freight subsidiary of South Africa's Transnet, held a minority share of 17 per cent (Bullock 2005: 23; OECD 2012: 155–56). Actual operation of the line was subcontracted to Spoornet (Bullock 2005: 22).[9] State-owned ZRL was installed as asset manager with 25 staff (IEG 2006: n.n.).

[9] In 2007, Spoornet was renamed Transnet Freight Rail (Bullock 2009: 4 n. 11).

Just as in the Tanzanian case, very soon after commencement of the concessions, contentions over the interpretation of the contractual obligations arose. Disputed issues were RSZ's failures to achieve agreed investment plans and to meet its reporting obligations (Bullock 2005: 23). According to a report by the Organisation for Economic Co-operation and Development, the concession was lacking "an appropriate regulatory framework that would address operational standards, safety, and the rigorous enforcement of investments into rehabilitation and expansion of track and rolling stock, which should be undertaken by RSZ" (OECD 2012: 156). As a result, the concession failed to meet the government's financial targets. Beyond the entry fee of $0.75m, the payment of the fixed concession fee was dependent on the achievement of a pre-defined threshold which was based on freight forecasts that soon turned out to be too optimistic (Bullock 2005: 23). Moreover, the concessionaire faced capacity constraints in terms of rolling stock which caused "deliberate withdrawal from local intermine traffic", as the concessionaire "gave priority to longer-distance traffic from the Copperbelt to South Africa at the expense of local intermine movement of bulk minerals and feeder traffic to Tazara" (Bullock 2009: 29, 49 n. 57; also interview Musonda, C.). Bullock (2009: 49 n. 57) suggests that this decision was driven by the rationale "to concentrate assets on the most profitable freight".

The RSZ concession had detrimental effects for TAZARA, too. For RSZ, the short-distance feeder traffic from Congolese or Zambian mines to the TAZARA interchange in Kapiri Mposhi was not lucrative compared to the southern route. Both RSZ shareholders had strong economic incentives to serve the southern corridor to increase the distance covered on their own rail lines, with NLPI controlling the operators of the Zimbabwean lines that connect Beitbridge and Victoria Falls and Spoornet operating lines to South Africa's ports (Bullock 2005: 24). Following a parliamentary inquiry into the benefits of the RSZ concession (OECD 2012: 156), the agreement was cancelled under late President Sata in 2012 (AfDB 2015: 189). Sata, a veteran trade unionist, was elected in 2011 after several electoral campaigns during which he criticised privatisation and pledged the nationalisation of key companies, such as ZRL, Zambia Telecommunications Company and Finance Bank (Bwalya and Maharaj 2018; Carmody and Kragelund 2016; Larmer 2011: 262; Lee 2017: 18).

Zambia's developmental state experiment was short-lived, as I will discuss in Chapter 6. The country's expansionary fiscal policy, not least to finance infrastructure, combined with neopatrimonial modes of governance, has driven the country's sovereign debt to unsustianable levels. The government has started to revert to PPPs as a means of constructing, operating and managing infrastructure. In a ministerial statement on the state of Zambia's railway system, then Transport Minister Mushimba outlined the government's strategy towards rail infrastructure development in times of scarce public funds, when he argued that "considering the high cost of new railway infrastructure […] developments, we shall encourage more public private partnership (PPP) initiatives for the construction of the planned new railway lines based on reasonable feasibility studies" (National Assembly of Zambia 2017: 4). Indeed, in March 2020 the government signed a PPP contract, reportedly worth $825m, with CCECC to rehabilitate the southern segment of the ZRL tracks (Livingstone-Lusaka) over a period of eight years (Lusaka Times 2020b; Reuters 2020; also interviews Musonda, C.; Mwila). Only a few days later the government announced that it had entered a memorandum of understanding with the US company Railnet International for a greenfield project that would connect Kafue with Lion's Den in Zimbabwe, thereby providing for the missing rail link along the Beira corridor, the closest route to the sea from Lusaka (Lusaka Times 2020a; also interview senior official Zambian MTC). Financial constraints were equally invoked as the main reason for Lusaka's persistent interest in privatising TAZARA, an aspect I will return to in the next chapter.

Conclusion

If there was an "archetype" of Sino-African cooperation in the infrastructure sector, it certainly would be the Tanzania–Zambia Railway. The railway was built to reduce Zambia's dependency on racist regimes to its south and to advance economic development along its route. Chinese support for the railway has had a lasting impact on China's relations with Zambia and Tanzania and the "TAZARA spirit" that was cultivated in the construction era resonates, to this day, with people across Africa and China (see Liu 2024). The historical cooperation constitutes a crucial path-dependency for Sino-African relations, which not least expresses itself in frequent discursive references in the context of contemporary Sino-African relations. This chapter established external and internal causes for the decade-long devaluation of the binational railway company, which, following Harvey's theory, could possibly be "bought up at fire-sale prices and profitably recycled back into the circulation of capital by overaccumulated capital" (Harvey 2003: 150). Yet, in this concrete case the Chinese infrastructural fix has hitherto not materialised.

The 2016 intergovernmental negotiations over a Chinese participation in TAZARA failed to reach an agreement. The Chinese side rejected a short-term management contract which was preferred by the shareholding governments. Instead, a Chinese consortium proposed a 30-year, large-scale investment in the form of a ROT PPP, whose profitability the investors wanted to be secured by means of financial concessions from the two states involved, notably tax breaks and the assumption of TAZARA's outstanding debts, and through major job rationalisations. Liu (2024: 82), a long-term observer of Sino-African relations and the TAZARA specifically, suggests that "[t]here is now a strong focus in China that the cooperation on TAZARA is in need of reform towards a full commercialisation of the railway along market lines". The Chinese proposal is in line with the structural tendencies inherent in the spatio-temporal fix, as it would "temporally fix" a large amount of Chinese surplus capital in a project with a long gestation time. An ROT contract also reflects the nascent shift in the financial governance of the BRI whereby Chinese firms have increasingly been encouraged by Beijing to increase equity investments in African infrastructures in a move to compensate for restricted loan financing due to economic risks and political backlashes (see Alden and Jiang 2019; van Wieringen and Zajontz 2023; Zhang 2023).

Following the logic of the spatio-temporal fix, "fixing" TAZARA by means of a Chinese equity investment would allow for a faster circulation of other mobile capitals. These could be (Chinese) investment goods or merchandise destined for markets along the TAZARA corridor or export goods produced in (Chinese-owned) mines, farms or agribusinesses in Tanzania, Zambia, Malawi or the DRC. Across Africa, the improvement of transport and corridor infrastructure has been considered as conducive to Chinese market expansion (Gambino 2022). Transferring the operation, management and (potentially) ownership of TAZARA would signify a concrete form of accumulation by dispossession, whereby a devalued publicly owned asset is expropriated from the commons at very low (or zero) costs with the aim of providing new profitable outlets for overaccumulated capital (see Harvey 2003: 149). Yet, the infrastructural fix has not (yet) materialised in this manner, partly because of path-dependencies of failed railway privatisations and counteracting strategic action on the part of the shareholding governments, which—in strategic-relational terms—affected their structurally oriented strategic calculations (see Hay 2002: 129; Jessop 2005: 48).

In both cases, state managers have proven reflective of strategic "mistakes" in the context of the failed privatisations of Tanzania's and Zambia's national railway companies in the 2000s. Hence, strategic learning informed the governments' negotiation strategies. Nonetheless, neither of the two governments has ruled out a PPP that entails an operational concession with a Chinese investor, granted it would yield mutual economic benefits. The strategic capacities of the shareholders to act upon their strategic learning have differed however, as it is influenced by strategic selectivities found in each state. Put differently, infrastructure states and their agents are differentially constrained. As I will elaborate on in Chapter 5, Zambia's sovereign debt had become a strategically constraining structural impediment which, from Lusaka's vantage point, left TAZARA's privatisation without any alternative. It was ultimately the rise of a decidedly nationalist infrastructure state in neighbouring Tanzania under the late President Magufuli which prevented the Chinese infrastructure fix from materialising in the case of TAZARA. In the meantime, Zambia under President Hichilema has come under the tutelage of IMF emergency facilities, whereas the economic nationalist Magufuli has died. TAZARA's privatisation is back on the negotiation table.

List of Interviews

Chilumbu, Delax, former chief mining engineer, Zambian Ministry of Mines and Minerals Development, Lusaka, Zambia, 21 July 2017.

Chinese journalist (anonymised), 8 February 2019.

Executive, China Civil Engineering Construction Corporation (CCECC) East Africa Ltd. (anonymised), 14 November 2019.

Kamata, Ng'wanza, head of department, Department of Political Science and Public Administration, University of Dar es Salaam (UDSM), Dar es Salaam, Tanzania, 5 February 2019.

Key informant 1 (anonymised), 4 February 2019.

Key informant 2 (anonymised), 26 November 2019.

Lusinde, Job Malecela, former Tanzanian cabinet minister (1961–1975) and former Tanzanian ambassador to China (1975–1984), Dodoma, Tanzania, 20 November 2019.

Mtonga, Robert, chief executive officer, Truckers Association of Zambia (TAZ), Lusaka, Zambia, 25 July 2017.
Musonda, Christopher, managing director, Zambia Railways Ltd. (ZRL), Kabwe, Zambia, 8 August 2017.
Mwila, Elias, general secretary, Railway Workers Union of Zambia (RWUZ), Kabwe, Zambia, 7 July 2017.
Official, Ministry of Works, Transport and Communication (MWTC) (anonymised), 18 November 2019.
Senior official, Tanzanian Ministry of Works, Transport and Communication (MWTC) (anonymised), 19 November 2019.
Senior official, Zambian Ministry of Transport and Communication (MTC) (anonymised), Lusaka, Zambia, 14 June 2017.
Senior TAZARA manager (anonymised), 10 August 2017.
Shivji, Issa, professor, Mwalimu Julius Nyerere Research Chair in Pan-African Studies, University of Dar es Salaam, Dar es Salaam, Tanzania, 1 February 2019.
Shone, Vernon, managing director, Advance Transport, Ndola, Zambia, 7 July 2017.
Tanzanian top official (anonymised), 15 November 2019.
TAZARA labour union executive (anonymised), 10 August 2017.
TAZARA manager (anonymised), 2 June 2017.

References

AfDB. 2015. *Rail Infrastructure in Africa: Financing Policy Options*. Abidjan: African Development Bank.
Africa-Asia Confidential. 2010. "TAZARA Troubles." *Africa-Asia Confidential* 4(1):6.
Alden, Chris, and Lu Jiang. 2019. "Brave New World: Debt, Industrialization and Security in China–Africa Relations." *International Affairs* 95(3):641–57.https://doi.org/10.1093/ia/iiz083.
Baregu, Mwesiga. 2006. "Tanzania-China Relations in Historical Perspective." Pp. 209–16 in *China in Africa: Mercantilist Predator, or Partner in Development*, edited by G. le Pere. Braamfontein: The Institute of Global Dialogue and The South African Institute of International Affairs.
Brautigam, Deborah. 2022. "China and Zambia: Creating a Sovereign Debt Crisis." *International Affairs* 98(4):1347–65. https://doi.org/10.1093/ia/iiac109.
Bullock, Richard. 2005. *Results of Railway Privatization in Africa*. Transport Paper. Washington: World Bank.

Bullock, Richard. 2009. *Off Track: Sub-Saharan African Railways*. Africa Infrastructure Country Diagnostic Background Paper 17. Washington: World Bank.

Bwalya, John, and Brij Maharaj. 2018. "Not to the Highest Bidder: The Failure of Incumbency in the Zambian 2011 Elections." *Journal of Contemporary African Studies* 36(1):71–86. https://doi.org/10.1080/02589001.2017.1369014.

Bwayla, Edgar. 2013. "China-Zambia Relations." Pp. 189–213 in *China's Diplomacy in Eastern and Southern Africa*, edited by S. Adem. Farnham: Ashgate.

Carmody, Pádraig. 2013. *The Rise of the BRICS in Africa: The Geopolitics of South-South Relations*. London: Zed Books.

Carmody, Pádraig, and Peter Kragelund. 2016. "Who Is in Charge? State Power and Agency in Sino-African Relations." *Cornell International Law Journal* 49(1):1–24. https://doi.org/10.1038/nmeth.2841.

Carmody, Pádraig, Tim Zajontz, and Ricardo Reboredo. 2022. "From 'Debt Diplomacy' to Donorship? China's Changing Role in Global Development." *Global Political Economy* 1(2):198–217. https://doi.org/10.1332/uzhw7185.

Chen, Yingqun, and Lucie Morangi. 2019. "Chinese Aid Helps Put African Nations on Track." *China Daily*. Retrieved February 29, 2020 (https://www.global.chinadaily.com.cn/a/201909/09/WS5d7593c9a310cf3e3556a5ed_4.html).

Chinese Ministry of Foreign Affairs. 2015. *A Monument to China-Africa Friendship: Firsthand Account of the Building of the TAZARA*. Beijing: World Affairs Press.

Craig, John. 2001. "Putting Privatisation into Practice: The Case of Zambia Consolidated Copper Mines Limited." *The Journal of Modern African Studies* 39(3):389–410. https://doi.org/10.1017/s0022278x01003652.

Domasa, Sylivester. 2016. "China in Rail Upgrade Talks with TAZARA Owners." *The Guardian*. Retrieved September 13, 2019 (https://www.ippmedia.com/en/news/china-rail-upgrade-talks-tazara-owners).

Duarte, Ana, Regina Santos, and Elling N. Tjønneland. 2014. "Angola's Lobito Corridor: From Reconstruction to Development." *Angola Brief* 4(5):1–4.

Erdmann, Gero. 2011. "Zambia." Pp. 525–34 in *Africa Yearbook: Politics, Economy and Society South of the Sahara in 2010*, edited by A. Mehler, H. Melber, and K. van Walraven. Leiden: Brill.

Essack, A. K. 1970. "The Tanzam Railway." *Economic and Political Weekly* 5(24):936–37.

Farquharson, Edward, Clemencia Torres de Mästle, E. R. Yescombe, and Javier Encinas. 2011. *How to Engage with the Private Sector in Public-Private Partnerships in Emerging Markets*. Washington: World Bank.

Friedman, Jeremy. 2021. *Ripe for Revolution: Building Socialism in the Third World*. Cambridge: Harvard University Press.

Gambino, Elisa. 2022. "Corridors of Opportunity? African Infrastructure and the Market Expansion of Chinese Companies." Pp. 286–316 in *Transport Corridors in Africa*, edited by H. Lamarque and P. Nugent. Woodbridge: James Currey.

Gleave, Michael B. 1992. "The Dar Es Salaam Transport Corridor: An Appraisal." *African Affairs* 91:249–67.

Gonzalez-Vicente, Ruben. 2019. "Make Development Great Again? Accumulation Regimes, Spaces of Sovereign Exception and the Elite Development Paradigm of China's Belt and Road Initiative." *Business and Politics* 21(4):487–513. https://doi.org/10.1017/bap.2019.20.

GPRC. 1964. "The Chinese Government's Eight Principles for Economic Aid and Technical Assistance to Other Countries." *Woodrow Wilson International Center for Scholars*. Retrieved March 18, 2020 (https://digitalarchive.wilsoncenter.org/document/121560).

Guo, Yu. 2019. "Development and Characteristics of China's Foreign Aid: The Tanzania–Zambia Railway." Pp. 23–34 in *South-South Cooperation and Chinese Foreign Aid*, edited by M. Huang, X. Xu, and X. Mao. Singapore: Palgrave Macmillan.

GURT. 2016. *National Five Year Development Plan: 2016/17–2020/21*. Dodoma: Ministry of Finance and Planning.

Hall, Richard, and Hugh Peyman. 1976. *The Great UHURU Railway: China's Showpiece in Africa*. London: Victor Gollancz.

Harvey, David. 2003. *The New Imperialism*. Oxford: Oxford University Press.

Hay, Colin. 2002. *Political Analysis: A Critical Introduction*. London: Red Globe Press.

Hildyard, Nicholas. 2016. *Licenced Larceny: Infrastructure, Financial Extraction and the Global South*. Manchester: Manchester University Press.

Hill, Matthew. 2016. "Zambia 2015 Copper Production Unexpectedly Rises on New Mine." *Bloomberg*. Retrieved February 28, 2020 (https://www.bloomberg.com/news/articles/2016-01-22/zambia-2015-copper-output-unexpectedly-increases-on-new-mine).

IEG. 2006. *ICR Review: Zambia Railways Restructuring Project: Report No: ICRR12336*. Independent Evaluation Group, World Bank.

Jessop, Bob. 2005. "Critical Realism and the Strategic-Relational Approach." *New Formations: A Journal of Culture, Theory and Politics* (56):40–53.

Jessop, Bob. 2006. "Spatial Fixes, Temporal Fixes and Spatio-Temporal Fixes." Pp. 142–66 in *David Harvey: A Critical Reader*, edited by N. Castree and D. Gregory. Malden: Blackwell Publishing.

Jessop, Bob. 2016. *The State: Past, Present, Future*. Cambridge: Polity Press.

Kahama, Joseph K. 2018. *The Challenge to China-Tanzania Relationship: To Enhance Cooperation and Mutual Benefits*. Dar es Salaam: Tema Publishers.

Kaiser, Paul J. 1996. "Structural Adjustment and the Fragile Nation: The Demise of Social Unity in Tanzania." *The Journal of Modern African Studies* 34(2):227–37. https://doi.org/10.1017/s0022278x00055300.

Kamata, Ng'wanza. 2013. "Perspectives on Sino-Tanzanian Relations." Pp. 87–106 in *China's Diplomacy in Eastern and Southern Africa*, edited by S. Adem. Farnham: Ashgate.

Kandoya, James. 2018. "RAHCO Disbanded as TRL Gives Way to TRC." *The Guardian*. Retrieved March 24, 2020 (https://www.ippmedia.com/en/news/rahco-disbanded-trl-gives-way-trc).

Kragelund, Peter. 2010. "The Price of 'Openness': Towards Chinese Economic Control in Zambia." Pp. 208–17 in *The Rise of China and India in Africa*, edited by F. Cheru and C. Obi. London: Zed Books.

Larmer, Miles. 2005. "Reaction & Resistance to Neo-Liberalism in Zambia." *Review of African Political Economy* 32(103):29–45. https://doi.org/10.1080/03056240500120992.

Larmer, Miles. 2011. *Rethinking African Politics: A History of Opposition in Zambia*. Surrey: Ashgate.

Lee, Ching Kwan. 2017. *The Specter of Global China: Politics, Labor, and Foreign Investment in Africa*. Chicago: University of Chicago Press.

Leslie, Agnes Ngoma. 2016. "Zambia and China: Workers' Protest, Civil Society and the Role of Opposition Politics in Elevating State Engagement." *African Studies Quarterly* 16(3–4):89–106.

Liu, Haifang. 2024. "The Freedom Railway Now and Then: The Enduring Relevance of the 'TAZARA Spirit' for South-South Cooperation." Pp. 68–88 in *Africa's Railway Renaissance: The Role and Impact of China*, edited by T. Zajontz, P. Carmody, M. Bagwandeen, and A. Leysens. Abingdon: Routledge.

Liu, Haifang, and Jamie Monson. 2011. "Railway Time: Technology Transfer and the Role of Chinese Experts in the History of TAZARA." Pp. 226–51 in *African Engagements: Africa Negotiating an Emerging Multipolar World*, edited by T. Dietz, K. Havnevik, M. Kaag, and T. Oestigaard. Leiden: Brill.

Lusaka Times. 2019. "Tanzania Orders Probe into $6.7 Million Funds for TAZARA." *Lusaka Times*. Retrieved August 19, 2019 (https://www.lusakatimes.com/2019/07/29/tanzania-orders-probe-into-6-7-million-funds-for-tazara/).

Lusaka Times. 2020a. "Government Signs a Railway MOU with Railnet International." *Lusaka Times*. Retrieved March 8, 2020 (https://www.lusakatimes.com/2020/03/07/government-signs-a-railway-mou-with/?fbclid=IwAR24TP-8QAIsW-MWERYfg3uGm0qnFxQ2Hi1OTnU9XrOQX-tLGit4YmiWVl4).

Lusaka Times. 2020b. "Zambia Signs over $824 Million Deal with China Railway for Line Upgrades." *Lusaka Times*. Retrieved March 8, 2020 (https://www.lusakatimes.com/2020/03/06/265085/?fbclid=IwAR3VebAqXdWL8o6SRXaGwT2xqeHGE16zUo0X8Eymy6UOzk5fLyfDZzjaPUw).

Monson, Jamie. 2006. "Defending the People's Railway in the Era of Liberalization: Tazara in Southern Tanzania." *Africa: Journal of the International African Institute* 76(1):113–30.

Monson, Jamie. 2009. *Africa's Freedom Railway: How a Chinese Development Project Changed Lives and Livelihoods in Tanzania*. Bloomington: Indiana University Press.

Monson, Jamie. 2013. "Remembering Work on the Tazara Railway in Africa and China, 1965–2011: When 'New Men' Grow Old." *African Studies Review* 56(1):45–64. https://doi.org/10.1017/asr.2013.5.

Mutesa, Fredrick. 2010. "China and Zambia: Between Development and Politics." Pp. 67–78 in *The Rise of China and India in Africa*, edited by F. Cheru and C. Obi. London: Zed Books.

Mwase, Ngila. 1987. "Zambia, the TAZARA and the Alternative Outlets to the Sea." *Transport Reviews* 7(3):191–206. https://doi.org/10.1080/01441648708716655.

Mwase, Ngila. 2003. "The Liberalisation, De-Regulation and Privatisation of the Transport Sector in Sub-Saharan Africa: Experiences, Challenges and Opportunities." *Journal of African Economies* 12(Supplement 2):ii153–92. https://doi.org/10.1093/jae/12.suppl_2.ii153.

National Assembly of Zambia. 2017. "Ministerial Statements: Railway Transport System in Zambia." *National Assembly of Zambia*. Retrieved May 19, 2019 (http://www.parliament.gov.zm/sites/default/files/images/publication_docs/MINISTERIAL/STATEMENT/ON/THE/STATE/OF/RAILWAY/TRANSPORT/BY/HON/MUSHIMBA.pdf).

Niemann, Michael. 2000. *A Spatial Approach to Regionalisms in the Global Economy*. Basingstoke: Macmillan Press.

Nkrumah, Kwame. 1965. *Neo-Colonialism: The Last Stage of Imperialism*. Edinburgh: Thomas Nelson and Sons.

Nugent, Paul. 2018. "Africa's Re-Enchantment with Big Infrastructure: White Elephants Dancing in Virtuous Circles?" Pp. 22–40 in *Extractive Industries and Changing State Dynamics in Africa*, edited by J. Schubert, U. Engel, and M. Elisio. Abingdon: Routledge.

Nyerere, Julius. 2015. "Speech at the Official Handover of the Tanzania Zambia Railway to Tanzania and Zambia, Kapiri Mposhi, Zambia, 14 July 1976." Pp. 64–71 in *Julius Nyerere: Asante sana, Thank You, Mwalimu*. Dar es Salaam: Mkuki na Nyota.

OECD. 2012. *OECD Investment Policy Reviews: Zambia*. Paris: Organisation for Economic Cooperation and Development Publishing.

Railway Gazette. 2018. “TRC Returns as Vertical Separation Ends.” *Railway Gazette*. Retrieved March 25, 2020 (https://www.railwaygazette.com/news/policy/single-view/view/trc-returns-as-vertical-separation-ends.html).

Rettman, Rosalyn J. 1973. “The TANZAM Rail Link: China’s ‘loss-Leader’ in Africa.” *World Affairs* 136(3):232–58.

Reuters. 2020. “Zambia Signs over $824 Million Deal with China Railway for Line Upgrades.” *Reuters*. Retrieved March 8, 2020 (https://uk.reuters.com/article/zambia-railways-idAFJ8N2AI007).

Scholvin, Sören. 2016. *The Geopolitics of Regional Power: Geography, Economics and Politics in Southern Africa*. Abingdon: Routledge.

Scott, Guy. 2019. *Adnetures in Zambian Politics: A Story in Black and White*. Boulder: Lynne Rienner.

Shangwe, Muhidin J. 2017. “China’s Soft Power in Tanzania: Opportunities and Challenges.” *China Quarterly of International Strategic Studies* 3(1):79–100. https://doi.org/10.1142/S2377740017500026.

Shlyk, Alexander. 2009. *Performance of the Contractual Arrangements of Public-Private Partnerships: Case of Railway Concession in Tanzania*. Master thesis, Lund University.

Simutanyi, Neo. 1996. “The Politics of Structural Adjustment in Zambia.” *Third World Quarterly* 17(4):825–39.

Sklar, Richard L. 1974. “Zambia’s Response to the Rhodesian Unilateral Declaration of Independence.” Pp. 320–62 in *Politics in Zambia*, edited by W. Tordoff. Berkeley: University of California Press.

Söderbaum, Fredrik. 2002. *The Political Economy of Regionalism in Southern Africa*. Göteborg: Department of Peace and Development Research Göteborg University.

Sum, Ngai-Ling, and Bob Jessop. 2013. *Towards a Cultural Political Economy: Putting Culture in Its Place*. Cheltenham: Edward Elgar.

Taylor, Ian. 2006. *China and Africa: Engagement and Compromise*. Abingdon: Routledge.

Taylor, Ian, and Tim Zajontz. 2020. “In a Fix: Africa’s Place in the Belt and Road Initiative and the Reproduction of Dependency.” *South African Journal of International Affairs* 27(3):277–295. https://doi.org/10.1080/10220461.2020.1830165.

TAZARA. 2018. “Annual Report Confirms a Rebound, Upward Trend Continues.” *TAZARA Newsletter* (April–June):6–7.

The Citizen. 2016. “China to Take over Tazara in New Plan.” *The Citizen*. Retrieved September 20, 2019 (https://www.thecitizen.co.tz/news/China-to-take-over-Tazara-in-new-plan/1840340-3205138-an93ljz/index.html).

The Citizen. 2017. “TZ-China Relations ‘Not on a Free Fall.’” *The Citizen*. Retrieved August 7, 2019 (https://www.thecitizen.co.tz/magazine/politicalreforms/TZ-China-relations--not-on-a-free-fall-/1843776-3823236-iu13m1z/index.html).

TSDI. 2016. *Renovation Project of Tanzania-Zambia Railway: Feasibility Study*. Tianjin: Third Railway Survey and Design Institute Group Corporation.

UNDP. 1976. *A Profile of the Zambian Economy*. Lusaka: United Nations Development Program.

Wang, Lily. 2018. "Making the Chinese Standard Shine in Africa." *China's Foreign Trade* (5):32.

van Wieringen, Kjeld, and Tim Zajontz. 2023. "From Loan-Financed to Privatised Infrastructure? Tracing China's Turn towards Public-Private Partnerships in Africa." *Journal of Current Chinese Affairs*, online first. https://doi.org/10.1177/18681026231188140.

World Bank. 2000. *Report No. PID9176: Zambia-Railway Restructuring Project*. Washington: World Bank.

World Bank. 2005. *United Republic of Tanzania: Privatization Impact Assessment: Report No: 69628*. Washington: World Bank.

World Bank. 2010. *Implementation Completion and Results Report (IDA-33040 & IDA-3304A; P0498838): Report No: ICR00001459*. Washington: World Bank.

World Bank. 2013. *Opening the Gates: How the Port of Dar Es Salaam Can Transform Tanzania*. Tanzania Economic Update. Dar es Salaam: World Bank.

World Bank. 2014. *International Development Association: Project Appraisal Document on a Proposed Credit: Report No: 78925-TZ*. Washington: World Bank.

World Bank. 2020. "Concessions, Build-Operate-Transfer (BOT) and Design-Build-Operate (DBO) Projects." *Public-Private Partnership Legal Resource Center*. Retrieved June 17, 2021 (https://ppp.worldbank.org/public-private-partnership/agreements/concessions-bots-dbos).

World Bank. n.d. "PPP Contract Types and Terminology." *PPP Knowledge Lab*. Retrieved September 15, 2019 (https://pppknowledgelab.org/guide/sections/6-ppp-contract-types-and-terminology#table-3).

Yescombe, E. R., and Edward Farquharson. 2018. *Public-Private Partnerships for Infrastructure: Principles of Policy and Finance*. 2nd edition. Oxford: Butterworth-Heinemann.

Yu, George T. 1971. "Working on the Railroad: China and the Tanzania-Zambia Railway." *Asian Survey* 11(11):1101–17.

Zajontz, Tim. 2022a. "Tanzania and Zambia Want to Upgrade the 'Uhuru Railway'—But Can They?" *The Conversation*. Retrieved June 22, 2023 (https://theconversation.com/tanzania-and-zambia-want-to-upgrade-the-uhuru-railway-but-can-they-190659).

Zajontz, Tim. 2022b. "The Chinese Infrastructural Fix in Africa: Lessons from the Sino-Zambian 'Road Bonanza.'" *Oxford Development Studies* 50(1):14–29. https://doi.org/10.1080/13600818.2020.1861230.

Zajontz, Tim. 2022c. "'Win-Win' Contested: Negotiating the Privatisation of Africa's Freedom Railway with the 'Chinese of Today.'" *Journal of Modern African Studies* 60(1):111–34. https://doi.org/10.1017/S0022278X21000446.

Zajontz, Tim, Pádraig Carmody, Mandira Bagwandeen, and Anthony Leysens. 2024. "Introduction: China's Role in Africa's Railway Renaissance." Pp. 1–25 in *Africa's Railway Renaissance: The Role and Impact of China*, edited by T. Zajontz, P. Carmody, M. Bagwandeen, and A. Leysens. Abingdon: Routledge.

Zhang, Hong. 2023. *From Contractors to Investors? Evolving Engagement of Chinese State Capital in Global Infrastructure Development and the Case of Lekki Port in Nigeria*. China Africa Research Initiative Working Paper No. 53. Washington: Johns Hopkins University.

CHAPTER 5

Divergent State Agency: Zambia's Debt Impasse and Magufuli's Nationalist Infrastructure State

> [W]hatever decision is made, is made between Zambia and Tanzania and we go together with whatever decision ends up being made. At the end of the day, what we want is the modern TAZARA, a TAZARA that you and me are going to be proud of. (Then Zambian Minister of Transport Mushimba, quoted in Mbewe 2018)

Both Zambian and Tanzanian politicians and officials, including one of my interviewees (Interview Tanzanian top official), have regularly emphasised the political unity between the shareholding governments when it comes to TAZARA's ongoing restructuration process. Beyond the official narrative, there were however strategic divergences during and following the 2016 negotiations about a Chinese investment in TAZARA. As one interviewee argued, "the biggest sticking point is that we have different ways, the two governments first of all – Tanzania and Zambia – they are not at the same level of looking at things. And the Chinese know" (Interview key informant 1). A CCECC executive confirmed that the differences were smaller between the Chinese consortium and the Zambian government than they were between the Chinese side and the Tanzanian administration (Interview executive CCECC). Despite similar path-dependencies in terms of failed railway privatisation, the interests and

T. Zajontz, *The Political Economy of China's Infrastructure Development in Africa*, International Political Economy Series,
https://doi.org/10.1007/978-3-031-44449-4_5

strategic capacities of the two shareholding governments diverged significantly as a result of different structural contexts in each state. In this chapter I discuss the strategically constraining impact of Zambia's indebtedness on the government's strategic scope to rehabilitate the historic railway and how neopatrimonial governance might have abetted Zambian calls for TAZARA's privatisation.

The Zambian government has over the past decade embarked on an ambitious state-steered transport infrastructure development. Lusaka fully embraced the role of an infrastructure state in that it actively mobilised foreign capital for its state spatial project of a "land-linked Zambia" and pursued a "development-through-infrastructure" agenda. I elaborate on this in Chapter 6. Loans for infrastructure projects, not least from Chinese banks, have driven up the country's sovereign debt (see Fig. 5.1). At the same time, both state-owned railway companies—ZRL and TAZARA—have been chronically undercapitalised for several decades (Interviews Musonda, C.; senior official Zambian MTC; TAZARA labour union executive; Mwila; senior TAZARA manager). In line with the assumptions of the strategic-relational approach (SRA), Zambia's indebtedness has limited the strategic scope for the government to rehabilitate TAZARA

Fig. 5.1 Tanzania's and Zambia's external debt (% of GDP), 2009–2019 (*Source* Author's compilation, based on data from World Bank [n.d.-a, n.d.-b])

significantly. The latter's devalued assets and corporate debts pose a strategically selective structural constraint which has affected Zambia more than Tanznian for fiscal reasons.

The second part of the chapter focuses on political developments leading up to the election of President Magufuli and the state transformation process from a neopatrimonial to an autocratic developmental state that followed Magufuli's election. Magufuli's economic nationalism had major impact on the government's negotiation strategy about TAZARA's privatisation and entailed measures to improve the state of the railway on Tanzanian terms. The chapter also discusses the controversy around the Bagamoyo port project and the role of Chinese firms in the construction of Tanzania's SGR.

TAZARA—"A Drain on Zambia's Coffers"

While both shareholding governments rejected the Chinese ROT proposal in 2016, the Zambian government under Lungu actively lobbied for reconsidering a concession-based PPP with a Chinese investor. In light of the failed ZRL concession, a senior official argued that the declared objective in the negotiations with the Chinese government is to "negotiate a better deal than we did last time [RSZ concession]". Hence, the official argued, "we need to learn from our previous concession. Just because the previous concession went bad, it doesn't mean concession is a bad thing in itself" (Interview senior official Zambian MTC). The interviewee underscored the political sensitivity of the participation of a Chinese company in TAZARA, when stating that any PPP model would have to ensure that the ownership of the company remains Tanzanian and Zambian, so that "TAZARA's concessioning [would] not look like they are giving it away to the Chinese but allowing the Chinese to invest into it" (Interview senior official Zambian MTC).

Zambia's strategy in the privatisation talks has been strongly affected by the country's increasing financial constraints. A well-placed interviewee argued that, whereas the Tanzanian leadership is "very careful" and thus "it is not easy to sell that idea [referring to the Chinese proposal] from China in Tanzania", the Zambian government, despite agreeing that the conditions initially put forward by the Chinese consortium were unacceptable, supported a Chinese long-term participation for financial reasons. The interviewee further described the strategic divergence between the shareholders as follows:

> We have a new president [Magufuli] and the politics, again, they play a big part in the life of TAZARA [...]. He is a nationalist [...]. He says: "Tanzania first. Am I – what am I going to benefit from this? I bring in a foreign company to come and manage this company [TAZARA]. I take out all my employees, all my nationals, I have to pay them and then they bring in 400 million dollars. I spend 800 million to clean this company and then this new company comes with 400 million dollars. What's the point?" So, that's the sticking point. So, this guy [Magufuli] has said: "No, it cannot work". But on the Zambian side, they have said: "No, no, no, let's [do it] – this company is too much of a drain on our coffers. [...] The money that they want us to invest – we don't have money for reinvestment. So, let's bring in a private [investor] – let's bring the Chinese." (Interview key informant 1)

The Chinese dismissal of a management contract during the 2016 negotiations, in the words of a Zambian official, resulted in a situation in which "now we [Zambian government] have to go and convince our Tanzanian colleagues that 'look, maybe we are better off having to concession this thing [TAZARA]'". For the interviewee, Zambia's "fiscal constraints" speak for a TAZARA concession for 20–25 years which should guarantee fixed amounts of yearly investment into the company as well as employment guarantees and technology transfer (Interview senior official Zambian MTC).

The Zambian government has failed to inject capital into the under-capitalised railway authority, despite investment pledges agreed upon by TAZARA's governing bodies, the council of ministers and the board of directors. As a result of TAZARA's deteriorating performance, since 2011 non-payment of salaries has become a regular quarrel between TAZARA management and its trade unions, and the "consistency of getting salaries started to give us [TAZARA employees] serious problems", as periods of non-payment rose up to five months (Interview TAZARA labour union executive). The situation culminated in a strike in January 2015 which brought the railway to a standstill for more than a week (BBC 2015; Oirere 2015). In order to redress the issue and avoid further strikes, the shareholding governments decided in 2015 to step in and to alleviate the company of the wage bill. However, as Zambia's fiscal space has rapidly shrunk in the 2010s, non-payment of salaries has remained an issue for TAZARA workers in Zambia. While the Tanzanian government has fulfilled its commitment, its Zambian counterpart delayed salary payments for several months in 2017 (Interview TAZARA labour union executive). In April 2019, unionised TAZARA workers in Zambia went on strike, as the Zambian government had again failed to pay salaries for four months in a row (The Mast 2019). Besides the Zambian government's recurring inability to pay the Zambian TAZARA staff, it has also failed to honour its investment pledges. In 2017, the two shareholding governments had agreed to each inject $5m over a period of two years as a form of immediate aid for urgent maintenance measures. While the Tanzanian government released the funds, the Zambian did not (Interview key informant 1). One Tanzanian official likened TAZARA's situation to that of a "stepson", whereby "every parent needs to make sure that the other parent puts in equally" (Interview official Tanzanian MWTC). However, due to Zambia's budgetary constraints this has not been the case in recent years (Interview senior official Tanzanian MWTC; interview official Tanzanian MWTC).

Zambia's fiscal situation and its mounting foreign and domestic debt have posed structural constraints that have directly affected the government's strategic leeway in the talks about TAZARA's restructuring. Figure 5.1 shows the development of Zambia's debt/GDP ratio throughout 2010, in comparison with Tanzania's. Within Zambian policy circles, Chinese investment by means of a concession is considered the most viable solution to recapitalise TAZARA, considering Zambia's shrinking capacity to borrow:

> Concerning the constraints the economy has right now and the fiscal space we are better off concessioning TAZARA. Otherwise, with about 1.2 billion, 1.6 billion dollars of fiscal space for borrowing – if you take in 200 million dollars for TAZARA and another 200 million for Zambia Railways, you are close to 30 per cent of the fiscal space. Yeah, so we have to think a bit more outside the box and see how the private sector could help us with a number of these issues. Plus having the Chinese clean up the institution [TAZARA] for us to a level where moving forward it would be much easier for us to be able to manage the issue – to manage the two companies [TAZARA and ZRL]. (Interview senior official Zambian MTC)

As elaborated on in Chapter 6, the Zambian government rediscovered PPPs as a policy alternative to debt financing after a decade of extensive borrowing for infrastructure development, not least from Chinese policy banks. This strategic shift is well exemplified in a statement by then Minister of Transport and Communication, Brian Mushimba, who commented on media reports which, in August 2018, falsely suggested that the Zambian government had agreed to concession TAZARA to a Chinese investor:

> Here is a true story; we as PF government, we are desirous to make sure that Tazara and Zambia [R]ailways are revamped and do their part in transporting heavy and bulk cargo, decongest our roads, spare our roads, also create employment in the railway sector. Railway sector is an important sector. [...] As we are studying the best ways to modernise Zambia Railways and revamp TAZARA, we look at all the options that are available to us. One option is borrowing, which is debt. You know how many people have raised concerns about borrowing and debt? The same people that brought this story [referring to TAZARA's supposed concession to a Chinese company], they are the same people that are screaming about borrowing and debt! So, we don't want to borrow. [...] So, in the discussions around how we will revamp and raise resources for TAZARA, the conversation came up to say "how about a concession to the Chinese?" They know TAZARA, they know how it was constructed, they know its gaps, they have money. They want to use TAZARA to move some of their cargo, so can't we create a win-win situation with the Chinese? [...] Can we concession it and put conditions to say "every year you are going to invest X amount of dollars into it and by the year X when we take it back, we would have invested all the money that we need invested without Zambia and Tanzania putting in anything." (quoted in Mbewe 2018)

The statement is instructive in both discursive and material terms. Discursively, Mushimba invokes the "win–win" narrative which features frequently in official narratives on Sino-African cooperation in general and infrastructure development in particular. His official emphasis that Chinese participation in TAZARA would be in the mutual interest of China and Zambia must be understood as the deliberate attempt to contain anti-Chinese sentiments and public resentment vis-à-vis China's increasing influence in Zambia's economy generally (see Brooks 2010; Leslie 2016; Negi 2008; Sautman and Hairong 2015) and regular speculations about alleged takeovers of Zambian state assets and enterprises as collateral for delinquent debt in particular (see Lusaka Times 2018).[1]

In material terms, Minister Mushimba's explicit reference to Zambia's lack of borrowing capacity to rehabilitate both its national railway

[1] Sum (2019) provides an instructive discussion of hope- and fear-based discourses related to Chinese (infrastructure) investment in Belt and Road countries.

company and TAZARA underscores the shift in terms of the financial governance of infrastructure development/rehabilitation that I discuss in greater detail in Chapter 6. Zambia's indebtedness effectively limits "all the options that are available to us", which the Minister refers to, to one: privatisation by means of PPPs. Concessions are conceived as a "budget-friendly" policy substitute for debt-financed infrastructure development. Thereby, Mushimba invokes common arguments about PPPs, viz. that they do not burden public budgets, while, at the same time, they allow for much needed investment into ailing infrastructures. As discussed, the concession of Zambia's national railway held neither of these promises. The Minister's insistence in a concession that prescribes fixed yearly investment sums can therefore be interpreted as the result of strategic reflection and learning from the RSZ concession. However, the extent to which a concession to a Chinese consortium would incur societal costs is highly dependent on its exact terms and conditions. The Chinese proposal of 2016 indicated some of these costs: sovereign debt guarantees, tax exemptions and job losses. Mushimba also explicitly refers to the capital disequilibrium between China and the shareholding governments and, thus, the structural dependency on foreign investments. As a quick conceptual reminder, spatio-temporal fixes thrive particularly well under conditions of uneven spatial development (Harvey 2004: 67). Given the limited fiscal room of manoeuvre to reinvest in TAZARA, a Chinese takeover of TAZARA's operations is seen by the Zambian government as indispensable.

Railway Privatisation as a Potential Source of Rents?

Zambia's financial constraints were not the only drivers behind Lusaka's keen interest to privatise TAZARA that were cited by well-informed interviewees. Generally, corruption was raised to have played a role in Zambia's previous railway privatisation. Reflecting upon the failed RSZ privatisation, one interviewee suggested that the concession might have been entered hastily due to vested interests among decision-makers: "We had very good advisors and we had the World Bank backing it. But I think due to personal interest and corruption people eventually just decided to do it – don't listen to the advisors" (Interview senior official Zambian MTC). While Zambian political elites frequently reiterate the mutual public benefits that arise from Sino-Zambian cooperation, another interviewee questioned "how genuine" the Zambian "push" for a concession to a Chinese investor actually is. The interviewee suggested that vested interests could be at its core:

> What is happening in Zambia right now is that there is a lot of corruption. Too much corruption, compared to what is happening in Tanzania [where] corruption has gone. It used to be the other way around. There used to be a lot of corruption in Tanzania but since the coming of the new president [Magufuli] corruption has been going down. He is trying. But on the Zambian side, it's different. There is a lot of corruption. So much as we appreciate that they want private sector [participation], especially the Zambian side. We believe that they could have been compromised. (Interview key informant 1)

The interviewee also stated that then Zambian Transport Minister Mushimba "has been jumping the gun on the concession", suggesting that it could "be that the Chinese have got to him. Corruption is part of [the] business for most Chinese" (Personal electronic communication with key informant 1, May 2019). While there is no legal evidence for political corruption in the context of the tripartite negotiations, the interviewee is not alone in his general assessment that corruption is on the rise in Zambia. As Fig. 5.2 shows, Zambia has fallen in Transparency International's Corruption Perception Index for the fifth consecutive year, while Tanzania, in contrast, has consecutively climbed over the same period.

Simultaneously, Chinese companies have developed a keen interest in Zambia's railway sector. In November 2016, a $2.3bn Engineering-Procurement-Construction+Finance (EPC+F) contract was signed between the Zambian government and CCECC for a green field project. It is planned to interlink the TAZARA line in Serenje with the Chipata-Mchinji railway, thereby closing the current "rail gap" along the Nacala corridor and thus creating the shortest rail link between Kapiri Mposhi and the Indian Ocean (Lusaka Times 2016; National Assembly of Zambia 2017: 6; interview senior official Zambian MTC). Yet, the project has since fallen victim to Chinese restrictions on further overseas loan finance, especially in financially distressed countries like Zambia (Zajontz et al. 2024: 20 n.1). Another greenfield project was tendered as a Design-Finance-Build-Operate-Transfer PPP. The 192 km Nseluka-Mpulungu railway in Northern Province is planned to connect the TAZARA station in Nseluka with Mpulungu port and, thus, with markets in the Democratic Republic of Congo (DRC), Burundi, Rwanda and Tanzania

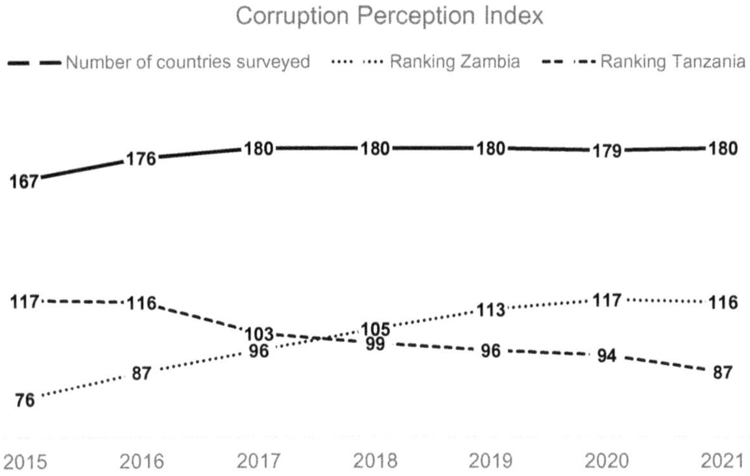

Fig. 5.2 Perceived levels of public sector corruption in Zambia and Tanzania (*Source* Author's compilation, based on data from Transparency International [n.d.])

(MTC n.d.). According to an informant, two Chinese companies were shortlisted for the project (Personal electronic communication with key informant 1, May 2019).

A senior official from the Ministry of Transport recalled a situation during the preparation of the tender process for said project. Against the predominant view at the working level within the ministry, the Permanent Secretary at the time gave the instruction to tender the project as a PPP, with the remark that he had "got instructions". The interviewee considered it disadvantageous for the rail sector to tender the project as a concession-based PPP, because the successful contractor would have to recover its investment by means of user charges, thus driving up the costs for rail transportation. "If you go and do it under PPP, basically you are tolling the rail line. Now the rail line is already disadvantaged as it is. Would you want to go and toll it?" (Interview senior official Zambian MTC). Of course, these statements are mere anecdotal "evidence"' that formal and informal processes have intertwined in negotiations of railway projects. Yet, they suggest that the neopatrimonial strategic selectivity of the Zambian state conditions the latter's agency and strategic engagement with Chinese investors in the infrastructure sector, something that is analysed more closely in Chapter 7.

While it was impossible to establish whether Zambia's keen interest to conclude a PPP for the rehabilitation of TAZARA has been motivated solely by public considerations, notably the country's inability to subsidise—let alone recapitalise—the parastatal, the neopatrimonial "institutional ensemble" of the Zambian state does provide potential gateways for the advancement of private, as opposed to public, interests in the context of TAZARA's privatisation. These gateways were widened throughout the 2010s through informal and personalised engagements between Zambian and Chinese elites in negotiating infrastructure projects, as discussed in Chapter 7. In contrast hereto, Tanzania's negotiation strategy was marked by utmost caution and scrutiny on the part of state managers involved in the negotiations and by official emphases on long-term developmental benefits, both a result of the economic nationalism pursued by the late President Magufuli and the autocratic developmental state form it generated.

From Neopatrimonialism to Autocratic Developmentalism: State Transformation under Magufuli

> Most importantly, we must seize control of our economy and destiny. This will require courageous leadership, self-confidence, ingenuity, hard work and economic patriotism. (Magufuli 2017: viii)

The fact that a Chinese equity investment in TAZARA did not materialise in the form proposed by the Chinese investors cannot be explained without looking into state transformation processes under the late President Magufuli that have accompanied the transition from Tanzania's "fourth" to its "fifth phase government", notably the centralisation of power in the presidency and a rigid approach against clientelistic and corrupt networks in Tanzanian politics.[2] To transcend reductionist and

[2] Tanzanians commonly distinguish their post-independence administrations by phases, with Nyerere's presidency constituting the first, Mwinyi's the second, Mkapa's the third, Kikwete's the fourth, Magufuli's the fifth and Hassan's the sixth.

voluntarist readings of state agency, the coming into office of President Magufuli and resultant institutional and strategic shifts must be understood as a result of a changing balance of political forces within Tanzania. This changing balance of forces has informed Magufuli's nationalist developmentalism. While the late president's "infrastructure nationalism" was arguably driven by Magufuli's "political vulnerability" (Barton 2023: 338), it nevertheless entailed state strategies oriented towards the transformation of particular structural constraints of the Tanzanian state which have crucially informed the government's positions in the negotiations about a Chinese participation in TAZARA and fostered state interventions aimed at reversing TAZARA's devaluation.

President Magufuli famously earned himself the nickname "Bulldozer" due to his uncompromising anti-corruption campaign, radical government interventions vis-à-vis foreign investors and domestic capital alike and an increasingly repressive handling of the political opposition, the media and civil society (Andreoni 2017: 32, 37; Nwapi and Andrews 2017; Polus and Tycholiz 2019). Magufuli's populist-nationalist policies and narrative were the result of longer-term shifts in the balance of political forces—both within the ruling party *Chama cha Mapinduzi* (CCM) and Tanzania's political system. Magufuli's very ascent into the highest office resulted from protracted party factionalism and the CCM's inability to discipline political corruption and clientelistic networks within its party structure (Andreoni 2017: 30; Barton 2023: 339). Corruption scandals were a "recurring feature of Tanzania's political landscape at the start of the twenty-first century, against a backdrop of rapid economic growth and global integration" (Gray 2015: 382). In 2008, Prime Minister Lowassa, alongside two cabinet ministers, were forced to resign over their involvement in a tender for the construction of a power plant. A parliamentary investigation, ordered by then President Kikwete, found evidence for corruption and the violation of procurement laws (Andreoni 2017: 49; Tsubura 2018: 70).

As a result of a series of high-profile corruption cases, the CCM, which had provided the president since the first multiparty election in 1995, saw its dominant political position in Tanzanian politics increasingly under challenge (Andreoni 2017: 29, 48–49; Tsubura 2018: 70). In 2010, Kikwete was reelected with only 63 per cent of the vote, down from 80 per cent in 2005. Simultaneously, voter turnout had dropped from 72.4 to 42.8 per cent and CCM's parliamentary majority decreased significantly between 2005 and 2010 (Tsubura 2018: 71; see also Andreoni

2017: 29). It is argued that "[p]ublic disappointment at CCM's response to grand corruption scandals and party infighting was among the key factors" for the ruling party's waning popular support (Tsubura 2018: 71). The biggest opposition party *Chama cha Demokrasia na Maendeleo* (CHADEMA) could increasingly capitalise on the "conflicts between the so called CCM-Safi (clean) and the CCM-Mafisadi (corrupted) factions" and growing anti-corruption sentiments among the electorate (Andreoni 2017: 29; see also Tsubura 2018: 70).

Kikwete's "clean" faction reacted by stepping up efforts to ban corrupt party members and politicians and to "break some of the clientelistic networks underpinning the pro-Lowassa faction" (Andreoni 2017: 29). In 2011, Kikwete's camp proclaimed the initiative "kujivua gamba", which translates into "shedding the old skin", with the aim to curb corrupt practices among the CCM elite (Tsubura 2018: 71 also interview Shangwe). Factional politics within CCM further intensified during the intraparty race for Kikwete's succession, with the allegedly corrupt Lowassa, despite being banned by the party's newly established ethics committee, retaining significant support for a presidential bid among CCM members and local and regional party functionaries (Andreoni 2017: 28; Tsubura 2018: 72). In July 2014, CCM's Central Committee presented five candidates to the party's national executive committee.[3] Lowassa was not among them. On 12 July, John Magufuli was elected presidential candidate by the party's national congress with 87 per cent of the votes (Tsubura 2018: 72–73). According to Tsubura (2018: 73), he was regarded as "diligent and competent but also expected to unite CCM members because he was known to have distanced himself from factional competition within the party".

Accompanied by a number of CCM politicians, Lowassa subsequently defected the party, joined CHADEMA and became presidential candidate of an alliance of four opposition parties which was formed in October 2014 (Andreoni 2017: 31; Tsubura 2018: 63).[4] The unprecedented strategic alliance among main opposition parties significantly threatened

[3] These were Bernard Membe, John Magufuli, Asha Migiro, January Makamba and Amina Salum Ali (Tsubura 2018: 72).

[4] The alliance *Umoja wa Katiba ya Wananchi* (UKAWA) includes, besides CHADEMA, the Civic United Front (CUF), the National Convention for Construction and Reform-*Mageuzi* (NCCR-Mageuzi) and the National League for Democracy (NLD) (Tsubura 2018: 71).

CCM's prospects for the 2015 general elections (Tsubura 2018: 71). In an attempt to accommodate the popular political agenda, Magufuli's election campaign centred around five key topics: the fight against corruption, the country's industrialisation, tax compliance, government efficiency and free access to education (Andreoni 2017: 31). He won the presidential elections with 58.8 per cent, a new all-time low for a CCM presidential candidate, with Lowassa polling second at 40 per cent (Andreoni 2017: 31; Tsubura 2018: 74). A Tanzanian scholar argued that Magufuli's fierce anti-corruption campaign and his belligerent approach towards foreign investment signified an "appropriation" of the opposition's agenda, in order to secure electoral support (Interview Shangwe; for a similar argument, see Andreoni 2017: 32). Magufuli "had pressure to prove himself – like he is different from his predecessor. And he is taking the country into a different direction" (Interview Shangwe).

Magufuli's developmentalist ambitions most clearly manifested in an intensification of resource nationalism which the country had embarked on under his predecessor Kikwete as a reaction to "widespread sentiment [amongst the populace] that Tanzania is not getting enough out of its natural resources" (Jacob and Pedersen 2018: 289, also interviews Shangwe; Wetengere; see Barton 2023; Kinyondo and Huggins 2019; Lange and Kinyondo 2016; Roder 2019). Reforms, such as the 2010 Mining Act and the new Petroleum Act of 2015, were intended to roll back a hyper-liberalised regulatory environment as well as to increase state revenues and promote local ownership and content in the extractive industries (Lange and Kinyondo 2016: 1098–99, 1102). However, these reforms were compromised by a lack of implementation and enforcement capacities and subverted by political corruption and tax evasion (Kinyondo and Huggins 2019: 184). As a result, the 2015 electoral campaign was marked by fierce political debates about the developmental effects of foreign investment, not least with regard to land acquisitions and natural resources, and by demands for an indigenisation of Tanzania's economy (Schlimmer 2018: 92–93). A Tanzanian academic described the "political climate" at the time as characterised by "a feeling that this country is losing a lot when it comes to foreign direct investment. [...] So, there was this kind of a demand for someone to stand up to these so-called investors" (Interview Shangwe). The scholar further suggested that Magufuli has actively tried to accommodate growing negative public sentiment vis-à-vis Chinese investments, which had become manifest in a popular narrative that "this country is going to be colonised again" and had been successfully taken up by the political opposition (Interview Shangwe; see Kinyondo 2019: 136). Such assumptions are backed by empirical research that has documented that Chinese investments have been associated by Tanzanians with nefarious practices such as bribery, price dumping and market distortion (Barton 2023: 348; see Kelly et al. 2016; Sigalla 2014).

Having campaigned on a populist platform that promised higher public revenues from foreign investment and a resolute fight against tax avoidance, Magufuli, once in office, pursued a "[c]onfrontational and authoritarian approach towards the private sector" (Andreoni 2017: 31, 37). In 2017, the presidency temporarily banned the export of gold and copper concentrate and set up two commissions to investigate minerals exports and alleged tax evasion by the country's biggest mining multinational Acacia, a subsidiary of Barrick Gold. The dispute resulted in the dismissal of senior officials in the relevant authorities and the dissolvement and protracted renegotiations of mining contracts (Jacob and Pedersen 2018: 287–89; Kinyondo and Huggins 2019: 184; Polus and Tycholiz 2019: 67; Roder 2019: 409). Following Magufuli's "bulldozer approach", Andreoni discerned a nascent "'builder' phase" (2017: 38, 37). Accordingly, the government has proven "willing to allocate rents to private investors", if and where investments are considered in line with the government's strategic goals of industrialisation, job creation and higher tax yields (Andreoni 2017: 40). Hence, the government engages in "[d]isciplining rents, with a direct [state] involvement in deal-making and infrastructures" (Andreoni 2017: 38). The extrajudicial settlement of the tax dispute with Barrick in late-2019 is a case in point that confirms Andreoni's conjecture. Whereas in terms of payment of tax arrears the deal stayed behind the government's initial demands, it granted the state means of control in Barrick's Tanzania operations and higher revenue prospects, as the settlement reportedly envisaged the establishment of a joint venture on the basis of parity (Reuters 2019a).

Magufuli's economic nationalism was characterised by rigid state interventionism, protectionist measures and efforts to increase state revenues, not least from foreign investments. At least according to official government narratives, the government's economic policies served the goals of industrialisation and the indigenisation of the economy. As one senior government official put it:

> We want the business. But apparently win-win – full stop. Not win-lose. Hapana [Swahili for 'no']. So, it's win-win. We are fighting for win-win and that's what the government is saying – always. Come, we need you [referring to foreign investors], but it should be a win-win. (Interview former Tanzanian top official)

Several authors suggested that Magufuli pursued a developmentalist state model (see Andreoni 2017; Kinyondo and Huggins 2019; Lange and Kinyondo 2016; Polus and Tycholiz 2019; Roder 2019). In fact, a strategic realignment towards developmentalist policies had already commenced under President Kikwete against the background of waning popular support for the ruling party (Barton 2023; Jacob and Pedersen 2018; Nwapi and Andrews 2017). However, the Magufuli administration significantly stepped up "state-led macroeconomic planning and management" (Polus and Tycholiz 2019: 67) and fostered state involvement in key industries "by increasing its stakes in operations through SOEs in the wider economy" (Jacob and Pedersen 2018: 290). Yet, Barton (2023: 341) remarks that Magufuli's economic policies were short of a consistent developmentalist strategy but rather opportunistically combined state interventionism and protectionism with investor-friendly signalling where this was politically opportune, amounting to what the author calls "pseudo-developmentalism". Crucially, the developmental state under Magufuli's administration took on increasingly autocratic forms, as national development was stylised as an overarching goal that should not be compromised by political debate and contestation (Chiyemura et al. 2023: 113). This resulted in frequent arrests, intimidation and harassment of supporters and politicians from opposition parties, journalists, scholars and activists (Barton 2023: 344; Paget 2021).

By centralising (economic) decision-making in the presidential office, Magufuli aimed at "rejigging"' clientelistic power structures that had previously linked state managers and CCM-aligned business interests (Andreoni 2017: 33, 36; see also Gray 2015). As Polus and Tycholiz (2019: 68) point out, in the past "decision-making processes within the Tanzanian government were highly decentralised and dependent on vested interests among various cliques within the ruling party". In order to disrupt entrenched clientelistic networks, Magufuli fired, demoted and/or prosecuted hundreds of top officials and civil servants who were allegedly involved in corruption or considered responsible for the mismanagement of state agencies, SOEs or public infrastructure

(Andreoni 2017: 33; Hönke 2018: 352; Polus and Tycholiz 2019: 67). The positions were filled with personally trusted individuals, some of whom Magufuli had been working with in previous government functions or at the University of Dar es Salaam (Andreoni 2017: 33–34; Polus and Tycholiz 2018).

Magufuli aligned his cabinet and newly installed top bureaucrats to his "economic patriotism", with the continual dismissal of top officials creating an atmosphere of constant threat of the president's zero-tolerance approach towards negligence and malfeasance (Andreoni 2017: 36; Polus and Tycholiz 2019: 67). This had major impact on the planning, negotiation and implementation of infrastructure projects, including those with Chinese participation. As Makundi et al. aptly summarise:

> Positive prospects reside in the strong faith of the current efforts under Magufuli to bring about transformations in the governance process, as part of his war on corruption, elitism and preferential tendering. However, these tendencies may over time also confront the notion of "win-win" which is argued to have predominantly benefited associated Chinese contractors and suppliers in the past. On the other hand, it can be argued that Magufuli's style is diverting the country away from the risk of long-term dependency on China. (2017: 346)

The rise of a decidedly nationalist infrastructure state under Magufuli and resultant state agency crucially affected how the Chinese infrastructural fix could play out in Tanzania.

The Rise of Tanzania's Nationalist Infrastructure State

Magufuli's economic nationalism was characterised by efforts to reduce the country's "dependence on FDI-driven growth towards one in which the state make[s] effort to regain the position it lost prior to liberalisation" and hence becomes the central actor in steering economic development (Jacob and Pedersen 2018: 289). Public procurement was therefore considered a key strategic tool to direct economic resources, including foreign capital, in ways that would foster the goal of industrialisation. Tanzania's Five Year Development Plan 2016/2017–2020/2021 spelled out the interventionist role of the state when it suggests that "successful industrialisation requires [a] smart developmental state role to spearhead strategic industrialization using various mechanisms including state procurement" (GURT 2016: 32).

The concentration of decision-making power in the presidential office was accompanied by a tightening of control and oversight of the treasury, line ministries and state agencies and a rigid scrutiny of public spending, borrowing and procurements. As Makundi et al. (2017: 345) note, the Magufuli administration "has demonstrated a firm position against corruption in public procurement". A senior official explained that the coming into office of Magufuli had a lasting impact on governmental practices in the context of negotiations of contracts, procurements and loans with external actors:

> When we were given offices, our Excellency [President Magufuli] told us: "I know you are educated enough and you won't be fooled by your fellow educators". So, that being the message, you have to read those documents [referring to contracts for infrastructure projects] properly [...] Although they are large, you know where the bodies are buried. [...] Now we think that we have to look more into the details in every particular project, irrespective of the origin – whether it is World Bank, it is AfDB, it is Chinese. (Interview top official)

Throughout the 2010s, the Tanzanian administration aimed at decreasing its dependence on foreign aid and loan finance. Under both Kikwete and Magufuli, Tanzanian borrowing has become increasingly conservative. As a result, the country's debt levels have stabilised, as Fig. 5.1 shows, and remained well below the IMF debt-to-GDP ceiling of 56 per cent (Makundi et al. 2017: 345). Under Magufuli, the government has aimed at "mobilising capital internally", not least by means of increasing tax revenues, from multinational corporations, local businesses, incomes and consumers equally (Interview Wetengere; see GURT 2016: 96–97; Roder 2019: 409–10). In this instance, the "fifth phase government" appeared to re-invoke the principle of self-reliance and the goal of independence from donors that were central to the 1967 Arusha Declaration (Kinyondo and Huggins 2019: 185; see Kahama 2018: 67; Lange and Kinyondo 2016: 1103; Nwapi and Andrews 2017: 247). Table 5.1 shows the steady increase of domestic revenues in the state budget.

It is evident that Tanzania's sovereign borrowing markedly differed from Zambia's throughout the 2010s. A statement by former President Kikwete at the National Economic Summit in Livingstone in July 2019,

Table 5.1 Projected domestic revenue in Tanzania's public budget

Fiscal year	*2014/2015*	*2015/2016*	*2016/2017*	*2017/2018*	*2018/2019*	*2019/2020*
Revenue[a] (in TSh bn)	12,178	13,476	17,798	19,289	20,159	22,280

Source PwC (2016: 20, 2017: 20, 2018: 16, 2019: 16)
[a] *Numbers include tax and non-tax revenues*

an event organised by the Economics Association of Zambia, underlined the divergent approaches towards sovereign borrowing in Tanzania and Zambia:

> In Tanzania, we have an audit management committee to look at every loan that we get and if it meets the required criteria, it has to have a concessional percentage and that concession should not be small. You need to look at the total loan criteria and total debt portfolio and GDP. Any country that gets a loan without the ability to pay back is crazy. You must have the capability to pay back the loan. (quoted in Mbulo 2019)

Not surprisingly the guest of honour from Tanzania got cut short by the master of ceremony (Mbulo 2019), since Kikwete overtly questioned the sustainability of Zambia's extensive external borrowing. A statement by one interviewee underlines Tanzania's pragmatic strategy regarding foreign investment and loan financing:

> The fifth [phase of government] what it says is: Where we can do and have money to do, let's do. Because you go into PPPs – at the end of the day, your partner also wants a profit out of it. And sometimes don't go for a loan, because if you go for a loan, you pay interest. So, if you have funds, why not do? But for areas where we have no funds, I am sure we opt for PPPs. (Interview former Tanzanian top official)

Another interviewee suggested that stricter and more centralised political control over state expenditures and sovereign borrowing had resulted in stringent inter-ministerial coordination in the context of cost–benefit analyses and financial agreements for infrastructure projects:

> Luckily enough, we are independent enough from the Ministry of Finance. We have to justify our cases to an acceptable level for it to be considered. Both ways – technologically and financially. [...] We come and sit together and then do the analysis and look at it, without bowing to external pressure. We want to make the decisions properly before we advise the politicians. Because it's the politicians who make the decisions. But the analysis should be proper. The pros and cons are laid down on the table and up to now they haven't let us down. And if we put the analysis properly, take it to them, their decisions are okay. [...] What we want to do is make sure that the analysis we make is for the benefit of the country, that it takes into account the country's interests and that's it. (Interview Tanzanian top official)

Barton convincingly reasons that, in the infrastructure sector, the conflation of state developmentalism, heightened nationalism and authoritarianism under Magufuli conflated into "infrastructure nationalism" (Barton 2023: 339). The emergence of a decidedly nationalist infrastructure state under Magufuli proved detrimental to Chinese investments in Tanzania's infrastructure sector and hence to the Chinese infrastructural fix at large. Masabo (2021: 151) argues in his study on the BRI in Tanzania that the Magufuli government gave BRI projects much lower priority than his predecessor. The state strategies regarding TAZARA had equally changed under Magufuli.

Scrutinising "Win–Win" Cooperation in the Freedom Railway

> They [the Chinese] have a long history when it comes to TAZARA. And I would say they are not ready to give it up. Because it's part of their history when it comes to Tanzania-Chinese relation – or Chinese-Africa relation. Because those were the very first arrangements with Chinese [...] in Africa. That's the first project that they have done. So, they don't want to lose it. They want to be part of TAZARA. But Chinese of that time are not Chinese of today. That's the problem. They are very much different and Chinese of today they are business-minded. And business is not bad, but we are also saying that we should be able to benefit from whatever kind of arrangement that we are going to agree. We also want to benefit. Benefits should not always be on their side. We should share. That's what we are saying. Maybe we might be seen as not cooperating, but we also want to benefit from whatever arrangement that they are proposing. (Interview senior official Tanzanian MWTC)

The quote above underscores a high degree of reflection and awareness on the part of Tanzanian state managers that the Chinese consortium—just as other investors—was pursuing commercial interests within the structural logics of a capitalist global economy. The statement also highlights the perceived distinctiveness between China's historical involvement in TAZARA and the contemporary approach of Chinese state capital to get involved in rehabilitating and operating TAZARA, a sentiment that was also expressed by other interviewees. The Secretary General of the Tanzania China Friendship Promotion Association (TCFPA), Joseph Kahama, who is an influential figure in Sino-Tanzanian relations declared that the "Chinese are new Chinese. They are more on just dealing with [the] market. And they move fast. So, Tanzanians need to catch up with that" (Interview Kahama).

Just as their Zambian counterparts, Tanzanian state managers are aware that a sufficient recapitalisation of TAZARA requires external funding, as a statement by the Director for Asia and Australasia Department in Tanzania's Ministry of Foreign Affairs and East African Cooperation of Tanzania, Justa Nyanga, underlines: "Tanzania and Zambia wanted to revamp the railway using 'own fund resources' but these were limited by the ongoing financial crunch" (quoted in Malanga 2017). In November 2019, senior officials confirmed that a concession agreement with a Chinese investor is still considered a possible option for TAZARA's rehabilitation (Interviews Tanzanian top official; senior official Tanzanian MWTC). However, Magufuli's administration remained adamant in its rejection of the Chinese proposal and simultaneously pursued alternative strategies to improve the condition of TAZARA. Recurrently, Tanzanian interviewees who were involved in the 2016 negotiations stressed that the proposed terms and conditions did not provide for a "win–win situation" (Interview Tanzanian top official) and failed to serve the "national interest" (Interview senior official Tanzanain MWTC). A Tanzanian official argued that "some of the recommendations from the study [referring to the TSDI feasibility study], to our view, were not in the public interest". The interviewee emphasised that the Tanzanian government did not generally rule out a concession as an option to rehabilitate TAZARA but that the "issue was on the terms": "If we would gain optimally from the arrangement but the problem is that we could not – when we assessed – the gain was not that much. So we thought: 'why shouldn't we look for other options?' Yeah. Better options than those which were given by the Chinese" (Interview senior official Tanzanian MWTC).

As discussed in Chapter 4, the strategic calculation of the Tanzanian government in the tripartite negotiations about a Chinese participation in TAZARA was strongly informed by the experience of the terminated TRL concession. The government's learning and reflection capacity in the context of infrastructure development generally and Chinese-funded projects in particular was arguably strengthened with the coming into power of President Magufuli. Not only did Magufuli oversee the TRL privatisation, several interviewees also pointed out that the President had vast experience in dealing with Chinese firms, as he held the ministerial portfolio of Works, Transport and Communication under presidents Mkapa from 2000 until 2005 and Kikwete between 2010 and 2015 (Interviews Kahama; Kamata; Lusinde). In the past two decades, the Tanzanian government invested heavily in the country's road infrastructure, with the lion's share of projects being implemented by Chinese companies (Interview senior official Tanzanian MWTC; see Flores 2017; Kahama 2018: 109–10). As one academic reasoned, "you have a president [Magufuli] who has been in the infrastructure sector throughout his political career over twenty years and he has dealt with Chinese companies. Maybe he knows how they deal with government" (Interview Kamata). Similarly, the Secretary General of TCFPA argued Magufuli's professional experience could mean that "he learnt a lot about China and the way they do things which probably has led him to be a little careful" (Interview Kahama). And political veteran Job Lusinde remarked that Magufuli "came into working relationship with the Chinese much, much earlier before he became the president. Therefore, by that time he must have made up his mind to say: 'Right, we'll do it this way and that way" (Interview Lusinde). Magufuli certainly made the tripartite negotiations a top-level issue, one which, in line with the general centralisation of political power during his presidency, he subjected to his direct control. It is not by chance that Magufuli charged his Chief Secretary Kijazi, a long-standing confidant who previously served under him as Permanent Secretary in the Ministry of Works, Transport and Communications, with leading the Tanzanian negotiation team in 2016.

During and after the negotiations, the strategic reflection and strategies of state officials were strongly informed by the economic nationalism postulated by the president and further consolidated Tanzania's nationalist infrastructure state. Magufuli's autocratic developmentalism translated into a negotiation strategy which was marked by utmost caution and scrutiny on the part of state managers involved in the negotiations and official emphases on long-term developmental benefits, as the following statement underlines:

> The change is obvious that this time around [referring to the Magufuli administration] the government is moving slowly but cautiously. Cautiously. We need to make sure that whatever decision we make, we should not come to regret. We should do it perfectly and for the benefit – for the interest of the nation. Yeah. I think you understand when I say 'for the interest of the nation'. It should not be for this current generation, it should be for the future generation. Because when it comes to those arrangements you might give the railway – say TAZARA – concession it for 30 years. 30 years – it's a long time. It's a long time. So, before you come into such decision, you should satisfy yourself. You should be pretty sure that the investment – or the arrangement – that you are going to enter into is of national interest, is of benefit to our side. It will move us from one point of development to the other. So those are the issues that we want to be sure of. (Interview senior official Tanzanian MWTC)

While the Tanzanian administration did not generally renunciate a concession-based PPP, as mentioned above, the government's engagement with Chinese investors over contractual terms, means of financing and the distribution of costs and benefits had changed under Magufuli. A Tanzanian top official put it as follows:

> The policy now [referring to the fifth phase of government under President Magufuli] is that we cannot be negotiating any contract, any deal as if we are desperate. No. It should be a win-win situation, yes. We are not that desperate. We are not in such a hurry to concede too much. That is the position of the government. That it should be a win-win situation and that's it. If it doesn't, we can wait. (Interview Tanzanian top official)

Enhanced scrutiny was also applied to the recurrent cooperation protocols which govern Chinese aid projects for TAZARA. In November 2019, the Magufuli administration still had not signed the 16th TAZARA protocol, although its intended project period was 2016–2017 and the Zambian government had signed it in 2017 (Interviews key informant 2; official Tanzanian MWTC; senior official Tanzanian MWTC). "That's how serious things are", commented a key informant (Personal electronic communication with key informant 1, May 2019). Just as previous cooperation protocols, the protocol was to be financed through an interest-free loan, this time for the purchase of spares for locomotives and wagons. A key informant argued that "[t]he Chinese set up the 16th protocol as a prelude to concession" (Personal electronic communication with key informant 1, May 2019). This was confirmed by a Chinese interviewee who argued that the three governments had in principle agreed that a major rehabilitation of TAZARA under Chinese participation, which later became subject of the 2016 tripartite negotiations, should "be implemented as soon as possible. That's why they said the 16th protocol will serve as a kind of a transition period. So, they said 'no, we are not going to invest too much on the 16th protocol, because all the problems will be solved under that rehabilitation project" (Interview key informant 2). Consequently, the scope of the 16th protocol was smaller compared to the 14th and 15th protocols and mainly included the acquisition of spare parts for rolling stock, equipment and the Mbeya concrete sleeper plant as well as for overhead costs for the CRET. Equally, the volume of the loan for the protocol was significantly lower compared to the 14th and 15th protocols, which both amounted to ¥270m (Interview key informant 2).

While delays in the ratification of protocols have been common in the past, "it has never been delayed so long" (Interview key informant 2). A Chinese interviewee explained in November 2019 that the Tanzanian Ministry of Works, Transport and Communications approved of the terms and conditions of the protocol. Yet, the interviewee stated that

> up to now the Tanzanian government, they are still going through the protocol. They said because there are some articles about tax exemption in the protocol. So, you know, before in Tanzania the Ministry of Finance they were authorised to decide whether the tax exemption can be allowed or not. Now, this kind of right is taken back to the cabinet. So that means if the protocol, if any agreement involv[es] tax exemption, the cabinet should go through and approve, then the Ministry can sign. It's the official reason up to now. (Interview key informant 2)

The statement points to institutional consequences of the centralisation of economic decision-making and the concentration of political control under President Magufuli, whereby the autonomy of the Ministry of Finance and line ministries had been restricted and major (loan) contracts ultimately required the approval from the cabinet and, hence, the presidential office.

The delay of the protocol ratification was also caused by the government's newfound scepticism about the limited local content in procurements related to TAZARA aid protocols. A key informant suggested that Magufuli "has been questioning why 80% of the money goes back to China […] [a]nd why they are given tax exemptions". The interviewee argued that

> [m]ost of the money is used by the personnel [referring to the CRET] – [u]pkeep for the project period. […] So, if say we get $20m [million] and the hardware costs $8m, the rest is spent on personnel. With lots of tax exemptions. Magufuli says the whole amount must be given to us and we decide how to use it because it is our loan. (Personal electronic communication with key informant 1, May 2019)

The statement underlines the nationalist character of Tanzania's infrastructure state under Magufuli which also came to the fore in measures to revamp the ailing railway by other means.

"Fixing" TAZARA on Tanzanian Terms

While waiting for the Chinese side to get back with a revised concession proposal, the Tanzanian government started to invest in TAZARA with its own resources. A top official reasoned that the Tanzanian government is committed to maintaining TAZARA's infrastructure and rolling stock to improve the overall state of the company for when "we make the big decisions". The interviewee emphasised that "we cannot be seen as neglecting the railway because without an injection of investments it will fade" (Interview Tanzanian top official). In 2017, the Tanzanian government allocated about $6.65m, over a period of two years, for urgent maintenance measures (Lusaka Times 2019; interviews Tanzanian top official; senior official Tanzanian MWTC). Parts of the funds were allocated to procure 42 traction motors, with which seven locomotives could be rehabilitated (Interview senior official MWTC; interview Tanzanian top official; interview TAZARA labour union executive). In July 2019, Magufuli, before travelling to Kisaki using TAZARA, personally inquired at the company's headquarters about the status of the investment (Lusaka Times 2019). While such visits not least served political communication objectives vis-à-vis the domestic political audience, they signified the high degree of control and scrutiny the presidency exercised over public spending.

In line with Magufuli's "infrastructure nationalism" (Barton 2023), the government mobilised additional resources for TAZARA. An executive of one of TAZARA's labour unions explained that:

> In the past few years, yes. There was that unwillingness to fund TAZARA. It wasn't an easy nut to crack. But in the late – I think starting 2015 there about – we saw that the political will started to change towards TAZARA. And what more now that the coming in of the new Head of State [Magufuli] has changed the way he thinks and the way the people in Tanzania are believed to think towards TAZARA. (Interview TAZARA labour union executive)

Besides efforts to address TAZARA's chronic shortness of rolling stock, the Tanzanian government, through the board of directors, urged the company to enter access agreements with private operators to create alternative revenue streams (Interview official Tanzanian MWTC). In February 2018, TAZARA started a pilot project with the South African railway logistics company Calabash Freight. In April 2019, the pilot project led to a permanent cooperation contract between the two companies. Interviewees revealed that the private operator Calabash transported similar—some weeks even higher—cargo volumes than TAZARA itself (Interviews official MWTC; key informant 2; Tanzanian top official). For private operators, fees incur per tonne and kilometre for accessing TAZARA rails as well as for the usage of fuel provided by TAZARA and the company's workshops (Interview key informant 2). TAZARA also leases locomotives (two, as at November 2019) from Calabash to increase its pulling power (Interviews official Tanzanian MWTC).

The Magufuli administration also expedited the protracted revision of the TAZARA Act of 1995. One element of the reform concerns the repeal of Paragraph 14 of the current act which prescribes that the company's managing director must be a Zambian national, while the deputy must be Tanzanian. Several interviewees argued that this rule, in the past, had weakened the company's performance, as it abetted the engagement of political appointees without the necessary qualification to manage the company (Interviews senior official Tanzanian MWTC; Lusinde; TAZARA labour union executive; key informant 1). Moreover, the reform intends to decentralise TAZARA's operation by strengthening the autonomous role of the cost and profit centres—the Zambian one in Mpika and the Tanzanian one in Dar es Salaam—and to restrict the duties of the company's headquarters to non-operative policy issues, to avoid inefficiencies that result from the duplication of structures (Interview official Tanzanian MWTC). The reform plans furthermore mandate Tanzania's and Zambia's national railway regulators, which are not recognised under the current act, with the regulatory authority for TAZARA (Interview official Tanzanian MWTC). Most importantly however, the revision of the act is intended to clarify and extend legal provisions on possible modes of private participation in TAZARA, in order to provide an appropriate legal framework for open access agreements, operation contracts, concessions, private or government investments into infrastructure rehabilitation or track expansions (Interviews Tanzanian top official; senior official Tanzanian MWTC; official Tanzanian MWTC).

Whereas the reform is necessary for a possible concession to a Chinese investor, Tanzanian interviewees stressed that private involvement and/or investment in TAZARA would be considered regardless of its origin and that there was "appetite from the private sector" (Interview senior official Tanzanian MWTC; also interview Tanzanian top official). Indeed, the reform process was already initiated by presidents Kikwete and Sata in 2013. Yet, President Magufuli discovered it as an opportunity to rehabilitate TAZARA on Tanzanian terms. In mid-July 2019, he urged the relevant authorities to speed up the revision process, arguing that

> [i]t was agreed that it was essential to review and restructure the legal frameworks so that any side that wants to invest can do so without hindrance. [...] Currently, neither country can invest without the consent of the other, but must do so together. We must restructure the laws; Tazara is for both countries but legal provisions should allow any of the two countries to be able to conduct investment activities. (quoted in Lusaka Times 2019)

The statement underlines the pivotal role attributed to the state in steering investments, be they ultimately private or public, into infrastructure assets. It also exemplifies the general objective of Magufuli's administration to broaden the state's strategic scope in fostering (infrastructure) development. This statist approach affected the political economy of Tanzania's transport sector.

Magufuli's attempts to disrupt clientelistic networks extended to the transport sector. In conceptual terms, state agency exerted by the government aimed at altering structural constraints and opportunities that have prevailed in Tanzania's political economy. By making the improvement of Tanzania's railway infrastructure and services a key priority of his administration, Magufuli openly confronted traditionally influential organised interests of Tanzania's road transporters (Interviews official Tanzanian MWTC; Wetengere; Kamata). Several interviewees suggested that vested interests of politicians have contributed to the devaluation of TAZARA over the decades. A Zambian railway union executive claimed that former Tanzanian presidents Mwinyi, Mkapa and Kikwete had heavily invested in the road transport and haulage sectors. "The major transporters in Tanzania are these three former leaders [...]. This is a cartel". He further suggested that it is due to the lasting political influence of these politicians that TAZARA had experienced difficulties to get loaded at Dar es Salaam port, since "these are the ones commanding the ports" (Interview Mwila).

Whereas it proved impossible to establish to what extent said elder statesmen and their families hold interests in trucking businesses, several interviewees confirmed the strong political influence of road transporters in Tanzanian politics. "Who are they? Some of them are members of parliament. [...] Either they were in politics before or they were in business and they became politicians. So, if you have anything in parliament to discuss against them, they won't allow it, they will block it". As a consequence, the interviewee argued that the country's railways have, among other reasons, chronically underperformed because of the strong trucking lobby, reasoning that "if you allow railway lines to operate, these guys with lorries will not have business. So, sabotage the railway line, including TAZARA" (Interview Kamata). Another Tanzanian interviewee argued in a similar vein, suggesting that Tanzania's railways were

> killed by corrupt private and government officials who wanted their lorries, tankers to operate. Train is 40 per cent cheaper than road transport but they wanted to kill it. This was the members of parliament. They are the ones who own lorries and tankers. They are in the parliament to make a decision. How would you make a decision? Make a decision that will take off your lorries and tankers? [...] They were killing railway purposely. (Interview Wetengere)

Guy Scott, Zambia's Vice-President under Michael Sata, provided a similar account: "There are considerable Tanzanian private interests in the trucking industry, and these usually work by effectively sabotaging the operations of Tazara" (2019: 183).

Magufuli's anti-corruption agenda, as well as his (presumably self-serving) objective to cut back the influence of clientelistic networks consiting of CCM and business elites, aimed at transforming strategically selective constraints which, in the past, had biased policy-making in favour of private interests in the trucking industry. An official from the Tanzanian transport ministry opined that Magufuli remained resolute in strengthening the railway sector, in the context of both the new SGR and TAZARA, and that road transporters could no longer informally influence government offices under Magufuli. The interviewee added that the president would immediately fire a minister if s/he was found to compromise on the government's priority. They know that "the president is watching 24/7" (Interview official Tanzanian MWTC). In SRA terminology, the changing balance of political forces before and during Magufuli's presidency has deprived this particular faction of capital of informal access to state institutions and, by extension, to state powers, which they previously enjoyed through patrimonial networks. The transformation of the Tanzanian state under Magufuli also affected other projects with Chinese involvement, such as the Bagamoyo port and special economic zone (SEZ).

The Bagamoyo Controversy

The Magufuli administration subjected a flagship project of China's BRI to a thorough reevaluation of its developmental effects, namely the planned development of a SEZ and a mega-port in Bagamoyo, 60 km north of Dar es Salaam (Barton 2023; Hönke 2018: 356; Kinyondo 2019: 152; Makundi et al. 2017: 345). Under Kikwete, in 2012, a memorandum of understanding was signed with China Merchants Holdings International (CMHI), a private entity headquartered and listed in Hong Kong. The signing of a framework agreement followed during Chinese President Xi Jinping's Tanzania visit in March 2013, with an implementation agreement being concluded in January 2014. Oman's State General Reserve joined the project by means of a tripartite agreement, signed in October 2014 (Interview former Tanzanian top official). The project envisaged an investment of $10bn into a 3000 hectares site which would be linked to Tanzania's new SGR and to TAZARA (Africa-Asia Confidential 2013: 7; interviews former Tanzanian top official; Tanzanian top official). Project implementation came to a halt under Magufuli who questioned the terms and conditions put forward by the investors. Magufuli's intervention was flanked by a populist-nationalist discourse that had become typical for his presidency. In May 2019, the Director General of the state-owned Tanzania Ports Authority (TPA) stated that "[t]he conditions that they have given us are commercially unviable. We said no, let's meet halfway [...]. It would have been a loss [...] they shouldn't treat us like schoolkids and act like our teachers" (Kakoko, quoted in Reuters 2019b). Magufuli himself outspokenly criticised the project's conditions in June 2019, after he had refrained from publicly commenting on the project since coming into office

> This project has very difficult conditions. They are exploitative and awkward. We can't allow it. [...] In fact, the investors wanted to tie our hands in developing Tanga port, which is very crucial for the oil pipeline from Uganda and others in Mtwara and Kilwa. These are our oldest ports. (quoted in The Citizen 2019)

Magufuli's statement indicates that the investors demanded so-called "stabilisation" or "adverse action" clauses, i.e. contractual provisions that protect the investor from revenue losses as a result of changing legislation/regulation or, as in the concrete case, the development of competing port infrastructure that could compromise the profitability of the project (see Hildyard 2016: 37–38). A former top official who was involved in the negotiations confirmed that CMHI requested the government not to develop ports within a radius of 300 miles (Interview former Tanzanian top official).

Furthermore, CMHI sought a BOT contract for the port with a duration of 99 years, the government however proposed a duration of 33 years (Interview former Tanzanian top official; see Barton 2023: 347; Kinyondo 2019: 153–54). The Tanzanian government was also apprehensive of a loss of sovereignty rights regarding the control of exports and imports as well as over customs and taxation, because CMHI sought the management of the port, "with taxes, calculations and audits [...] set to be undertaken in China" (Kakoko, quoted in Musa 2019). A former top official confirmed that "they wanted to collect revenue themselves" (Interview former Tanzanian top official). The investors also expected state-guaranteed compensations of any losses incurred during the implementation of the project, a "demand [that] can render the country bankrupt" (Kakoko, quoted in Musa 2019; see also The Citizen 2019). A further controversy was caused by substantial tax exemptions that CMHI demanded, based on the argument that expected cargo volumes were still too low for the port to run profitably (The Citizen 2019). The TPA Director at the time stated that "it seems they wanted to invest for free, which would be akin to selling our freedom" (Kakoko, quoted in Musa 2019).

Demands for regulatory exemptions caused further controversy. An interviewee who is familiar with the agreements argued that "they wanted not to be touched by the labour laws, not to be touched by immigration laws. [...] We said: 'No, this is a country – you can't be given that freedom'" (Interview former Tanzanian top official). A Tanzanian academic suspected that the question of who would be in control of the port could have been decisive for the renunciation of the Bagamoyo project: "One of the things China is interested in—worldwide—is ports and control of major ports. So, it is not just a question of assisting to construct a port but eventually who owns it and who controls it". The interviewee conjectured that relinquishing the operation of Bagamoyo port to a foreign corporation is incompatible with the "kind of nationalism" pursued by the Magufuli administration (Interview Kamata; see Masabo 2021: 138). Ultimately, the conditions put forward by China Merchants were incompatible with the nationalist developmentalism the Magufuli administration envisaged. The Bagamoyo case is instructive as it graphically exemplifies the contradiction between the capitalist and the territorial logic of power. As discussed in Chapter 2, Shivji (2009: 57, italics added) argues that this contradiction "presents itself in the periphery as the contradiction between accumulation by dispossession and accumulation by expanded reproduction on the one hand (capitalist logic), and the contradiction between nation and imperialism (territorial logic), on the other". The dispute between the investors and the Magufuli administration was arguably one between imperial and national social formations to determine whether a port investment would follow the logic of accumulation by dispossession or expanded reproduction. Another Chinese loan-debt investment foundered on the agency exerted by Tanzania's nationalist infrastructure state.

The Standard Gauge Railway: From Confrontation to Pragmatism

Chinese involvement in another large-scale project, Tanzania's SGR, fell victim to anti-corruption investigations instructed by Magufuli early into his first term in office which, along with other highly publicised government interventions, served the purpose of signalling to the electorate that his administration was serious about eliminating informal and illegal conduct in government. In May 2015, then Transport Minister Samuel Sitta had announced in parliament that the Tanzanian government had awarded a $7.6bn contract for a new SGR along the country's Central Corridor to a Chinese consortium (Reuters 2015). Months after coming into office, Magufuli revoked the contract following an investigation that had established irregularities in the tender process. An interviewee revealed that two Chinese companies, CCECC and China Railway Jianchang Engineering, had been fiercely competing for the project, with the former eventually winning the contract. The interviewee with close connections to executives of said companies argued that "in that competition there was a lot of corruption that took place" (Interview anonymised). According to a senior government official, who was quoted in *The East African* on condition of anonymity, "[t]he initial contract [...] had been awarded, but the president cancelled it following irregularities. The Chinese consortium was disqualified from re-entering the race" (quoted in Olingo 2017).

A well-connected Chinese interviewee confirmed that public procurements for infrastructure projects had changed under Magufuli, arguing that "there are no existing channels" anymore for Chinese contractors to influence tender processes. The interviewee explicitly contrasted the situation with Ethiopia, Kenya and Zambia, where there are "a lot of [local] companies that broker relations to government" and "help you" with the "project tender". Conversely, in Tanzania, while they also existed, such "service providers" would no longer have influence on the outcome of public tenders. The interviewee named two individuals, both sons of former Tanzanian presidents, who had previously served as important interlocutors for Chinese corporations, helped the latter to get access to decision-makers and charged a "consultant fee" in return. Yet, these channels had become ineffective under President Magufuli, according to the interviewee. The latter added that even Chinese diplomats would face "closed doors" in their attempts to get access to the Tanzanian government (Interview Chinese journalist).

For Tanzania's SGR, a new invitation to tender was issued in 2016 and, in February 2017, a consortium of the Turkish company Yapı Merkezi and Portuguese Mota-Engil was awarded a $1.2bn Build-Transfer contract for phase 1 of the project between Dar es Salaam and Morogoro (Zajontz 2024: 37–38). Yapı Merkezi also won the contracts for the second (Morogoro-Makutupora), third (Makutupora-Tabora) and fourth (Tabora-Isaka) phases of the project (Tanzania Invest 2023). In July 2023, the construction of phase 1 and phase 2 was completed, phase 3 was close to completion and phases 4 and 5 were under construction. Figure 5.3 depicts the construction phases of the SGR. The cancellation of the initial contract with CCECC implied the opting out from a $7.6bn loan from China Exim Bank. Instead, the Magufuli administration started off financing the construction of the first segment of the railway from the state budget (Interview senior official Tanzanian MWTC). Polus and Tycholiz (2018: 160) interpret this as "part of its efforts to reduce dependency on foreign aid".[5] Importantly, according to one interviewee, re-awarding the contract brought down the project costs from $6 to $4m per rail kilometre (Interview key informant 1).

When I asked a Tanzanian top official whether there was a risk that African states ended up indebted as a result of loan-debt investment that is driven by Chinese overaccumulation, the interviewee reiterated that the Tanzanian government assessed the viability and benefits of each project thoroughly:

> Some of the financing has strings attached – most of the financing which comes as aid and grants. Even some of the loans have got strings attached. So, that being the case, if you analyse properly and make it neutral, you are not prone to be a victim of that movement of the overaccumulation there [referring to the export of Chinese overcapacities in the infrastructure and construction sectors]. Because you will be making decisions based on the parameters you have set on the ground. And that is what we are doing here now. We are not for the dangling carrots, because we think: "No, we should analyse properly what is on the ground for our particular case". (Interview Tanzanian top official)

[5] Tanzania's Parliament allocated $1.1bn for the SGR construction in the 2019/2020 budget (Onyango 2019). In February 2020, a facility agreement with Standard Chartered for a $1.46 loan for finalising phases 1 and 2 was signed (Xinhua 2020).

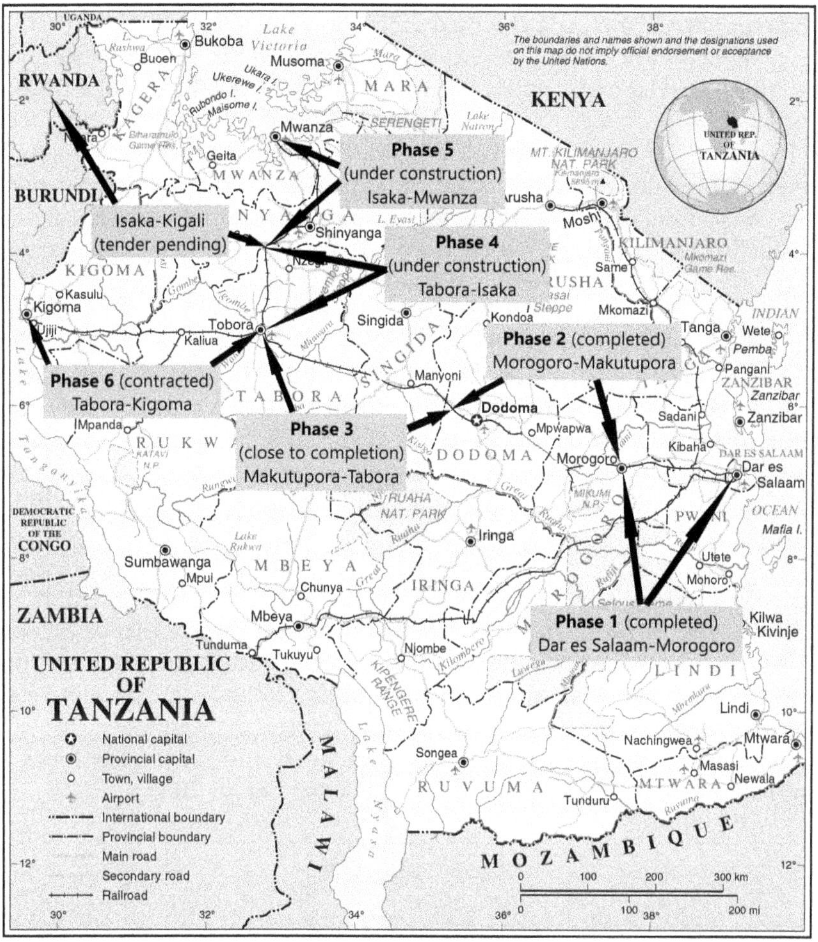

Fig. 5.3 Construction phases of Tanzania's Standard Gauge Railway (*Source* Author's own depiction based on UN map Tanzania, No. 3667, Rev. 6, January 2006 [Permission to reproduce obtained])

This statement is in line with findings that, under Magufuli, the Ministry of Finance and Planning "maintained a tight control on Chinese projects" and, to avoid debt distress, delayed or terminated projects (Makundi et al. 2017: 345). The review of the procurement process for the first phase of the SGR and the cancellation of the contract obstructed the materialisation of the Chinese infrastructural fix in the concrete case and strained relations between Tanzania and China (Interview Chinese journalist).

However, as noted above, Magufuli's engagement with foreign investors became less openly confrontational and more pragmatic over time, at least in cases in which foreign firms furthered the president's nationalist-populist developmentalism (Andreoni 2017: 37, 38; Barton 2023: 341). Developmental pragmatism was certainly applied in the context of the SGR, which should become Magufuli's legacy project. After his re-election in 2020, which saw him win 84 per cent of the vote,[6] and months before his death in March 2021, Magufuli witnessed the signing of a contract with CCECC and CRCC which had won the tender for the fifth construction phase of the SGR from Isaka to Mwanza (Cuenca 2021). The two companies were also awarded a $2.2bn contract for the SGR extension between Tabora and Kigoma in December 2022 (Mhagama 2022). The SGR demonstrates that the Tanzanian government did not entirely shun but rather pragmatically drew on foreign capital, including Chinese firms and loans, for the implementation of infrastructure projects that were deemed to have a transformative impact on the country's economy. Magufuli's nationalist infrastructure state and the changes it entailed within the institutions of the state and in relation to foreign capital demonstrate how dependent Chinese firms are on strategic action pursued by host governments and, by implication, on national politics in African states (see Chiyemura et al. 2023).

Conclusion

Despite similar path-dependencies regarding railway privatisations and evident strategic reflection on the part of both governments, the capacity of TAZARA's shareholders to act upon their strategic learning has diverged as a result of differential structural constraints prevalent in each state. Although both governments declined the terms of a concession-based PPP proposed by a Chinese consortium in 2016, the Zambian government has maintained a keen interest in a Chinese investment in TAZARA, predominantly due to the country's indebtedness

[6] For a critical discussion of the electoral process and infringements of democratic rights in the context of the 2020 elections, see Paget (2021).

which ultimately does not allow for a rehabilitation through other means. As such, sovereign debt has become a structural constraint for Zambian state agency in the infrastructure sector. Zambia's new government under the leadership of Hakainde Hichilema not only inherited the country's immense external debt, which in 2023 amounted to about $13bn, but also strategic selectivities this debt imposes. It therefore does not come as a surprise that, during Hichilema's state visit to Tanzania in August 2022, TAZARA was back on top of the agenda. Hichilema and his counterpart Samia Suluhu Hassan of Tanzania agreed to re-engage the Chinese side to solicit options for a rehabilitation of the historic railway (Liu 2024; Zajontz 2022).

During the 2016 negotiations it was Tanzanian state agency which ultimately hindered an agreement with the Chinese investor. The resolute stance of the Tanzanian government in the negotiations was a clear manifestation of the nationalist infrastructure state that had emerged under the late President Magufuli in the context of a wider transformation of the Tanzanian state from neopatrimonial to autocratic-developmental. Magufuli's populist economic nationalism was a reaction to a changing balance of social and political forces, which had compromised the dominant position of the ruling party CCM in Tanzanian politics. The centralisation of political power in and tightened control by the presidency reduced the influence of clientelistic networks that have traditionally determined the distribution of both state resources and rents. Magufuli's autocratic leadership created an atmosphere of constant threat of the president's uncompromising dealings with negligence and malfeasance within government which caused a relative strengthening of legal-bureaucratic institutions, norms and procedures, not least in the context of public procurement processes. Magufuli's economic nationalism indicated strategic awareness of existing structural constraints flowing from Tanzania's dependent integration into global markets and capital flows. In the official discourse at least, the Magufuli administration aimed at transforming existing structural constraints by strengthening the interventionist role of the state in steering and conditioning investments in key industries, such as the extractive industries and the infrastructure sector, with the aim of increasing public revenues and developmental benefits. The emergence of a decidedly nationalist infrastructure state under Magufuli significantly decelerated the Chinese infrastructural fix, as the "lost" SGR contract and the suspension of the Bagamoyo port and special economic zone exemplified.

Discussed transformations within the Tanzanian state crucially affected the government's strategy and priorities vis-à-vis TAZARA and resulted in a contestation over the prerogative of interpretation of "win–win" cooperation. Tanzania's clear rejection of the conditions proposed by the Chinese consortium in the 2016 tripartite negotiations and the long delay of the ratification of the 16th cooperation protocol sent an unambiguous signal to Beijing that Chinese infrastructure finance and investments were only welcome if they were considered to serve Tanzanian national interests. The Magufuli administration also fostered alternative initiatives to improve TAZARA's condition. Investing additional government funds was an "economic nationalist" attempt to reverse TAZARA's longstanding devaluation. While the Tanzanian government under Magufuli did not rule out the option of granting a concession to a Chinese investor, it was keen to improve the state of the company (Interview Tanzanian top official), so that it would not have to be sold at "fire-sale prices", the destiny that Harvey (2003: 150) predicts for devalued capital assets.

The nationalist form Tanzania's infrastructure state took on under Magufuli implied an abrupt readjustment for Chinese (state) capital which had over the past two decades significantly expanded its presence in Tanzania's infrastructure and construction sectors. However, Magufuli's infrastructure statism was not only nationalist but also pragmatic, as long as the involvement of foreign firms and finance was conducive to national development goals and the president's personal political agenda (see Barton 2023). As discussed in this chapter, Chinese firms and banks are now involved in laying the tracks of the SGR, the late president's legacy project, all the way to his home region of Mwanza. Chinese presence in Tanzania's infrastructure sectors is likely to further recover under Magufuli's successor. President Hassan has, at least partially, started to turn back both Magufuli's autocratic developmentalism and economic nationalism and has emphasised Tanzania's openness to foreign investment and the importance of PPPs for economic development (see Wambura 2022). With regard to TAZARA, considering Zambia's financial straightjacket and Tanzania's rediscovered friendliness towards foreign investors, it seems likely that the Chinese infrastructural fix will soon materialise by means of equity investment in a privatised "Freedom Railway".

List of Interviews

Chinese journalist (anonymised), 8 February 2019.

Executive, China Civil Engineering Construction Corporation (CCECC) East Africa Ltd. (anonymised), 14 November 2019.

Former Tanzanian top official (anonymised), Dar es Salaam, Tanzania, 27 November 2019.

Kahama, Joseph Kulwa, secretary general, Tanzania China Friendship Promotion Assocation (TCFPA), Dar es Salaam, Tanzania, 28 November 2019.

Kamata, Ng'wanza, head of department, Department of Political Science and Public Administration, University of Dar es Salaam (UDSM), Dar es Salaam, Tanzania, 5 February 2019.

Key informant 1 (anonymised), 4 February 2019.

Key informant 2 (anonymised), 26 November 2019.

Lusinde, Job Malecela, former Tanzanian cabinet minister (1961–75) and former Tanzanian ambassador to China (1975–84), Dodoma, Tanzania, 20 November 2019.

Musonda, Christopher, managing director, Zambia Railways Ltd. (ZRL), Kabwe, Zambia, 8 August 2017.

Mwila, Elias, general secretary, Railway Workers Union of Zambia (RWUZ), Kabwe, Zambia, 7 July 2017.

Official, Ministry of Works, Transport and Communication (MWTC) (anonymised), 18 November 2019.

Senior official, Tanzanian Ministry of Works, Transport and Communication (MWTC) (anonymised), 19 November 2019.

Senior official, Zambian Ministry of Transport and Communication (MTC) (anonymised), Lusaka, Zambia, 14 June 2017.

Senior TAZARA manager (anonymised), 10 August 2017.

Shangwe, Muhidin, lecturer, Department of Political Science and Public Administration, University of Dar es Salaam, Dar es Salaam, Tanzania, 15 November 2019.

Tanzanian top official (anonymised), 15 November 2019.

TAZARA labour union executive (anonymised), 10 August 2017.

Wetengere, Kitojo, former deputy director, Mozambique-Tanzania Centre for Foreign Relations (CFR), Dar es Salaam, Tanzania, 13 November 2019.

References

Africa-Asia Confidential. 2013. "Pipeline and Transparency Protests." *Africa-Asia Confidential* 6(9):7.

Andreoni, Antonio. 2017. *Anti-Corruption in Tanzania: A Political Settlements Analysis*. AEC Working Paper 1. London: Anti-Corruption Evidence (AEC) Research Consortium.

Barton, Benjamin. 2023. "Infrastructure Nationalism and Political Vulnerability—Examining the Stalled Negotiations Over the Bagamoyo Port Project During Magufuli's Reign." *Journal of Asian and African Studies* 58(3):338–53. https://doi.org/10.1177/00219096211062471.

BBC. 2015. "Tanzania-Zambia Train Route Hit by Strike." *BBC News*. Retrieved March 4, 2020 (https://www.bbc.co.uk/news/world-africa-30786039).

Brooks, Andrew. 2010. "Spinning and Weaving Discontent: Labour Relations and the Production of Meaning at Zambia-China Mulungushi Textiles." *Journal of Southern African Studies* 36(1):113–32. https://doi.org/10.1080/03057071003607360.

Chiyemura, Frangton, Elisa Gambino, and Tim Zajontz. 2023. "Infrastructure and the Politics of African State Agency: Shaping the Belt and Road Initiative in East Africa." *Chinese Political Science Review* 8(1):105–31. https://doi.org/10.1007/s41111-022-00214-8.

Cuenca, Oliver. 2021. "Chinese Contractors Awarded Contract for Tanzanian SGR." *International Railway Journal*. Retrieved August 1, 2022 (https://www.railjournal.com/africa/chinese-contractors-awarded-contract-for-tanzanian-sgr/).

Flores, Isabel. 2017. *Dissecting Chinese Involvement in Road Construction Projects in Tanzania: Strategic Roadways and Resources*. Bachelor of Arts thesis, University of Iowa.

Gray, Hazel S. 2015. "The Political Economy of Grand Corruption in Tanzania." *African Affairs* 114(456):382–403. https://doi.org/10.1093/afraf/adv017.

GURT. 2016. *National Five Year Development Plan: 2016/2017–2020/2021.* Dodoma: Ministry of Finance and Planning.

Harvey, David. 2003. *The New Imperialism.* Oxford: Oxford University Press.

Harvey, David. 2004. "The 'New' Imperialism: Accumulation by Dispossession." *Socialist Register* 40:63–87.

Hildyard, Nicholas. 2016. *Licenced Larceny: Infrastructure, Financial Extraction and the Global South.* Manchester: Manchester University Press.

Hönke, Jana. 2018. "Beyond the Gatekeeper State: African Infrastructure Hubs as Sites of Experimentation." *Third World Thematics: A TWQ Journal* 3(3):347–63. https://doi.org/10.1080/23802014.2018.1456954.

Jacob, Thabit, and Rasmus Hundsbæk Pedersen. 2018. "New Resource Nationalism? Continuity and Change in Tanzania's Extractive Industries." *Extractive Industries and Society* 5(2):287–92. https://doi.org/10.1016/j.exis.2018.02.001.

Kahama, Joseph K. 2018. *The Challenge to China-Tanzania Relationship: To Enhance Cooperation and Mutual Benefits*. Dar es Salaam: Tema Publishers.

Kelly, Gina, Samuel Brazys, and Johan A. Elkink. 2016. *The Dragon's Curse? China, the World Bank, and Perceptions of Corruption in Tanzania*. AidData Working Paper 26.

Kinyondo, Abel. 2019. "Is China Recolonizing Africa? Some Views from Tanzania." *World Affairs* 182(2):128–64. https://doi.org/10.1177/0043820019839331.

Kinyondo, Abel, and Christopher Huggins. 2019. "Resource Nationalism in Tanzania: Implications for Artisanal and Small-Scale Mining." *Extractive Industries and Society* 6(1):181–89. https://doi.org/10.1016/j.exis.2018.08.005.

Lange, Siri, and Abel Kinyondo. 2016. "Resource Nationalism and Local Content in Tanzania: Experiences from Mining and Consequences for the Petroleum Sector." *Extractive Industries and Society* 3(4):1095–104. https://doi.org/10.1016/j.exis.2016.09.006.

Leslie, Agnes Ngoma. 2016. "Zambia and China: Workers' Protest, Civil Society and the Role of Opposition Politics in Elevating State Engagement." *African Studies Quarterly* 16(3–4):89–106.

Liu, Haifang. 2024. "The Freedom Railway Now and Then: The Enduring Relevance of the 'TAZARA Spirit' for South-South Cooperation." Pp. 68–88 in *Africa's Railway Renaissance: The role and impact of China*, edited by T. Zajontz, P. Carmody, M. Bagwandeen, and A. Leysens. Abingdon: Routledge.

Lusaka Times. 2016. "Government Signs a $2.3 Billion Deal with a Chinese Firm to Construct a Chipata-Serenje Railway Line." *Lusaka Times*. Retrieved July 25, 2019 (https://www.lusakatimes.com/2016/11/03/government-signs-a-2-3-billion-deal-with-a-chinese-firm-to-construct-a-chipata-serenje-railway-line/).

Lusaka Times. 2018. "Kenneth Kaunda International Airport Will Not Be Surrendered to China-Dora Siliza." *Lusaka Times*. Retrieved July 25, 2019 (https://www.lusakatimes.com/2018/09/10/kenneth-kaunda-international-airport-will-not-be-surrendered-to-china-dora-siliya/).

Lusaka Times. 2019. "Tanzania Orders Probe into $6.7 Million Funds for TAZARA." *Lusaka Times*. Retrieved August 19, 2019 (https://www.lusakatimes.com/2019/07/29/tanzania-orders-probe-into-6-7-million-funds-for-tazara/).

Magufuli, John Joseph Pombe. 2017. "Foreword." Pp. viii–ix in *Tanzania's Industrialisation Journey, 2016–2056: From Agrarian to a Modern Industrialised State in Forty Years*, edited by A. A. Mufuruki, R. Mawji, M. Marwa, and G. Kasiga. Nairobi: Moran Publishers.

Makundi, Hezron, Huib Huyse, and Patrick Develtere. 2017. "Negotiating the Technological Capacity in Chinese Engagements: Is the Tanzanian Government in the Driving Seat?" *South African Journal of International Affairs* 24(3):331–53. https://doi.org/10.1080/10220461.2017.1391116.

Malanga, Alex. 2017. "China, Tanzania in Fresh Talks on Tazara Revitalisation Plan." *The Citizen*. Retrieved August 4, 2019 (https://www.thecitizen.co.tz/News/China--Tanzania-in-fresh-talks-on--Tazara-revitalisation-plan/1840340-4173116-e6pcnbz/index.html).

Masabo, Conrad John. 2021. "Tanzania in China's MSRI: The 'Chinese Dream' Awaits Alignment with the African One." Pp. 137–64 in *China's Maritime Silk Road Initiative, Africa, and the Middle East: Feats, Freezes, and Failures*, edited by J.-M. F. Blanchard. Singapore: Palgrave Macmillan.

Mbewe, Zondiwe. 2018. "Govt Refutes TAZARA Concession Claims." *News Diggers*. Retrieved March 24, 2020 (https://diggers.news/?p=30394 Accessed on: 28.02.2019).

Mbulo, Edwin. 2019. "It's Crazy for a Country to Get in Debt without Capability to Repay, Says Kikwete." *The Mast*. Retrieved August 10, 2019 (https://www.themastonline.com/2019/07/28/its-crazy-for-a-country-to-get-in-debt-without-capability-to-repay-says-kikwete/?fbclid=IwAR0sCaZIReAuUCbhjGd85Tm4Kn2tE5e2cL_U11flFkiVL8UuB0iSjUpiWUw).

Mhagama, Hilda. 2022. "Strategic Projects: Samia Goes for Healthy Borrowing." *Daily News*. Retrieved July 15, 2023 (https://dailynews.co.tz/strategic-projects-samia-goes-for-healthy-borrowing/).

MTC. n.d. *Request for Expressions of Interest for Public-Private Partnerships for the Financing, Construction, Operation and Maintenance of the Nseluka to Mpulungu Railway Spur in Zambia*. Lusaka: Ministry of Transport and Communications.

Musa, Jonathan. 2019. "Why Talks on Port Stalled—Video." *The Citizen*. Retrieved July 27, 2019 (https://www.thecitizen.co.tz/news/1840340-5124384-8pdm7b/index.html).

National Assembly of Zambia. 2017. "Ministerial Statements: Railway Transport System in Zambia." *National Assembly of Zambia*. Retrieved May 19, 2019 (http://www.parliament.gov.zm/sites/default/files/images/publication_docs/MINISTERIAL/STATEMENT/ON/THE/STATE/OF/RAILWAY/TRANSPORT/BY/HON/MUSHIMBA.pdf).

Negi, Rohit. 2008. "Beyond the 'Chinese Scramble': The Political Economy of Anti-China Sentiment in Zambia." *African Geographical Review* 27(1):41–693. https://doi.org/10.1080/19376812.2008.9756209.

Nwapi, Chilenye, and Nathan Andrews. 2017. "A 'New' Developmental State in Africa? Evaluating Recent State Interventions Vis-a-Vis Resource Extraction in Kenya, Tanzania, and Rwanda." *Journal of Sustainable Development* 13(2):223–67.

Oirere, Shem. 2015. "Court Declares Tazara Staff Strike Illegal." *International Railway Journal*. Retrieved March 4, 2020 (https://www.railjournal.com/africa/court-declares-tazara-staff-strike-illegal/).

Olingo, Allan. 2017. "Tanzania's Turn to Turkey for SGR Funds Leaves China in Limbo." *The East African*. Retrieved August 2, 2019 (https://www.theeastafrican.co.ke/business/Tanzania-SGR-funds-/2560-3793116-m75574/index.html).

Onyango, Emmanuel. 2019. "China Could Finance Part of Tanzania's SGR Project." *The East African*. Retrieved August 2, 2019 (https://www.theeastafrican.co.ke/business/China-could-finance-part-of-tanzania-sgr-project/2560-5185404-1e7c77/index.html).

Paget, Dan. 2021. "Tanzania: The Authoritarian Landslide." *Journal of Democracy* 32(2):61–76. https://doi.org/10.1353/jod.2021.0019.

Polus, Andrzej, and Wojciech Tycholiz. 2018. "Gold, Gas and Lies: Extractive Sector in a Sub-Saharan Functional State. The Case of Natural Resource Sector in Tanzania." *Politeja* 15(56):151–68. https://doi.org/10.12797/politeja.15.2018.56.09.

Polus, Andrzej, and Wojciech Tycholiz. 2019. "David versus Goliath: Tanzania's Efforts to Stand up to Foreign Gas Corporations." *Africa Spectrum* 54(1):61–72. https://doi.org/10.1177/0002039719848507.

PwC. 2016. "Budget 2016: PwC Insight and Analysis." *PricewaterhouseCoopers Tanzania*. Retrieved February 29, 2020 (https://www.pwc.co.tz/assets/pdf/budget-2016-presentations.pdf).

PwC. 2017. "Budget 2017: PwC Insight and Analysis." *PricewaterhouseCoopers Tanzania*. Retrieved February 29, 2020 (https://www.pwc.co.tz/assets/pdf/budget-2017-presentation.pdf).

PwC. 2018. "Reimagine the Possible: Budget 2018/2019." *PricewaterhouseCoopers Tanzania*. Retrieved February 29, 2020 (https://www.pwc.co.tz/assets/pdf/2018-19-budget.pdf).

PwC. 2019. "Sustaining the Momentum National Budget Bulletin 2019/20." *PricewaterhouseCoopers Tanzania*. Retrieved February 29, 2020 (https://www.pwc.co.tz/assets/pdf/2019-2020-budget.pdf).

Reuters. 2015. "Tanzania Awards $9 Bln Rail Projects to Chinese Companies." *Reuters*. Retrieved August 4, 2019 (https://www.reuters.com/article/tanzania-railways/tanzania-awards-9-bln-rail-projects-to-chinese-companies-idUSL5N0YM09H20150531).

Reuters. 2019a. "Barrick Gold Reaches Deal with Tanzania over Acacia Mining." *Reuters*. Retrieved February 18, 2020 (https://www.reuters.com/article/us-barrick-gold-tanzania/barrick-gold-reaches-deal-with-tanzania-over-acacia-mining-idUSKBN1WZ0DL).

Reuters. 2019b. "Tanzania's China-Backed $10 Billion Port Plan Stalls over Terms: Official." *Reuters*. Retrieved July 26, 2019 (https://www.reuters.com/article/us-tanzania-port/tanzanias-china-backed-10-billion-port-plan-stalls-over-terms-official-idUSKCN1ST084).

Roder, Kai. 2019. "'Bulldozer Politics', State-Making and (Neo-)Extractive Industries in Tanzania's Gold Mining Sector." *Extractive Industries and Society* 6(2):407–12. https://doi.org/10.1016/j.exis.2018.10.012.

Sautman, Barry, and Yan Hairong. 2015. "Bashing 'the Chinese': Contextualizing Zambia's Collum Coal Mine Shooting." Pp. 138–57 in *China in*

Africa: Strategic Motives and Economic Interests, edited by S. Zhao. Abingdon: Routledge.

Schlimmer, Sina. 2018. "Talking 'land Grabs' Is Talking Politics: Land as Politicised Rhetoric during Tanzania's 2015 Elections." *Journal of Eastern African Studies* 12(1):83–101. https://doi.org/10.1080/17531055.2017.1410757.

Scott, Guy. 2019. *Adventures in Zambian Politics: A Story in Black and White*. Boulder: Lynne Rienner.

Shivji, Issa G. 2009. *Accumulation in an African Periphery: A Theoretical Framework*. Dar es Salaam: Mkuki na Nyota Publishers.

Sigalla, Huruma Luhuvilo. 2014. "Changing Trends in the Tanzania–China Relationship: A Sociological Inquiry into the Mixed Perceptions of the Tanzania–China Relationship on the Eve of Globalization." *Österreichische Zeitschrift Für Soziologie* 39(1):61–78. https://doi.org/10.1007/s11614-014-0118-6.

Sum, Ngai-Ling. 2019. "The Intertwined Geopolitics and Geoeconomics of Hopes/ Fears: China's Triple Economic Bubbles and the 'One Belt One Road' Imaginary." *Territory, Politics, Governance* 7(4):528–52. https://doi.org/10.1080/21622671.2018.1523746.

Tanzania Invest. 2023. "SGR: Tanzania Standard Gauge Railway." *Tanzania Invest*. Retrieved July 14, 2023 (https://www.tanzaniainvest.com/sgr).

The Citizen. 2019. "How the Dream for a Port in Bagamoyo Became Elusive." *The Citizen*. Retrieved July 26, 2019 (https://www.thecitizen.co.tz/news/1840340-5124384-8pdm7b/index.html).

The Mast. 2019. "TAZARA Workers down Tools over Salaries." *The Mast*. Retrieved March 25, 2020 (https://www.themastonline.com/2019/04/03/tazara-workers-down-tools-over-salaries/).

Transparency International. n.d. "Corruption Perceptions Index." *Transparency International*. Retrieved February 20, 2020 (https://www.transparency.org/research/cpi/overview).

Tsubura, Machiko. 2018. "'Umoja Ni Ushindi (Unity Is Victory)': Management of Factionalism in the Presidential Nomination of Tanzania's Dominant Party in 2015." *Journal of Eastern African Studies* 12(1):63–82. https://doi.org/10.1080/17531055.2017.1410758.

Wambura, Bethsheba. 2022. "Private-Public Partnership Has Not Been Realized as Envisioned by Mkapa, Says Samia." *The Citizen*. Retrieved July 15, 2023 (https://www.thecitizen.co.tz/tanzania/news/national/private-public-partnership-has-not-been-realized-as-envisioned-by-mkapa-says-samia-3880726).

World Bank. n.d.-a. "Tanzania." *World Bank Public Documents*. Retrieved February 21, 2020 (https://pubdocs.worldbank.org/en/278341492207296350/data-tza.pdf).

World Bank. n.d.-b. "Zambia." *World Bank Public Documents*. Retrieved February 21, 2020 (https://pubdocs.worldbank.org/en/359911492207299026/data-zmb.pdf).

Xinhua. 2020. "Standard Chartered Bank, Tanzania Sign Facility Agreement for SGR Project." *XinhuaNet*. Retrieved February 26, 2020 (http://www.xinhuanet.com/english/2020-02/14/c_138781409.htm).

Zajontz, Tim. 2022. "Tanzania and Zambia Want to Upgrade the 'Uhuru Railway'—But Can They?" *The Conversation*. Retrieved June 22, 2023 (https://theconversation.com/tanzania-and-zambia-want-to-upgrade-the-uhuru-railway-but-can-they-190659).

Zajontz, Tim. 2024. "The Political Economy of China's Globalising Railways – And their Arrival in Africa." Pp. 26–48 in *Africa's Railway Renaissance: The role and impact of China*, edited by T. Zajontz, P. Carmody, M. Bagwandeen, and A. Leysens. Abingdon: Routledge.

Zajontz, Tim, Pádraig Carmody, Mandira Bagwandeen, and Anthony Leysens. 2024. "Introduction: China's Role in Africa's Railway Renaissance." Pp. 1–25 in *Africa's Railway Renaissance: The role and impact of China*, edited by T. Zajontz, P. Carmody, M. Bagwandeen, and A. Leysens. Abingdon: Routledge.

CHAPTER 6

The Price of the Sino-Zambian "Road Bonanza"

If you want to be rich, first build a road. (Chinese proverb)

Chinese sun-hatted supervisors instructing foremen on one of the continent's countless road construction sites have become a regular sight for travellers on African roads.[1] According to one report, Chinese companies had built or upgraded around 30,000km of highways on the African continent by 2018 (Edinger and Labuschagne 2019). As one of Africa's 16 landlocked countries, Zambia and its minerals-dependent economy are particularly reliant on transport infrastructure that links its economic heartlands, the capital Lusaka as well as the Copper Belt, with ports in neighbouring countries (see Bach 2016: 79; Nugent 2018: 23). Road infrastructure has therefore been the sector in which the emergence of the Zambian infrastructure state has been most evident throughout the 2010s.

This and the following chapter scrutinise the involvement of Chinese firms and banks in Zambia's road sector and how Zambian actors have facilitated and conditioned the Chinese spatio-temporal fix in the concrete

[1] Some sections in this chapter and in Chapter 7 were previously published under the title "The Chinese infrastructural fix in Africa: lessons from the Sino-Zambian 'road bonanza'" in *Oxford Development Studies* and are reprinted with permission.

T. Zajontz, *The Political Economy of China's Infrastructure Development in Africa*, International Political Economy Series,
https://doi.org/10.1007/978-3-031-44449-4_6

case. I first discuss the "development-through-infrastructure" strategy pursued by the Patriotic Front (PF) government and how it has been fuelled by peculiar characteristics of Chinese loan financing and informal procurements, before problematising the financial implications of this "road bonanza". The second part of the chapter documents the gradual shift in the financial governance of road development from debt financing towards project finance PPPs, a trend which has been expedited by Zambia's unsustainable accumulation of debt throughout the 2010s. PPPs are likely to become a "fix" for the Chinese infrastructural fix in Zambia's road sector, as privatisation is a likely form of accumulation by dispossession in times of a debt crisis and the recovery period from the same. The last part of this chapter problematises the rapid scaling up of road tolling that has paralleled the Sino-Zambian "road bonanza".

Build Now, Pay Later: The Costly Ambition of a "Land-Linked Zambia"

An ambitious state-led infrastructure development agenda formed a central element of the late Michael Sata's successful presidential campaign of 2011. Following the change of government from the Movement for Multi-Party Democracy (MMD) to the PF in 2011, road development was significantly stepped up under Sata (Cheelo and Liebenthal 2018: 3; Lee 2017: 18). Framed by the imaginary of a "land-linked Zambia", the country-wide Link Zambia 8000 programme, also known as Accelerated National Roads Construction Programme (ANRCP), was launched in 2012. It envisaged the construction, rehabilitation and/or upgrade of some 8,000km of roads to bitumen standard (Cheelo and Liebenthal 2018: 3; Lee 2014: 41; RDA n.d.-b; Saasa 2018: 17). One official from Zambia's Road Development Agency (RDA) described the project's objectives as follows:

> [T]he Link Zambia had a specific purpose, yes. Being landlocked we were looking at ways of opening up the country to make it a truly land-linked country. Trying to take advantage of our situation. So, under the Link Zambia the objective was to link all major economic centres and any place with potential. That's why you will see that even in places where there isn't much economic activity at the moment, you find that we've planned some roads in that area in order to achieve the whole purpose of linking the

country that you have access to basically all the places. (Interview RDA official)

The statement is exemplary for the pervasive conviction among Zambian technocrats (and decision-makers) that the improvement of transport infrastructure would create spill-over effects into other sectors of the economy and unlock the country's economic potentials. As noted in the introduction, with the global (re-)emergence of the "infrastructure-led development" paradigm, state-steered spatial planning (not least in the so-called Global South) has aimed at "getting the territory right" for its smooth integration with global value chains by means of cross-border and (trans)regional connectivity (Schindler and Kanai 2021: 40, 41; see Nugent 2018; Wethal 2019; Zajontz et al. 2024).

The Zambian infrastructure state that emerged, from 2011 onwards, under the PF-led government hoped to boost the country's competitiveness by improving transport infrastructure, especially as the landlocked country was seen as being at a geographical disadvantage compared to other major copper exporters such as Chile "who [sic!] can convey our product [copper] to the sea – who still get the same price at half the cost of yours" (interview Musonda, C.). At the same time, public investments in transport infrastructure were expected to boost growth in economic sectors other than mining. The programme served as a counter-cyclical measure against the background of dwindling commodity prices after 2011, as the "massive bond-financed road and infrastructure programme [...] provided some short term cushion against a persistent weakening of the global copper price" (Fraser 2017: 465). Zambia's 7th National Development Plan 2017–2021 suggested that "[i]nvestment in improved transport systems and infrastructure will drive wider economic benefits, including supporting growth and creation of jobs, raising the productive capacity of the economy, driving efficiency and boosting international competitiveness" (GRZ 2017: 72). In the construction sector, the ANRCP was expected to create 24,000 jobs, "especially among the youths", and at boosting growth in the "local contracting industry" (RDA n.d.-b).

Lusaka's ambitious road development agenda coalesced with enhanced Chinese efforts to "move out" surplus capital and material in the construction and infrastructure sectors to address domestic overaccumulation problems (see Chapter 2). Both China's state-owned infrastructure giants and private companies tapped into Zambia's growing road construction market. According to one source, by April 2016 16 out of the 23 contracts under the Link Zambia programme had been awarded to Chinese contractors (Simumba 2018: 22). At 30 June 2018, the National Construction Council (NCC) listed a total of 71 "grade one" contractors that qualify for large-scale works, in the category "R—general roads and earthworks". 39 thereof were Chinese, whereas only 21 were classified as "Zambian citizen owned", with 11 being other foreign companies (NCC 2019).[2] Table 6.1 shows select road projects with Chinese participation that were commenced during the 2010s.

Besides concessional loans and grants from multilateral financial institutions, whose lending to Zambia largely stagnated in the 2010s (Ofstad and Tjønneland 2019: 5), the massive hike in road development in Zambia was rendered possible by eager lending practices on the side of China's policy banks, which boosted "[c]redit-fuelled construction" (Lee 2014: 41). As Carmody and Kragelund (2016: 17) underscore, China's leverage in Zambia stems inter alia from its "ability to grant or deny new loans or investments of importance for the Zambian government in its quest for modernization and economic development". It became common practice in Zambia's road sector that Chinese contractors facilitated loans from China's policy banks. Ofstad and Tjønneland have raised concerns about the distribution of costs and benefits of such lending, arguing that

> China is [...] less transparent in its finances and aid, and these challenges are apparent in Zambia. It is difficult to obtain information about the actual figures and the full terms and conditions for their loans and development support. In many cases, contracts were awarded to Chinese contractors without public tendering. Accusations regarding "gifts" and corruption are rife. The Chinese packages may seem to be "too good" not to be accepted. It is nevertheless the responsibility of the Zambian decision-makers to ensure that they get value for money, to make a full assessment of the terms of any contract and loan agreement and to make sure that the borrowing is sustainable. (2019: 7)

The authors point to the agency of Zambian decision-makers in the negotiation and appraisal of infrastructural loans. Brautigam (2021) similarly argues that Chinese and Zambians have effectively "co-created a debt

[2] For a list of Chinese grade 1 contractors, see Table A.2 in the annex.

Table 6.1 Major road construction projects with Chinese participation commenced in the 2010s

Project	*Projected total costs*	*Source of funding*	*Contractor*
Trunk road network			
Chinsali-Nakonde (T2, 210km): Rehabilitation of single carriageway	$182.4m	African Development Bank (AfDB), Africa Growing Together Fund (funded by the People's Bank of China, administered by AfDB), Zambian government	Lot 1 (Chinsali-Isoka): China State Construction Engineering Lot 2 (Isoka-Nakonde): China Railway Seventh Group
Kitwe-Chingola (T3, 45km): Upgrade to dual carriageway	Kwacha844m (≈$75m at the time)	National Pensions Scheme Authority (NAPSA)	Sino-Hydro Zambia
Ndola-Kitwe (T3, 63km): Upgrade to dual carriageway	Unclear	NAPSA	China Jiangxi
Chingola-Solwezi (T5):Rehabilitation single carriageway (lots 1&3, 128km)	Kwacha1.067bn (≈$150m at the time)	NAPSA	China Geo Engineering
Lusaka-Chirundu (T2): Rehabilitation of 96.5km single carriageway	$104.5m	World Bank; Department for International Development (DFID), DFID funds administered by Development Bank of Southern Africa	China Henan International
Local road networks			
Lusaka 400	$348.29m	China Exim Bank (loan of $295.8m), Zambian government	Aviation Industry Corporation of China (AVIC)
Copperbelt 400	$493m	China Development Bank	China Henan International
Regional roads			
Mansa-Luwingu: Upgrade of 175km single carriageway	$207m	China Development Bank ($180m commercial loan), Zambian government	China Henan International

(continued)

Table 6.1 (continued)

Project	*Projected total costs*	*Source of funding*	*Contractor*
Nakonde-Mbala: Rehabilitation of 172km single carriageway	$180m	China Development Fund (Concessional loan, disbursed by China Exim Bank)	China CAMC Engineering
Mongu-Kalabo: 34km single carriageway, including 26 bridges	$286.94m	China Exim Bank (loan of $244m), Zambian government	AVIC

Source Author's compilation, based on numerous official and media sources; the table was previously published in a slightly different version in Zajontz (2022b) and is reprinted with the publisher's permission

'tragedy of the commons'". The particularities of Chinese loan financing have contributed to this co-creation.

Loan Financing with Chinese Characteristics

> China is a useful partner. China advocates a win-win situation, but the thing we are failing as Africans is the same issue of shifting the blame. When you are at the table with China, it's said win-win but the reality is that sitting on opposite ends of the table, all of you can't win. Somebody must win, the other must lose because it's a negotiation, isn't it? So we shouldn't blame China for our own inadequacies. We are passing our own inadequacies to China saying China is wrong, we are at the table negotiating and when they defeat us, we say China is there to blame. […] Let us have our own understanding of a win-win situation. Sometimes let us also learn to say no to some of the loans. Let's show off. When you show off they will come to you and when they come to you, you have greater capacity to negotiate better, isn't it! But when you go to the table begging almost crawling and kneeling saying "I beg you, I beg you," they will say "yes we are winning together" [meanwhile] who is winning? (Mutati, quoted in Phiri 2018)

These are the words of Felix Mutati, who served, among others, as Minister of Commerce, Trade and Industry (2006–2011) under Presidents Mwanawasa and Banda and as Minister of Finance (2016–2018) under President Lungu. Mutati was at the forefront in negotiating financial arrangements for infrastructure projects, among them the Lusaka-Ndola dual carriageway, which is discussed below. Mutati's description of Sino-African relations as a zero-sum game and Africa's perceived "defeat" in (loan) negotiations with the Chinese allude to controversies related to Chinese infrastructure lending on the continent. "Easy money" for road construction, in the form of loans as well as export and supplier credits, has become a prime means of how the Chinese infrastructural fix has played out in the Zambian context. However, what might have been considered by some decision-makers as "too good to decline" has come at a price.

To begin with, and Mutati's statement underscores this, the terms and conditions of Chinese infrastructure loans have not necessarily been beneficial for Zambia. This even applies to concessional loans that the Zambian government signed. As Lee (2014: 41) points out, "[o]ften touted by Beijing as a form of assistance, Chinese concessional loans actually charge higher interest rates than the World Bank (2 per cent vs 1.7 per cent), have a smaller grant element (23 per cent vs 35 per cent), [and] shorter repayment periods (10–15 years vs 20–50 years)". In his memoirs, Zambia's former Vice-President Scott remembers as the "outstanding feature" of the Chinese engagement in Zambia's construction industry "the long-term and apparently 'soft' financing that comes through, say, the Bank of China". Yet, Scott alludes to the 'real' costs of Chinese loans:

> Of course, if you do the discounting to get net present cost you will find that the Chinese are overpricing to compensate for the generous terms of the loan. But at least you can build something, even if it is burdensome to your children to pay the loan back. Rule of thumb calculations indicate that Chinese financed capital projects cost about double what they would if paid for in cash. (2019: 190)

Besides the cost aspect, Chinese loan financing usually rules out competitive bidding and thus compromises conventional public procurement procedures—with a number of detrimental effects. Indeed, the Chinese government has often stressed the "non-conditionality" of Chinese loans and has contrasted its lending practices to that of Western donors and multilateral development banks, which typically attach conditionalities regarding good governance as well as labour and environmental standards to their loans. Yet, Chinese loans have come with "commercial conditions" (Mohan and Tan-Mullins 2019: 1373; see Alden and Jiang 2019). Chinese concessional loans are usually tied to the non-competitive single sourcing of Chinese contractors (Corkin 2012; Lee 2014, 2017: 48; Mohan and Tan-Mullins 2019).

As Corkin (2013: 64) points out, concessional loans from China's Exim Bank resemble "preferential commercial lending". Exim Bank's loan requirements prescribe that projects funded by the bank are awarded to Chinese contractors. Moreover, the loans are designed to fund projects in the manufacturing, infrastructure or social welfare sectors that "can generate promising economic returns or good social benefits" as well as "finance the procurement of Chinese mechanical, electronic products, complete sets of equipment, technology and service and other goods by the borrowing country" (Corkin 2013: 64; see Corkin 2012). At least 50 per cent of procured materials, equipment and services are expected to be sourced from China (Corkin 2012, 2013: 66). In the case of Chinese concessional loans and export credits, the link between Harvey's temporal fix and the spatial fix could not get more obvious.

Due to the discussed commercial conditionalities, road construction projects that are financed through Chinese concessional loans or export credits are generally not openly tendered but the result of closed-door government-to-government negotiations (Gonzalez-Vicente 2019). Several large-scale projects in Zambia's road sector have been "package deals" in that financing of projects was tied to the selection of particular contractors or even facilitated by the same. Chinese state-owned banks and the country's SOEs in construction have acted in close coordination, thereby offering one-stop shop services to Zambian decision-makers, notwithstanding the rather diffuse corporate structures that govern China's SOEs. In 2015, for instance, the Zambian government signed a $493m contract with China Henan for the rehabilitation of about 400 km of township roads in the Copper Belt. According to then Minister of Works and Supply, Yamfwa Mukanga, the contractor "facilitated" the corresponding "Export Credit Offer/loan" from the Development Bank of China (National Assembly of Zambia 2015). The Lusaka 400 programme, dedicated to the improvement of about 400 km of urban roads in Zambia's capital, was, for example, financed through a $348m loan from China's Exim Bank (Saasa 2018: 17). As a result, the main contractor Aviation Industry Corporation of China (AVIC) International was single-sourced (Auditor General n.d.: 48–50).

The "peculiarity of the Chinese way of noncompetitive bidding" is a major reason for inflated project costs in Zambian road construction, as single-sourced contractors determine the costs, in some cases without feasibility studies being conducted (Lee 2017: 51). A 172 km feeder road, that links Nakonde at the Tanzanian-Zambian border with Mbala, close to Mpulungu port at Lake Tanganyika, was implemented through a concessional loan from the China Development Fund, disbursed by Exim Bank. It was carried out by China CAMC Engineering Corporation, a Shanghai-listed parastatal (NRFA n.d.: 27; RDA 2016b: 5, 15, n.d.-a: 10). An RDA director suggested that the road, under an open and competitive tender, would have cost about $100m, instead of $180m. But "the contractor had already secured the agreement with the Ministry of Finance when they came to us [RDA]" (quoted in Lee 2017: 51). This points to the circumvention of formal and due legal-bureaucratic procurement processes in the context of Chinese-funded road projects, an issue I will return to in Chapter 7.

Chinese-funded road projects, some of which were pre-agreed at the highest levels of intergovernmental exchange, have not necessarily aligned with the road development priorities set out at the working level within the relevant ministries and government agencies. In Zambia, the Chinese quest for infrastructure and construction markets overseas has also resulted in the implementation of road projects that were criticised for being driven by Chinese supply and not necessarily by Zambian demand. Chinese contractors in the Zambian market have actively lobbied officials within line ministries and specialised agencies by proposing particular projects, with the promise that they can facilitate tailor-made loans for their implementation. This supply-driven, or rather supplier-driven, mode of engagement has turned conventional policy planning on its head (Lee 2017: 50).

One case in point is the 175 km Mansa-Luwingu road. China Henan Corporation secured the $207m contract which came with a $180m commercial loan from China Development Bank (AidData n.d.). Not only was the project considered overpriced by RDA officials due to single sourcing of the contractor, the road was also not prioritised by RDA. Still, Zambian politicians insisted in its implementation (Lee 2017: 51). As a 2013 World Bank report suggests, "[o]ne of the most notable examples of single sourcing has been the contract award for the Mongu-Kalabo road to a Chinese firm with a limited experience in road contracting" (Raballand et al. 2013: 16). AVIC constructed the road for $287m,

$244m thereof financed through an Exim Bank loan (NRFA, n.d.-a: 27). The 34 km of single carriageway between Mongu and Kalabo, including 26 bridges across the Barotse plains, was still initiated under the MMD government in an attempt to secure electoral support in the Western Province and became "one of the most expensive roads per kilometer in the world" (Raballand et al. 2013: 14). The conjuncture of the discussed particularities of Chinese lending and oftentimes uncritical financial and economic appraisals of debt-financed road projects on the part of Zambian decision-makers has contributed to Zambia's debt crisis (see Brautigam 2022).

The Price of Chinese Road Investment

In 2005, a lion's share of Zambia's external debt, namely $3.9bn, was cancelled by the World Bank and the IMF under the Highly Indebted Poor Countries initiative. In the sequel, the MMD government under presidents Levy Mwanawasa and Rupiah Banda restrained external borrowing, while the economy recorded steady economic growth rates of 6–7 per cent since 2002 (Fraser 2017: 458; Ofstad and Tjønneland 2019: 4). In September 2011, the PF took over government with relatively low levels of external debt which amounted to 8.4 per cent of the GDP by the end of 2011 (Ofstad and Tjønneland 2019: 4). The PF's 2011 electoral platform banked on state-steered development, particularly in the form of infrastructure development. The party was explicit in its assessment that its development-through-infrastructure approach required a more expansive fiscal policy than under the MMD. The party's 2011–2016 Manifesto of 2011 reads as follows:

> Under the MMD government, investment in infrastructure development has been limited and the pace of development slow. Part of this is due to an obsession with maintaining 'tight money' through fiscal and monetary policies. This has resulted in many parts of Zambia resembling ghost towns despite more than five years of record mineral prices and a production boom. (Patriotic Front 2011: 29; also cited in Cheelo and Liebenthal 2018: 3)

After the change in government, the PF's demands for a less restrictive fiscal policy were quickly reflected institutionally within the Ministry of Finance and State House, where "[a]fter a decade of dominance of fiscal conservatives, the expansionists came to the fore" (Hinfelaar and Sichone 2019: 18). Road development became a top priority in Zambia's budget and constituted by far the largest non-financial capital expenditure item, averaging 42 per cent of all expenditures on non-financial assets between 2011 and 2017 (Cheelo and Liebenthal 2018: 4). In order to finance its ambitious infrastructure agenda, the PF-led government borrowed extensively from both "traditional" lenders, particularly multilateral financial institutions, but increasingly also from so-called non-traditional and commercial creditors (Hinfelaar and Sichone 2019: 6; Ofstad and Tjønneland 2019: 5). This policy change consolidated the emergence of the Zambian "infrastructure state" (see DiCarlo and Schindler 2022), a state form that has corresponded with the worldwide emergence of an "infrastructure-led development" (Schindler and Kanai 2021) paradigm following the global financial crisis of 2007–08 and China's central role in promoting the same through the BRI.

In the Zambian infrastructure state, the high concentration of economic decision-making power in the presidential office has expedited expansive borrowing, as the Treasury has refrained from opposing ever-growing "wish lists" under presidents Sata and Lungu. This was specifically pronounced in the case of former Finance Minister Chikwanda (2011–16) who put up little opposition to rapidly growing debt obligations (Ofstad and Tjønneland 2019: 6). *Africa Confidential* ascertained in 2018 that:

> The Ministry of Finance's economists are competent enough, insiders say, but political interference from State House is the problem. Typically, ministries make their own financing arrangements and then use the clout of the head of state to force the finance ministry to authorise their frequently questionable credit arrangements. The departments will announce projects so as to encourage the politicians to avoid the embarrassment of rowing back on popular promises. (2018a: 8–9)

Especially large-scale infrastructure projects have been brokered by the office of the president (Ofstad and Tjønneland 2019: 6). Once agreement was reached at the highest intergovernmental level, Zambia's Treasury was instructed to negotiate loan agreements and credit lines with China's policy banks, in some cases without necessary and up-to-date information on costing and viability. Line ministries and specialised agencies only got involved after a financial framework had been agreed on in top-level government-to-government negotiations (Lee 2017: 50–51).

MMD politician Mutati's greater hesitancy to sign off on loans can reasonably be assumed to have been a reason for his replacement. Nonetheless, external debt has further risen under him and his successor Margaret Mwanakatwe (2018–19). Bwalya Ng'andu, in turn, who replaced Mwanakatwe in July 2019, appears to have been called in as a "fire fighter" who was expected to turn around the country's looming debt crisis, shortly after Zambia had been downgraded by Moody's to a "Caa2 negative" rating, which indicates "the probability of default over the near term" (Africa Confidential 2019a: 8). A default followed shortly into the COVID-19 pandemic when, in November 2020, the Zambian treasury was unable to service a $42.5 million Eurobond payment (Large 2021: 96). As Table 6.2 shows, Zambia's external has risen significantly during the 2010s. According to World Bank data, the country's debt-to-GDP ratio climbed from to 20.5 per cent in 2009 to 78.1 per cent in 2018 (World Bank, n.d.; see also Fig. 5.1).

China has become Zambia's largest bilateral creditor. Chinese lenders accounted for 28 per cent of Zambia's external debt in February 2018. In 2016 alone, Zambia borrowed $1.7bn from Chinese lenders (Simumba 2018: 5); see also Alden and Jiang 2019: 645). It is essential to acknowledge that Zambia has also borrowed extensively from other lenders in recent years. Most notably, three Eurobonds at a total value of $3bn were issued in 2012 ($750m at an interest rate of 5.6 per cent), 2014 ($1bn, 8.6 per cent) and 2015 ($1.25bn, 9.4 per cent) (Ofstad and Tjønneland 2019: 5; Simumba 2018: 16 n. 14). Yet, about half of $2.64bn in loans contracted by the Zambian government in 2018 came from Chinese financial institutions: $908m from the Chinese Exim Bank, $401m from the Industrial and Commercial Bank of China and $36m from the Bank of China (Ministry of Finance 2019a: 48). Export and supplier's credit amounted to about a fourth of Zambia's external debt stock in 2018,

Table 6.2 Zambia's external debt, 2015–2019

	2015	*2016*	*2017*	*2018*	*06/2019*	*12/2019*
External debt (in $bn)	6.70	6.95	8.74	10.05	10.23	11.2

Source Lusaka Times (2019), Ministry of Finance (2018, 2019a), and Mitimingi and Hill (2020)

with China's Exim Bank holding $2.27bn of the same, 90 per cent of the total (Ministry of Finance 2019a: 47).

Between 2016 and 2018, Zambia's commercial debt rose from $3.3bn to $5.31bn. While the lion's share of commercial debt is made up of $3bn in Eurobonds, Chinese creditors also own significant amounts of it. In 2018, the government owed $325 m in commercial loans to China Development Bank alone (Ministry of Finance 2019a: 47). Some estimates suggest that the Zambian government, between 2015 and 2018, has signed off on Chinese loan arrangements that are worth at least $8bn, of which $5bn are not reflected in official statistics, because they have not been disbursed yet (Africa Confidential 2018b). In August 2021, researchers from the China–Africa Research Initiative (CARI) at Johns Hopkins estimated Zambia's public or publicly guaranteed debt owed to China at $6.6 billion, almost double the figure which was officially circulated by the PF government at the time (Brautigam 2021).

Zambia's accumulation of Chinese loans became a highly controversial political issue and both civil society actors and the opposition regularly accused the PF-led government to delude the public with regard to the actual amounts owed to or guaranteed vis-à-vis Chinese creditors. Speculations about Chinese "takeovers" of Zambia's state energy company Zambia Electricity Supply Corporation (ZESCO), Lusaka's International Airport or Zambia National Broadcasting Corporation, as a result of the government's inability to service its debts, have periodically flared up in the newspapers, social media and in Parliament, with the government hastily refuting such claims (Lusaka Times 2018a). In December 2018, U.S. National Security Advisor John Bolton further fuelled the "debt trap" narrative when he argued that Zambia's actual debt to China stood between $6 and 10bn and that ZESCO was being seized as collateral (Reuters 2018). These fear-based discourses resemble developments in the public realm of countries that are central to China's BRI, as described by Sum (see 2019). While some of these fears might not be fact-based or exaggerated for (geo)political reasons, valid scrutinising of the "debt trap" narrative (see Brautigam 2019) should not cloud potential legal and financial risks related to Chinese loan-debt investment. The latter is based on "bilateral loan-debt contractuality" which implies legal-disciplinary rules that regulate the relationship between creditor and lender. In case of default, "loan-debt obligations allow China to renegotiate the terms, collateralize the debt and claim assets/resources by converting debt into equity" (Sum 2019: 545).

The IMF concluded after its Article IV visit to Zambia in April 2019 that "Zambia's development strategy targeting a rapid scaling up in infrastructure spending has resulted in large fiscal deficits, financed by nonconcessional debt" (Goodman, quoted in IMF 2019). In a statement on Zambia's economic performance from 11 March 2019, then Finance Minister Mwanakatwe attributed the rise "to increased disbursements on previously contracted loans for on-going economic infrastructure programmes aimed at supporting economic diversification and structural transformation" (Ministry of Finance 2019b). In a response to growing domestic and international political pressure over its unsustainable fiscal situation, the government has announced a break on further debt accumulation, a reevaluation and restructuring of loan commitments already taken on and a postponement or delay of projects that are far from completion (Ofstad and Tjønneland 2019: 9; see also Africa Confidential 2018b). First day in office, then Finance Minister Ng'andu reiterated that

> [g]overnment has taken measures for management of project disbursements, debt cancellation and rescheduling to bring down deficits to sustainable levels. [...] This will be supported by measures to postpone and cancel some contracted but not disbursed loans, which is in line with the directive by the President from the special Cabinet Meeting of 27th May, 2019. This is an activity which I intend to actively engage my fellow Cabinet Ministers. (quoted in Lusaka Times 2019)

Besides the (declared) objective of fiscal consolidation, which implies the scaling down of infrastructure development, a second strategy has been pursued with enhanced efforts, namely the privatisation of infrastructure development by means of PPPs that encompass project finance. This trend I shall discuss in the next section.

The Renaissance of Public–Private Partnerships

Zambia has in recent years experienced a renaissance of PPPs which has been catalysed by the country's rapidly deteriorating public finances culminating in a default on a Eurobond payment in November 2020. From the mid-2010s onwards, the Zambian government has tried to gradually shift the financial governance of road infrastructure development by complementing sovereign borrowing for road projects with private project finance. Conventional discourse, both in academia and at NEPAD and World Bank roundtables, has long suggested that PPPs are particularly suitable for "Sub-Sahara Africa", where strained public budgets are deemed to coincide with a "huge transport investment gap" (Osei-Kyei and Chan 2016: 172; see Biau et al. 2008; Ngoma et al. 2014; Shendy et al. 2011). In order to meet Africa's projected infrastructural needs, PPPs are commonly considered to be without alternative: "The high cost of public debts, public budgetary constraints and the increasing demand for transport services have left many governments with no option than to leverage the private sector's expertise and finance through Public–Private Partnership (PPP) approach" (Osei-Kyei and Chan 2016: 170–71). Consequently, development banks, think tanks and governments alike advocate PPPs as the "vanguard vehicle" to attract private investment in infrastructure (Hildyard 2016: 31). As Kjeld van Wieringen and myself elaborate elsewhere (van Wieringen and Zajontz 2023), the Chinese government for its part has started to subscribe to the dominant neoliberal discourse around PPPs and has, since the second half of the 2010s, actively promoted PPPs as a supposedly debtless alternative to sovereign loans and encouraged Chinese firms to invest in infrastructure PPPs across Africa.

Zambia has a long history of privatising state assets across all sectors of the economy as a result of IFI-sponsored structural adjustment programmes. The World Bank-orchestrated privatisation of ZCCM between 1992 and 2000 constituted the single most important nail in the coffin of Zambia's statist political economy (see Craig 2001; Fraser 2010; Kragelund 2010; Larmer 2005; Lee 2014). In the 2000s, further efforts were undertaken to liberalise Zambia's economy as well as to attract FDI and foster PPPs. The establishment of the Zambian Development Agency (ZDA) in 2006 aimed at creating a governmental "one stop facility" with the mandate to "ensure, among other matters, client focus, dialogue with the private sector and [to] create confidence in public sector support for business" (GRZ 2006: 73). The PPP Act of 2009, in turn, intends

> to promote and facilitate the implementation of privately financed infrastructure projects and effective delivery of social services by enhancing transparency, fairness and long term sustainability and removing undesirable restrictions on private sector participation in the provision of social sector services and the development and operation of public infrastructure. (GRZ 2009: 79)

Despite such legislation, Zambia's privatisation agenda stalled towards the end of the 2000s and was rolled back in some cases against the background of a changing political *Zeitgeist*. Late President Sata's populist-nationalist presidential campaigns were marked by a counter-hegemonic discourse that was decidedly critical of privatisations and of foreign, not least Chinese, investment in key sectors of the economy, promising a "Zambia for Zambians" (Kopinski and Polus 2011: 188; see Hampwaye and Kragelund 2013; Lee 2014). By bringing Zamtel, a telecommunications firm, and Zambia Railways back into state ownership, the PF under Sata, a former labour union executive, tried to roll back the privatisation agenda. Sata's economic policies signified a "re-inscription of African nationalism" (Carmody and Kragelund 2016:13; see Lee 2014). Larmer (2011: 262) argues that Sata's rise to power "was the clearest sign of a renewed political discourse of national developmentalism that transgressed party boundaries and suggested an emerging political consensus that the worst results of neo-liberalism needed to be reversed". As a result, both the ZDA and the PPP Act were largely sidelined in economic policy-making during Sata's presidency. Besides these domestic political developments, PPPs suffered a slump globally in the wake of the 2008 global financial crisis (Hildyard 2016: 31).

But not only did Zambia's PPP agenda stall due to Sata's statist developmentalism, Zambian scholars have also criticised the lack of "specific project strategies and expected results from the PPP process" and the "absence of adequate technical expertise" within the relevant government agencies (Ngoma et al. 2014: 19). In a policy brief from January 2014, the ZDA admitted that, since the passing of the PPP Act in 2009, "only one concession agreement" had been initiated under its provision, namely in the tourism sector (ZDA 2014: 4). Echoing neoliberal discourses, the ZDA argued the case for PPPs to help to close "Zambia's Infrastructure Funding Gap" which, drawing on World Bank data, it estimated at $500m per year for the years 2006–2015 (ZDA 2014: 4). As one of the benefits of PPPs the ZDA lists that they

> will enable government to accelerate the development of infrastructure by tapping into the private sector's financial resources, as well as its skills in designing, building, and operating infrastructure on a whole life-cycle cost basis. Because PPPs are financed by the private sector and Government pays for the facility over the life of the project, PPPs enable Government to have

> access to the infrastructure facility while paying for it. The public therefore benefits from *faster implementation of infrastructure projects* because *Government would not have to wait until it can afford the construction of the facility to address the matter*. (ZDA 2014: 11; italics added).

Project finance through PPPs is portrayed here as the solution to the dilemma of addressing projected infrastructure needs in times of constrained public budgets. Onerous infrastructure financing is simply "outsourced" to the private sector, whereas the public enjoys prompt access to infrastructures—so the neoliberal theory at least. As Hall (2015: 7) points out, PPP models that involve project finance can be seen as "an accounting trick, a way round the government's own constraints on public borrowing. This remains the overwhelming attraction for governments and international institutions". A statement by a ZDA official confirms the attraction that private project finance has wielded in Lusaka:

> We have now got the PPP initiative [PPP Act of 2009] which basically is one area, one instrument we're using to sort of attract investors to sort of look at our infrastructure needs in the country. Rail infrastructure is in a deplorable state, road infrastructure we have done a lot of work, we've done a lot of borrowing, we've gotten into it. But we still need more resources and the private sector, we feel, will provide those resources. (Interview Banda)

As sovereign borrowing was becoming increasingly costly for Lusaka in the second half of the 2010s, both economically and politically, PPPs re-entered Zambian policy-making as a panacea. The PF-led government shed previous scepticism about the privatisation of commons and, henceforth, saw in PPPs a possibility to continue to pursue its "development-through-infrastructure" strategy. In the 7th National Development Plan 2017–21, the government committed to "continue to develop tolls and collect road user charges to finance its programmes in the road sub-sector as well as pursuing PPPs as a financing mechanism for road construction" (GRZ 2017: Paragraph 7.9.3). Then Finance Minister Mwanakatwe underscored this shift towards infrastructure PPPs by emphasising that Zambia's PPP Act was amended in July 2018 in order to "strengthen the implementation of public–private sector development financing models in meeting the country's needs for public goods and services" (Ministry of Finance 2019b). Privatising infrastructure development was now portrayed as a fiscally sustainable alternative to attain the country's perceived "infrastructural needs"—very much in line with globally dominant development financing discourses and Chinese narratives promoting overseas PPPs that had emerged at around the same time (see van Wieringen and Zajontz 2023).

The described shift within the Zambian infrastructure state has had implications for the Chinese infrastructural fix, as it currently unfolds in Zambia. By no means, it has implied the end of the "fix". Project finance PPPs provide new opportunities for Chinese capital to invest in projects with long gestation times. Hence, in theoretical terms, the "temporal fix" comes in a new guise. Infrastructure PPPs simultaneously uphold demand for Chinese construction firms that are widely mobilised across Zambia and other African markets. Alden and Jiang observe

> a new trend among Chinese companies that are involved in the infrastructure and power sectors (where the majority of African sovereign debts to China are located) [which] is to change their role from *contractors* on the previously dominant EPC model to *operators* and *investors* on the BOT/BOOT model. (2019: 647–48, original italics)

Reminiscent of the organic relationship between spatio-temporal fixes and accumulation by dispossession (Harvey 2003: 141–42; see also Shivji 2009: 34), privatising public infrastructure sets free new assets for Chinese surplus capital. Zambian road PPPs are increasingly integrated into Chinese accumulation strategies and serve as outlets for equity investment. In his study aptly headlined *Licensed Larceny*, Hildyard shows that PPPs are lucrative means for "financial extraction". In 2014, annual returns of toll roads in developing countries ranged between 8 and 26 per cent (Hildyard 2016: 48–49). Hildyard (2016: 32) further emphasises that "such extraction is not just normalised but encouraged, even at the expense of some of the poorest people in the world". Generally secured by an entire series of state-backed guarantees, PPPs as a governance modality have transformed infrastructure into an "asset class capable of providing yield-hungry investors with the returns that they seek" (Hildyard 2016: 31). Consequently, PPPs incur significant financial liabilities and risks for public authorities, as discussed in the following.

Accumulating by dispossessing Zambian roads

As a reaction to Zambia's deteriorating financial situation (see Fig. 5.1), the Zambian government, as of the mid-2010s, started to consider PPPs as an alternative to loan-financed infrastructure. This policy shift concurred with Beijing's own efforts to restrain lending which had become increasingly economically risky and politically costly following allegations about China's supposed "debt trap" diplomacy in the context of the BRI (see Bräutigam 2020). Since 2016, Chinese government agencies have actively promoted PPPs as financially sustainable alternatives for infrastructure financing in Africa, fostering a gradual and pragmatic shift in the financial governance of the BRI (van Wieringen and Zajontz 2023).

In Zambia's road sector, the most frequently used form of project finance arrangements has been Engineering-Procurement-Construction + Finance (EPC+F) contracts. EPC+F contracts fall under the rubric of "Private Finance Initiatives" or what Yescombe and Farquharson (2018:17) call "availability PPPs".[3] Zambia's RDA labels EPC+F contracts as contractor facilitated initiatives (CFIs). One RDA official explicated the advantage of CFIs as follows:

> So basically, it's *some form of a loan*. However, what happens is that, of course, we are again trying to tap into the expertise of the private sector. They are able to identify and find cheap financing. So, what we do in the CFI is: The contractor, because for some reason the government may not be able to pay the money upfront. We allow the contractor to mobilize financing at competitive rates and then government reimburses through agreed terms. So, *it's basically a way of being able to do more projects, but we defer the payment, because government cannot pay for all the projects*

[3] In political and popular parlance, EPC+F contracts are typically not considered PPPs, as the latter are commonly reduced to contracts that entail operating concessions. Indeed, classical EPC contracts are agreements typical for the Design-Bid-Build (or Build-Transfer) model of public-sector procurement, according to which the public authority is solely responsible for funding the project (Yescombe and Farquharson 2018: 18; see Deloitte 2006: 5; Pratap and Chakrabarti 2017: 129). EPC contracts are therefore confined to the design and construction of infrastructure and thus generally short-term contractual arrangements that foresee neither transfer of ownership and/or management nor project financing through the private contractor. In contrast, in EPC+F arrangements project finance is subject matter of the contract. Consequently, EPC+F contracts establish long-term financial contractual obligations between public authorities and private investors. It is their "project finance" element which justifies to subsume them under the PPP label (Yescombe and Farquharson 2018: 14–15).

immediately. So, we say we are budgeting for them subsequently, but we need the road today. So, the contractor mobilizes financing, then we pay the contractor. (Interview RDA official)

The statement reveals that project finance PPPs have been considered a means to sustain high levels of road development despite serious budgetary constraints and waning debt sustainability. Yet implicitly, it also points to financial risks for governments that flow from long-term repayment obligations. Hildyard (2016: 39) warns of "burgeoning off-balance-sheet liabilities that countries have incurred through PPPs, storing up debt crises for future generations". By 2017, CFIs made up 35 per cent of the Zambian road budget, and, by 2019, the Zambian government had signed CFIs worth $900 million with eight Chinese companies, most of which were ultimately cancelled due to fiscal pressures (Brautigam 2022: 1356). The upgrade of the trunk road between Lusaka and Ndola in Zambia's Copper Belt into a dual carriageway became a highly controversial case of a CFI, which I discuss in Chapter 7 in detail.

Besides CFIs, Lusaka also tendered key segments of Zambia's trunk road network as concession-based PPPs (see RDA 2015, 2016a).[4] The PPP scheme that was advertised in 2015 and 2016 was a comprehensive variant of a Build-Operate-Transfer (BOT) arrangement and encompassed project financing, design, construction to dual carriageway, operation, maintenance and tolling of the selected roads (FDCOMT). According to a ZDA official, in June 2019, three of the six trunk road projects tendered in 2016 had reached an advanced stage of negotiations with "preferred bidders". First, the T5 segment between Chingola and Solwezi in Zambia's so-called New Copper Belt in North-Western Province was negotiated with Bert Motors Zambia Limited. Second, contract negotiations were ongoing in February 2020 with the Zambian-owned company Zamtoll Management Limited for the T3 segment between Chingola and Kasumbalesa, the main road link between the Zambian and the Congolese

[4] The RDA's 2016 request for proposals included the following roads: (1) Lusaka to Ndola (T2/T3), approximately 321 km, including Kafulafuta to Luanshya Town (M6), approximately 45 km; (2) Ndola to Kasumbalesa Border (T3), approximately 150 km; (3) Kazungula via Livingstone to Turnpike (M10/T1) approximately 488 km (including a potential Livingstone Town Bypass road from Kazungula); (4) Chirundu Border to Chilanga in Lusaka (T2), approximately 124 km; (5) Chingola to Mutanda via Solwezi (T5), approximately 205 km; (6) Kapiri Mposhi to Nakonde (T2), approximately 855 km. (RDA 2016a).

parts of the Copper Belt (Personal electronic communications with RDA official, June 2019 and February 2020). Neither Zamtoll nor Bert Motors had been registered contractors with the NCC in 2019 (see NCC 2019), which suggested that the actual construction works would be subcontracted if negotiations were successful. In both cases, financing facilities were expected to be arranged by the contractor (Personal electronic communication with RDA official, June 2019).

Preferred bidder for a third project, the upgrade of the T2 between Chilanga and Chirundu along the road corridor to Beira, was China Railway Seventh Group. The Chinese SOE intended to provide 25 per cent of the contract sum as equity investment, while the remaining 75 per cent were to be raised through a loan towards a Special Purpose Vehicle (SPV) that was envisaged (Personal electronic communication with RDA official, June 2019). Although, at the time of writing in June 2023, a PPP for the Chilanga-Chirundu was still not concluded, China Railway Seventh Group's initial interest in investing in the project indicates that road projects (in Zambia) no longer only create welcome demand for Chinese construction companies and suppliers but also serve as asset class for Chinese surplus capital. Operating the road between Chilanga, south of Lusaka, and Chirundu at Zambia's border with Zimbabwe, can be expected to potentially yield high returns, considering that the Beira corridor constitutes the shortest road link from Lusaka to the Indian Ocean.

The upgrade of the Chingola-Solwezi-Mutanda road was eventually awarded as a Design-Finance-Build-Operate-Transfer (DFBOT) PPP, with a concession duration of 30 years, in May 2021 to Bert Pave and Maintenance Limited, a SPV set up to implement the project (Bert Pave and Maintenance n.d.). PF veteran politician Given Lubinda used the PPP agreement for campaign purposes when, in June 2021, he stated that "I can assure the people of North [W]estern province that before the end of this year, the project is commencing because President Edgar Lungu has already authorized to have the road worked on under the Public Private Partnership (PPP) arrangement" (quoted in Mapapayi 2021). The statement underlines that infrastructure development, especially roads, have remained central to Zambian electoral politics (see Brautigam 2022). Amidst Zambia's sovereign debt crisis, Zambia's infrastructure state and those with access to state powers did not abandon the "development-through-infrastructure" strategy but rather altered its institutional forms—from sovereign debt to private project finance. In June

2023, the concessionaire was still busy mobilising equipment and had not yet set up camp along the road (ZNBC 2023). It seems likely that the firm will draw on subcontractors, potentially Chinese firms, to do the actual construction. What becomes apparent is that the government, by privatisating the financing, rehabilitation and maintenance of roads, has created new rents for both domestic and foreign capital alike.

In the case of the Chingola-Kasumbalesa road, negotiations between RDA and the preferred bidder Zamtoll had not concluded when the PF was voted out of power in August 2021. Instead, the United Party for National Development (UPND) government announced, in late 2022, that a DFBOT PPP was entered with the Chinese-financed Turbo-Ka-Chin Investment Consortium to upgrade the chronically congested Chingola-Kasumbalesa road which links Zambia with the DRC (Lusaka Times 2022). At the signing ceremony, Infrastructure, Housing, and Urban Development Minister, Charles Miliupi, remarkably one of four cabinet ministers attending the signing ceremony, emphasised the new government's intention to increasingly draw on road PPPs:

> The new government plans to build or repair these high-traffic roads using the public-private partnership financing model. This is in a bid to get around the challenges caused by hindered financial resources and reduce related financial pressure. [...] The private sector will therefore work with the government by investing in public infrastructure and receiving compensation in the form of toll fees for a given period of time. Carrying out sustainable public-private partnership projects for better infrastructure development and service delivery would be improved by this financing model. (quoted in Wanjala 2022)

In April 2023, President Hichilema instructed the main contractor constructing the Chingola-Kasumbalesa road, AVIC International, to deliver high-quality work (Muswala 2023). The self-declared "New Dawn government" under Hichilema's leadership has concluded a second major road PPP with a Chinese investment consortium, namely for the Lusaka-Ndola dual carriageway. This project had caused major controversies under the previous government, as I discuss in Chapter 7. In March 2023, Lusaka announced that a PPP with a project volume of $650 million and a concession period of 25 years had been agreed with Macro Ocean Investment Consortium, which consists of AVIC International Project

Engineering, Zhenjiang Communications Construction Group and China Railway Seventh Group (Nyabiage 2023).

Long-term concession-based project finance arrangements like the ones discussed are emblematic of the global trend of "development of infrastructure-as-asset-class" whereby traditional forms of infrastructure finance, notably multilateral and bilateral loans, are increasingly substituted by a "push for Public–Private Partnerships [...] to provide both an enticement to private investors and the foundation stone on which other extractive forms of finance can be built" (Hildyard 2016: 83). To exploit economic opportunities arising from the privatisation of infrastructure development, Chinese investors have complemented their accumulation strategies towards equity investment in African infrastructure markets (Alden and Jiang 2019; Gonzalez-Vicente 2019; van Wieringen and Zajontz 2023). Both Chinese SOEs and financial institutions have proven adaptive to the change in the financial governance of road development in Zambia. By means of fixed availability payments or toll-sharing agreements, PPPs provide more secure means to guarantee revenues for Chinese investors, not least in highly indebted countries like Zambia. Project finance PPPs come with a "security" for Chinese contractors, as payments occur directly between project firms, usually SPVs, or Chinese banks and contractors. By implication, contractors are independent of the solvency of African governments. Chinese contractors, such as AVIC, Henan and China Jiangxi Corporation for International Economic and Technical Cooperation (CJIC), repeatedly experienced delayed payments or non-payment by the Zambian government (Daily Star 2019; Lusaka Times 2018b; Phiri 2019). The problem had become so widespread that, in early-2019, a delegation from China Exim Bank reportedly engaged the Zambian government on the issue of overdue payments to Chinese contractors (Africa Confidential 2019b: 10). The incremental privatisation of the country's road infrastructure seems to be an unavoidable consequence of an unsustainable debt-financed road bonanza. It has been paralleled by an acceleration in the roll-out of the "user pays principle", i.e. road tolling.

The Commodification of Zambia's Roads

Zambia's ambitious road development agenda has been paralleled by the introduction of road tolling along Zambian trunk roads. The National Road Tolling Programme was formally introduced by the Tolls Act No.

14 of 2011. Statutory Instrument No. 73 of 2013 specified the toll points as well as the fee structure. The Tolls Act stipulates toll collection for foreign-registered vehicles at 37 border post, whereas drivers of Zambian vehicles are required to pay tolls at 26 inland toll gates (GRZ 2013).[5] The implementation of the Tolls Act has remained long in the coming, one reason for this being the initial scepticism of the PF-led government towards the user-pays principle and, more generally, the legacy of the ruling party's developmentalist, read statist, agenda under late President Sata. The latter in 2006, 2008 and 2011 consistently campaigned under the campaign slogan "lower taxes, more jobs, and more money in your pockets" (Resnick 2017: 113).

Yet, mounting fiscal pressures arising from rising debt financing costs for infrastructure development have accelerated the roll-out of tolling infrastructure across the country. As Tembo (2015: 42) argues, "[t]he actualization of the Tolls Act No. 14 of 2011 came, of course, against the backdrop of a huge infrastructure funding gap identified in the 2014 national budget". The government intended to have all 26 toll gates operative by the end of 2019 (Personal communication with anonymised RDA official, June 2019). In January 2021, 27 inland toll points and 10 toll points at ports of entry were operational. The National Road Fund Agency, which is in charge of the roll-out of the tolling programme, plans to "expand the Road Tolling footprint to 40 Toll Stations across the country of different types according to Traffic Volumes" (NRFA n.d.-b). The toll structure for inland vehicles was initially stipulated in Statutory Instrument 73/2013 but, with effect from 1 January 2017, the rates were doubled by means of Statutory Instrument 85/2016 (for the current toll structure, see Table A.3). In reaction to public pressure, the latter also introduced discounted toll rates for local users who are domiciled within a ten kilometre radius of a particular toll gate (GRZ 2016).

The PF-led government portrayed road tolling as a fiscal necessity to meet costs related to road maintenance and development. At the RDA booth at the 2017 Ndola International Trade Fair, the agency promoted the introduction of "the road user pay principle as an innovative and self-financing mechanism for sustainable road rehabilitation and maintenance" (Field notes). Critique has come from both civil society actors and the parliamentary opposition, one contentious aspect being the

[5] The toll point in Mumbwa was added by Statutory Instrument No. 85 of 2016, which brought the total of inland toll points to 27.

lack of accountability and transparency with regard to tolling revenues. Isaac Mwaipopo from the non-governmental Centre for Trade Policy and Development (CTPD) stated:

> Because the whole idea of setting up things like a toll gate from our understanding is that the government wants to create another avenue through which it can collect some money or resources and those resources are to be ploughed back to maintain the same roads. Those resources have to be ploughed back to construct new roads. But is that how it is being used? This far we do not know. (Interview Mwaipopo)

A Member of Parliament from the then oppositional UPND equally raised concerns about the usage of toll revenues and suggested that tolling revenues might be used to plug budgetary holes:

> It is one thing to collect revenue, it's another to convert that revenue into infrastructure development [...] Right now, there is speculation that that money is going into the general account for government called Control 99, with the bulk of everything else that is being collected. That's poor accountability, if that assertion is true. Money that is being collected from the toll gates should have a specific account with a proper audit trail. If it's meant for the roads, it should stick to the roads. (Interview Kakubo)

Indeed, toll revenues have become an increasingly important stream of income for the government, considering the latter's limited fiscal space. According to the National Road Fund Agency, ZMK 926m were collected in 2018 and ZMK 1.2bn in 2019 (Lusaka Times 2020).[6] The Zambia Institute for Policy Analysis and Research reported even higher revenues for 2018, namely ZMK 1.6bn. To put these numbers into relation, Zambia's proposed budget for 2020 aggregated ZMK 106bn (ZIPAR 2019: 4, 2). Between 2016 and 2021, the government collected Kwacha 6.3bn in tolls (Daily Mail 2022).

The introduction of the user-pays principle as a means to finance road construction and maintenance has prompted broader controversies related to the distribution of costs and benefits in relation to the commodification of commons. Some of the costs for Zambia's expansionary borrowing for infrastructure are now being shifted towards road

[6] In February 2020, this was equivalent to about $63m and $82m respectively.

users, with highly uneven impact. Then opposition Member of Parliament Stanley Kakubo criticised the uneven socio-economic impact the introduction of tolling has had on the Zambian population:

> The mines have been having a field day in this country for a long time. […] The mines need to be taxed heavily in terms of transport. They are the biggest users of our roads. The vast majority of the heavy goods that are being carried are not being produced by Zambians, it's the mines. […] Are they paying enough? Or are the Zambians again, in inverted commas, subsidising the mines on the toll gates? […] So, you find the grandmother in my village who tries to come to Lusaka will pay more. She has no choice. […] Already Zambians are paying a lot and I said this again in parliament […]. There is road tax being paid already, apart from the toll fees […]. Yes, it's the same pocket that is paying out. So, if it is a solution to gain government revenue, it should be specific to a specific sector that can be held hugely responsible for the tear and damage that you see on the Zambian roads. Yeah, that's how it ought to be. (Interview Kakubo)

Besides creating revenues for covering road-related expenses, tolling has become an important aspect in the negotiations of road development PPPs. Whereas, thus far, the tolling system has been administered by the RDA and the National Road Fund Agency (Tembo 2015: 43), the road PPPs tendered by the government in 2016 foresaw operational concessions that included the tolling of the roads. The legal basis for this move is given, since the Tolls Act explicitly "provides for private sector participation in the tolling of roads" (GRZ 2011: 195). Yet, one interviewee described it as "politically undesirable to ask these people [foreign concessionaires]" to operate and toll the road (Interview senior official Zambian MTC). Potential political costs of having foreign corporations operating, maintaining and possibly tolling Zambian roads appear not least relevant in PPPs with Chinese participation, considering the persistence of anti-Chinese sentiments in the Zambian population (see Leslie 2016; Negi 2008; Sautman and Hairong 2015).

Economically, future tolling revenues will be decisive as to how "beneficial" road PPPs will be for the Zambian government. Hall (2015: 33) cautions that "[r]oad traffic forecasts for toll road PPPs are systematically exaggerated everywhere". Indeed, the "usage risk" in the context of PPPs that entail operational concessions usually remains with the concessionaire (Yescombe and Farquharson 2018: 20). However, investors usually diminish this risk significantly by insisting on a number of state-backed guarantees, such as guaranteed minimum income streams, minimum service charge payments and guarantees of compensation if legislation should affect their returns adversely (Hildyard 2016: 32). Considering Zambia's limited traffic volumes, even along the country's trunk roads, investors are likely to demand state-backed guarantees in order to ensure profitability of their investments in road PPPs. In 2011, a government-commissioned study on the feasibility of tolling established "the broad rule of thumb that about 15,000 veh/day is required for conventional concession to cover full cost, 6,500 veh/day to cover rehabilitation, operation and maintenance costs, and 3,500 veh/day to cover operation and maintenance costs only" (cited in Tembo 2015: 44). According to the 2013 Toll Revenue Projections Report, compiled by the RDA, the country's busiest road, the T3 segment between Chingola and Kitwe, only carried 7,790 vehicles per day in both directions (Tembo 2015: 43). The fact that the Zambian government has embarked on major programmes to move cargo traffic from the road to the rail adds additional uncertainty on future traffic volumes and thus on the "success" of road PPPs.

Conclusion

This chapter explained the Sino-Zambian "road bonanza" as a conjuncture of the state strategy of debt-financed infrastructure development, initiated under late President Sata and accelerated under President Lungu, on the one hand and China's keen interest in loan-debt investments in Zambia's road sector on the other hand. In line with Harvey's reasoning that spatio-temporal fixes materialise particularly well under conditions of uneven geographical development (Harvey 2004: 67), Zambia's dependence on foreign capital for its ambitious road programmes has been readily met by Chinese excess capital. Thereby, as discussed in this chapter, the characteristics of Chinese loan financing have ensured that Chinese capital remains in China-centred circuits of accumulation. The absence of open tendering as well as opaque and informal negotiations between Chinese SOBs and contractors and Zambian officials have furthermore accelerated procurements, curtailed project appraisals and driven up project costs. The Sino-Zambian "road bonanza" has contributed to rapidly increasing, meanwhile unsustainable, sovereign debt levels. Zambian state agency is now heavily curtailed by structural constraints emanating from its debt obligations vis-à-vis a diverse set of creditors and by austerity measures that naturally follow sovereign debt crises (see Bagwandeen et al. 2023; Brautigam 2022; Zajontz 2022a).

There have been readjustments in the (financial) governance of road development in Zambia as a result of the country's indebtedness. Zambia's deteriorating financial situation, alongside the devaluation of its currency and credit rating downgrades, imposed major structural constraints to the continuation of the infrastructure development agenda pursued by the PF-led government, as further debt financing had become politically and economically increasingly costly. As a result, the Zambian administration pursued a strategic shift from public debt finance to private project finance, in order to be able to uphold high levels of infrastructure development in spite of the country's rapid fiscal decline. Yet, project finance PPPs have incurred significant long-term financial liabilities and risks and the introduction of road tolling, accelerated by deteriorating public finances, has had highly unequal socio-economic effects.

For the Chinese infrastructural fix, the nascent privatisation of Zambian roads heralds a new era. The current realignment in the financial governance of Zambia's road sector implies that the "temporal fix" comes in a new guise. I established that Chinese SOEs and SOBs have proven favourable towards the change in governance "methodology", particularly as PPPs promise to be more secure investments for Chinese companies. The Chinese interest in PPPs reveals new temporal horizons on the part of Chinese SOEs in Zambia's road sector. Zambian road PPPs provide for long-term investments and for possible outlets for equity investment. These recent developments in the Zambian road sector are reflective of the general trend among Chinese construction companies to engage in projects on longer terms as investors and operators (Alden and Jiang 2019: 647–48; see Zhang 2023). In fact, debt sustainability concerns in a number of countries that heavily borrowed from Chinese banks have resulted in Chinese efforts to meta-govern the financial governance of the BRI by actively promoting supposedly "debtless" alternatives to fund infrastructure in the form of PPPs (van Wieringen and Zajontz 2023).

The present chapter allows for valuable conclusions about the degree of African state agency in the manifestation of the Chinese infrastructural fix. It has become evident that the Chinese infrastructural fix in Zambia has been fostered by the government's det-financed "development-through-infrastructure" strategy. Yet, this strategy became financially unsustainable and politically costly, as both domestic political forces and external actors, such as the IMF and rating agencies, started to exert pressure on the

PF-led government to avoid further debt accumulation. While Zambia's sovereign debt, which amounted to $13bn in 2023, certainly constitutes a structural constraint that limits the government's strategic scope in developing infrastructure, it has not inhibited, yet altered, the concrete manifestation of the infrastructural fix. Very much in line with Harvey's theory, the "fix" is sustained by the gradual transition in the dominant form of accumulation—from expanded reproduction to forms of accumulation by dispossession (see Harvey 2003: 139, 149–53, 2004: 64, 76). Again, this transition is dependent on structurally oriented strategic action of Zambian state actors, who, in the light of fiscal constraints, have started to orchestrate accumulation by dispossession by expediting the commodification and privatisation of Zambian roads. As shown in this chapter, this trend has continued under the UPND-led government. It is likely to accelerate, as Zambia's debt restructuring agreements with its creditors and the IMF under the Common Framework are likely to clearly restrict public spending (on infrastructure), thus expediting new rounds of privatisation. The Sino-Zambian "road bonanza" has entered its next stage.

List of Interviews

Banda, Robert, manager infrastructure development, Zambia Development Agency (ZDA), Lusaka, Zambia, 7 June 2017.

Kakubo, Stanley Kasongo, Member of Parliament, National Assembly of Zambia, United Party for National Development (UPND), Lusaka, Zambia, 4 August 2017.

Musonda, Christopher, managing director, Zambia Railways Ltd. (ZRL), Kabwe, Zambia, 8 August 2017.

Mwaipopo, Isaac, executive director, Centre for Trade Policy and Development (CTPD), Lusaka, Zambia, 12 July 2017. Official, Road Development Agency (RDA) (anonymised), Lusaka, Zambia, 2 August 2017.

Senior official, Zambian Ministry of Transport and Communication (MTC) (anonymised), Lusaka, Zambia, 14 June 2017.

References

AidData. n.d. "CDB Loans $179.5 Million USD for Mansa-Luwingu Road." AidData. Retrieved May 25, 2019 (https://china.aiddata.org/projects/30719).

Africa Confidential. 2018a. “A Swirling Fog of Debt.” *Africa Confidential* 59(10):8–9.

Africa Confidential. 2018b. “Bonds, Bills and Ever Bigger Debts.” *Africa Confidential* 59(18).

Africa Confidential. 2019a. “Little Cash, No Credit.” *Africa Confidential* 60(11):8–9.

Africa Confidential. 2019b. “Treasury in the Red.” *Africa Confidential* 60(9):9–10.

Alden, Chris, and Lu Jiang. 2019. “Brave New World: Debt, Industrialization and Security in China–Africa Relations.” *International Affairs* 95(3):641–57. https://doi.org/10.1093/ia/iiz083.

Auditor General. n.d. *Report of the Auditor General on the Road Projects under the Road Development Agency (RDA) for the Period January 2012 to December 2015*. Lusaka: Office of the Auditor General.

Bach, Daniel C. 2016. “Cross-Border Interactions and Regionalism.” Pp. 71–88 in *Region-building in Africa: Political and Economic Challenges*, edited by D. H. Levine and D. Nagar. Basingstoke: Palgrave Macmillan.

Bagwandeen, Mandira, Christopher Edyegu, and Oscar M. Otele. 2023. “African Agency, COVID-19 and Debt Renegotiations with China.” *South African Journal of International Affairs* 30(1):1–27. https://doi.org/10.1080/10220461.2023.2180083.

Bert Pave and Maintenance. n.d. “About Us.” Retrieved July 11, 2023 (https://bertpave.com/about-us/).

Biau, Carole, Karim Dahou, and Toru Homma. 2008. “How to Increase Sound Private Investment in Africa’s Road Infrastructure: Building on Country Successes and OECD Policy Tools.” Proceedings from the Expert Roundtable Investment in Transport Infrastructure, 11 December 2008, NEPAD-OECD Africa Investment Initiative.

Brautigam, Deborah. 2019. “Is China the World’s Loan Shark?” *The New York Times*. Retrieved August 13, 2019 (https://www.nytimes.com/2019/04/26/opinion/china-belt-road-initiative.html).

Bräutigam, Deborah. 2020. “A Critical Look at Chinese ‘Debt-Trap Diplomacy’: The Rise of a Meme.” *Area Development and Policy* 5(1):1–14. https://doi.org/10.1080/23792949.2019.1689828.

Brautigam, Deborah. 2021. *How Zambia and China Co-Created a Debt “Tragedy of the Commons.”* China-Africa Research Initiative Working Paper 51. Washington: Johns Hopkins University.

Brautigam, Deborah. 2022. “China and Zambia: Creating a Sovereign Debt Crisis.” *International Affairs* 98(4):1347–65. https://doi.org/10.1093/ia/iiac109.

Carmody, Pádraig, and Peter Kragelund. 2016. "Who Is in Charge? State Power and Agency in Sino-African Relations." *Cornell International Law Journal* 49(1):1–24. https://doi.org/10.1038/nmeth.2841.

Cheelo, Caesar, and Robert Liebenthal. 2018. *The Role of the Construction Sector in Influencing Natural Resource Use, Structural Change, and Industrial Development in Zambia*. WIDER Working Paper 2018/172. Helsinki: UNU WIDER.

Corkin, Lucy. 2012. "Chinese Construction Companies in Angola: A Local Linkages Perspective." *Resources Policy* 37(4):475–83. https://doi.org/10.1016/j.resourpol.2012.06.002.

Corkin, Lucy. 2013. *Uncovering African Agency: Angola's Management of China's Credit Lines*. Farnham: Ashgate.

Craig, John. 2001. "Putting Privatisation into Practice: The Case of Zambia Consolidated Copper Mines Limited." *The Journal of Modern African Studies* 39(3):389–410. https://doi.org/10.1017/s0022278x01003652.

Daily Mail. 2022. "Use Road Tolls for Roads." *Daily Mail*. Retrieved July 12, 2023 (http://www.daily-mail.co.zm/use-road-tolls-for-roads/).

Daily Star. 2019. "Avic, China Henan Abandon Works Over Non Payment." *Daily Star*. Retrieved May 31, 2019 (https://www.dailystar.news/Articles/Index/50?articleType=TodaysNewsArticle&fbclid=IwAR3dEitkeDg9jP4nl5rsVoQ7-xNqfuGyAT5TUhCHTN7GOM_41_Zkh7UlZEE).

Deloitte. 2006. "Closing the Infrastructure Gap: The Role of Public-Private Partnerships." *Deloitte*. Retrieved May 15, 2019 (https://www2.deloitte.com/content/dam/Deloitte/ie/Documents/Finance/CorporateFinance/2006_closing_infrastructure_gap_deloitte_ireland.pdf).

DiCarlo, Jessica, and Seth Schindler. 2022. "Introduction: Geopolitics, Infrastructure, and the Emergent Geographies of US-China Competition." Pp. 1–10 in *The Rise of the Infrastructure State: How US-China Rivalry Shapes Politics and Place Worldwide*, edited by S. Schindler and J. DiCarlo. Bristol: Bristol University Press.

Edinger, Hannah, and Jean-Pierre Labuschagne. 2019. "If You Want to Prosper, Consider Building Roads: China's Role in African Infrastructure and Capital Projects." *Deloitte Insights*. Retrieved July 2, 2019 (https://www2.deloitte.com/insights/us/en/industry/public-sector/china-investment-africa-infrastructure-development.html).

Fraser, Alastair. 2010. "Introduction: Boom and Bust on the Zambian Copperbelt." Pp. 1–30 in *Zambia, Mining, and Neoliberalism: Boom and Bust on the Globalized Copperbelt*, edited by A. Fraser and M. Larmer. New York: Palgrave Macmillan.

Fraser, Alastair. 2017. "Post-Populism in Zambia: Michael Sata's Rise, Demise and Legacy." *International Political Science Review* 38(4):456–72. https://doi.org/10.1177/0192512117720809.

Gonzalez-Vicente, Ruben. 2019. "Make Development Great Again? Accumulation Regimes, Spaces of Sovereign Exception and the Elite Development Paradigm of China's Belt and Road Initiative." *Business and Politics* 21(4):487–513. https://doi.org/10.1017/bap.2019.20.

GRZ. 2006. *The Zambia Development Agency Act: No. 11 of 2006*. Lusaka: National Assembly of Zambia.

GRZ. 2009. *The Public-Private Partnership Act: No. 14 of 2009*. Lusaka: National Assembly of Zambia.

GRZ. 2011. *The Tolls Act: No. 14 of 2011*. Lusaka: National Assembly of Zambia.

GRZ. 2013. "Statutory Instrument No. 73 of 2013." *Government Gazette*, August 9, 605–10.

GRZ. 2016. "Statutory Instrument No. 85 of 2016." *Government Gazette*, November 11, 927–34.

GRZ. 2017. *The Seventh National Development Plan 2017–2021*. Lusaka: Ministry of National Development Planning.

Hall, David. 2015. *Why Public-Private Partnerships Don't Work: The Many Advantages of the Public Alternative*. Greenwich: Public Services International Research Unit.

Hampwaye, Godfrey, and Peter Kragelund. 2013. "Trends in Sino-Zambian Relations." Pp. 27–40 in *China's Diplomacy in Eastern and Southern Africa*, edited by S. Adem. Farnham: Ashgate.

Harvey, David. 2003. *The New Imperialism*. Oxford: Oxford University Press.

Harvey, David. 2004. "The 'New' Imperialism: Accumulation by Dispossession." *Socialist Register* 40:63–87.

Hildyard, Nicholas. 2016. *Licenced Larceny: Infrastructure, Financial Extraction and the Global South*. Manchester: Manchester University Press.

Hinfelaar, Marja, and Justine Sichone. 2019. *The Challenge of Sustaining a Professional Civil Service amidst Shifting Political Coalitions: The Case of the Ministry of Finance in Zambia, 1991–2018*. ESID Working Paper No. 122. Manchester: Effective States and Inclusive Development Research Centre.

IMF. 2019. "IMF Staff Completes 2019 Article IV Visit to Zambia." *International Monetary Fund*. Retrieved April 30, 2019 (https://www.imf.org/en/News/Articles/2019/04/30/pr19130-zambia-imf-staff-completes-2019-article-iv-visit?fbclid=IwAR0LLB3WYsWz4Yc404nUBaY4s942AmxPYbAnGmiF5S1N4ZPSge3nYVOEw9U).

Kopinski, Dominik, and Andrzej Polus. 2011. "Sino-Zambian Relations: 'An All-Weather Friendship' Weathering the Storm." *Journal of Contemporary African Studies* 29(2):181–92. https://doi.org/10.1080/02589001.2011.555193.

Kragelund, Peter. 2010. "The Price of 'Openness': Towards Chinese Economic Control in Zambia." Pp. 208–17 in *The Rise of China and India in Africa*, edited by F. Cheru and C. Obi. London: Zed Books.

Large, Daniel. 2021. *China and Africa: The New Era*. Cambridge: Policy Press.

Larmer, Miles. 2005. "Reaction & Resistance to Neo-Liberalism in Zambia." *Review of African Political Economy* 32(103):29–45. https://doi.org/10.1080/03056240500120992.

Larmer, Miles. 2011. *Rethinking African Politics: A History of Opposition in Zambia*. Surrey: Ashgate.

Lee, Ching Kwan. 2014. "The Spectre of Global China." *New Left Review* September(89):29–66.

Lee, Ching Kwan. 2017. *The Specter of Global China: Politics, Labor, and Foreign Investment in Africa*. Chicago: University of Chicago Press.

Leslie, Agnes Ngoma. 2016. "Zambia and China: Workers' Protest, Civil Society and the Role of Opposition Politics in Elevating State Engagement." *African Studies Quarterly* 16(3–4):89–106.

Lusaka Times. 2018a. "Kenneth Kaunda International Airport Will Not Be Surrendered to China-Dora Siliza." *Lusaka Times*. Retrieved July 25, 2019 (https://www.lusakatimes.com/2018/09/10/kenneth-kaunda-international-airport-will-not-be-surrendered-to-china-dora-siliya/).

Lusaka Times. 2018b. "Kitwe-Ndola Dual Carriageway Is Funded by the Zambian Government." *Lusaka Times*. Retrieved May 31, 2019 (https://www.lusakatimes.com/2018/06/24/kitwe-ndola-dual-carriageway-project-is-funded-by-the-zambian-government/).

Lusaka Times. 2019. "Zambia's Debt Continues Pilling Up as First Half Growth Shrinks." *Lusaka Times*. Retrieved July 17, 2019 (https://www.lusakatimes.com/2019/07/17/zambias-debt-continues-pilling-up-as-first-half-growth-shrinks/).

Lusaka Times. 2020. "National Road Fund Agency Collects K1.2 Billion in Toll Fees in 2019." *Lusaka Times*. Retrieved February 9, 2020 (https://www.lusakatimes.com/2020/02/08/262747/?fbclid=IwAR2s8S5I6KC5W1ldPdH27C_W7fQbPH9VTgznGsrtT810Wz_ImHXsOQyveio).

Lusaka Times. 2022. "Chingola-Kasumbalesa PPP Concession Agreement Inked." *Lusaka Times*. Retrieved July 11, 2023 (https://www.lusakatimes.com/2022/11/01/chingola-kasumbalesa-ppp-concession-agreement-inked/).

Mapapayi, Jackson. 2021. "US$250 Millian Road Deal Sealed." *Daily Nation*. Retrieved July 11, 2023 (https://dailynationzambia.com/2021/06/us250-million-road-deal-sealed/).

Ministry of Finance. 2018. *Annual Economic Report 2017*. Lusaka: Ministry of Finance.

Ministry of Finance. 2019a. *Annual Economic Report 2018*. Lusaka: Ministry of Finance.

Ministry of Finance. 2019b. *Highlights on the Performance of the Economy in 2018*. Lusaka: Ministry of Finance.

Mitimingi, Taonga Clifford, and Matthew Hill. 2020. "Zambia Wants to Forgo $5 Billion in Contracted External Debt." *Bloomberg*. Retrieved March 1, 2020 (https://www.bloomberg.com/news/articles/2020-02-12/zambia-plans-to-cut-undisbursed-external-debt-by-5-billion).

Mohan, Giles, and May Tan-Mullins. 2019. "The Geopolitics of South–South Infrastructure Development: Chinese-Financed Energy Projects in the Global South." *Urban Studies* 56(7):1368–85. https://doi.org/10.1177/0042098018794351.

Muswala, Tamara. 2023. "HH Demands Quality on Chingola-Kasumbalesa Road." *ZNBC*. Retrieved July 11, 2023 (https://www.znbc.co.zm/news/hh-demands-quality-on-chingola-kasumbalesa-road/).

National Assembly of Zambia. 2015. "Ministerial Statement on the Procurement of The Copperbelt 400 (C400) Road Rehabilitation Project in United States Dollars Currency." *National Assembly of Zambia*. Retrieved May 15, 2019 (http://www.parliament.gov.zm/sites/default/files/images/publication_docs/WorksandSupplyStatement.pdf).

NCC. 2019. "List of Contractors: Registrations as at 30 June 2018." *National Council for Construction*. Retrieved June 22, 2019 (http://www.ncc.org.zm/classified/contractors/).

Negi, Rohit. 2008. "Beyond the 'Chinese Scramble': The Political Economy of Anti-China Sentiment in Zambia." *African Geographical Review* 27(1):41–693. https://doi.org/10.1080/19376812.2008.9756209.

Ngoma, Sydney, Muya Mundia, and Chabota Kaliba. 2014. "Benefits, Constraints and Risks in Infrastructure Development via Public-Private Partnerships in Zambia." *Journal of Construction in Developing Countries* 19(1):15–33.

NRFA. n.d.-a. *National Road Fund Agency: Annual Report 2017*. Lusaka: National Road Fund Agency.

NRFA. n.d.-b. "NRTP (PHASE II)." Retrieved July 12, 2023 (https://nrfa.org.zm/nrtp-phase-ii/).

Nugent, Paul. 2018. "Africa's Re-Enchantment with Big Infrastructure: White Elephants Dancing in Virtuous Circles?" Pp. 22–40 in *Extractive Industries and Changing State Dynamics in Africa*, edited by J. Schubert, U. Engel, and M. Elisio. Abingdon: Routledge.

Nyabiage, Jevans. 2023. "Chinese Consortium to Build US$650 Million Toll Road in Cash-Strapped Zambia, but Will It Pay Off?" *South China Morning Post*. Retrieved July 12, 2023 (https://www.scmp.com/news/china/diplomacy/article/3213048/chinese-consortium-build-us650-million-toll-road-cash-strapped-zambia-will-it-pay).

Ofstad, Arve, and Elling Tjønneland. 2019. *Zambia's Looming Debt Crisis—Is China to Blame?* CMI Insight No. 1. Bergen: Chr. Michelsen Institute.

Osei-Kyei, Robert, and Albert P. C. Chan. 2016. "Developing Transport Infrastructure in Sub-Saharan Africa through Public–Private Partnerships: Policy Practice and Implications." *Transport Reviews* 36(2):170–86. https://doi.org/10.1080/01441647.2015.1077288.

Patriotic Front. 2011. *2011–2016 Manifesto*. Lusaka: Patriotic Front.

Phiri, Tobias. 2018. "African Govts Weak in Negotiations with China Because They Go Crawling to Beg—Mutati." *The Mast*. Retrieved July 17, 2019 (https://www.themastonline.com/2018/11/24/african-govts-weak-in-negotiations-with-china-because-they-go-crawling-to-beg-mutati/?fbclid=IwAR2mK4aUaTowwAMEhP0fpm071kiMFAZe-Rg6UaHyKRZiokZaaaUVhMD-nPg).

Phiri, Chris. 2019. "AVIC Partially Resumes Kitwe Road Works." *Zambia Reports*. Retrieved May 31, 2019 (https://zambiareports.com/2019/05/06/avic-partially-resumes-kitwe-road-works/).

Pratap, Kumar V., and Rajesh Chakrabarti. 2017. *Public-Private Partnerships in Infrastructure: Managing the Challenges*. Singapore: Springer Nature.

Raballand, Gaël, Kate Bridges, Monica Beuran, and Audrey Sacks. 2013. *Does the Semi-Autonomous Agency Model Function in a Low-Governance Environment? The Case of the Road Development Agency in Zambia*. Word Bank Policy Research Working Paper 6585. https://doi.org/10.1596/1813-9450-6585.

RDA. 2015. *Request for Expression of Interest for Public-Private Partnerships for the Financing, Design, Construction to Dual Carriageway, Operation, Maintenance and Tolling of Selected Roads in Zambia*. Lusaka: Road Development Agency.

RDA. 2016a. *Request for Proposals (RFP) for Public Private Partnerships for the Financing, Design, Construction to Dual Carriageway, Operation, Maintenance and Tolling of Selected Roads in Zambia*. Lusaka: Road Development Agency.

RDA. 2016b. *Roads: January-March 2016*. Lusaka: Road Development Agency.

RDA. n.d.-a. "2016 Road Sector Annual Work Plan." *Road Development Agency*. Retrieved March 25, 2020 (http://www.rda.org.zm/jdownloads/Programmes/RSAWP2016finalDec31.pdf).

RDA. n.d.-b. *Link Zambia 8000: "Transforming Zambia into a Truly Landlinked Country."* Lusaka: Road Development Agency.

Resnick, Danielle E. 2017. "Populism in Africa." Pp. 101–20 in *The Oxford Handbook of Populism*, edited by C. Rovira Kaltwasser, P. Taggart, P. Choa Espejo, and P. Ostiguy. Oxford: Oxford University Press.

Reuters. 2018. "Zambia Denies White House Claim China Taking over Power Utility." *Reuters*. Retrieved July 25, 2019 (https://www.reuters.com/article/us-zambia-economy/zambia-denies-white-house-claim-china-taking-over-power-utility-idUSKBN1OE0LD).

Saasa, Oliver S. 2018. *Pro-Growth Road Infrastructure Development in Zambia: Challenges, Opportunities and Policy Options*. Lusaka: Premier Consult Limited.

Sautman, Barry, and Yan Hairong. 2015. "Bashing 'the Chinese': Contextualizing Zambia's Collum Coal Mine Shooting." Pp. 138–57 in *China in Africa: Strategic Motives and Economic Interests*, edited by S. Zhao. Abingdon: Routledge.

Schindler, Seth, and J. Miguel Kanai. 2021. "Getting the Territory Right: Infrastructure-Led Development and the Re-Emergence of Spatial Planning Strategies." *Regional Studies* 55(1):40–51. https://doi.org/10.1080/00343404.2019.1661984.

Scott, Guy. 2019. *Adnetures in Zambian Politics: A Story in Black and White*. Boulder: Lynne Rienner.

Shendy, Riham, Zachary Kaplan, and Peter Mousley. 2011. *Toward Better Infrastructure: Conditions, Constraints, and Opportunities in Financing Public-Private Partnerships in Select African Countries*. Washington: World Bank.

Shivji, Issa G. 2009. *Accumulation in an African Periphery: A Theoretical Framework*. Dar es Salaam: Mkuki na Nyota Publishers.

Simumba, Trevor. 2018. *He Who Pays The Piper: Zambia's Growing China Debt Crisis*. Lusaka: Centre for Trade Policy and Development.

Sum, Ngai-Ling. 2019. "The Intertwined Geopolitics and Geoeconomics of Hopes/ Fears: China's Triple Economic Bubbles and the 'One Belt One Road' Imaginary." *Territory, Politics, Governance* 7(4):528–52. https://doi.org/10.1080/21622671.2018.1523746.

Tembo, Yohane. 2015. *A Look at Zambia's Road Financing Strategies: The Impact of Incongruent Policies and Budgets*. Hamburg: Anchor Academic Publishing.

van Wieringen, Kjeld, and Tim Zajontz. 2023. "From Loan-Financed to Privatised Infrastructure? Tracing China's Turn towards Public-Private Partnerships in Africa." *Journal of Current Chinese Affairs*, online first. https://doi.org/10.1177/18681026231188140.

Wanjala, Peter. 2022. "Chingola-Kasumbalesa Road Concession Agreement Signed, Zambia." *Construction Review*. Retrieved July 11, 2023 (https://constructionreviewonline.com/news/chingola-kasumbalesa-road-concession-agreement-signed-zambia/).

Wethal, Ulrikke. 2019. "Building Africa's Infrastructure: Reinstating History in Infrastructure Debates." *Forum for Development Studies* 46(3):473–99. https://doi.org/10.1080/08039410.2019.1616609.

World Bank. n.d. "Zambia." *World Bank Public Documents*. Retrieved February 21, 2020 (https://pubdocs.worldbank.org/en/359911492207299026/data-zmb.pdf).

Yescombe, E. R., and Edward Farquharson. 2018. *Public-Private Partnerships for Infrastructure: Principles of Policy and Finance*. 2nd ed. Oxford: Butterworth-Heinemann.

Zajontz, Tim, Pádraig Carmody, Mandira Bagwandeen, and Anthony Leysens. 2024. "Introduction: China's Role in Africa's Railway Renaissance." Pp. 1–25 in *Africa's Railway Renaissance: The role and impact of China*, edited by T. Zajontz, P. Carmody, M. Bagwandeen, and A. Leysens. Abingdon: Routledge.

Zajontz, Tim. 2022a. "Debt, Distress, Dispossession: Towards a Critical Political Economy of Africa's Financial Dependency." *Review of African Political Economy* 49(171):173–83. https://doi.org/10.1080/03056244.2021.1950669.

Zajontz, Tim. 2022b. "The Chinese infrastructural fix in Africa: lessons from the Sino-Zambian 'road bonanza'." *Oxford Development Studies* 50(1):14–29. https://doi.org/10.1080/13600818.2020.1861230.

ZDA. 2014. "Public-Private-Partnerships in Infrastructure Development in Zambia." *Zambia Development Agency*. Retrieved March 25, 2020 (https://www.zda.org.zm/?q=download/file/fid/60www.zda.org.zm/?q=content/zambia-triple-power-generation-two-years-solar).

Zhang, Hong. 2023. *From Contractors to Investors? Evolving Engagement of Chinese State Capital in Global Infrastructure Development and the Case of Lekki Port in Nigeria*. China-Africa Research Initiative Working Paper No. 53. Washington: Johns Hopkins University.

ZIPAR. 2019. *Nurturing the Seeds of Humanity: Analysis of the 2020 National Budget*. Lusaka: Zambia Institute for Policy Analysis and Research.

ZNBC. 2023. "Chingola-Mutanda Dual Carriage Road Works On Cards." *ZNBC News*. Retrieved July 11, 2023 (https://www.znbc.co.zm/news/139507-2/).

CHAPTER 7

The Political Economy of "Not so Public" Procurement

Spatio-temporal fixes are necessarily characterised by contentions about the distribution of related benefits and costs. Consequently, they require particular social, organisational and institutional compromises which mediate their inherent contradictions (Jessop 2006: 162; Sum and Jessop 2013: 242–43, 248). This includes, in the case of China's infrastructural fix, social and class alliances, most notably between Chinese (state) capital and Zambian political elites, as well as between the latter and social and economic forces within Zambia. Strategic selectivities inherent in the Zambian state have thus crucially affected the manifestation of the Chinese infrastructural fix in Zambia's road sector. As I shall argue in this chapter, the coexistence and interpenetration of legal-rational and patrimonial logics within the institutional set-up of the Zambian infrastructure state has provided a fluid strategic-relational realm which certain actors with access to state powers have strategically exploited to further private, at the expense of public interests (Fig. 7.1).

In this chapter, I first historicise the neoptarimonial form of the Zambian state and problematise the practice of "not so public" procurement that has been reinforced by highly personalised exchanges among Chinese and Zambian elites and opaque, partly informal procurements for road projects. Looking at the concrete case of the "20 per cent subcontracting policy", the chapter illustrates how Zambian state actors

T. Zajontz, *The Political Economy of China's Infrastructure Development in Africa*, International Political Economy Series,
https://doi.org/10.1007/978-3-031-44449-4_7

Fig. 7.1 President Edgar Lungu at a groundbreaking ceremony for a Chinese road project in Zambia's Northern Province, 11 August 2017 (© Tim Zajontz)

have strategically employed a combination of both formal and informal modes of governance to "zambianise" the Chinese infrastructural fix. The chapter then examines the case of the Lusaka-Ndola dual carriageway. This analysis, at a more concrete level, illustrates arguments I developed in the present and previous chapters, namely the strategic shift towards project finance arrangements and the interweaving of formal and informal institutions in the appraisal and procurement of road projects.

Zambia's Neopatrimonial Infrastructure State

Chinese-financed road development in Zambia has been conditioned by the strategic selectivities of the Zambian state. As conceptualised in Chapter 3, the state is an institutional ensemble with a particular set of structural constraints and opportunities which privilege some strategic actors, some political strategies and some policies over others (see Hay 1996: 7; Jessop 1990: 269–70 n.13, 2007: 37). As I will show in this chapter, neopatrimonial modes of governance imply a particular set of structural biases which have provided access to state powers to specific strategic actors in Zambia's infrastructure sector. Before detailing "not so public" procurement in Zambia's road sector, some historicisation of Zambia's neopatrimonial state, the country's political class and its clients seems indicated.

In 2017, one oppositional politician described the prevalence of informal institutions and patrimonial modes of domination in the relationship between Zambia's political elite and the country's citizenry as follows:

> You leave a system complicated so that you can have a lot of people in the dependence syndrome, so that you can keep patronizing them. You can keep them looking up to you for certain incentives or services. [...] Deliberately – and I say deliberately – it has been kept that way so that they [referring to the ruling elites] can maintain that dependence syndrome. Because it's the same dependence syndrome that wins them the votes. (Interview Ngulube)

As access to state institutions provides access to economic resources, clientelism and patronage have pervaded the Zambian state and "political competition takes place largely on the basis of distribution of patronage/targeted resources to allies and supporters" (Hinfelaar and Achberger 2017: 24). In the Zambian political system, party cadres play a particularly pronounced role as intermediaries between the populace and political patrons (Bwalya 2017; Bwalya and Maharaj 2018; Fraser 2017).

The distribution of economic resources in Zambia is commonly marked by a combination of formal and regulated processes of allocation with informal or even illicit practices, with the dividing line between the former and the latter generally being blurred. The pertinence of clientelism and patronage as a means of domination, alongside rational-bureaucratic norms and procedures, is first and foremost a legacy of racist colonial rule and the long-standing "singular exclusion of Zambians from social and economic resources" (Szeftel 2000: 209). Multinational mining houses and other foreign capital retained a tight grip on Zambia's economy after the formal end of colonial exploitation. This has left Zambians without control over the means of production. Consequently, the post-independence state was quasi overnight considered the central driver of social and economic development. The state provided "a mechanism for ensuring personal upward mobility and private access to public resources" (Szeftel 2000: 209) and thus became a "resource in itself" (Szeftel 1982: 4).

This affected Zambia's class structure lastingly. What Shivji (2009: 71) calls a "political-bureaucratic class" emerged whose legitimacy depended on the distribution of resources to individuals and groups (Szeftel 2000: 209). Under Zambia's one-party state (the so-called Second Republic between 1972 and 1991) the allocation of social and economic rewards along patron-client networks did not vanish but was monopolised by the United National Independence Party. Szeftel points out that

> [t]he one-party patronage state expanded the public sector in order to share out jobs and pay off supporters. In hindsight, it became more than a patronage system, almost a rudimentary welfare state in which those with party credentials and access were rewarded with jobs, salaries and other opportunities and protected from economic forces in the private sector. (2000: 214)

The reintroduction of a multiparty system in 1991 and Zambia's political and economic liberalisation in the 1990s caused another modification of the neopatrimonial state form. Despite a political platform that promised decisive action against entrenched corruption and patronage, as well as official commitments to good governance agendas promoted by Western donors, the MMD succumbed to patrimonial distributional politics soon after coming into power in 1991 (Bwalya and Maharaj 2018; Szeftel 2000). Chikulo (2000: 161) furthermore attests that, "[c]ontrary to conventional wisdom, corruption, under the multiparty state, has become pervasive, uncontrollable, and unrestrained" (see also van Donge 2009; Momba 2007). This, and here I agree with Scott Taylor (2006b: 283), does not suggest that corruption is somehow "an innate, cultural characteristic" of the Zambian society. Taylor rightly underscores late President Mwanawasa's efforts to prosecute his predecessor's regular misconduct, in order to re-establish public trust in Zambia's political institutions, not least the presidential office, and to mitigate corruption (Taylor 2006b; see Bwalya and Maharaj 2018). However, recent studies suggest that levels of public sector corruption have rebounded in the 2010s (see Hinfelaar and Sichone 2019: 10; Isbell 2018). Transparency International's Corruption Perception Index suggests that political corruption in Zambia might have worsened under President Lungu, as the country has fallen for five consecutive years in the ranking since 2015 (see Fig. 5.2, p. 155).

In the realm of economic governance, reforms of the 1990s which aimed at economic liberalisation and deregulation have compromised regulatory and enforcement capacities of the state and opened up niches for fraudulent business activities. Furthermore, waves of privatisation provided political office-holders with ample possibilities for personal enrichment by acquiring state assets or getting involved in economic activities that previously were under state tutelage (Hinfelaar and Achberger 2017: 25; Szeftel 2000). Privatising the mines and other state-owned enterprises, through which patronage traditionally took place, made Zambia's political elites "more susceptible to the interest of politico-economic entrepreneurs [...] and undermined the relatively formal structures that previously guided accountability and oversight of business lobby and deals" (Hinfelaar and Achberger 2017: 5). Zambia's shift towards more interventionist economic policies under Sata has opened up yet new economic opportunities for a newly emerging rentier class, which, in turn, has strengthened the latter's political influence. These Zambian rentiers have since acquired interests in the export–import sector and the mining supply industry and "make claims on the now expanded state" (Mosley 2017: 47; see also Hinfelaar and Achberger 2017: 25). The "expansion" of the state under the PF, not least by means of expansive state spending (on infrastructure), has been paralleled by a reinforcement of clientelism and efforts on the part of the ruling party to monopolise access to state powers to a small circle of individuals with close ties to President Lungu and his cabinet ministers. At the same time, infrastructure development, not least road projects, has become an important means of patronage through which the PF tried to secure political support. As one Zambian observer put it: "When you look at the Link Zambia 8000 project, you find that the township roads where some of these people have been voting heavily [for the PF] are the ones that are being developed, whereas economic roads are being neglected" (Interview key informant 3). Hinfelaar and Sichone (2019: 5) argue that, "[w]hile continuing to reflect the features of competitive clientelism, from 2015 onwards, Zambia has been showing signs of becoming a vulnerable/unstable [political] settlement, increasingly authoritarian in character". The significant hike in public works and procurements under the PF-led government has fostered personalised, opaque and, in some cases, allegedly corrupt practices of economic "resource allocation" in the road sector.

"Not so Public" Procurement as a Win-Win-Lose Strategy

Whereas the coexistence and interpenetration of formal and informal norms and practices is a general characteristic of neopatrimonial states (see Chapter 3), strategic action oriented towards the strategically selective structural constraints and opportunities inherent in the neopatrimonial state has taken on specific forms in the context of Sino-Zambian relations. As discussed in Chapter 3, Sino-African intergovernmental relations are often highly personalised, as the dividing lines between the state and government as well as between the government and the ruling party are fluid, in some cases arguably purely cosmetic, in both China and in many African polities (see also Taylor 2007, 2009: 11). As Carmody and Taylor (2010: 500) argue, high-level state visits are an integral part of China's public diplomacy aimed at building trust between Chinese political elites and their African counterparts—"the political 'coming out', as a complement to economic 'going out'".

This certainly applies in the Zambian case, where close ties between Chinese and Zambian political elites date back to China's support for liberation movements in the region and the "TAZARA experience" discussed in Chapter 4 (see, for instance, Baregu 2006; Taylor 2006a: 26–31). In Lusaka, visits from high-ranking Chinese officials have been frequent. Despite growing anti-Chinese sentiments in the political and public realms in the 2000s, fueled not least by the PF's electoral campaigns (see Brautigam 2022; Hampwaye and Kragelund 2013; Kopinski and Polus 2011), close and often informal relations between Chinese and Zambian elites have not ceased under late President Sata. In fact, Sata's China-critical "position shifted immediately on assumption of the presidency, as he was structurally enrolled and inducted into the elite actor network" (Carmody and Kragelund 2016: 12; see Hampwaye and Kragelund 2013). The latter was thoroughly maintained and expanded under Sata's successor whose first state visit outwith Africa led him to China in late March 2015 when Lungu and Xi witnessed the signing of further "cooperative documents covering economy, technique, infrastructure construction, telecommunications and so on" (Chinese Foreign Ministry 2015). Througout his term, Lungu met Xi on several other occasions and Lungu regularly received Chinese top officials in Lusaka, including Foreign Minister Wang Yi and State Councillor Yang Jiechi.

The expanded role of the Zambian state in the infrastructure sector and the inflow of Chinese capital into Zambia's road sector have created new sources of rents, some of which, under the banner of "local participation", have served capital accumulation strategies of a small but politically well-connected rentier class. In this sense, Zambia's market for infrastructure and construction (and China's keen interest in it) has become what Peiffer and Englebert term an "extraversion asset" (Peiffer and Englebert 2012: 362; see also Alves and Chichava 2019), a means through which Zambian political elites could extract economic resources to bolster political power and increase personal wealth. Simultaneously, there is evidence that the permeation of the Zambian state apparatus by informal institutions has been strategically exploited by Chinese economic actors. As Schoneveld and colleagues (2014: 1) point out, "considering the high levels of corruption within Zambia's institutional structures, the increasing Chinese participation in Zambia's economy arguably carries with it a number of risks should Chinese companies indeed be more inclined to exploit clientelist regimes".

The exploitation of particularistic economic opportunities that arise from the social relations that constitute Zambia's neopatrimonial infrastructure state has been facilitated by the practice of "not so public" procurement. The latter is marked by a high degree of informality. This is however not to say that binding law or existing regulations are altogether abandoned. "Not so public" procurement rather combines, at varying degrees, formal procedures and legal-rational norms with informal, personalised and often clandestine negotiations about the terms and conditions as well as the distribution of costs and (private) benefits of infrastructure projects. Zambia's "road bonanza" has been fostered by informal, high-level exchanges between Zambian decision-makers, on the one hand, and Chinese government agencies, SOEs and SOBs, on the other. Both the particularities of Chinese loan financing, most notably the absence of public tendering, and rent-seeking strategies on the part of Zambian political elites and their clients have further fuelled road development. Price-inflated construction contracts are suspected to have provided room for corruption. In a study on the Zambian road construction sector, Cheelo and Liebenthal have noticed "some seemingly overpriced roads". The authors suggest that overvaluation of construction contracts potentially allows for malfeasance, whereby "room for corruption is created by the over-design and over-specification of construction projects at inception" (Cheelo and Liebenthal 2018: 16). Considering that large-scale infrastructure projects are usually approved in the uppermost echelons of leadership, relatively high construction costs in regional comparison have caused "strong suspicion that decision-makers in or close to the President's office benefited from such contracts" (Ofstad and Tjønneland 2019: 7).

"Not so public" procurement in the context of Chinese road projects commonly implies the effective circumvention of legal norms that are codified in Zambian procurement law, notably the Public Procurement Act of 2008, the complementary Public Procurement Regulations of 2011 and, in the case of PPPs, the Public-Private Partnership Act of 2009. Strongly informed by European procurement laws, these acts and regulations meticulously stipulate rules and requirements to ensure transparent, competitive, cost-effective and accountable public procurements and mandate relevant authorities to monitor the same (see Mwamba 2017). However, the characteristics of Chinese loan financing, discussed above, ex ante rule out competitive bidding and public tendering (see Corkin 2012: 476, Lee 2014, 2017: 48, Mohan and Tan-Mullins 2019). In the context of Chinese preferential loans for African infrastructure projects, Zhao (2011: 67) describes a "practice of secret government-to-government agreements and the requirement that foreign aid contracts be awarded to Chinese contractors, through a closed-door bidding process. Competitive bidding is discouraged and China pulls a veil over vital data such as project costs, loan terms and repayment conditions". Ofstad and Tjønneland (2019: 7) assert that infrastructure contracts are "in many cases awarded without proper tendering, partly because of tied funding from Chinese banks".

A case in point has been the $348m Lusaka 400 programme, funded by China's Exim Bank. Zambia's Auditor General found that the main contractor AVIC was single-sourced despite its non-responsiveness to tender requirements (Auditor General n.d.: 48–50). As shown in Chapter 6, Chinese-sponsored road projects were commonly (pre-) agreed in opaque government-to-government negotiations. Subsequently, procuring agencies had to work with terms and conditions that were not the result of formal procurement procedures but personalised bargaining between Zambian political elites and Chinese SOEs and SOBs. When controversies about procurements and awards of contracts to Chinese companies arose, Zambian officials upheld the veneer of formality by emphasising that applicable laws and procurement procedures were complied with. As the case of the Lusaka-Ndola dual carriageway discussed below substantiates, "not so public" procurement results in a very "flexible" application of legal norms and regulations, which implies a significant loss of monitoring and control mechanisms and swings the pendulum from formal to informal bureaucratic practices.

"Not so public" procurment has not only fostered the actualisation of the Chinese infrastructural fix in Zambia's road sector, it has also provided for the distribution of a share of foreign capital along clientelistic networks. This has become apparent with regard to the "20 per cent subcontracting" policy that I discuss next. Intended as a formal policy to boost the local construction sector, it has been exploited by politically well-connected rentiers as well as by Chinese-owned companies which engage in illegal contract trading, underlying further contradictions in the political economy of "not so public" procurement.

Seeking rents from roads

The "development-through-infrastructure" strategy pursued by the Zambian infrastructure state has officially aimed at creating jobs, boosting the local construction sector and creating spill-over effects into other sectors of the economy. However, especially Chinese-funded road projects have received sustained critique for their Chinese-dominated supply chains, which has substantiated calls for policies to "zambianise" the construction sector. During Zambia's infrastructure boom of the 2010s, the "20 per cent subcontracting policy" became the main politico-institutional instrument to increase "local content" in the construction and infrastructure sectors. The heavy reliance on Chinese capital goods and material in the context of Chinese-funded road projects is itself a logical necessity of the spatio-temporal fix. The Zambian government has tried to increase local participation in the construction sector by means of a subcontracting policy which, however, has been subverted by clientelistic networks of state managers and rentiers.

In Search of "Local Content": Zambianising Chinese Circuits of Capital

Chinese-sponsored infrastructure projects have faced criticism for the limited degree to which African businesses are integrated into supply and value chains (see Corkin 2012). The Director of the Foreign Trade Department in Zambia's Ministry of Commerce, Trade and Industry confirmed that this concern is shared and addressed by the government which "is trying […] to make sure that you're not just inviting the Chinese to construct using their materials, but how does it link to the local industry and make sure that there's local content in what they are doing" (Interview Bwayla). Limited intra-sectoral spill-over effects and predominantly Chinese supply chains in infrastructure projects highlight a central contradiction inherent to the Chinese infrastructural fix (Mohan and Tan-Mullins 2019). The latter is driven by the structural necessity to expand the geographical circuits of Chinese capital to address over-capacities in China's construction and infrastructure sectors (Carmody and Wainwright 2022; Taylor and Zajontz 2020; Zhang 2017). For the spatio-temporal fix to successfully address China's overaccumulation problems, Chinese companies and suppliers must necessarily maximise both market shares in overseas infrastructure markets and Chinese content in concrete infrastructure projects. One means to do so has been by tying infrastructure funding to the selection of Chinese companies and, by extension, the procurement of materials through Chinese supply chains (Corkin 2012, 2013: 64, 66, Mohan and Tan-Mullins 2019: 1373–74). One interviewee described this contradiction quite vividly and urged the Zambian government to make local content an essential component of infrastructural loans:

> The other disadvantage with some of the loans that we have been acquiring as a country, especially those that are coming from China, is that they seem to be tied. Tied to conditions like in terms of procurement. Procurement, you can do the procurement maybe locally, but the tools, the materials that you are going to use are materials that still come from China […]. [Y]ou might have gotten a loan. A loan which is not just given as a grant. It's something that you pay back. But even as you are going to pay back it's like you are still giving business to the same people that have given you that loan. Meaning that China is giving business to its local industry, because they've given Zambia money and that money that they've given Zambia is still going back to China. And on top of that we pay back that money with interest. So it would have been good if these loans are negotiated in such a way that, beyond acquisition, there's also leverage for us to spend that money within the local economy so that a local manufacturer […] can benefit from that resource. It will have a multiplier effect. By the time you are paying back you would have already serviced some local industry, you would have left that in such a space that they would have actually

grown their businesses and they're able to hold the economy. (Interview Mwaipopo)

Single sourcing from China, as discussed above, is often a condition of Chinese loans and export credits and an important reason for predominantly Chinese supply and value chains in Zambia's road sector. Yet, it is of course not the only one. Besides significant capacity constraints within the industry (for studies on this, see Cheelo and Liebenthal 2018; Saasa 2018), lack of affordable credit and finance has hindered greater Zambian participation in Zambia's road construction boom and further tilted competition towards Chinese companies. The situation has worsened as a result of Zambia's mounting domestic debt, which has further curbed credit supply at reasonable rates to local construction businesses (CUTS International 2019: 14–15; Ofstad and Tjønneland 2019: 4).[1] As a labour union executive argued:

> In a way, they [Chinese contractors] are the ones that are taking the money back to China. For instance, the road construction. Most of the roads are done by Chinese today and it's huge, huge money, because of their support from the Chinese government. Most Zambian companies cannot compete. The banks here cannot assist them with finance. (Interview Chewe)

Even in cases of competitive public tendering, local construction businesses often do not stand a chance against their Chinese competitors, one reason being the competitive advantage that arises from Chinese export credits (Schoneveld et al. 2014: 11). Burke's (2007: 332) assessment has remained apt: "Once established, the only serious competition Chinese companies appear to face is from one another and it can be extremely fierce". A McKinsey report attests to a drop in profit margins among Chinese SOEs in the infrastructure construction sector, as a result of fierce competition from private Chinese corporations that have entered the African market (Sun et al. 2017: 31). The current slowing-down of Zambia's infrastructure and construction boom will further increase the competition among Chinese companies, while, at the same time, it will prolong the sidelining of local businesses.

[1] While having slightly dropped from 27 per cent in 2017, the average annual commercial bank lending rate was still at a staggering 24 per cent in 2018 (PWC 2019: 4).

Designed as a countermeasure against the dominance of Zambia's construction sector by foreign, not least Chinese, companies, late President Sata decreed a policy to increase local content. The subcontracting policy was introduced in 2012 and aimed at increasing local content in public procurements and boosting capacity and growth in Zambia's construction sector. Officially, the policy applies to all civil works contracts that exceed a contract volume of ZMK 30m[2] (RDA 2015a: 1). According to the RDA, 600 opportunities for local contractors were created under the subcontracting policy by May 2018 (Lusaka Times 2018b). The Chief Executive Officer (CEO) of Zambia's Chamber of Commerce and Industry, Prisca Chikwashi, assessed the policy positively, arguing that "we do have the policies in place for the private sector to benefit from the Zambian-Chinese investment. In the construction sector, for instance, there's a policy preferential procurement where there is 20 per cent reserved for Zambians. So that benefits the Zambians" (Interview Chikwashi). However, the policy has received sustained criticism because of the absence of a legally binding regulatory framework and allegedly opaque and unlawful awarding practices. The policy has thus been exemplary for the interplay of formal and informal practices in the procurement of road projects in Zambia. The policy has been strategically subverted by members of patrimonial networks to exploit opportunities that arise from the strategic selectivity of Zambia's neopatrimonial infrastructure state.

Subcontracting as (In)formal "Trickle-Down" Strategy

Local content policies are generally advocated by IFIs and development banks "as a magic bullet for broad-based development and structural transformation in resource-rich African economies" (Kragelund 2017: 57). Yet, neopatrimonial governance has significantly undermined the effectiveness of the subcontracting policy in Zambia's construction sector. The PF-led government did little to legally clarify its provisions and to ensure accountability in its application. By the end of 2019, the "local content" policy, introduced in 2012, was still not legally codified in a parliamentary act or a statutory instrument. It was introduced by means of a presidential policy directive and "did not have any measures or implementation framework for how its objectives would be achieved" (Cheelo

[2] Equal to about $2.17m in May 2019.

and Liebenthal 2018: 9). Meanwhile, without a legal basis, the RDA provided guidelines for the road sector on eligibility requirements as well as selection procedures and administration of contracts under the policy (see RDA 2015a). Yet, in the absence of a legal regulatory framework and monitoring mechanisms, local contractors and their associations have continuously criticised the government for the insufficient and non-transparent implementation and enforcement of the policy (Saasa 2018: 25–26). In a reaction to mounting public criticism, then Acting Minister for Housing and Infrastructure Development Katambo in 2018 publicly denounced non-compliance with the policy and urged that "[t]he policy decree on awarding the 20 per cent of works on all road contracts to Zambian Citizens owned companies must be adhered to because failure to do so is tantamount to breaking the law" (quoted in Lusaka Times 2018b). Andrew Chellah, special assistant to the president for project implementation and monitoring, reiterated the call for compliance a few months later (Lusaka Times 2018a).

Misconduct has been reported regarding the selection of subcontractors. Saasa (2018: 25) argues that "there are no indications that the selection of local firms that are invited to partner with foreign contractors is transparent or merit-based". In contrast, the policy has been a means for the government to direct capital flows towards politically affiliated rentiers. Condemning rent-seeking behaviour in public procurement procedures, the president of Transparency International Zambia, Rueben Lifuka, warned that "cadreism has become another cancerous form of corruption where it has become a norm that political party cadres should be given construction contracts regardless of their ability to service this contract" (quoted in The Zambian Observer 2018). An opposition politician argued that it was the "so-called party cadres of the ruling party [at the time the PF]" that are "mostly benefitting" from the subcontracting policy (Interview Ngulube).

The sparsely regulated "local content" policy furthermore boosted "cadre-preneurial contract trading", a practice which Cheelo and Liebenthal (2018: 17) describe as "the specialization by politically connected cadres in the illicit capture of public tenders and their sale on illegal secondary tender markets". An interviewee with long-standing experience in Zambia's construction sector confirmed that contract trading has been "very, very common" in the industry. Thereby, companies would commonly bid for contracts without the intent to actually implement the project. The interviewee described the reasoning behind the practice as follows:

> Because as a contractor who has won the contract there is a time frame to do the work. If I don't deliver on the work, I will be black-listed and next time I won't be awarded a contract. So, if I don't have the capacity or the finances better give it to somebody who can do the work for me and I get a fee and I don't have to worry about the hustle and bustle of doing the work. (Interview Managing Director Zambian construction business association)

Furthermore, the interviewee pointed out that it was also common to register several companies, "one in your name, maybe one in your children's name and you bid using three or four companies to stand a chance" (Interview Managing Director Zambian construction business association). Generally, the "non-disclosure of beneficial owners" of bidding companies is considered to aggravate opacity in public procurement and to make corrupt practices easier (Cheelo and Liebenthal 2018: 17).

Under Lungu, mandatory subcontracting became a largely informal "trickle-down" mechanism in the context of Chinese-sponsored road construction. Trickling down, in this context, meant that a slice of Chinese capital that flowed into the development of Zambia's roads was being dispersed along clientelistic networks of politically well-connected individuals. The opacity related to the practice of non-competitive bidding common to Chinese-sponsored road projects was thus amplified by a largely informal subcontracting policy. The latter provided Zambian political elites with an administrative, prima facie legal-rational, instrument for rent-seeking, particularly because subcontractors are not selected by the main contractor but by RDA (Saasa 2018: 25). As Lee documents (2017: 50–51), high-level political interference into decision-making and project selection procedures within RDA has been common. Political interference has also occurred in the selection of local contractors under the subcontracting policy. The President of the Zambian National Association for Medium and Small-Scale Contractors, Edward Mpepo, criticised this, stating that the "RDA nominates political cadres with no qualifications and knowledge in construction but [who] may produce NCC [National Construction Council] registration certificate. These politically-inclined beneficiaries normally trade-off the 20 percent with Chinese contractors" (quoted in Saasa 2018: 26). Where works are subcontracted to political affiliates, the contract sum, minus a "fair" share—or in economic terms: a rent—for the successful "tenderpreneur", often finds its way back to Chinese companies after all. A politician from an opposition party described contradictions related to the subcontracting policy as follows:

> They [Zambian government] will put up a deliberate policy to say 'we want to empower Zambians to get these contracts'. Even the same Zambians that they want in power they have not been given an opportunity to be trained and understand the task that they are trying to undertake. They end up getting a contract, sell it to a Chinese national. [...] Now when they get the contract, they will sell it to this particular Chinese company, they need themselves, as the one that won that contract in the construction industry, they want to remain with some profits. So, by the time the contract lands with a Chinese investor, he also wants to make a profit. What is he going to give you? Sub-standard type of a construction. (Interview Ngulube)

Particularly Chinese small- and medium-sized businesses that fall into the category of *minying qiye*, i.e. companies not managed by the Chinese state, have been ready to buy contracts that were awarded to local businesses under the subcontracting rule. An interviewee confirmed that construction contracts are frequently sold to Chinese companies. However, the interviewee also stated that "it does not mean that every contract that is awarded, the Chinese run for them". Rather, it "depends on how they assess the risk and how much profit is in it for them. It depends on the contract, the amount of money awarded and how much that contractor who is selling the contract is asking for" (Interview Managing Director Zambian construction business association). The malfeasant application of the subcontracting policy can be assumed to have been significantly higher in the context of Chinese loan-financed road construction, compared to IFI-funded projects which generally require open tendering and meticulous documentation and disclosure of the application of funds. This, of course, is not to suggest that IFI-financed development projects are immune to corruption.

In January 2019, then Minister of Housing and Infrastructure Development, Ronald Chitotela, announced that his ministry was directed by President Lungu to provide a legal basis, in the form of a statutory instrument, for the subcontracting policy. Interestingly, the presidency directed the Ministry to increase the local share applicable under the policy from 20 to 30 per cent (Jere 2019). This happened in spite of significant capacity constraints among local construction companies, not least as a result of their limited access to affordable credit and equipment (Saasa 2018: 19). It is questionable whether increasing the local share was timely and if it was the right measure to address the challenges Zambian local contractors face. However, in the light of clientelistic rent-seeking practices in the infrastructure and construction sectors, increasing the share of "local content" in public procurements presumably allowed for a larger share of foreign capital to "trickle-down" along patrimonial networks ahead of presidential elections in 2021.

The President himself publicly admitted that the subcontracting policy had been unlawfully exploited by PF cadres and ministers, when he stated in September 2019 that:

> I do not want to get reports that people from Lusaka especially ministers and senior officials in the party are insisting on getting 20 percent when they are not even eligible. That is the corruption we do not want. [...] I have heard that some party officials, Ministers and other people from Lusaka want to withhold the contracts. The intention is that the contracts should be distributed so that other Zambians can benefit so I want Copperbelt Minister Japhen Mwakalombe, Permanent [S]ecretary Bright Nundwe and Copperbelt Chairperson Nathan Chanda to sit together with others and ensure that there is fairness and equity in giving of the 20 percent subcontracts. (Lungu, quoted in Lusaka Times 2019c)

The statement casts into doubt how serious President Lungu was about clarifying the regulatory confines by placing the subcontracting policy on a statutory footing. His instruction towards a coterie of PF politicians in the Copperbelt Province to "sit down with others and ensure" a fair distribution of subcontracts conveys an overt commitment to informal and "not so public" procurement processes and prebendalism. In the absence of a legal basis for the subcontracting policy, the role of provincial ministers and local politicians in the procurement of public works remained unclear. The explicit inclusion of PF functionary Chanda[3] perfects the conflation between government and political party in the context of the "20 per cent subcontracting policy". The President's statement in the media can only be interpreted as a rhetoric attempt to appease voters in

[3] At the time, Chanda was also mayor of the mining town Luanshya.

the Copperbelt Province, Zambia's fiercely contested "swing state" (see Bwalya 2017; Bwalya and Maharaj 2018).

The subcontracting policy has become the most vivid case of how the Zambian government combined legal-bureaucratic state capacities with informal and patrimonial practices, notably undefined and unregulated decision-making procedures that govern the implementation of the policy. Evidently, it has also provided for rentier activities which Boone (1990: 427) defines as "politically mediated opportunities for obtaining wealth through non-productive economic activity". These findings coincide with Corkin's (2013: 116–17) in the Angolan context where existing local content policies have not been enforced due to a lack of political will and vested interests on the part of political elites. But not only corrupt officials and party cadres were involved in the informalisation of the formally declared, but not legally codified, policy. The interest of privately owned Chinese companies in illegally traded subcontracts, discussed above, underline that the actualisation of the Chinese spatio-temporal fix in the political-economic context of the Zambian neopatrimonial infrastructure state has produced a "win–win cooperation" of a special kind. In conjunction with the procedural opacity owed to the economic conditionalities attached to Chinese loans, i.e. non-competitive bidding and single sourcing, the subcontracting policy has amplified "not so public" procurement processes in Zambia's road sector. The following in-depth analysis of the Lusaka-Ndola dual carriageway project rounds up the case study of Zambia's road sector by illustrating propositions made in Chapter 6 and in this chapter at a yet more concrete-complex level.

The Lusaka-Ndola Dual Carriageway

The Lusaka-Ndola trunk road that stretches along parts of the T2 and T3, is a key segment of all major road corridors (Fig. 7.2), towards southern ports in Durban and Richards Bay, to Dar es Salaam, to Nacala, Beira and Walvis Bay. The road is of utmost importance for Zambia's economy, as most of the country's mining exports as well as most imports for the heavily populated Copperbelt Province and its mines are being transported on this road. Hitherto a single carriageway, the condition of the road has deteriorated under high traffic volumes, especially heavy goods traffic, and the road is frequently congested, especially in suburban Lusaka and in other urban centres it traverses (Field notes). The contractual arrangement the PF-led government opted for in 2017 to upgrade

Fig. 7.2 Route of the Lusaka-Ndola dual carriageway (*Source* Author's depiction based on UN map Zambia, No. 3731, Rev. 4, January 2004)

the road marked a shift towards project finance in transport infrastructure development in Zambia due to debt sustainability concerns. This shift in the financial governance of road construction has exposed new contradictions some of which will be discussed below.

Moreover, the procurement process for the Lusaka-Ndola project was characterised by the coexistence and interpenetration of legal-rational procedures and informal practices. In May 2017, the project was awarded to CJIC, although the company had been repeatedly criticised by both government and opposition for delivering sub-standard and behind-schedule works in the context of the construction of the Ndola-Kitwe dual carriageway, a road of similar economic importance (Lusaka Times 2017, 2018c). The announcement caused fierce public debate about a supposed cost explosion, the opaque tender process and the obscure terms of the contract, particularly with regard to financial obligations that it incurred for the Zambian government (The Zambian Observer

2017). After a years-long delay in project commencement and the change of government of 2021, the new UPND-led administration announced in March 2022 that it had cancelled the project due to "overpricing" (Sinyangwe 2022). The fact that former Finance Minister Bwalya Ng'andu insisted that the PF-led government had never signed a contract for the Lusaka-Ndola road and that the project had been cancelled before the change of government only adds to the opacity that had surrounded the project (Mofya 2022). After taking office, the UPND government re-tendered the project. In early 2023, it was publicised that a PPP with a 25 years operational concession and a project volume of $650 million had been agreed. The successful bidder is the Chinese consortium Macro Ocean Investment which includes AVIC International Project Engineering, Zhenjiang Communications Construction Group and China Railway Seventh Group (Nyabiage 2023). The genesis of the road project is a prime example of "not so public" procurement practices that have characterised Zambia's infrastructure sector, and Chinese involvement in it, throughout the 2010s.

A Case of "Not so Public" Procurement

In June 2015, the upgrade of the Lusaka-Ndola road to a dual carriageway was, for the first time, tendered as a FDCOMT PPP (National Assembly of Zambia 2017: n.n.; see RDA 2015b). According to a government source, the RDA unsuccessfully tendered the project six times as a PPP that includes finance, operation and tolling. As a result, the FDCOMT scheme was abandoned and replaced by an EPC+F arrangement (Interview senior official Zambian MTC). Media reports suggested however that RDA had received offers for the initial tenders. The South African company Group Five Construction Pty was reportedly selected as the preferred bidder but contract negotiations were abruptly cancelled in February 2017. A contract sum of $600m circulated in the media (see The Zambian Observer 2017). According to the RDA's Annual Report 2016, the agency had commenced negotiations over a Design-Finance-Build-Operate-Transfer contract with Group Five on 10 August 2016, after it had received authority from the PPP Council to do so on 26 July 2016. However, the PPP Council "terminated the negotiation" on 13 December 2016 and "at its meeting on December 14, 2016 directed that RDA enter into negotiations with Messrs China Jiangxi Corporation". In the sequel, "[a]n inter-sectoral negotiating team including three members from the private sector was constituted and the first negotiation meeting was scheduled for January 18, 2017" (RDA 2017: 27). The annual report does not state reasons why the negotiations with Group Five were terminated.

The antecedents to the selection of CJIC were not mentioned by then Minister of Housing and Infrastructure Development, Ronald Chitotela, in his statement on the project in parliament on 3 October 2017. The minister revealed however that the contract with CJIC was signed on 30 May 2017 (National Assembly of Zambia 2017). This meant the contract, including a change in implementation models, was negotiated in less than four and a half months. Minister Chitotela addressed speculations as to whether the competitive bidding process might have been a mere façade and the Chinese contractor selected unlawfully. Chitotela explicated that CJIC "was selected as a preferred bidder by the PPPs Council" in December 2016 and subsequently engaged by RDA for contract negotiations. According to the minister, during these negotiations "the implementation mode was changed from PPPs [sic!] Model to Engineering Procurement and Construction plus Finance (EPC+F)" (National Assembly of Zambia 2017). This course of action raises the question as to whether a change in the project implementation mode from a PPP that included operation and tolling (FDCOMT scheme), as tendered by RDA in January 2016 (RDA 2016), to an EPC+F arrangement would have required a new public tender process. In June 2019, the Office of the Public Protector (OPP) instituted investigations into the procurement process. The OPP asserted, prima facie, that the scope and contractual model was irregularly changed, as the Ministry of Housing and Infrastructure Development had failed to publicly tender the project under the altered contractual framework (The Zambian Observer 2019).

In September 2017, CJIC was publicly announced as the contractor and the contract amount was stated as $1.246bn (Reuters 2017). The RDA's request for proposals from January 2016 had estimated the construction costs at ZMK 930m, which amounts to about $83.5 m at the time, and an economic internal rate of return of 29 per cent (RDA 2016: 14). Indeed, this original cost estimate was highly unrealistic and can be explained by what Saasa learned from the Director of Policy and Monitoring at the Ministry of Transport and Communications, namely "that there are no detailed designs and engineering drawings for the Lusaka-Ndola Highway" (Saasa 2018: 29 n. 30). Drawing on Collier et al. who use data from the World Bank's Road Costs Knowledge

System, Chelwa comes to the conclusion that "the road should cost about US$1.04billion instead of US$1.2billion" (Chelwa 2017; see Collier et al. 2015). Minister Chitotela justified the discrepancy between initial estimated costs and the agreed contract sum with additional contractual items, such as one weighbridge, three service stations, an office building for RDA and "satellite cities" (National Assembly of Zambia 2017). Equally vague remained then Finance Minister Mutati in his 2018 budget address when he explained that the project "consists of two phases", the first one being the construction of the dual carriageway, "while phase II will involve the construction of auxiliary infrastructure which includes hotels, toll gates and service stations", which will be "financed through private sector participation" (Mutati 2017: 13).

The "not so public" procurement process and the presumably overpriced contract made the Lusaka-Ndola dual carriageway subject to fierce political debate about the costs of Chinese-sponsored road projects and caused suspicion of corruption among the political opposition (see, for instance, Lupupa 2017; Ncube 2018). Corruption allegations were not new to the minister in charge. Whereas Chitotela was sacked by late President Sata, in whose cabinet he served as Deputy Labour Minister, over corruption charges (Africa Confidential 2019: 10), President Lungu appointed him as Minister of Infrastructure and Housing in 2016. For three years, Chitotela held a key position in the procurement of public works, including in the road sector, as the RDA falls under the auspices of his former ministry. In February and May 2019, he was repeatedly temporarily detained by the Anti-Corruption Commission on charges of corruption in which two Chinese SOEs, AVIC International and China Harbour, were allegedly implicated (Lusaka Times 2019a; Mwenda 2019a; Reuters 2019). Shell companies owned by the minister and some accomplices reportedly received payments and subcontracts from Chinese contractors (Africa Confidential 2019: 10). Invoking the principle of the presumption of innocence, President Lungu refrained from removing Chitotela (Sishuwa 2019). The cases against the minister were dropped in July 2019 by the Lusaka Magistrate Court on grounds of the state having failed to substantiate them (Lusaka Times 2019b). A few days later Chitotela got demoted to Minister of Tourism and Arts in a major cabinet reshuffle (Mwenda 2019b).

The Lusaka-Ndola road project is not only exemplary for "not so public" procurement procedures in the context of the Sino-Zambian road bonanza, it also exposes the financial and economic risks that can arise from public–private project finance arrangements and, thus, some of the contradictions related to the privatisation of infrastructure financing, that I discussed in Chapter 6.

The Fallacy of Project Finance at No Cost

While then Minister Chitotela hailed the change of implementation models from a BOT variant that includes financing, construction, operation and tolling (FDCOMT scheme) to an EPC+F contract, since "all revenues from the project in the form of toll fees would accrue to the Government instead of the revenue going to the private sector" (National Assembly of Zambia 2017), particulars of the contractual arrangement between CJIC and the Zambian government remained undisclosed. In a study on Zambia's growing debt burden vis-à-vis China, published by the non-governmental CTPD and titled *He Who Pays The Piper*, Zambian economist Simumba argues that the Lusaka-Ndola dual carriageway

> is another example of funds being funnelled into Zambia from China but going directly to Chinese owned and operated companies – in this case China Jiangxi – instead of to the government or directly to Zambian firms. [...] Not only is the size of this Chinese loan tremendous, but its terms remain opaque. (2018: 23)

The opacity of financial agreements constitutes a common thread of project finance through PPPs. For Hildyard (2016: 10), lack of transparency is a main characteristic of PPPs, as "[c]ommercial confidentiality ensures that many of the financial arrangements underlying the deals remain secret". Such opacity can potentially reinforce strategic selectivities inherent in neopatrimonial governance contexts and encourage state managers to orient their strategic action towards opportunities that arise from informal government conduct that is hidden from public and legal-bureaucratic control.

Indeed, Minister Chitotela had to explain the agreement with CJIC in Parliament where he stated that "the selected financial model has a payback period of seventeen years, with an internal rate of return of 15 per cent" and that it "will generate gross revenues of approximately US$3.5 billion over a period of seventeen years after commencement of operations" (National Assembly of Zambia 2017). This indicates that the contract of 2017 bound the Zambian government to availability payments to the contractor for a duration of 17 years upon completion, which the government expected to amortise through road tolling revenues. Despite this, a statement on the Lusaka-Ndola dual carriageway by then Minister of Finance, Felix Mutati, underlines the euphoria of government about private sector project finance: "Government will not borrow or spend a single ngwee, this will be a PPP" (The Zambian Observer 2017). Mutati's enthusiasm reflects the perceived advantages of PPPs that encompass project finance over debt-financed road development. Since under the EPC+F scheme the contractor acts as the borrower, project-related loans do not further strain the public budget.

However, project financing and construction under EPC+F contracts is obviously not undertaken at no cost. In contrast to BOT variants, private finance initiatives (in Zambian policy jargon: CFIs) do not entail an operation contract and/or a concession agreement between the public authority and the contractor (Yescombe 2007: 8–10). The contractor is not compensated through the collection of user charges but "the private-sector investor is paid by the contracting authority for 'availability', *i.e.* constructing the facility to the required specification and making it available for the period of the PFI [private finance initiative] contract" (Yescombe and Farquharson 2018: 17). Such fees are pre-agreed for a certain period to compensate the private investor for financing and construction costs (Yescombe and Farquharson 2018: 19).

Then Minister Chitotela's remarks in parliament give reason to assume that the Chinese firm CJIC favoured an EPC+F model over a PPP that entails operation and tolling (as the project was initially tendered in 2016) and convinced the Zambian government accordingly. Favourable revenue projections for the government are invoked as the decisive factor that led to the change in the implementation scheme. Minister Chitotela stated: "[A]s a responsible Government, we accepted the change in the mode of implementation, given the substantial revenue estimates" (National Assembly of Zambia 2017). Yet, EPC+F contracts bear significant financial and economic risks for public authorities. First, as availability payments are contractually fixed and independent of usage (Hildyard 2016: 35), the "usage risk" lies with the public authority, not with the contractor (Yescombe and Farquharson 2018: 20). For the government, the success of the EPC+F arrangement was therefore highly dependent on whether the projected internal rate of return of 15 per cent and gross revenues of $3.5bn would have materialised. Such estimates depend on a myriad of variables, such as future economic growth rates, copper prices and not least potentially competing transport infrastructure development that might compromise expected traffic volumes and related cash flows from tolling. The project finance arrangement for the Lusaka-Ndola dual carriageway is based on revenue estimates from tolling that, in turn, require particular traffic throughputs. If the projected tolling revenues should turn out lower than estimated, the Zambian government would have faced challenges to refinance its payments to the contractor CJIC.

CJIC's push for an EPC+F contract, instead of a FDCOMT PPP as initially intended, gives reason to assume that the company assessed the project's economic return through tolling unfavourably. One interviewee confirmed that, during the initial tender process, firms had expressed interest in implementing projects that were tendered as FDCOMT PPPs by means of CFIs instead (Interview RDA official). Fixed availability payments, secured through sovereign guarantees, appear to be a more secure and more profitable source of return than user charges from an operating and tolling concession. In turn, had the contract lasted, the government would have had a heightened interest that the Lusaka-Ndola road creates enough tolling revenues to be able to meet agreed availability payments. Hildyard (2016: 35) rightly points to contradictions that can arise from availability PPPs: "Locked into contracts that oblige payments for a given project, the pressure is on to make sure that the project is used, even if that means competing projects that might serve the public better are allowed to deteriorate". In the concrete case, this could undermine recent policies to bring cargo from the road to the rail, which, of course, would prolong the lifetime of roads as well as broader societal goals, such as carbon emission reduction. Another adjustment screw to ensure that collected revenues meet pre-specified payments to the contractor is the upward adjustment of the toll fee structure.

A second risk arose from the loan guarantee provided by the Zambian government. Simumba (2018: 23) finds that the government provided a $1.2bn sovereign guarantee for the project, whereby "exact terms of this security are unknown". A characteristic of project finance PPPs is the "lack of recourse to the project sponsors" who usually do not guarantee the debt raised by the contractor (Yescombe and Farquharson 2018: 14). Instead, sovereign loan guarantees have become a standard means of securing private investments in PPPs. They imply that governments are liable for servicing loans if a contractor fails to do so (Hildyard 2016: 35–36). But guaranteed debt not only bears potential debt servicing obligations. As a component of the government's financial account it has also affected Zambia's creditworthiness and thus drove up the rates at which the Zambian state has borrowed on global and domestic money markets. And caused the Kwacha to devaluate.

The 2017 funding arrangement for the Lusaka-Ndola dual carriageway constitutes a key example for the gradual organisational alteration of the temporal fix, from debt to project finance. It exemplifies the fallacy and deception in the Zambian political discourse that project finance PPPs reprieve the public budget. Yet, EPC+F contracts incur long-term financial obligations and fiscal risks, while they guarantee low-risk surplus creation for investors far into the future. It, therefore, was not surprising that the new UPND-led government, which has faced enormous economic pressure due to Zambia's indebtedness since coming into office in 2021, reassessed the controversial contract and cancelled it in 2022 (Sinyangwe 2022). It remains to be seen whether the terms and conditions of the PPP agreed in 2023 with Macro Ocean Investment Consortium will provide for a win–win situation for both the Chinese investor and the Zambian government.

Conclusion

This chapter has highlighted how Chinese engagements in Zambia's road sector have interrelated with structural biases inherent to Zambia's neopatrimonial infrastructure state. The chapter first briefly contextualised informal institutions and patron-client relationships within the Zambian state, before discussing how they have been reinforced by the informality that characterises Sino-Zambian intergovernmental relations. The conjuncture of patrimonial modes of governance and the peculiarity of Chinese loan-debt investment, notably the absence of public tendering and related single sourcing of contractors, has reinforced "not so public" procurement processes in Zambia's road sector. "Not so public" procurement has become a joint Sino-Zambian elite strategy which has sustained the Chinese infrastructural fix and has distributed its benefits among Chinese capital and Zambian political elites and rentiers. Thereby, it effectively circumvented existing bureaucratic-legal norms and procedures stipulated in Zambian (procurement) law in favour of non-transparent, personalised bargaining over the terms and conditions of road projects. "Not so" public procurement has furthermore made Chinese investment in Zambia's road sector particularly vulnerable to interference from corrupt individuals.

The influx of Chinese capital into Zambia's road sector has provided informal "trickle-down" effects by opening up new sources of rents which have been exploited by clientelistic networks that traverse the Zambian state. As Chinese investment in Zambia's road sector serves the purpose of "moving out" overcapacities in China's construction and infrastructure sectors, supply and value chains in road projects have unsurprisingly remained predominantly Chinese, with little Zambian input beyond labour. The PF-led Zambian government tried to redress the dominance of the construction market by foreign firms by means of a mandatory subcontracting policy. However, the latter has not been adequately regulated and has become a prime example for the retention of patrimonial strategies and "not so public" procurement. Due to the lack of a regulatory framework, the policy has been exploited by individuals within the Zambian government to channel contracts to politically well-connected "tenderpreneurs". Moreover, it has allowed for the creation of rents, whereby successful Zambian bidders have illegally sold contracts to other, not least Chinese-owned, companies—quite clearly a non-productive economic activity. Hence, the formal policy initiative, aimed at boosting Zambia's construction sector, has been permeated by informal, personalised distributional logics. Overall, Chinese-funded road development has caused an increasing informalisation of procurement processes, which secured both the awarding of contracts to Chinese SOEs and the distribution of a share of Chinese capital along clientelistic networks with the aim of consolidating the political power of the ruling party at the time.

The case study of the Lusaka-Ndola dual carriageway has concretised two main arguments developed in Chapter 6 and in this chapter, viz. the strategic shift from public debt finance to private project finance and the practice of "not so public" procurement. Whereas formal procurement procedures were initially followed and the project was publicly tendered, the abrupt cancellation of negotiations with a preferred bidder, and the selection of a Chinese SOE instead, suggest a deviance from rational-legal procedures towards informal agreements. At the urge of the Chinese contractor, the mode of implementation was allegedly irregularly changed and suspicion has been raised about inflated project costs and the role of Zambian top officials in the negotiations. The project also reveals contradictions that arise from the recent trend to finance road infrastructure by means of project finance PPPs. It can reasonably be assumed that profitability concerns made the contractor shy away from a concession-based

PPP considering the operational and maintenance costs such an arrangement entails as well as the exposure to usage risk. Both would have fallen to the Zambian government, whereas the contractor would have received fixed availability payments, backed by a state guarantee. The fact that new government cancelled and reawarded the contract in 2022 and 2023 respectively speaks for itself.

Chapter 6 and this chapter have documented how the Chinese infrastructural fix has unfolded in Zambia's road sector and how it has been facilitated, mediated and institutionalised by Zambian state actors. Zambia's state strategy of debt-financed infrastructure development corresponded to both the spatial displacement of Chinese surplus capital and the logic of the "temporal fix", in terms of Chinese loan financing. Both the Zambian infrastructure state that emerged under the PF and Chinese (state) capital have proven adaptable to mounting structural constraints that arose from Zambia's indebtedness. The recent shift in the financial governance of road development will sustain demand for Chinese construction firms and offer opportunities for equity investment—at the price of the gradual privatisation of Zambian roads. The case study has furthermore revealed that African (state) actors have exerted agency by "zambianising" the Chinese infrastructural fix to the extent that specific social forces, namely political elites and politically well-connected local capital, have managed to benefit from the influx of Chinese capital into Zambia's road sector by means of "not so public" procurement and patrimonial modes of governance. The Chinese proverb I quoted at the outset of Chapter 6 definitely proves true—some people do get rich, once a road is built.

List of Interviews

Bwayla, Lillian, director, Foreign Trade Department, Zambian Ministry of Commerce, Trade and Industry, Lusaka, Zambia, 18 July 2017.

Chewe, Joseph, general secretary, Mineworkers Union of Zambia (MUZ), Kitwe, Zambia, 6 July 2017.

Chikwashi, Prisca, chief executive officer, Zambia Chamber of Commerce and Industry (ZACCI), Lusaka, Zambia, 16 May 2017.

Key informant 3 (anonymised), 16 December 2020.

Managing Director of a Zambian construction business association and building contractor (anonymised), Lusaka, Zambia, 29 May 2017.

Mwaipopo, Isaac, executive director, Centre for Trade Policy and Development (CTPD), Lusaka, Zambia, 12 July 2017.

Ngulube, Ezra, general secretary, National Restoration Pary (NAREP), Lusaka, Zambia, 7 June 2017.

Official, Road Development Agency (RDA) (anonymised), Lusaka, Zambia, 2 August 2017.

Senior official, Zambian Ministry of Transport and Communication (MTC) (anonymised), Lusaka, Zambia, 14 June 2017.

References

Africa Confidential. 2019. "Cash in the Cabinet." *Africa Confidential* 60(4):9–10.

Alves, Cristina, and Sérgio Chichava. 2019. "Neo-Patrimonialism and Extraversion in China's Relations with Angola and Mozambique: Is Beijing Making a Difference?" Pp. 243–59 in *New Directions in Africa-China Studies*, edited by C. Alden and D. Large. Abingdon: Routledge.

Auditor General. n.d. *Report of the Auditor General on the Road Projects under the Road Development Agency (RDA) for the Period January 2012 to December 2015*. Lusaka: Office of the Auditor General.

Baregu, Mwesiga. 2006. "Tanzania-China Relations in Historical Perspective." Pp. 209–16 in *China in Africa: Mercantilist Predator, or Partner in Development*, edited by G. le Pere. Braamfontein: The Institute of Global Dialogue and The South African Institute of International Affairs.

Boone, Catherine. 1990. "The Making of a Rentier Class: Wealth Accumulation and Political Control in Senegal." *The Journal of Development Studies* 26(3):425–49.

Brautigam, Deborah. 2022. "China and Zambia: Creating a Sovereign Debt Crisis." *International Affairs* 98(4):1347–65. https://doi.org/10.1093/ia/iiac109.

Burke, Christopher. 2007. "China's Entry into Construction Industries in Africa: Tanzania and Zambia as Case Studies." *China Report* 43(3):323–36. https://doi.org/10.1177/000944550704300304.

Bwalya, John. 2017. "Unravelling Clientelism in the Zambian Electoral Campaigns." *Third World Quarterly* 38(7):1551–65. https://doi.org/10.1080/01436597.2016.1229568.

Bwalya, John, and Brij Maharaj. 2018. "Not to the Highest Bidder: The Failure of Incumbency in the Zambian 2011 Elections." *Journal of Contemporary African Studies* 36(1):71–86. https://doi.org/10.1080/02589001.2017.1369014.

Carmody, Pádraig, and Ian Taylor. 2010. "Flexigemony and Force in China's Resource Diplomacy in Africa: Sudan and Zambia Compared." *Geopolitics* 15(3):496–515. https://doi.org/10.1080/14650040903501047.

Carmody, Pádraig, and Peter Kragelund. 2016. "Who Is in Charge? State Power and Agency in Sino-African Relations." *Cornell International Law Journal* 49(1):1–24. https://doi.org/10.1038/nmeth.2841.

Carmody, Pádraig, and Joel Wainwright. 2022. "Contradiction and Restructuring in the Belt and Road Initiative: Reflections on China's Pause in the 'Go World.'" *Third World Quarterly* 43(12):2830–51. https://doi.org/10.1080/01436597.2022.2110058.

Cheelo, Caesar, and Robert Liebenthal. 2018. The Role of the Construction Sector in Influencing Natural Resource Use, Structural Change, and Industrial Development in Zambia. WIDER Working Paper 2018/172. Helsinki: UNU WIDER.

Chelwa, Grieve. 2017. "Is the Lusaka-Ndola Dual Carriageway Overpriced?" *Africa Watch*. Retrieved June 1, 2019 (http://gchelwa.blogspot.com/2017/09/is-lusaka-ndola-dual-carriageway.html).

Chikulo, Bornwell C. 2000. "Corruption and Accumulation in Zambia." Pp. 161–82 in *Corruption and Development in Africa: Lessons from Country Case-Studies*, edited by K. R. Hope and B. C. Chikulo. Basingstoke: Macmillan Press.

Chinese Foreign Ministry. 2015. "Xi Jinping Holds Talks with President Edgar Lungu of Zambia, Stressing to Cherish Traditional Friendship and Advance China-Zambia Relations." *Chinese Foreign Ministry*. Retrieved June 24, 2023 (https://www.fmprc.gov.cn/mfa_eng/gjhdq_665435/2913_665441/3114_664254/3116_664258/201504/t20150401_547636.html).

Collier, Paul, Martina Kirchberger, and Måns Söderbom. 2015. *The Cost of Road Infrastructure in Low and Middle Income Countries*. World Bank Policy Research Working Paper 7408. Washington.

Corkin, Lucy. 2012. "Chinese Construction Companies in Angola: A Local Linkages Perspective." *Resources Policy* 37(4):475–83. https://doi.org/10.1016/j.resourpol.2012.06.002.

Corkin, Lucy. 2013. *Uncovering African Agency: Angola's Management of China's Credit Lines*. Farnham: Ashgate.

CUTS International. 2019. *#DebtConcernsMe: Understanding the Impact of Zambia's Growing Debt on Different Stakeholders*. Lusaka: Consumer Unity & Trust Society International.

Fraser, Alastair. 2017. "Post-Populism in Zambia: Michael Sata's Rise, Demise and Legacy." *International Political Science Review* 38(4):456–72. https://doi.org/10.1177/0192512117720809.

Hampwaye, Godfrey, and Peter Kragelund. 2013. "Trends in Sino-Zambian Relations." Pp. 27–40 in *China's Diplomacy in Eastern and Southern Africa*, edited by S. Adem. Farnham: Ashgate.

Hay, Colin. 1996. *Re-Stating Social and Political Change*. Milton Keynes: Open University Press.

Hildyard, Nicholas. 2016. *Licenced Larceny: Infrastructure, Financial Extraction and the Global South*. Manchester: Manchester University Press.

Hinfelaar, Marja, and Jessica Achberger. 2017. *The Politics of Natural Resource Extraction in Zambia*. ESID Working Paper No. 80. Manchester: Effective States and Inclusive Development Research Centre.

Hinfelaar, Marja, and Justine Sichone. 2019. *The Challenge of Sustaining a Professional Civil Service amidst Shifting Political Coalitions: The Case of the Ministry of Finance in Zambia, 1991–2018*. ESID Working Paper No. 122. Manchester: Effective States and Inclusive Development Research Centre.

Isbell, Thomas. 2018. *Zambians See Corruption Rising, Government Failing in Anti-Graft Fight*. Afrobarometer Dispatch No. 213. Cape Town.

Jere, Joshua. 2019. "20% Subcontracting Policy to Be Legal." *ZNBC*. Retrieved April 14, 2019 (https://www.znbc.co.zm/20-subcontracting-policy-to-be-legal/).

Jessop, Bob. 1990. *State Theory: Putting the Capitalist State in Its Place*. Cambridge: Polity Press.

Jessop, Bob. 2006. "Spatial Fixes, Temporal Fixes and Spatio-Temporal Fixes." Pp. 142–66 in *David Harvey: A Critical Reader*, edited by N. Castree and D. Gregory. Malden: Blackwell Publishing.

Jessop, Bob. 2007. *State Power: A Strategic-Relational Approach*. Cambridge: Polity Press.

Kopinski, Dominik, and Andrzej Polus. 2011. "Sino-Zambian Relations: 'An All-Weather Friendship' Weathering the Storm." *Journal of Contemporary African Studies* 29(2):181–92. https://doi.org/10.1080/02589001.2011.555193.

Kragelund, Peter. 2017. "The Making of Local Content Policies in Zambia's Copper Sector: Institutional Impediments to Resource-Led Development." *Resources Policy* 51(March):57–66. https://doi.org/10.1016/j.resourpol.2016.11.008.

Lee, Ching Kwan. 2014. "The Spectre of Global China." *New Left Review* September(89):29–66.

Lee, Ching Kwan. 2017. *The Specter of Global China: Politics, Labor, and Foreign Investment in Africa*. Chicago: University of Chicago Press.

Lupupa, Frank. 2017. "Kambwili Tells Lungu to Resign over 'Corrupt' Lusaka-Ndola Road Project." *The Mast*. Retrieved October 26, 2019 (https://www.themastonline.com/2017/09/13/kambwili-tells-lungu-to-resign-over-corrupt-lusaka-ndola-road-project/).

Lusaka Times. 2017. "Construction of the $1.2 Billion Ndola-Lusaka Dual Carriageway Is a Scandal-GBM." *Lusaka Times*. Retrieved May 5, 2019 (https://www.lusakatimes.com/2017/09/16/construction-1-2-billion-ndola-lusaka-dual-carriageway-road-contract-scandal-gbm/).

Lusaka Times. 2018a. "Foreign Contractors Disobeying Presidential Directive to Employ Local Contractors." *Lusaka Times*. Retrieved July

5, 2019 (https://www.lusakatimes.com/2018/07/09/foreign-contractors-disobeying-presidential-directive-to-employ-local-contractors/).

Lusaka Times. 2018b. "Government Directs All Foreign Contractors to Adhere to the 20% Subcontracting Policy." *Lusaka Times*. Retrieved May 20, 2019 (https://www.lusakatimes.com/2018/05/23/government-directs-all-foreign-contractors-to-adhere-to-the-20-sub-contracting-policy/).

Lusaka Times. 2018c. "On-Going Works on the Ndola-Kitwe Dual Carriageway Are a Serious Diplomatic Scandal-Sinkamba." *Lusaka Times*. Retrieved May 13, 2019 (https://www.lusakatimes.com/2018/06/21/on-going-works-on-the-ndola-kitwe-dual-carriageway-are-a-serious-diplomatic-scandal-sinkamba/).

Lusaka Times. 2019a. "ACC Arrests, Charges Minister Chitotela with 9 More Counts of Corruption." *Lusaka Times*. Retrieved July 17, 2019 (https://www.lusakatimes.com/2019/05/24/acc-arrests-charges-minister-chitotela-with-9-more-counts-of-corruption/).

Lusaka Times. 2019b. "Lusaka Magistrate Court Clears Chitotela, He Has No Case to Answer." *Lusaka Times*. Retrieved July 12, 2019 (https://www.lusakatimes.com/2019/07/11/lusaka-magistrate-court-clears-chitotela-he-has-no-case-to-answer/?fbclid=IwAR0BDdcsfsAXrUPZz-UvwCuccTBDB58MvSEzHYG_KRoRlEPQFWXLkWDCaBQ).

Lusaka Times. 2019c. "President Lungu Warns Ministers and PF Officials Abusing the 20% Meant for Local Contractors." *Lusaka Times*. Retrieved September 30, 2019 (https://www.lusakatimes.com/2019/09/30/president-lungu-warns-ministers-and-pf-officials-abusing-the-20-meant-for-local-contractors/?fbclid=IwAR2lBO2rmJA1c2KI2fU-10pHJT-YR1bSQgGt8RtrLHTjtzvr-PHyUMJAbWc).

Mofya, Mwenya. 2022. "Lusaka-Ndola Highway Was Never Signed as a Contract, It Never Existed – Ng'andu." *News Diggers*. Retrieved July 12, 2023 (https://diggers.news/local/2022/08/08/lusaka-ndola-highway-was-never-signed-as-a-contract-it-never-existed-ngandu/).

Mohan, Giles, and May Tan-Mullins. 2019. "The Geopolitics of South–South Infrastructure Development: Chinese-Financed Energy Projects in the Global South." *Urban Studies* 56(7):1368–85. https://doi.org/10.1177/0042098018794351.

Momba, Jotham C. 2007. "The Intersection between Politics and Corruption in Zambia." *South African Journal of International Affairs* 14(1):115–25. https://doi.org/10.1080/10220460709545486.

Mosley, Paul. 2017. *Fiscal Policy and the Natural Resources Curse: How to Escape from the Poverty Trap*. Abingdon: Routledge.

Mutati, Felix. 2017. "2018 Budegt Address: 'Accelerating Fiscal Fitness for Sustained Inclusive Growth, Without Leaving Anyone Behind.'" *National*

Assembly of Zambia. Retrieved March 25, 2020 (http://www.parliament.gov.zm/sites/default/files/images/publication_docs/2018Budget.pdf).

Mwamba, Gilbert K. 2017. "Public Procurement in Zambia: A Commentary on the Law and Practice." *IJRDO Journal of Business Management* 3(9):24–44.

Mwenda, Joseph. 2019a. "Chitotela Probe Implicates Chinese, Lawyers, Fellow MP, Ministers and Others." *News Diggers*. Retrieved July 17, 2019 (https://diggers.news/local/2019/02/07/investigation-reveals-millions-linked-to-chitotela/).

Mwenda, Joseph. 2019b. "Lungu Fires Mawere, Transfers Chitotela, Luo." *News Diggers*. Retrieved July 19, 2019 (https://diggers.news/local/2019/07/19/lungu-fires-mawere-transfers-chitotela-luo/).

National Assembly of Zambia. 2017. "Ministerial Statement on the Lusaka/Ndola/Dual Carriageway Project Given by the Hon. Minister of Housing and Infrastructure Development, Mr. Chitotela, MP." *National Assembly of Zambia*. Retrieved May 19, 2019 (http://www.parliament.gov.zm/sites/default/files/images/publication_docs/MINISTERIALSTATEMENTBYTHEHON.MINISTEROFHOUSINGANDINFRA.DEV.pdf).

Ncube, Sipilisiwe. 2018. "Lusaka-Ndola Road Project Riddled with Corruption, Insists Simumba." *News Diggers*. Retrieved October 26, 2019 (https://diggers.news/local/2018/07/17/lusaka-ndola-road-project-riddled-with-corruption-insists-simumba/).

Nyabiage, Jevans. 2023. "Chinese Consortium to Build US$650 Million Toll Road in Cash-Strapped Zambia, but Will It Pay Off?" *South China Morning Post*. Retrieved July 12, 2023 (https://www.scmp.com/news/china/diplomacy/article/3213048/chinese-consortium-build-us650-million-toll-road-cash-strapped-zambia-will-it-pay).

Ofstad, Arve, and Elling Tjønneland. 2019. *Zambia's Looming Debt Crisis—Is China to Blame?* CMI Insight No. 1. Bergen: Chr. Michelsen Institute.

Peiffer, Caryn, and Pierre Englebert. 2012. "Extraversion, Vulnerability to Donors, and Political Liberalization in Africa." *African Affairs* 111(444):355–78. https://doi.org/10.1093/afraf/ads029.

PwC. 2019. *2018 Zambia Banking and Non-Banking Industry Survey*. Lusaka: Pricewaterhouse Coopers.

RDA. 2015a. "20 Percent Mandatory Sub-Contracting Guidlines." *Road Development Agency*. Retrieved March 25, 2020 (http://www.rda.org.zm/jdownloads/Publications/RDA20PERCENTMANDATORYSUB-CONTRACTINGGUIDELINES.pdf).

RDA. 2015b. *Request for Expression of Interest for Public-Private Partnerships for the Financing, Design, Construction to Dual Carriageway, Operation, Maintenance and Tolling of Selected Roads in Zambia*. Lusaka: Road Development Agency.

RDA. 2016. *Request for Proposals (RFP) for Public Private Partnerships for the Financing, Design, Construction to Dual Carriageway, Operation, Maintenance and Tolling of Selected Roads in Zambia*. Lusaka: Road Development Agency.

RDA. 2017. *Road Development Agency 2016: Annual Report*. Lusaka: Road Development Agency.

Reuters. 2017. "Zambia Awards Chinese Firm $1.2 Billion Road Expansion Project." *Reuters*. Retrieved May 15, 2019 (https://www.reuters.com/article/us-zambia-road/zambia-awards-chinese-firm-1-2-billion-road-expansion-project-idUSKCN1BJ1OT).

Reuters. 2019. "Zambia Infrastructure Minister Arrested on Corruption Charge." *Reuters*. Retrieved May 15, 2019 (https://www.reuters.com/article/us-zambia-corruption/zambia-infrastructure-minister-arrested-on-corruption-charge-idUSKCN1PU20G).

Saasa, Oliver S. 2018. *Pro-Growth Road Infrastructure Development in Zambia: Challenges, Opportunities and Policy Options*. Lusaka: Premier Consult Limited.

Schoneveld, George, Laura German, and Davison Gumbo. 2014. *The Developmental Implications of Sino-African Economic and Political Relations: A Preliminary Assessment for the Case of Zambia*. CIFOR Working Paper 133. Bogor: Center for International Forestry Research.

Shivji, Issa G. 2009. *Accumulation in an African Periphery: A Theoretical Framework*. Dar es Salaam: Mkuki na Nyota Publishers.

Simumba, Trevor. 2018. *He Who Pays The Piper: Zambia's Growing China Debt Crisis*. Lusaka: Centre for Trade Policy and Development.

Sinyangwe, Chiwoyu. 2022. "Zambia Cancels $1.2bn Chinese Road Project Linking Lusaka and Ndola." *The Africa Report*. Retrieved June 29, 2023 (https://www.theafricareport.com/185538/zambia-cancels-1-2bn-chinese-road-project-linking-lusaka-and-ndola/).

Sishuwa, Sishuwa. 2019. "The Real Reasons Why Lungu Won't Fire Chitotela." *Lusaka Times*. Retrieved July 4, 2019 (https://www.lusakatimes.com/2019/02/12/the-real-reasons-why-lungu-wont-fire-chitotela/).

Sum, Ngai-Ling, and Bob Jessop. 2013. *Towards a Cultural Political Economy: Putting Culture in Its Place*. Cheltenham: Edward Elgar.

Sun, Irene Yuan, Kartik Jayaram, and Omid Kassiri. 2017. *Dance of the Lions and Dragons: How Are Africa and China Engaging, and How Will the Partnership Evolve?* New York: McKinsey & Company.

Szeftel, Morris. 1982. "Political Graft and the Spoils System in Zambia: The State as a Resource in Itself." *Review of African Political Economy* 9(24):4–21.

Szeftel, Morris. 2000. "'Eat with Us': Managing Corruption and Patronage under Zambia's Three Republics, 1964-99." *Journal of Contemporary African Studies* 18(2):207–24. https://doi.org/10.1080/713675624.

Taylor, Ian. 2006a. *China and Africa: Engagement and Compromise*. Abingdon: Routledge.

Taylor, Scott D. 2006b. "Divergent Politico-Legal Responses to Past Presidential Corruption in Zambia and Kenya: Catching the 'Big Fish', or Letting Him off the Hook?" *Third World Quarterly* 27(2):281–301. https://doi.org/10.1080/01436590500432325.

Taylor, Ian. 2007. "Governance in Africa and Sino-African Relations: Contradictions or Confluence?" *Politics* 27(3):139–46. https://doi.org/10.1111/j.1467-9256.2007.00293.x.

Taylor, Ian. 2009. *China's New Role in Africa*. Boulder: Lynne Rienner Publishers.

Taylor, Ian, and Tim Zajontz. 2020. "In a Fix: Africa's Place in the Belt and Road Initiative and the Reproduction of Dependency." *South African Journal of International Affairs* 27(3): 277–295. https://doi.org/10.1080/10220461.2020.1830165.

The Zambian Observer. 2017. "Mutati Throws the $1.2billion Lusaka-Ndola Dual Carriage Way into Funding Confusion." *The Zambian Observer*. Retrieved May 15, 2019 (https://www.zambianobserver.com/mutati-throws-the-1-2billion-lusaka-ndola-dual-carriage-way-into-funding-confusion/).

The Zambian Observer. 2018. "Cadreism a Source of Construction Sector Corruption in Zambia—TIZ." *The Zambian Observer*. Retrieved May 20, 2019 (https://www.zambianobserver.com/cadreism-a-source-of-construction-sector-corruption-in-zambia-tiz/).

The Zambian Observer. 2019. "Scope For Lusaka-Ndola Dual Carriage Was Irregularly Changed—Public Protector." *The Zambian Observer*. Retrieved June 29, 2019 (https://www.zambianobserver.com/scope-for-lusaka-ndola-dual-carriage-was-irregularly-changed-public-protector/).

van Donge, Jan Kees. 2009. "The Plundering of Zambian Resources by Frederick Chiluba and His Friends: A Case Study of the Interaction between National Politics and the International Drive towards Good Governance." *African Affairs* 108(430):69–90. https://doi.org/10.1093/afraf/adn073.

Yescombe, E. R. 2007. *Public-Private Partnerships: Principles of Policy and Finance*. Oxford: Butterworth-Heinemann.

Yescombe, E. R., and Edward Farquharson. 2018. *Public-Private Partnerships for Infrastructure: Principles of Policy and Finance*. 2nd ed. Oxford: Butterworth-Heinemann.

Zhang, Xin. 2017. "Chinese Capitalism and the Maritime Silk Road: A World-Systems Perspective." *Geopolitics* 22(2):310–31. https://doi.org/10.1080/14650045.2017.1289371.

Zhao, Suisheng. 2011. "China's African Relations and the Balance with Western Powers." Pp. 61–80 in *China and the European Union in Africa*, edited by J. Men and B. Barton. Farnham: Ashgate.

CHAPTER 8

Towards a "New Era" of Sino-African Infrastructure Cooperation

Rooted in the critical realist tradition within the philosophy of science, this book scrutinised Sino-African cooperation in the infrastructure sector through a combination of conceptual abstraction and causal analysis with reference to the cases of Zambia's road sector and the Tanzania-Zambia Railway Authority (TAZARA). The aim of the study was to discern structural determinants that underlie Africa's recent, Chinese-sponsored infrastructure boom and to assess the degree to and the ways in which African actors co-determine and condition Chinese engagements in infrastructure projects. I posited David Harvey's spatio-temporal fix, i.e. the structural tendency towards the "temporal deferral and geographical expansion" of capital as a result of overaccumulation (Harvey 2003: 115, see also 2004: 65), as a key generative mechanism involved in China's rise in Africa's infrastructure sector. Driven by mounting overaccumulation in China's infrastructure and construction sectors, the Chinese government, SOEs and SOBs, as well as private Chinese capital, have undertaken coordinated (thought not always concerted) to spatially reorganise the Chinese growth model. African infrastructural "needs" and the continent's often-invoked "infrastructure finance gap" have offered convenient outlets for Chinese surplus capital, goods and material. The iterative movement between the "explanatory model" of the spatio-temporal fix and the concrete cases under investigation revealed the

T. Zajontz, *The Political Economy of China's Infrastructure Development in Africa*, International Political Economy Series,
https://doi.org/10.1007/978-3-031-44449-4_8

necessity for further theorisation, as Harvey's theory did not provide sufficiently rich conceptualisations to account for the co-determining role of African (state) actors in facilitating, mediating and regulating the actualisation of the "fix" in concrete spatio-temporal conjunctures. In the remainder of this concluding chapter, I extrapolate from the most central theoretical arguments and empirical findings some generalising claims (of a non-empiricist kind) and prospects for Sino-African cooperation in the infrastructure sector that I consider relevant—or believe to become increasingly relevant.

African State Agency Matters—Yet It Matters Differentially

Complementing the spatio-temporal fix with Jessop's strategic-relational approach (SRA) to state power allowed me to assess particular African state strategies that have shaped the concrete forms the Chinese infrastructural fix has taken on in the empirical cases under scrutiny. This, in turn, suggests that "the" "infrastructure state" (Schindler et al. 2022) in Africa and the agency it exerts in the context of Chinese-funded infrastructure projects are contingent upon historically and spatio-temporally specific political and economic context factors. In Zambia's road sector, the infrastructural fix has been strongly fostered by the conjuncture of the government's expansive, debt-financed "development-through-infrastructure" strategy and the particularities of Chinese loan financing, most notably the tying of funding to the selection of particular contractors. Chapter 6 has shown that the Sino-Zambian "road bonanza" and the corresponding rise in public debt have increasingly constrained the strategic scope of the Zambian government in the infrastructure sector (and beyond). This structural constraint has caused a nascent shift in the governance of Chinese road projects, from public debt finance to private project finance and has accelerated the gradual commodification and privatisation of the country's trunk road network.

Chapter 7 has illustrated how strategic opportunities which have arisen from Zambia's neopatrimonial state form have provided (private) economic incentives for Zambian political elites and rentiers to agree with Chinese contractors on road projects in "not so public" procurement processes. The study found that Zambia's underregulated "local content" policy has served as a neopatrimonial elite strategy through which a share of Chinese capital "trickles down" along clientelistic networks. In this instance, African elite agency has exploited the inflow of Chinese capital into Zambia's road sector to stabilise the institutional ensemble of the neopatrimonial state. The analysis of the Lusaka-Ndola dual carriageway project has exemplified "not so public" procurement and the shift towards private project finance, both of which have ensured the realisation of the "fix"—at significant public costs.

Chapters 4 and 5 concerned a case in which African state strategies obstructed the Chinese infrastructural fix from materialising, namely the hitherto unsuccessful privatisation of the TAZARA. Chapter 4 revealed that the Chinese proposal for a 30 year Rehabilitate-Operate-Transfer PPP typifies the logic of temporally deferring surplus capital by "fixing" it in a long-term investment, whose profitability the Chinese terms and conditions intended to secure. The two shareholding governments exerted "African agency" by firmly rejecting the Chinese proposal on the grounds that the proposed terms and conditions were not mutually beneficial. I illustrated how the path-dependency of previous, unsuccessful railway privatisations has caused strategic cautiousness on the part of the Tanzanian and Zambian governments. Yet, as shown in Chapter 5, the two governments are differentially constrained in acting upon their strategic learning. Again a result of unsustainable levels of public debt, the Zambian government has considered a Chinese participation in TAZARA by means of a concession as indispensable.

The decisive factor for the impasse of the Chinese infrastructural fix in the case of TAZARA had been the position of the Tanzanian government. The study traced the shift in Tanzania's state strategies towards economic nationalist policies back to a change in the balance of political forces in the Tanzanian political system over the past decade and a half. The Magufuli administration challenged social forces that hitherto profited from patrimonial modes of governance through a rigid anti-corruption campaign and the centralisation of political power and control in the presidency. Magufuli's autocratic leadership created an atmosphere of constant threat of the president's uncompromising dealings with negligence and malfeasance within government which caused a relative strengthening of legal-bureaucratic institutions and norms, not least in the context of public procurement processes. As a consequence, the Tanzanian government exercised increasing scrutiny and pragmatism with regard to the prioritisation, selection, loan financing and governance of infrastructure projects.

Doubtlessly, Magufuli's authoritarian tendencies curtailed the political space for the political opposition, civil society actors and the media and gave reason to worry about the state of democracy in Tanzania, something which is only very slowly reversed by his successor President Hassan (see Minde 2023). In the economic realm, the government's autocratic developmentalism and its oftentimes confrontational strategy vis-à-vis foreign investors aimed at ameliorating structural constraints which the government considered to result from Tanzania's disadvantageous integration into the global economy. Consequently, the government's engagement with China was marked by cautious and pragmatic negotiations, based on the government's declared infrastructural and developmental priorities and on more "nationalist" cost–benefit analyses. This has significantly decelerated Chinese involvement in the infrastructure sector, as the protracted TAZARA negotiations as well as the stalled Bagamoyo port project and the re-tendering of the SGR construction have exemplified. Magufuli's nationalist infrastructure state proved incompatible with some of the conditions and practices related to Chinese projects. Yet, over time Magufuli's strategy towards foreign investors had became more pragmatic and Chinese firms are now constructing parts of the country's SGR, the legacy project of the late president.

Overall, this study has shown that the strategic selectivity of prevailing forms of states, i.e. specific structural constraints and opportunities inherent in the social relations that constitute the state (Jessop 2016: 54; Koivisto 2010: 79–80), conditions both the forms and degree of African state agency in facilitating, negotiating and implementing infrastructure projects in collaboration with Chinese (state) capital. By implictaion, state transformations, such as the one from a neopatrimonial to an autocratic developmental state under President Magufuli, affect the processes, outcomes and the distribution of costs and benefits of Sino-African infrastructure projects and, hence, call for further theoretically informed (comparative) case studies. This is not least relevant in the light of mounting controversies about debt and the privatisation of African infrastructure.

Debt and the Renaissance of PPPs

The findings of this study provide a more nuanced understanding of the function of debt in relation to Sino-African cooperation in the infrastructure sector. The case study of Zambia's road sector has revealed that growing African debt owned by China does not result in asset expropriations and colonial-style takeovers of African economies, as some China critics in the West, including US President Biden, polemically suggest (see White House 2023). In fact, the detrimental structural effects of Africa's growing indebtedness to China (and other creditors) are more subtle, inherent in structural tendencies of capitalist accumulation and, yet, contingent upon the strategic reflection and capacities of African states. In the Zambian case, the unsustainable accumulation of debt from Chinese SOBs to finance infrastructure has reduced the government's strategic capacities and catalysed the gradual commodification and privatisation of formerly public assets, viz. Zambia's trunk roads. In line with Harvey's theory, it is likely that these new rounds of accumulation by dispossessing African infrastructure will first afflict those states that are particularly indebted.

As discussed in Chapter 2.1, Chinese loan commitments to African countries have dropped by 93 per cent between 2016 and 2020 (Carmody et al. 2022: 206; see Figure 2.1). Sovereign lending to countries like Zambia, for example, has simply become economically too risky and politically costly because of backlashes related to the discussed "debt trap" narrative. To keep up demand and ensure surplus creation, Chinese firms and banks have started to adapt their accumulation strategies from hitherto dominant EPC contracts, usually financed through sovereign loans, to PPPs that include project finance, operation and, in some cases, tolling (see Alden and Jiang 2019; Zhang 2023). Since the mid-2000s, the Chinese government has, in line with neoliberal discourse, actively promoted PPPs as a supposedly "debtless" alternative to loan-financed infrastructure through their embassies on the continent and at gatherings such as the FOCAC (van Wieringen and Zajontz 2023). One of the main objectives of the China Overseas Infrastructure Development and Investment Corporation, which opened its Africa headquarters in Johannesburg in April 2017, is the facilitation of PPPs (ICA 2018: 54). The 2019 BRI Forum "encourage[d] third-market, tripartite cooperation and Public Private Partnership (PPP) cooperation" (BRI 2019: Paragraph 29). The "dominant form of accumulation" (Harvey 2003: 153) within the Chinese infrastructural fix across Africa gradually shifts from expanded reproduction to accumulation by dispossession. It is likely that we will be witnessing a renaissance of PPPs—this time driven not least by Chinese (state) capital in alliance with indebted African governments which have "run out of alternatives".

Alden and Jiang see a chance that China's gradual move from loan-debt investment to equity investment might allow for a reconciliation of sustainable public budgets and continued infrastructure development in Africa:

> If equity investment, regarded by China as the future direction for financing in Africa, could gradually overtake traditional loans as one of the main financing methods, especially in the infrastructure and power sectors, this may help alleviate the dilemma posed by the combination of the need for infrastructure development and deepening debt difficulties. (2019: 648)

Brautigam (2020) likewise suggests that "we should be encouraging more of them [PPPs]. Equity investments are a smart way for countries to finance the operation of badly needed infrastructure, while also helping repay loans". Yet, this implies the privatisation of African roads, railways and other commons. The recent trend in Zambia's road sector reveals that the change in financial governance of road projects, from loan finance to Chinese-run project finance PPPs, amounts to new forms of accumulation by dispossession with detrimental effects for those people with the smallest disposable incomes—the small-scale traders on their way to market places or working-class commuters. Skyrocketing costs of living already immensely affect African citizens. Adding toll fees will in all likelihood spark further popular contestation against PPPs, as in the case of the Nairobi Expressway which was built and is now operated and tolled by China Road and Bridge Corporation under a 30 year BOT contract (van Wieringen and Zajontz 2023). Furthermore, as the now cancelled EPC+F contract for the Lusaka-Ndola dual carriageway has shown, private project finance PPPs can incur major liabilities for public authorities. Even Uganda's country director of the IMF, usually an institution which actively promotes PPPs, declared to be "very uneasy when we talk about PPPs in terms of debt instruments" (Karpowicz, quoted in Barigaba 2021). It remains to be seen how mutually beneficial the two DFBOT road PPPs (Chingola-Kasumbalesa, Lusaka-Ndola), into which the new Zambian government recently entered, will turn out. Sino-African infrastructure PPPs therefore constitute instructive objects for future research, as they herald a "new era" in the governance of the Chinese infrastructural fix.

A new era has also come regarding the increasing geopoliticisation of infrastructure and the intensifying competition among China and

"Western" powers for shares in and the control of infrastructure markets across Africa. Both the European Union and the US government have announced their own connectivity initiatives, the Global Gateway and the Partnership for Global Infrastructure and Investment which is actually a Group of 7 (G7) initiative. Both initiatives must be understood as geopolitical-cum-geoeconomical reactions to China's influence in the "Global South". They have been explicitly promoted by top officials as socially, environmentally and financially more sustainable as well as more transparent and high-quality alternatives to the BRI. Both initiatives pledge tens of billions of dollars in investments for transport, green energy and ICT infrastructures, with Africa playing a central role in both strategies (Zajontz 2022: 130–32). When US President Biden spoke, on the margins of COP26 in Glasgow in November 2021, about the G7 initiative he stated among other things: "Being transparent about how we're financing our projects, we offer positive alternatives to debt—to debt traps and corruption. We can hold entire countries back if we don't do that. Transparency is critically important" (Biden 2021). Two weeks later Secretary of State Antony Blinken travelled to Kenya, Nigeria and Senegal for a "listening session" to discuss African infrastructure needs. In Abuja, Blinken tellingly told his Nigerian audience that the US government "doesn't want to limit your partnerships with other countries. We want to make your partnerships with us even stronger. We don't want to make you choose. We want to give you choices".

While Biden's statement is further evidence that Chinese-owned debt has become a highly geopoliticised, as discussed in the introduction of this book, Blinken alludes to a second central theme this book covered, African state agency. It is too early to tell whether the political economy of competing connectivity initiatives will afford African governments more strategic space and capacities to develop infrastructure in times of tight public budgets. In the current global political environment, it seems likely that the "Global Race to Build Africa's Infrastructure" (Gil et al. 2019: 1) will intensify and that said infrastructure initiatives will be used to wield geopolitical influence and to control critical value chains against the background of a looming Second Cold War (see Gort and Brooks 2023; Schindler et al. 2022; Zajontz and Bagwandeen 2023).

The "Fragility" of the "Fix" and the Regional Dimension

Returning once again to Chinese capital and its spatio-temporal fix: As shown in this study, for their continuity spatio-temporal fixes require organisational and institutional compromises among various social forces that aim at establishing (always temporary) "structured coherence" within territories that are incorporated into spatially expanding accumulation systems (Harvey 2001: 329, 2003: 102; Sum and Jessop 2013: 248). Yet, the issues of sovereign indebtedness, privatisations, "not so public" procurement and corruption have exposed "systematic contradictions or patterned incoherence" (Jessop 2005: 50) and, hence, the inherent "fragility" (Jessop 2013: 303) of the Chinese infrastructural fix in Africa. Debt distress among some recipient states, the debatable economic feasibility of some projects as well as recurrent corruption allegations in public tenders and procurements no longer only damage the legitimacy of Chinese infrastructure development abroad but hold the potential to cause major economic backlashes—both for recipient countries and for China. This is why the Chinese government has (discursively) reacted and elevated debt sustainability as a cornerstone for cooperation under both the BRI and FOCAC (see BRI 2019: Paragraph 30; FOCAC 2018: Paragraphs 3.3.1, 3.9.2). Materially, Chinese lending has decreased substantially, as discussed in Chapter 2. Equally, Beijing has stepped up (declaratory) efforts to curb graft and corrupt practices. The Joint Communique of the April 2019 BRI Forum expresses support for "international anti-corruption cooperation and work towards zero tolerance in anti-corruption, consistent with national laws and regulations" (BRI 2019: Paragraph 25; see Weinland 2019).

While the effectiveness of these measures is hard to measure, Jessop and Sum have pioneered an interesting research agenda in this context. They aptly describe China's enhanced efforts to regulate and monitor more closely the conduct of Chinese-run infrastructure projects and investments abroad as "multi-spatial metagovernance" (2018: 474). Meta-governance "in its most basic [...] sense [...] denotes the governance of governance" (Jessop 2016: 169). It comprises the modification of organisational, regulatory and institutional parameters with the aim of eradicating failures that arise from existing forms of coordination and exchange (Jessop 2016: 169–70; see Meuleman 2008). China's increasing meta-governance efforts aim at containing negative political and economic repercussions from China's "moving out" strategy and to uphold the image of a benevolent world power (see Carmody et al. 2022; van Wieringen and Zajontz 2023). Further research should focus on African (state) strategies against the background of China's multi-spatial meta-governance as well as to what extent coordination in multilateral fora, especially the BRI Forum, the FOCAC and the BRICS grouping, affects regional cooperation and integration among African states, not least in the infrastructure sector (see Zajontz 2024).

The case study of TAZARA has elucidated politico-economic challenges to the organisation and institutionalisation of China's spatio-temporal fix that arise from the railway's binational governance structure. Different structural contexts, differential strategic capacities on the part of African governments and resultant strategic divergences in the context of Chinese infrastructure projects pose challenges for the Chinese government and capital in the implementation of cross-border and regional infrastructure projects. Kenya's SGR is another case in point where a combination of opaque procurements, waning debt sustainability and a lack of regional cooperation has hitherto hampered the realisation of this *regional* railway along the Northern Corridor (Taylor 2020; Wang and Wissenbach 2019). China's infrastructure bilateralism with African states has equally not helped to ensure a coordinated approach among the countries of the Northern Corridor (Otele 2020). To address the "regional dimension", China has recently stepped up efforts to enhance cooperation among and between BRI and FOCAC signatory states as well as with the African Union and regional economic communities (Zajontz 2024: 117). Particularly the BRI "aims to constitute and (meta)govern relations among territories, places, scales and networks" (Jessop and Sum 2018: 477).

Further analysis should therefore be directed towards the interrelation between the Chinese infrastructural fix and African regionalisation generally and regional infrastructural planning in particular. The fierce competition between Kenya and Tanzania for the dominant position as the Eastern "gateway to Africa" is an intriguing case in point (see Kahama 2018: 56, 64, 74). The countries' new SGR lines are intended to serve, at least partially, the same landlocked destinations (Rwanda, Uganda, Burundi, Eastern DRC) (see Onyango 2019), Nairobi and Dodoma are also in a race to expand their respective port infrastructure (see BBC 2016; Hönke and Cuesta-Fernandez 2017: 1082) and have competed over the oil pipeline from Hoima (see Blair 2016). Infrastructure development in Africa has re-entered the realm of "high politics". Sino-African cooperation in the infrastructure realm is therefore not least dependent on political developments within Africa's regional economic communities and, ultimately, the extent to which African governments are willing to coordinate regional infrastructure development. The overall absence of regional coordination with respect to large-scale infrastructure projects certainly fuels the risk of erecting "white elephants" (Nugent 2018: 38) which, in Harveyean terms, would be subject to particularly rapid devaluation—at significant societal costs. In summary, the Chinese infrastructural fix across Africa is likely to remain what it was posited to be in this book: A highly contentious, strategic-relational process that is co-determined by differentially constrained African agency, yet characterised by contradictions inherent in global capitalism.

References

Alden, Chris, and Lu Jiang. 2019. "Brave New World: Debt, Industrialization and Security in China–Africa Relations." *International Affairs* 95(3):641–57.https://doi.org/10.1093/ia/iiz083

Barigaba, Julius. 2021. "Kenya in Debt Distress, as All EA Economies Facing Risks Too." *The East African*, September 18, 4–5.

BBC. 2016. "The Race to Become East Africa's Biggest Port." *BBC News*. Retrieved March 10, 2020 (https://www.bbc.co.uk/news/world-africa-36458946).

Biden, Joseph. 2021. "Remarks by President Biden in Meeting on the Build Back Better World Initiative." *The White House*. Retrieved March 31, 2021 (https://www.whitehouse.gov/briefing-room/speeches-remarks/2021/11/02/remarks-by-president-biden-in-meeting-on-the-build-back-better-world-initiative/).

Blair, Edmund. 2016. "Uganda Picks Tanzania for Oil Pipeline Route Rather than Kenya." *Reuters*. Retrieved March 10, 2020 (https://www.reuters.com/article/us-energy-uganda/uganda-picks-tanzania-for-oil-pipeline-route-rather-than-kenya-idUSKCN0XK0DT).

Brautigam, Deborah. 2020. "Chinese Debt Relief: Fact and Fiction." *The Diplomat*. Retrieved May 26, 2020 (https://thediplomat.com/2020/04/chinese-debt-relief-fact-and-fiction/).

BRI. 2019. "Joint Communique of the Leaders' Roundtable of the 2nd Belt and Road Forum for International Cooperation." *The Belt and Road Forum*. Retrieved August 14, 2019 (http://www.beltandroadforum.org/english/n100/2019/0427/c36-1311.html).

Carmody, Pádraig, Tim Zajontz, and Ricardo Reboredo. 2022. "From 'Debt Diplomacy' to Donorship? China's Changing Role in Global Development." *Global Political Economy* 1(2):198–217. doi: https://doi.org/10.1332/uzhw7185.

FOCAC. 2018. "Beijing Action Plan (2019–2021)." *Forum on China-Africa Cooperation*. Retrieved June 1, 2019 (https://www.focac.org/eng/zywx_1/zywj/t1594297.htm).

Gort, Joris, and Andrew Brooks. 2023. "Africa's Next Debt Crisis: A Relational Comparison of Chinese and Western Lending to Zambia." *Antipode* 55(3):830–52. doi:https://doi.org/10.1111/anti.12921

Gil, Nuno, Anne Stafford, and Innocent Musonda. 2019. "Duality by Design: The Global Race to Build Africa's Infrastructure." Pp. 1–30 in *Duality by Design: The Global Race to Build Africa's Infrastructure*, edited by N. Gil, A. Stafford, and I. Musonda. Cambridge: Cambridge University Press.

Harvey, David. 2001. *Spaces of Capital: Towards a Critical Geography*. Edinburgh: Edinburgh University Press.

Harvey, David. 2003. *The New Imperialism*. Oxford: Oxford University Press.

Harvey, David. 2004. "The 'New' Imperialism: Accumulation by Dispossession." *Socialist Register* 40:63–87.

Hönke, Jana, and Ivan Cuesta-Fernandez. 2017. "A Topolographical Approach to Infrastructure: Political Topography, Topology and the Port of Dar Es Salaam." *Environment and Planning D: Society and Space* 35(6):1076–95. https://doi.org/10.1177/0263775817707762.

ICA. 2018. *Infrastructure Financing Trends in Africa – 2017*. Abidjan: Infrastructure Consortium for Africa.

Jessop, Bob. 2005. "Critical Realism and the Strategic-Relational Approach." *New Formations: A Journal of Culture, Theory and Politics* (56):40–53.

Jessop, Bob. 2016. *The State: Past, Present, Future*. Cambridge: Polity Press.

Jessop, Bob, and Ngai-Ling Sum. 2018. "Geopolitics: Putting Geopolitics in Its Place in Cultural Political Economy." *Environment and Planning A: Economy and Space* 50(2):474–78. https://doi.org/10.1177/0308518X17731106.

Kahama, Joseph K. 2018. *The Challenge to China-Tanzania Relationship: To Enhance Cooperation and Mutual Benefits*. Dar es Salaam: Tema Publishers.

Koivisto, Marjo. 2010. "State Theory in International Relations: Why Realism Matters." Pp. 69–87 in *Scientific Realism and International Relations*, edited by J. Joseph and C. Wight. Basingstoke: Palgrave Macmillan.

Meuleman, Louis. 2008. *Public Management and the Metagovernance of Hierarchies, Networks and Markets*. Heidelberg: Springer.

Minde, Nicodemus. 2023. "Samia Suluhu Hassan Is Reforming Tanzania—It's Winning Her Fans but Boosting the Opposition." *The Conversation*. Retrieved July 17, 2023 (https://theconversation.com/samia-suluhu-hassan-is-reforming-tanzania-its-winning-her-fans-but-boosting-the-opposition-198793).

Nugent, Paul. 2018. "Africa's Re-Enchantment with Big Infrastructure: White Elephants Dancing in Virtuous Circles?" Pp. 22–40 in *Extractive Industries and Changing State Dynamics in Africa*, edited by J. Schubert, U. Engel, and M. Elisio. Abingdon: Routledge.

Onyango, Emmanuel. 2019. "Blow to Northern Corridor as Tanzania Signs Deal to Link SGR to Burundi, DRC." *The East African*. Retrieved March 10, 2020 (https://www.theeastafrican.co.ke/business/Tanzania-signs-mega-sgr-deal-with-burundi-drc/2560-5377324-75ujpd/index.html?fbclid=IwAR172nOaD4742dRHckKA0Yr3XbfD-8ZqpUoEuRckpK2EIMYSk9CKF-mGhnA).

Otele, Oscar M. 2020. "China, Region-Centric Infrastructure Drives and Regionalism in Africa." *South African Journal of International Affairs* 27(4):511–32. https://doi.org/10.1080/10220461.2020.1856179.

Schindler, Seth, Jessica DiCarlo, and Dinesh Paudel. 2022. "The New Cold War and the Rise of the 21st-Century Infrastructure State." *Transactions of the Institute of British Geographers* 47(2):331–46. https://doi.org/10.1111/tran.12480.

Sum, Ngai-Ling, and Bob Jessop. 2013. *Towards a Cultural Political Economy: Putting Culture in Its Place*. Cheltenham: Edward Elgar.

Taylor, Ian. 2020. "Kenya's New Lunatic Express: The Standard Gauge Railway." *African Studies Quarterly* 19(3–4):29–52.

Wang, Yuan, and Uwe Wissenbach. 2019. "Clientelism at Work? A Case Study of Kenyan Standard Gauge Railway Project." *Economic History of Developing Regions* 34(3):280–99. https://doi.org/10.1080/20780389.2019.1678026.

Weinland, Don. 2019. "China to Tackle Corruption in Belt and Road Projects." *Financial Times*. Retrieved March 14, 2020 (https://www.ft.com/content/a5815e66-a91b-11e9-984c-fac8325aaa04).

White House. 2023. "Remarks by President Biden and Prime Minister Rishi Sunak of the United Kingdom in Joint Press Conference." Retrieved July 16, 2023 (https://www.whitehouse.gov/briefing-room/speeches-remarks/2023/06/08/remarks-by-president-biden-and-prime-minister-rishi-sunak-of-the-united-kingdom-in-joint-press-conference/).

van Wieringen, Kjeld, and Tim Zajontz. 2023. "From Loan-Financed to Privatised Infrastructure? Tracing China's Turn towards Public-Private Partnerships in Africa." *Journal of Current Chinese Affairs*, online first. https://doi.org/10.1177/18681026231188140.

Zajontz, Tim. 2022. "Infrastructure." Pp. 120–38 in *Yearbook on the African Union*. Vol. 2, edited by U. Engel. Leiden: Brill.

Zajontz, Tim. 2024. "Chinese Globalism, African Regionalisms and State Spatial Strategies: The Intricacies of Regionalising Africa's Railway Renaissance." Pp. 112–36 in *Africa's Railway Renaissance: The role and impact of China*, edited by T. Zajontz, P. Carmody, M. Bagwandeen, and A. Leysens. Abingdon: Routledge.

Zajontz, Tim, and Mandira Bagwandeen. 2023. "Infrastructure." Pp. 134–58 in *Yearbook on the African Union*. Vol. 3, edited by U. Engel. Leiden: Brill.
Zhang, Hong. 2023. *From Contractors to Investors? Evolving Engagement of Chinese State Capital in Global Infrastructure Development and the Case of Lekki Port in Nigeria*. China Africa Research Initiative Working Paper No. 53. Washington: Johns Hopkins University.

Appendix

See (Tables A.1, A.2, and A.3)

T. Zajontz, *The Political Economy of China's Infrastructure Development in Africa*, International Political Economy Series,
https://doi.org/10.1007/978-3-031-44449-4

Table A.1 Funding commitments for African infrastructure by source (in $m)

	2020	*2019*	*2018*	*2017*	*2016*	*2015*
ICA members[a] total	**18,142**	**26,863**	**20,243**	**19,650**	**18,615**	**19,832**
Selected ICA members						
France	966	1932	1936	2123	2887	2445
Germany	588	739	1608	838	1127	1139
Japan	532	751	517	2361	1941	1768
USA	243	227	297	292		307
South Africa	1078	1480	1055	497	1211	929
AfDB	1176	5365	4538	3364	3956	4166
European Investment Bank	2225	1590	2225	1852	1250	1414
World Bank Group	7178	6634	7989	7516	4055	6285
Non-ICA members total	**43,846**	**47,346**	**68,736**	**59,592**	**45,766**	**51,687**
Selected non-ICA members						
African governments	33,406	34,866	37,525	34,345	30,700	24,000
China	6480	6715	25,680	19,403	6413	20,868
India	1318	803	762	704	1197	524
South Korea				10	432	88
Non-ICA European bilaterals	347	553	282	277	287	238
African regional development banks	242		328	541	924	419
Arab Coordination Group[b]	631	2200	2442	2985	5528	4412
European Bank for Reconstruction and Development	422	344	744	1327	105	638
New Development Bank	1000	1715	500		180	
Asian Infrastructure Investment Bank		150	300			
Private sector	**19,010**	**10,817**	**11,824**	**2320**	**2600**	**7400**
TOTAL financing	**80,998**	**85,026**	**100,803**	**81,562**	**66,981**	**78,919**

Source Author's compilation, based on data from (ICA 2018b: 8, 2022: 71)*; empty fields stand for either no commitments made or no data available*

[a]Membership: All G8 members (Canada, France, Germany, Italy, Japan, Russia, United Kingdom, USA), South Africa, the World Bank, International Finance Corporation (IFC), European Commission (EC), European Investment Bank (EIB), Islamic Development Bank (IsDB), African Development Bank (AfDB), Development Bank of Southern Africa (DBSA)

[b]Membership: Kuwait Fund for Arab Economic Development (KFAED), Saudi Fund for Development (SFD), Abu Dhabi Fund for Development (ADFD), Qatar Development Fund (QDF), Arab Fund for Economic and Social Development (AFESD), Islamic Development Bank (IsDB), OPEC Fund for International Development (OFID), Arab Bank for Economic Development in Africa (BADEA), Arab Gulf Program for United Nations Development Organizations (AGFUND), Arab Monetary Fund (AMF)

Table A.2 Chinese-owned companies registered with the Zambian National Construction Council in grade 1, category R - general roads and earthworks (as at 30 June 2018)

1	CHINA HENAN INTERNATIONAL COOPERATION GROUP COMPANY LIMITED
2	ZHONGMEI ENGINEERING GROUP LIMITED
3	AVIC-INTL PROJECT ENGINEERING COMPANY
4	CHINA GEO ENGINEERING CORPORATION SOUTHERN AFRICAN LIMITED
5	CHINA GEO-ENGINEERING CORPORATION LIMITED
6	CHINA HARBOUR ENGINEERING COMPANY LIMITED
7	WAH KONG ENTERPRISES LIMITED
8	FIFTEEN MCC AFRICA CONSTRUCTION AND TRADE LIMITED
9	SINOHYDRO ZAMBIA LIMITED
10	CHINA CAMC ENGINEERING CO., LIMITED
11	UNIK CONSTRUCTION ENGINEERING ZAMBIA LIMITED
12	CHINA STATE CONSTRUCTION ENGINEERING CORPORATION LIMITED
13	HUA-JIANG INVESTMENTS LIMITED
14	SEPCO ZAMBIA LIMITED
15	HEBEI BUILDING MATERIALS INDUSTRY DESIGN AND RESEARCH INSTITUTE (ZAMBIA)
16	ZHONGAN HUALI ZAMBIA CORPORATION LIMITED
17	VOTO ENGINEERING EQUIPMENT ZAMBIA LIMITED
18	CHINA CIVIL ENGINEERING CONSTRUCTION CORPORATION (ZAMBIA) LIMITED
19	COVEC (ZAMBIA) LIMITED
20	HENAN ZHONGMENG CONSTRUCTION AND ENGINEERING COMPANY LIMITED
21	SHANGHAI CONSTRUCTION GROUP COMPANY LIMITED
22	CHINA JIANGXI CORPORATION FOR INTERNATIONAL ECONOMIC AND TECHNICAL COOPERATION ZAMBIA LIMITED
23	SOGECOA ZAMBIA LIMITED
24	ZAMBIAN NONFERROUS METALS EXPLORATION AND CONSTRUCTION COMPANY
25	CHINA RAILWAY TWENTY FOURTH BUREAU ZAMBIA ENGINEERING COMPANY
26	CHINA RAILWAY SEVENTH GROUP (ZAMBIA) LIMITED
27	ZAMBIAN JIHAI AGRICULTURE COMPANY LIMITED
28	ANHUI SHUIAN CONSTRUCTION GROUP CORPORATION (ZAMBIA) LIMITED
29	DATONG CONSTRUCTION LIMITED
30	CHINA NATIONAL COMPLETE ENGINEERING CORPORATION ZAMBIA

(continued)

Table A.2 (continued)

31	CBMI AFRICA LIMITED
32	SUNSHARE CONSTRUCTION LIMITED
33	ZHONGYANG CONSTRUCTION GROUP (ZAMBIA) COMPANY LIMITED
34	POLY TECHNOLOGIES INC (ZAMBIA) LIMITED
35	CHINA JIANGSU INTERNATIONAL ECONOMIC TECHNICAL CO ZAMBIA
36	LUSHION INVETSMENTS LIMITED
37	HENGXIN INFRASTRUCTURE ENGINEERING COMPANY LIMITED
38	CHINA COMMUNICATIONS CONSTRUCTION COMPANY LIMITED
39	HUATE-ZAMBIAN INTERNATIONAL INDUSTRIAL COMPANY LIMITED

Source NCC (2019)

Table A.3 Toll structure for Zambia-registered vehicles

Vehicle category	*Single-access charge (Zambian Kwacha)*
Private small vehicles	20
Buses (including minibuses 16–30 seats)	45
Light vehicles with 2–3 axles	50
Buses (including buses over thirty seats)	80
Heavy vehicle with 4 axles	150
Heavy vehicles with multiple axles above 4 axles	150
All abnormal loads	500

Source Author's compilation, based on Statutory Instrument No. 85 of 2016 (GRZ 2016)

List of Interviews

Anand, Rahim, director, Phoenix Freight Ltd. Clearing & Forwarding Agent, Dar es Salaam, Tanzania, 8 November 2017.

Banda, Robert, manager infrastructure development, Zambia Development Agency (ZDA), Lusaka, Zambia, 7 June 2017.

Bwayla, Lillian, director, Foreign Trade Department, Zambian Ministry of Commerce, Trade and Industry, Lusaka, Zambia, 18 July 2017.

Chewe, Joseph, general secretary, Mineworkers Union of Zambia (MUZ), Kitwe, Zambia, 6 July 2017.

Chileshe, Francis, general secretary, Cross-Border Traders Assocation (CBTA), Lusaka, Zambia, 11 July 2017.

Chilumbu, Delax, former chief mining engineer, Zambian Ministry of Mines and Minerals Development, Lusaka, Zambia, 21 July 2017.

Chikwashi, Prisca, chief executive officer, Zambia Chamber of Commerce and Industry (ZACCI), Lusaka, Zambia, 16 May 2017.

Chinese journalist (anonymised), 8 February 2019.

Chungu, Imelda, activist, Jesuit Centre for Theological Reflection, Lusaka, Zambia, 21 June 2017.

Clowes, Robert, commercial farmer, Tukuyu, Tanzania, 24 August 2017.

Consultant and political commentator (anonymised), Dar es Salaam, Tanzania, 3 February 2019.

Dungarsi, Firoz, managing director, JAAF Logistics Ltd., Ndola, Zambia, 30 June 2017.

Economist, Japan International Cooperation Agency (JICA) (anonymised), Lusaka, Zambia, 16 May 2017.

T. Zajontz, *The Political Economy of China's Infrastructure Development in Africa*, International Political Economy Series,
https://doi.org/10.1007/978-3-031-44449-4

Executive, China Civil Engineering Construction Corporation (CCECC) East Africa Ltd. (anonymised), 14 November 2019.

Executive manager, Chinese Logistics and Transport Company (anonymised), Lusaka, Zambia, 17 June 2017.

Former Tanzanian top official (anonymised), Dar es Salaam, Tanzania, 27 November 2019.

Hampwaye, Godfrey, senior lecturer, Department of Geography and Environmental Studies, University of Zambia, Lusaka, Zambia, 24 May 2017.

Imasiku, Richard, manager, Planning and Investment Promotion Department, Zambia-China Economic and Trade Cooperation Zone (ZCCZ), Lusaka, Zambia, 4 August 2017.

Kahama, Joseph Kulwa, secretary general, Tanzania China Friendship Promotion Association (TCFPA), Dar es Salaam, Tanzania, 28 November 2019.

Kaluba, Lucky, trader, COMESA Market, Lusaka, Zambia, 23 June 2017.

Kakubo, Stanley Kasongo, Member of Parliament, National Assembly of Zambia, United Party for National Development (UPND), Lusaka, Zambia, 4 August 2017.

Kamata, Ng'wanza, head of department, Department of Political Science and Public Administration, University of Dar es Salaam (UDSM), Dar es Salaam, Tanzania, 5 February 2019.

Key informant 1 (anonymised), 4 February 2019.

Key informant 2 (anonymised), 26 November 2019.

Key informant 3 (anonymised), 16 December 2020.

Kumwenda, Yewa, director of research, Mineworkers Union of Zambia (MUZ), Kitwe, Zambia, 8 May 2017.

Labour union representative at Chambishi Copper Smelter of China Nonferrous Metal Mining (CNMC) (anonymised), Kitwe, Zambia, 5 July 2017.

Lappeman, Garth, senior manager, Trident Foundation of First Quantum Minerals, Lusaka, Zambia, 21 June 2017.

Lindunda, Steven, chief financial officer, Zambia-China Economic and Trade Zone (ZCCZ), Ndola, Zambia, 30 June 2017.

Liu, Haifang, executive director, Centre for African Studies, Peking University, Edinburgh, United Kingdom, 5 October 2019.

Lusinde, Job Malecela, former Tanzanian cabinet minister (1961–1975) and former Tanzanian ambassador to China (1975–1984), Dodoma, Tanzania, 20 November 2019.

Mbulo, Jordan, general secretary, Federation of Small Scale Mining Associations of Zambia, Lusaka, Zambia, 21 June 2017.

Managing Director of a Zambian construction business association and building contractor (anonymised), Lusaka, Zambia, 29 May 2017.

Mtonga, Robert, chief executive officer, Truckers Association of Zambia (TAZ), Lusaka, Zambia, 25 July 2017.

Muchimba, Charles, deputy director of research, Mineworkers Union of Zambia (MUZ), Kitwe, Zambia, 8 May 2017.
Mudenda, Sydney, manager, Nakonde Trade Information Desk, Cross-Border Traders Association (CBTA), Nakonde, Zambia, 17 August 2017.
Mulenga, Chiti, senior economist, Ministry of Commerce, Trade and Industry, Lusaka, Zambia, 18 July 2017.
Musonda, Christopher, managing director, Zambia Railways Ltd. (ZRL), Kabwe, Zambia, 8 August 2017.
Musonda, John, programme manager, Labour Institute of Zambia (LIZ), Ndola, Zambia, 2 June 2017.
Muzorori, Tasara, senior trade officer, Common Market for Eastern and Southern Africa (COMESA), Lusaka, Zambia, 1 August 2017.
Mwaipopo, Isaac, executive director, Centre for Trade Policy and Development (CTPD), Lusaka, Zambia, 12 July 2017.
Mwansakombe, Gabriel, general manager, Sherwood Greene Properties at Mei Mei Ndola Hill Wholesale City, Ndola, Zambia, 2 June 2017.
Mwila, Elias, general secretary, Railway Workers Union of Zambia (RWUZ), Kabwe, Zambia, 7 July 2017.
Ngulube, Ezra, general secretary, National Restoration Pary (NAREP), Lusaka, Zambia, 7 June 2017.
Njovu, Elaston, deputy secretary general, Zambia Congress of Trade Unions (ZCTU), Lusaka, Zambia, 2 August 2017.
Nyrienda, Sam, former member of Ndola city council, Ndola, Zambia, 28 June 2017.
Official, Ministry of Works, Transport and Communication (MWTC) (anonymised), 18 November 2019.
Official, Road Development Agency (RDA) (anonymised), Lusaka, Zambia, 2 August 2017.
Phiri, Boniface, director of research, Zambia Congress of Trade Unions (ZCTU), Lusaka, Zambia, 2 August 2017.
Phiri, Yvette, senior manager, Bridge Shipping Zambia C. Steinweg Group, Lusaka, Zambia, 7 June 2017.
Sagar, Ashu, president, Ndola and District Chamber of Commerce and Industry, Ndola, Zambia, 29 June 2017.
Senior executive of a Tanzanian corporate group (anonymised), Dar es Salaam, Tanzania, 7 February 2019.
Senior manager, Zambia Cargo & Logistics, Mukuba Depot (anonymised), Ndola, Zambia, 30 June 2017.
Senior official, Tanzanian Ministry of Works, Transport and Communication (MWTC) (anonymised), 19 November 2019.
Senior official, Zambian Ministry of Transport and Communication (MTC) (anonymised), Lusaka, Zambia, 14 June 2017.

Senior TAZARA manager (anonymised), 10 August 2017.
Shangwe, Muhidin, lecturer, Department of Political Science and Public Administration, University of Dar es Salaam, Dar es Salaam, Tanzania, 15 November 2019.
Shivji, Issa, professor, Mwalimu Julius Nyerere Research Chair in Pan-African Studies, University of Dar es Salaam, Dar es Salaam, Tanzania, 1 February 2019.
Shone, Vernon, managing director, Advance Transport, Ndola, Zambia, 7 July 2017.
Sinyangwe, Kenny, investment consultant, Solwezi, Zambia, 4 July 2017.
Tanzanian top official (anonymised), 15 November 2019.
TAZARA labour union executive (anonymised), 10 August 2017.
TAZARA labour union executive 2 (anonymised), 10 August 2017.
TAZARA manager (anonymised), 2 June 2017.
TAZARA manager 2 (anonymised), 12 August 2017.
TAZARA manager 3 (anonymised), 17 August 2017.
Tembo, Sydney, president, Kabwe Chamber of Commerce and Industry, Kabwe, Zambia, 10 May 2017.
Trader, COMESA Market, Lusaka, Zambia, 20 July 2017.
Wetengere, Kitojo, former deputy director, Mozambique-Tanzania Centre for Foreign Relations (CFR), Dar es Salaam, Tanzania, 13 November 2019.

Bibliography

Ackroyd, Stephen, and Jan Ch. Karlsson. 2014. "Critical Realism, Research Techniques, and Research Designs." Pp. 21–45 in *Studying Organizations Using Critical Realism: A Practical Guide*, edited by P. K. Edwards, J. O'Mahoney, and S. Vincent. Oxford: Oxford University Press.
AfDB. 2015. *Rail Infrastructure in Africa: Financing Policy Options*. Abidjan: African Development Bank.
AfDB. 2018. *African Economic Outlook 2018*. Abidjan: African Development Bank.
Africa Confidential. 2018a. "A Swirling Fog of Debt." *Africa Confidential* 59(10):8–9.
Africa Confidential. 2018b. "Bonds, Bills and Ever Bigger Debts." *Africa Confidential* 59(18).
Africa Confidential. 2019a. "Cash in the Cabinet." *Africa Confidential* 60(4):9–10.
Africa Confidential. 2019b. "Little Cash, No Credit." *Africa Confidential* 60(11):8–9.
Africa Confidential. 2019c. "Treasury in the Red." *Africa Confidential* 60(9):9–10.

Africa-Asia Confidential. 2010. "TAZARA Troubles." *Africa-Asia Confidential* 4(1):6.

Africa-Asia Confidential. 2013. "Pipeline and Transparency Protests." *Africa-Asia Confidential* 6(9):7.

African Union. 2015. *Agenda 2063: The Africa We Want*. Addis Ababa: African Union Commission.

Agnew, John. 1998. "Political Power and Geographical Scale." Paper presented at the Third Pan-European IR Conference and Joint Meeting with ISA, 16–19 September, Vienna.

Agnew, John. 2010. "Still Trapped in Territory?" *Geopolitics* 15(4):779–84. https://doi.org/10.1080/14650041003717558.

AidData. n.d. "CDB Loans $179.5 Million USD for Mansa-Luwingu Road." *AidData*. Retrieved May 25, 2019 (https://china.aiddata.org/projects/30719).

Alden, Chris, and Daniel Large. 2019. "Studying Africa and China." Pp. 3–35 in *New Directions in Africa-China Studies*, edited by C. Alden and D. Large. Abingdon: Routledge.

Alden, Chris, and Lu Jiang. 2019. "Brave New World: Debt, Industrialization and Security in China–Africa Relations." *International Affairs* 95(3):641–57.https://doi.org/10.1093/ia/iiz083.

Alden, Chris, and Daniel Large. 2019a. "Conclusion." Pp. 329–42 in *New Directions in Africa-China Studies*, edited by C. Alden and D. Large. Abingdon: Routledge.

Alden, Chris, and Daniel Large. 2019b. "Studying Africa and China." Pp. 3–35 in *New Directions in Africa-China Studies*, edited by C. Alden and D. Large. Abingdon: Routledge.

Alves, Ana Cristina. 2013. "China's 'Win-Win' Cooperation: Unpacking the Impact of Infrastructure for-Resources Deals in Africa." *South African Journal of International Affairs* 20(2):207–26. https://doi.org/10.1080/10220461.2013.811337.

Alves, Cristina, and Sérgio Chichava. 2019. "Neo-Patrimonialism and Extraversion in China's Relations with Angola and Mozambique: Is Beijing Making a Difference?" Pp. 243–59 in *New Directions in Africa-China Studies*, edited by C. Alden and D. Large. Abingdon: Routledge.

Amin, Samir. 1976. *Unequal Development: An Essay on the Social Formations of Peripheral Capitalism*. Sussex: The Harvester Press.

Amin, Samir. 1990. *Maldevelopment: Anatomy of a Global Failure*. Tokyo: United Nations University Press.

Andreoni, Antonio. 2017. *Anti-Corruption in Tanzania: A Political Settlements Analysis*. AEC Working Paper 1. London: Anti-Corruption Evidence (AEC) Research Consortium.

Arber, Sara. 1993. “Designing Samples.” Pp. 68–93 in *Researching Social Life*, edited by N. Gilbert. London: Sage Publications.

Arrighi, Giovanni. 1994. *The Long Twentieth Century: Money, Power and the Origin of Our Times*. London: Verso.

Arrighi, Giovanni. 2005. “Hegemony Unravelling 1.” *New Left Review* 32:23–80.

Arrighi, Giovanni. 2007. *Adam Smith in Beijing: Lineages of the Twenty-First Century*. London: Verso.

Ashman, Sam, and Alex Callinicos. 2006. “Capital Accumulation and the State System: Assessing David Harvey’s The New Imperialism.” *Historical Materialism* 14(4):107–31.

Auditor General. n.d. *Report of the Auditor General on the Road Projects under the Road Development Agency (RDA) for the Period January 2012 to December 2015*. Lusaka: Office of the Auditor General.

Ayers, Alison J. 2013. “Beyond Myths, Lies and Stereotypes: The Political Economy of a ‘New Scramble for Africa.’” *New Political Economy* 18(2):227–57. https://doi.org/10.1080/13563467.2012.678821.

Bach, Daniel C. 2012. “Conclusion: Neopatrimonialism and Developmental—The Emerging States’ Syndrome.” Pp. 221–24 in *Neopatrimonialism in Africa and Beyond*, edited by D. C. Bach and M. Gazibo. Abingdon: Routledge.

Bach, Daniel C. 2016. “Cross-Border Interactions and Regionalism.” Pp. 71–88 in *Region-building in Africa: Political and Economic Challenges*, edited by D. H. Levine and D. Nagar. Basingstoke: Palgrave Macmillan.

Bagwandeen, Mandira, Christopher Edyegu, and Oscar M. Otele. 2023. “African Agency, COVID-19 and Debt Renegotiations with China.” *South African Journal of International Affairs* 30(1):1–27. https://doi.org/10.1080/10220461.2023.2180083.

Baregu, Mwesiga. 2006. “Tanzania-China Relations in Historical Perspective.” Pp. 209–16 in *China in Africa: Mercantilist Predator, or Partner in Development*, edited by G. le Pere. Braamfontein: The Institute of Global Dialogue and The South African Institute of International Affairs.

Barigaba, Julius. 2021. “Kenya in Debt Distress, as All EA Economies Facing Risks Too.” *The East African*, September 18, 4–5.

Barton, Benjamin. 2023. “Infrastructure Nationalism and Political Vulnerability—Examining the Stalled Negotiations Over the Bagamoyo Port Project During Magufuli’s Reign.” *Journal of Asian and African Studies* 58(3):338–53. https://doi.org/10.1177/00219096211062471.

BBC. 2015. “Tanzania-Zambia Train Route Hit by Strike.” *BBC News*. Retrieved March 4, 2020 (https://www.bbc.co.uk/news/world-africa-30786039).

BBC. 2016. "The Race to Become East Africa's Biggest Port." *BBC News*. Retrieved March 10, 2020 (https://www.bbc.co.uk/news/world-africa-36458946).

Beckmann, Björn. 1993. "The Liberation of Civil Society: Neo-Liberal Ideology and Political Theory." *Review of African Political Economy* 20(58):20–33.

Bert Pave and Maintenance. n.d. "About Us." Retrieved July 11, 2023 (https://www.bertpave.com/about-us/).

Bhaskar, Roy. 1978. *A Realist Theory of Science*. Hemel Hempstead: Harvester.

Bhaskar, Roy. 2008 [1975]. *A Realist Theory of Science*. Abingdon: Routledge.

Biau, Carole, Karim Dahou, and Toru Homma. 2008. "How to Increase Sound Private Investment in Africa's Road Infrastructure: Building on Country Successes and OECD Policy Tools." Proceedings from the Expert Roundtable Investment in Transport Infrastructure, 11 December 2008, NEPAD-OECD Africa Investment Initiative.

Biden, Joseph. 2021. "Remarks by President Biden in Meeting on the Build Back Better World Initiative." *The White House*. Retrieved March 31, 2021 (https://www.whitehouse.gov/briefing-room/speeches-remarks/2021/11/02/remarks-by-president-biden-in-meeting-on-the-build-back-better-world-initiative/).

Bieler, Andreas, and Adam David Morton. 2014. "Uneven and Combined Development and Unequal Exchange: The Second Wind of Neoliberal 'Free Trade'?" *Globalizations* 11(1):35–45. https://doi.org/10.1080/14747731.2014.860334.

Bieler, Andreas, and Adam David Morton. 2018. *Global Capitalism, Global War, Global Crisis*. Cambridge: Cambridge University Press.

Blair, Edmund. 2016. "Uganda Picks Tanzania for Oil Pipeline Route Rather than Kenya." *Reuters*. Retrieved March 10, 2020 (https://www.reuters.com/article/us-energy-uganda/uganda-picks-tanzania-for-oil-pipeline-route-rather-than-kenya-idUSKCN0XK0DT).

Bond, Patrick. 2015. "BRICS and the Sub-Imperial Location." Pp. 15–26 in *BRICS: An Anti-Capitalist Critique*, edited by A. Garcia and P. Bond. London: Pluto Press.

Boone, Catherine. 1990. "The Making of a Rentier Class: Wealth Accumulation and Political Control in Senegal." *The Journal of Development Studies* 26(3):425–49.

Boston University Global Development Policy Center. 2022. "Chinese Loans to Africa Database." Retrieved July 15, 2023 (https://www.bu.edu/gdp/chinese-loans-to-africa-database).

Bratton, Michael, and Nicolas van de Walle. 1997. *Democratic Experiments in Africa: Regime Transitions in Comparative Perspective*. Cambridge: Cambridge University Press.

Brautigam, Deborah. 2019. "Is China the World's Loan Shark?" *The New York Times*. Retrieved August 13, 2019 (https://www.nytimes.com/2019/04/26/opinion/china-belt-road-initiative.html).

Bräutigam, Deborah. 2020. "A Critical Look at Chinese 'Debt-Trap Diplomacy': The Rise of a Meme." *Area Development and Policy* 5(1):1–14. https://doi.org/10.1080/23792949.2019.1689828.

Brautigam, Deborah. 2020. "Chinese Debt Relief: Fact and Fiction." *The Diplomat*. Retrieved May 26, 2020 (https://www.thediplomat.com/2020/04/chinese-debt-relief-fact-and-fiction/).

Brautigam, Deborah. 2021. *How Zambia and China Co-Created a Debt "Tragedy of the Commons."* China-Africa Research Initiative Working Paper 51. Washington: Johns Hopkins University.

Brautigam, Deborah. 2022. "China and Zambia: Creating a Sovereign Debt Crisis." *International Affairs* 98(4):1347–65. https://doi.org/10.1093/ia/iiac109.

Brautigam, Deborah, and Kevin Acker. 2021. "Chinese Lending to Africa in the Pandemic Era." Pp. 165–77 in *Shaping Africa's Post-Covid Recovery*, edited by R. Arezki, S. Djankov, and U. Panizza. London: Centre for Economic Policy Research.

Brenner, Neil. 1999. "Beyond State-Centrism? Space, Territoriality, and Geographical Scale in Globalization Studies." *Theory and Society* 28(1):39–78. https://doi.org/10.1023/A:1006996806674.

Brenner, Neil. 2004. *New State Spaces: Urban Governance and the Rescaling of Statehood*. Oxford: Oxford University Press.

Brenner, Neil. 2009. "A Thousand Leaves: Notes on the Geographies of Uneven Spatial Development." Pp. 27–49 in *Leviathan Undone? Towards a Political Economy of Scale*. Vancouver: University of British Columbia Press.

Brenner, Neil, Bob Jessop, Martin Jones, and Gordon MacLeod. 2003. "Introduction: State Space in Question." Pp. 1–26 in *State/Space: A Reader*, edited by N. Brenner, B. Jessop, M. Jones, and G. MacLeod. Malden: Blackwell Publishing.

Breslin, Shaun. 2021. *China Risen? Studying Chinese Global Power*. Bristol: Bristol University Press.

BRI. 2019. "Joint Communique of the Leaders' Roundtable of the 2nd Belt and Road Forum for International Cooperation." *The Belt and Road Forum*. Retrieved August 14, 2019 (http://www.beltandroadforum.org/english/n100/2019/0427/c36-1311.html).

Brooks, Andrew. 2010. "Spinning and Weaving Discontent: Labour Relations and the Production of Meaning at Zambia-China Mulungushi Textiles." *Journal of Southern African Studies* 36(1):113–32. https://doi.org/10.1080/03057071003607360.

Bryan, Richard. 1987. "The State and the Internationalisation of Capital: An Approach to Analysis." *Journal of Contemporary Asia* 17(3):253–75.
Bullock, Richard. 2005. *Results of Railway Privatization in Africa*. Transport Paper. Washington: World Bank.
Bullock, Richard. 2009. *Off Track: Sub-Saharan African Railways*. Africa Infrastructure Country Diagnostic Background Paper 17. Washington: World Bank.
Burke, Christopher. 2007. "China's Entry into Construction Industries in Africa: Tanzania and Zambia as Case Studies." *China Report* 43(3):323–36. https://doi.org/10.1177/000944550704300304.
Bwalya, John. 2017. "Unravelling Clientelism in the Zambian Electoral Campaigns." *Third World Quarterly* 38(7):1551–65. https://doi.org/10.1080/01436597.2016.1229568.
Bwalya, John, and Brij Maharaj. 2018. "Not to the Highest Bidder: The Failure of Incumbency in the Zambian 2011 Elections." *Journal of Contemporary African Studies* 36(1):71–86. https://doi.org/10.1080/02589001.2017.1369014.
Bwayla, Edgar. 2013. "China-Zambia Relations." Pp. 189–213 in *China's Diplomacy in Eastern and Southern Africa*, edited by S. Adem. Farnham: Ashgate.
Cai, Kevin G. 2018. "The One Belt One Road and the Asian Infrastructure Investment Bank: Beijing's New Strategy of Geoeconomics and Geopolitics." *Journal of Contemporary China* 27(114):831–47. https://doi.org/10.1080/10670564.2018.1488101.
Callaghy, Thomas M. 1988. "The State and the Development of Capitalism in Africa: Theoretitorical, Historical, and Comparative Reflections." Pp. 67–99 in *The Precarious Balance: State and Society in Africa*, edited by D. Rothchild and N. Chazan. Boulder: Westview Press.
Carmody, Pádraig. 2009. "An Asian-Driven Economic Recovery in Africa? The Zambian Case." *World Development* 37(7):1197–1207. https://doi.org/10.1016/j.worlddev.2008.12.002.
Carmody, Pádraig. 2011. *The New Scramble for Africa*. Cambridge: Polity Press.
Carmody, Pádraig. 2013. *The Rise of the BRICS in Africa: The Geopolitics of South-South Relations*. London: Zed Books.
Carmody, Pádraig. 2020. "Dependence Not Debt-Trap Diplomacy." *Area Development and Policy* 5(1):23–31. https://doi.org/10.1080/23792949.2019.1702471.
Carmody, Pádraig, Godfrey Hampwaye, and Enock Sakala. 2012. "Globalisation and the Rise of the State? Chinese Geogovernance in Zambia." *New Political Economy* 17(2):209–29. https://doi.org/10.1080/13563467.2011.552107.

Carmody, Pádraig, and Peter Kragelund. 2016. "Who Is in Charge? State Power and Agency in Sino-African Relations." *Cornell International Law Journal* 49(1):1–24. https://doi.org/10.1038/nmeth.2841.

Carmody, Pádraig, Peter Kragelund, and Ricardo Reboredo. 2020. *Africa's Shadow Rise: China and the Mirage of African Economic Development*. London: Zed Books.

Carmody, Pádraig, and Ian Taylor. 2010. "Flexigemony and Force in China's Resource Diplomacy in Africa: Sudan and Zambia Compared." *Geopolitics* 15(3):496–515. https://doi.org/10.1080/14650040903501047.

Carmody, Pádraig, and Joel Wainwright. 2022. "Contradiction and Restructuring in the Belt and Road Initiative: Reflections on China's Pause in the 'Go World.'" *Third World Quarterly* 43(12):2830–51. https://doi.org/10.1080/01436597.2022.2110058.

Carmody, Pádraig, Ian Taylor, and Tim Zajontz. 2022a. "China's Spatial Fix and 'Debt Diplomacy' in Africa: Constraining Belt or Road to Economic Transformation?" *Canadian Journal of African Studies* 56(1):57–77. https://doi.org/10.1080/00083968.2020.1868014.

Carmody, Pádraig, Tim Zajontz, and Ricardo Reboredo. 2022b. "From 'Debt Diplomacy' to Donorship? China's Changing Role in Global Development." *Global Political Economy* 1(2):198–217. https://doi.org/10.1332/uzhw7185.

Castree, Noel. 2009. "The Spatio-Temporality of Capitalism." *Time & Society* 18(1):26–61. https://doi.org/10.1177/0961463X08099942.

Chabal, Patrick, and Jean-Pascal Daloz. 1999. *Africa Works: Disorder as Political Instrument*. London: James Currey.

Cheelo, Caesar, and Robert Liebenthal. 2018. *The Role of the Construction Sector in Influencing Natural Resource Use, Structural Change, and Industrial Development in Zambia*. WIDER Working Paper 2018/172. Helsinki: UNU WIDER.

Chellaney, Brahma. 2017. "China's Debt-Trap Diplomacy." *Project Syndicate*. Retrieved May 19, 2019 (https://www.project-syndicate.org/commentary/china-one-belt-one-road-loans-debt-by-brahma-chellaney-2017-01?barrier=accesspaylog).

Chelwa, Grieve. 2017. "Is the Lusaka-Ndola Dual Carriageway Overpriced?" *Africa Watch*. Retrieved June 1, 2019 (https://www.gchelwa.blogspot.com/2017/09/is-lusaka-ndola-dual-carriageway.html).

Chen, Yingqun, and Lucie Morangi. 2019. "Chinese Aid Helps Put African Nations on Track." *China Daily*. Retrieved February 29, 2020 (https://www.global.chinadaily.com.cn/a/201909/09/WS5d7593c9a310cf3e3556a5ed_4.html).

Cheru, Fantu. 2016. "Emerging Southern Powers and New Forms of South–South Cooperation: Ethiopia's Strategic Engagement with China and

India." *Third World Quarterly* 37(4):592–610. https://doi.org/10.1080/01436597.2015.1116368.
Chikulo, Bornwell C. 2000. "Corruption and Accumulation in Zambia." Pp. 161–82 in *Corruption and Development in Africa: Lessons from Country Case-Studies*, edited by K. R. Hope and B. C. Chikulo. Basingstoke: Macmillan Press.
Chinese Foreign Ministry. 2015. "Xi Jinping Holds Talks with President Edgar Lungu of Zambia, Stressing to Cherish Traditional Friendship and Advance China-Zambia Relations." *Ministry of Foreign Affairs of the People's Republic of China*. Retrieved June 24, 2023 (https://www.fmprc.gov.cn/mfa_eng/gjhdq_665435/2913_665441/3114_664254/3116_664258/201504/t20150401_547636.html).
Chinese Ministry of Foreign Affairs. 2015. *A Monument to China-Africa Friendship: Firsthand Account of the Building of the TAZARA*. Beijing: World Affairs Press.
Chiyemura, Frangton, Elisa Gambino, and Tim Zajontz. 2023. "Infrastructure and the Politics of African State Agency: Shaping the Belt and Road Initiative in East Africa." *Chinese Political Science Review* 8(1):105–31. https://doi.org/10.1007/s41111-022-00214-8.
Chu, Yin-wah, and Alvin Y. So. 2010. "State Neoliberalism: The Chinese Road to Capitalism." Pp. 46–72 in *Chinese Capitalisms: Historical Emergence and Political Implications*, edited by Y. Chu. Basingstoke: Palgrave Macmillan.
Collier, Paul. 2006. "African Growth: Why a 'Big Push'?" *Journal of African Economies* 15(suppl_2):188–211.
Collier, Paul, Martina Kirchberger, and Måns Söderbom. 2015. *The Cost of Road Infrastructure in Low and Middle Income Countries*. World Bank Policy Research Working Paper 7408. Washington.
Corkin, Lucy. 2012. "Chinese Construction Companies in Angola: A Local Linkages Perspective." *Resources Policy* 37(4):475–83. https://doi.org/10.1016/j.resourpol.2012.06.002.
Corkin, Lucy. 2013. *Uncovering African Agency: Angola's Management of China's Credit Lines*. Farnham: Ashgate.
Corkin, Lucy. 2015. "Understanding Angolan Agency: The Luanda-Beijing Face-Off." Pp. 61–84 in *Africa and China: How Africans and their Governments are Shaping Relations with China*, edited by A. W. Gadzala. Lanham: Rowman & Littlefield.
Cowaloosur, Honita. 2015. *Re-Inscribing Dependency: The Political Economy of Mauritius Jinfei Economic and Trade Cooperation Zone Co. Ltd*. PhD dissertation, University of St Andrews.
Craig, John. 2001. "Putting Privatisation into Practice: The Case of Zambia Consolidated Copper Mines Limited." *The Journal of Modern African Studies* 39(3):389–410. https://doi.org/10.1017/s0022278x01003652.

Cuenca, Oliver. 2021. "Chinese Contractors Awarded Contract for Tanzanian SGR." *International Railway Journal*. Retrieved August 1, 2022 (https://www.railjournal.com/africa/chinese-contractors-awarded-contract-for-tanzanian-sgr/).

CUTS International. 2019. *#DebtConcernsMe: Understanding the Impact of Zambia's Growing Debt on Different Stakeholders*. Lusaka: Consumer Unity & Trust Society International.

Daily Mail. 2022. "Use Road Tolls for Roads." *Daily Mail*. Retrieved July 12, 2023 (http://www.daily-mail.co.zm/use-road-tolls-for-roads/).

Daily Star. 2019. "Avic, China Henan Abandon Works over Non Payment." *Daily Star*. Retrieved May 31, 2019 (https://www.dailystar.news/Articles/Index/50?articleType=TodaysNewsArticle&fbclid=IwAR3dEitkeDg9jP4nl5rsVoQ7-xNqfuGyAT5TUhCHTN7GOM_41_Zkh7UlZEE).

Danermark, Berth, Mats Ekström, Liselotte Jakobsen, and Jan Ch. Karlsson. 2002. *Explaining Society: Critical Realism in the Social Sciences*. London: Routledge.

deGrassi, Aaron. 2008. "'Neopatrimonialism' and Agricultural Development in Africa: Contributions and Limitations of a Contested Concept." *African Studies Review* 51(3):107–33. https://doi.org/10.1353/arw.0.0087.

Deloitte. 2006. "Closing the Infrastructure Gap: The Role of Public-Private Partnerships." *Deloitte*. Retrieved May 15, 2019 (https://www2.deloitte.com/content/dam/Deloitte/ie/Documents/Finance/CorporateFinance/2006_closing_infrastructure_gap_deloitte_ireland.pdf).

Deloitte. 2016. *Africa's Changing Infrastructure Landscape: Africa Construction Trends Report*. Diegem: Deloitte University.

Denzin, Norman K. 1989. *The Research Act: A Theoretical Introduction to Sociological Methods*. 3rd edition. Englewood Cliffs: Prentice Hall.

DiCarlo, Jessica, and Seth Schindler. 2022. "Introduction: Geopolitics, Infrastructure, and the Emergent Geographies of US-China Competition." Pp. 1–10 in *The Rise of the Infrastructure State: How US-China Rivalry Shapes Politics and Place Worldwide*, edited by S. Schindler and J. DiCarlo. Bristol: Bristol University Press.

Domasa, Sylivester. 2016. "China in Rail Upgrade Talks with TAZARA Owners." *The Guardian*. Retrieved September 13, 2019 (https://www.ippmedia.com/en/news/china-rail-upgrade-talks-tazara-owners).

van Donge, Jan Kees. 2009. "The Plundering of Zambian Resources by Frederick Chiluba and His Friends: A Case Study of the Interaction between National Politics and the International Drive towards Good Governance." *African Affairs* 108(430):69–90.https://doi.org/10.1093/afraf/adn073.

Duarte, Ana, Regina Santos, and Elling N. Tjønneland. 2014. "Angola's Lobito Corridor: From Reconstruction to Development." *Angola Brief* 4(5):1–4.

Easton, Geoff. 2010. "Critical Realism in Case Study Research." *Industrial Marketing Management* 39(1):118–28. https://doi.org/10.1016/j.indmarman.2008.06.004.

Edinger, Hannah, and Jean-Pierre Labuschagne. 2019. "If You Want to Prosper, Consider Building Roads: China's Role in African Infrastructure and Capital Projects." *Deloitte Insights*. Retrieved July 2, 2019 (https://www2.deloitte.com/insights/us/en/industry/public-sector/china-investment-africa-infrastructure-development.html).

Eisenstadt, Samuel N. 1973. *Traditional Patrimonialism and Modern Neopatrominialism*. London: Sage Publications.

Elder-Vass, Dave. 2010. *The Causal Power of Social Structures: Emergence, Structure and Agency*. Cambridge: Cambridge University Press.

Erdmann, Gero. 2011. "Zambia." Pp. 525–34 in *Africa Yearbook: Politics, Economy and Society South of the Sahara in 2010*, edited by A. Mehler, H. Melber, and K. van Walraven. Leiden: Brill.

Erdmann, Gero. 2013. "Neopatrimonialism and Political Regimes." Pp. 59–69 in *Routledge Handbook of African Politics*, edited by N. Cheeseman, D. M. Anderson, and A. Scheibler. Abingdon: Routledge.

Erdmann, Gero, and Ulf Engel. 2006. *Neopatrimonialism Revisited: Beyond a Catch-All Concept*. GIGA Working Paper No. 16. Hamburg: German Institute of Global and Area Studies.

Erdmann, Gero, and Ulf Engel. 2007. "Neopatrimonialism Reconsidered: Critical Review and Elaboration of an Elusive Concept." *Commonwealth and Comparative Politics* 45(1):95–119. https://doi.org/10.1080/14662040601135813.

Essack, A. K. 1970. "The Tanzam Railway." *Economic and Political Weekly* 5(24):936–37.

Farquharson, Edward, Clemencia Torres de Mästle, E. R. Yescombe, and Javier Encinas. 2011. *How to Engage with the Private Sector in Public-Private Partnerships in Emerging Markets*. Washington: World Bank.

Fatton, Robert. 1988. "Bringing the Ruling Class Back in: Class, State, and Hegemony in Africa." *Comparative Politics* 20(3):253–64.

Fletcher, Amber J. 2017. "Applying Critical Realism in Qualitative Research: Methodology Meets Method." *International Journal of Social Research Methodology* 20(2):181–94. https://doi.org/10.1080/13645579.2016.1144401.

Flick, Uwe. 2018. *An Introduction to Qualitative Research*. 6th edition. London: Sage Publications.

Flores, Isabel. 2017. *Dissecting Chinese Involvement in Road Construction Projects in Tanzania: Strategic Roadways and Resources*. Bachelor thesis, University of Iowa.

Flyvbjerg, Bent. 2010. "Five Misunderstandings about Case-Study Research." Pp. 133–56 in *Realist Methodology Volume II: Realist Methods*, edited by W. Olsen. London: Sage Publications.

FOCAC. 2018. "Beijing Action Plan (2019–2021)." *Forum on China-Africa Cooperation*. Retrieved June 1, 2019 (https://www.focac.org/eng/zywx_1/zywj/t1594297.htm).

Frank, André Gunder. 1972. *Lumpenbourgeoisie and Lumpendevelopment: Dependency, Class and Politics in Latin America*. New York: Monthly Review Press.

Fraser, Alastair. 2010. "Introduction: Boom and Bust on the Zambian Copperbelt." Pp. 1–30 in *Zambia, Mining, and Neoliberalism: Boom and Bust on the Globalized Copperbelt*, edited by A. Fraser and M. Larmer. New York: Palgrave Macmillan.

Fraser, Alastair. 2017. "Post-Populism in Zambia: Michael Sata's Rise, Demise and Legacy." *International Political Science Review* 38(4):456–72. https://doi.org/10.1177/0192512117720809.

Freeman, Duncan. 2020. "The Belt and Road Initiative and the Overcapacity Connection." Pp. 120–138 in *The Belt and Road Initiative and Global Governance*, edited by M. A. Carrai, J.-C. Defraigne, and J. Wouters. Cheltenham: Edward Elgar.

Friedman, Jeremy. 2021. *Ripe for Revolution: Building Socialism in the Third World*. Cambridge: Harvard University Press.

Gadzala, Aleksandra W. 2015. "Introduction." Pp. xv–xxix in *Africa and China: How Africans and their Governments are Shaping Relations with China*, edited by A. W. Gadzala. Lanham: Rowman & Littlefield.

Gambino, Elisa. 2022. "Corridors of Opportunity? African Infrastructure and the Market Expansion of Chinese Companies." Pp. 286–316 in *Transport Corridors in Africa*, edited by H. Lamarque and P. Nugent. Woodbridge: James Currey.

Gelpern, Anna, Sebastian Horn, Scott Morris, Brad Parks, and Christoph Trebesch. 2021. *How China Lends: A Rare Look into 100 Debt Contracts with Foreign Government*. Peterson Institute for International Economics, Kiel Institute for the World Economy, Center for Global Development and AidData at William & Mary.

Gil, Nuno, Anne Stafford, and Innocent Musonda. 2019. "Duality by Design: The Global Race to Build Africa's Infrastructure." Pp. 1–30 in *Duality by Design: The Global Race to Build Africa's Infrastructure*, edited by N. Gil, A. Stafford, and I. Musonda. Cambridge: Cambridge University Press.

Gleave, Michael B. 1992. "The Dar Es Salaam Transport Corridor: An Appraisal." *African Affairs* 91:249–67.

Gonzalez-Vicente, Ruben. 2019. "Make Development Great Again? Accumulation Regimes, Spaces of Sovereign Exception and the Elite Development Paradigm of China's Belt and Road Initiative." *Business and Politics* 21(4):487–513. https://doi.org/10.1017/bap.2019.20.

Gort, Joris, and Andrew Brooks. 2023. "Africa's Next Debt Crisis: A Relational Comparison of Chinese and Western Lending to Zambia." *Antipode* 55(3):830–52. https://doi.org/10.1111/anti.12921.

GPRC. 1964. "The Chinese Government's Eight Principles for Economic Aid and Technical Assistance to Other Countries." *Woodrow Wilson International Center for Scholars*. Retrieved March 18, 2020 (https://digitalarchive.wilsoncenter.org/document/121560).

Gramsci, Antonio. 1971. *Selections from the Prison Notebooks*. London: Lawrence and Wishart.

Gray, Hazel S. 2015. "The Political Economy of Grand Corruption in Tanzania." *African Affairs* 114(456):382–403. https://doi.org/10.1093/afraf/adv017.

GRZ. 2006. *The Zambia Development Agency Act: No. 11 of 2006*. Lusaka: National Assembly of Zambia.

GRZ. 2009. *The Public-Private Partnership Act: No. 14 of 2009*. Lusaka: National Assembly of Zambia.

GRZ. 2011. *The Tolls Act: No. 14 of 2011*. Lusaka: National Assembly of Zambia.

GRZ. 2013. "Statutory Instrument No. 73 of 2013." *Government Gazette*, August 9, 605–10.

GRZ. 2016. "Statutory Instrument No. 85 of 2016." *Government Gazette*, November 11, 927–34.

GRZ. 2017. *The Seventh National Development Plan 2017–2021*. Lusaka: Ministry of National Development Planning.

Gu, Jing, Chuanhong Zhang, Alcides Vaz, and Langton Mukwereza. 2016. "Chinese State Capitalism? Rethinking the Role of the State and Business in Chinese Development Cooperation in Africa." *World Development* 81:24–34. https://doi.org/10.1016/j.worlddev.2016.01.001.

Guo, Yu. 2019. "Development and Characteristics of China's Foreign Aid: The Tanzania–Zambia Railway." Pp. 23–34 in *South-South Cooperation and Chinese Foreign Aid*, edited by M. Huang, X. Xu, and X. Mao. Singapore: Palgrave Macmillan.

GURT. 2016. *National Five Year Development Plan: 2016/2017–2020/2021*. Dodoma: Ministry of Finance and Planning.

Hall, David. 2015. *Why Public-Private Partnerships Don't Work: The Many Advantages of the Public Alternative*. Greenwich: Public Services International Research Unit.

Hall, Richard, and Hugh Peyman. 1976. *The Great UHURU Railway: China's Showpiece in Africa*. London: Victor Gollancz.

Hammersley, Martyn, and Paul Atkinson. 1995. *Ethnography: Principles in Practice*. 2nd edition. London: Routledge.
Hampwaye, Godfrey, and Peter Kragelund. 2013. "Trends in Sino-Zambian Relations." Pp. 27–40 in *China's Diplomacy in Eastern and Southern Africa*, edited by S. Adem. Farnham: Ashgate.
Harvey, David. 1982. *The Limits to Capital*. Oxford: Basil Blackwell.
Harvey, David. 2001. *Spaces of Capital: Towards a Critical Geography*. Edinburgh: Edinburgh University Press.
Harvey, David. 2003. *The New Imperialism*. Oxford: Oxford University Press.
Harvey, David. 2004a. "Retrospect on the Limits to Capital." *Antipode* 36(3):544–49. https://doi.org/papers2://publication/uuid/97396CC0-28E6-4674-9D45-0BDAA3110F4D.
Harvey, David. 2004b. "The 'New' Imperialism: Accumulation by Dispossession." *Socialist Register* 40:63–87.
Harvey, David. 2006. *Spaces of Global Capitalism: Towards a Theory of Uneven Geographical Development*. London: Verso.
Harvey, David. 2010. *A Companion to Marx's Capital*. London: Verso.
Harvey, David. 2020. *The Anti-Capitalist Chronicles*. London: Pluto Press.
Hay, Colin. 1996. *Re-Stating Social and Political Change*. Milton Keynes: Open University Press.
Hay, Colin. 2002. *Political Analysis: A Critical Introduction*. London: Red Globe Press.
Hay, Colin. 2014. "Levels of Governance and Their Interaction." Pp. 32–47 in *Handbook of the International Political Economy of Governance*, edited by A. Payne and N. Phillips. Cheltenham: Edward Elgar.
Hay, Colin, and Michael Lister. 2006. "Introduction: Theories of the State." Pp. 1–20 in *The State: Theories and Issues*, edited by C. Hay, M. Lister, and D. Marsh. London: Red Globe Press.
He, Yafei. 2014. "China's Overcapacity Crisis Can Spur Growth through Overseas Expansion." *South China Morning Post*. Retrieved May 25, 2019 (https://www.scmp.com/comment/insight-opinion/article/1399681/chinas-overcapacity-crisis-can-spur-growth-through-overseas).
Heigl, Miriam C. 2011. "An Operationalization of the Strategic-Relational Approach: The Contested Privatization of the Mexican Oil Sector (1982–2006)." *Globalizations* 8(1):81–96. https://doi.org/10.1080/14747731.2011.545663.
Henn, Matt, Mark Weinstein, and Nick Foard. 2009. *A Critical Introduction to Social Research*. London: Sage Publications.
Hildyard, Nicholas. 2016. *Licenced Larceny: Infrastructure, Financial Extraction and the Global South*. Manchester: Manchester University Press.

Hill, Matthew. 2016. "Zambia 2015 Copper Production Unexpectedly Rises on New Mine." *Bloomberg*. Retrieved February 28, 2020 (https://www.bloomberg.com/news/articles/2016-01-22/zambia-2015-copper-output-unexpectedly-increases-on-new-mine).

Hinfelaar, Marja, and Jessica Achberger. 2017. *The Politics of Natural Resource Extraction in Zambia*. ESID Working Paper No. 80. Manchester: Effective States and Inclusive Development Research Centre.

Hinfelaar, Marja, and Justine Sichone. 2019. *The Challenge of Sustaining a Professional Civil Service amidst Shifting Political Coalitions: The Case of the Ministry of Finance in Zambia, 1991–2018*. ESID Working Paper No. 122. Manchester: Effective States and Inclusive Development Research Centre.

Hodzi, Obert. 2018. "China and Africa: Economic Growth and a Non-Transformative Political Elite." *Journal of Contemporary African Studies* 36(2):191–206. https://doi.org/10.1080/02589001.2017.1406191.

Hönke, Jana. 2018. "Beyond the Gatekeeper State: African Infrastructure Hubs as Sites of Experimentation." *Third World Thematics: A TWQ Journal* 3(3):347–63. https://doi.org/10.1080/23802014.2018.1456954.

Hönke, Jana, and Ivan Cuesta-Fernandez. 2017. "A Topolographical Approach to Infrastructure: Political Topography, Topology and the Port of Dar Es Salaam." *Environment and Planning D: Society and Space* 35(6):1076–95. https://doi.org/10.1177/0263775817707762.

Horn, Sebastian, Carmen Reinhart, and Christoph Trebesch. 2019. *China's Overseas Lending*. Kiel Working Paper No. 2132. Kiel Institute for the World Economy.

Humphrys, Elizabeth. 2018. "Anti-Politics, the Early Marx and Gramsci's 'Integral State.'" *Thesis Eleven* 147(1):29–44. https://doi.org/10.1177/0725513618787638.

Hung, Ho Fung. 2008. "Rise of China and the Global Overaccumulation Crisis." *Review of International Political Economy* 15(2):149–79.https://doi.org/10.1080/09692290701869654

Hung, Ho-fung. 2022. *Clash of Empires: From "Chimerica" to the "New Cold War."* Cambridge: Cambridge University Press.

Hyden, Göran. 1983. *No Shortcuts to Progress: African Development Management in Perspective*. Berkeley: University of California Press.

Hyden, Göran. 2000. "The Governance Challenge in Africa." Pp. 5–32 in *African Perspectives on Governance*, edited by G. Hyden, D. Olowu, and H. W. O. Okoth Ogendo. Trenton: African World Press.

ICA. 2018a. *Infrastructure Financing Trends in Africa—2017*. Abidjan: Infrastructure Consortium for Africa.

ICA. 2018b. *Infrastructure Financing Trends in Africa—2018*. Abidjan: Infrastructure Consortium for Africa.

ICA. 2022. *Infrastructure Financing Trends in Africa: 2019–2020*. Abidjan: Infrastructure Consortium for Africa.

IEG. 2006. *ICR Review: Zambia Railways Restructuring Project: Report No: ICRR12336*. Independent Evaluation Group, World Bank.

IMF. 2019. "IMF Staff Completes 2019 Article IV Visit to Zambia." *International Monetary Fund*. Retrieved April 30, 2019 (https://www.imf.org/en/News/Articles/2019/04/30/pr19130-zambia-imf-staff-completes-2019-article-iv-visit?fbclid=IwAR0LLB3WYsWz4Yc404nUBaY4s942AmxPYbAnGmiF5S1N4ZPSge3nYVOEw9U).

Isbell, Thomas. 2018. *Zambians See Corruption Rising, Government Failing in Anti-Graft Fight*. Afrobarometer Dispatch No. 213. Cape Town.

Jackson, Patrick Thaddeus. 2016. *The Conduct of Inquiry in International Relations: Philosophy of Science and Its Implications for the Study of World Politics*. 2nd edition. Abingdon: Routledge.

Jacob, Thabit, and Rasmus Hundsbæk Pedersen. 2018. "New Resource Nationalism? Continuity and Change in Tanzania's Extractive Industries." *Extractive Industries and Society* 5(2):287–92. https://doi.org/10.1016/j.exis.2018.02.001.

Jäger, Johannes, Laura Horn, and Joachim Becker. 2016. "Critical International Political Economy and Method." Pp. 101–18 in *The Palgrave Handbook of Critical International Political Economy*, edited by A. Cafruny, L. S. Talani, and G. P. Martin. London: Palgrave Macmillan.

Jensen, Klaus Bruhn. 1995. *The Social Semiotics of Mass Communication*. London: Sage Publications.

Jere, Joshua. 2019. "20% Subcontracting Policy to Be Legal." *ZNBC*. Retrieved April 14, 2019 (https://www.znbc.co.zm/20-subcontracting-policy-to-be-legal/).

Jessop, Bob. 1982. *The Capitalist State: Marxist Theories and Methods*. Oxford: Blackwell.

Jessop, Bob. 1990. *State Theory: Putting the Capitalist State in Its Place*. Cambridge: Polity Press.

Jessop, Bob. 2001. "Institutional Re(Turns) and the Strategic-Relational Approach." *Environment and Planning A* 33(7):1213–35. https://doi.org/10.1068/a32183.

Jessop, Bob. 2002. "Capitalism, the Regulation Approach, and Critical Realism." Pp. 88–115 in *Critical Realism and Marxism*, edited by A. Brown, S. Fleetwood, and J. M. Roberts. London: Routledge.

Jessop, Bob. 2003. "The Political Economy of Scale and the Construction of Cross-Border Micro-Regions." Pp. 179–96 in *Theories of New Regionalism: A Palgrave Reader*, edited by F. Söderbaum and T. M. Shaw. Basingstoke: Palgrave Macmillan.

Jessop, Bob. 2004a. *From Localities via the Spatial Turn to Spatial-Temporal Fixes: A Strategic-Relational Odyssey*. SECONS Discussion Forum Contribution No. 6. Socio-Economics of Space, University of Bonn.
Jessop, Bob. 2004b. "On the Limits of The Limits to Capital." *Antipode* 36(3):480–96. doi: https://doi.org/10.1111/j.1467-8330.2004.00427.x.
Jessop, Bob. 2005. "Critical Realism and the Strategic-Relational Approach." *New Formations: A Journal of Culture, Theory and Politics* (56):40–53.
Jessop, Bob. 2006a. "Spatial Fixes, Temporal Fixes and Spatio-Temporal Fixes." Pp. 142–66 in *David Harvey: A Critical Reader*, edited by N. Castree and D. Gregory. Malden: Blackwell Publishing.
Jessop, Bob. 2006b. "The Strategic-Relational Approach: An Interview with Bob Jessop (by Joo-Hyoung Ji and Sandra Kytir)." Retrieved January 14, 2020 (https://bobjessop.wordpress.com/2014/12/02/the-strategic-relational-approach-an-interview-with-bob-jessop/).
Jessop, Bob. 2007. *State Power: A Strategic-Relational Approach*. Cambridge: Polity Press.
Jessop, Bob. 2010. "World Market, World State, World Society: Marxian Insights and Scientific Realist Interrogations." Pp. 186–202 in *Scientific Realism and International Relations*, edited by J. Joseph and C. Wight. Basingstoke: Palgrave Macmillan.
Jessop, Bob. 2013. "Finance-Dominated Accumulation and the Limits to Institutional and Spatio-Temporal Fixes in Capitalism." Pp. 303–28 in *Fragile Stabilität—stabile Fragilität*, edited by S. A. Jansen, E. S. Schröter, and N. Stehr. Wiesbaden: Springer VS.
Jessop, Bob. 2016a. "Territory, Politics, Governance and Multispatial Metagovernance." *Territory, Politics, Governance* 4(1):8–32. https://doi.org/10.1080/21622671.2015.1123173.
Jessop, Bob. 2016b. *The State: Past, Present, Future*. Cambridge: Polity Press.
Jessop, Bob, and Ngai-Ling Sum. 2017. "Putting the 'Amsterdam School' in Its Rightful Place: A Reply to Juan Ignacio Staricco's Critique of Cultural Political Economy." *New Political Economy* 22(3):342–54. https://doi.org/10.1080/13563467.2017.1286639.
Jessop, Bob, and Ngai-Ling Sum. 2018. "Geopolitics: Putting Geopolitics in Its Place in Cultural Political Economy." *Environment and Planning A: Economy and Space* 50(2):474–78. https://doi.org/10.1177/0308518X17731106.
Jones, Lee, and Shahar Hameiri. 2020. *Debunking the Myth of "Debt-Trap Diplomacy": How Recipient Countries Shape China's Belt and Road Initiative*. Asia-Pacific Programme Research Paper. London: Chatham House.
Jones, Lee, and Jinghan Zeng. 2019. "Understanding China's 'Belt and Road Initiative': Beyond 'Grand Strategy' to a State Transformation Analysis." *Third World Quarterly* 40(8):1415–39. https://doi.org/10.1080/01436597.2018.1559046.

Jones, Martin, and Bob Jessop. 2010. "Thinking State/Space Incompossibly." *Antipode* 42(5):1119–49. https://doi.org/10.1111/j.1467-8330.2010.00796.x.

Joseph, Jonathan. 2008. "On the Limits of Neo-Gramscian International Relations: A Scientific Realist Account of Hegemony." Pp. 101–24 in *Gramsci, Political Economy, and International Relations Theory: Modern Princes and Naked Emperors*, edited by A. J. Ayers. Basingstoke: Palgrave Macmillan.

Kahama, Joseph K. 2018. *The Challenge to China-Tanzania Relationship: To Enhance Cooperation and Mutual Benefits*. Dar es Salaam: Tema Publishers.

Kaiser, Paul J. 1996. "Structural Adjustment and the Fragile Nation: The Demise of Social Unity in Tanzania." *The Journal of Modern African Studies* 34(2):227–37. https://doi.org/10.1017/s0022278x00055300.

Kamata, Ng'wanza. 2013. "Perspectives on Sino-Tanzanian Relations." Pp. 87–106 in *China's Diplomacy in Eastern and Southern Africa*, edited by S. Adem. Farnham: Ashgate.

Kandoya, James. 2018. "RAHCO Disbanded as TRL Gives Way to TRC." *The Guardian*. Retrieved March 24, 2020 (https://www.ippmedia.com/en/news/rahco-disbanded-trl-gives-way-trc).

Kelly, Duncan. 1999. "The Strategic-Relational View of the State." *Politics* 19(2):109–15. https://doi.org/10.1111/1467-9256.00093.

Kelly, Gina, Samuel Brazys, and Johan A. Elkink. 2016. *The Dragon's Curse? China, the World Bank, and Perceptions of Corruption in Tanzania*. AidData Working Paper 26.

Kimari, Wangui, and Henrik Ernstson. 2020. "Imperial Remains and Imperial Invitations: Centering Race within the Contemporary Large-Scale Infrastructures of East Africa." *Antipode* 52(3):825–46. https://doi.org/10.1111/anti.12623.

Kinyondo, Abel. 2019. "Is China Recolonizing Africa? Some Views from Tanzania." *World Affairs* 182(2):128–64. https://doi.org/10.1177/0043820019839331.

Kinyondo, Abel, and Christopher Huggins. 2019. "Resource Nationalism in Tanzania: Implications for Artisanal and Small-Scale Mining." *Extractive Industries and Society* 6(1):181–89. https://doi.org/10.1016/j.exis.2018.08.005.

Koivisto, Marjo. 2010. "State Theory in International Relations: Why Realism Matters." Pp. 69–87 in *Scientific Realism and International Relations*, edited by J. Joseph and C. Wight. Basingstoke: Palgrave Macmillan.

Koivisto, Marjo. 2012. *Normative State Power in International Relations*. Oxford: Oxford University Press.

Konings, Piet. 2007. "The Neoliberalising African State and Private Capital Accumulation: The Case of Cameroon." Pp. 251–73 in *Big Business and Economic Development: Conglomerates and Economic Groups in Developing Countries and Transition Economies under Globalisation*, edited by A. E. Fernández Jilberto and B. Hogenboom. Abingdon: Routledge.

Kopinski, Dominik, and Andrzej Polus. 2011. "Sino-Zambian Relations: 'An All-Weather Friendship' Weathering the Storm." *Journal of Contemporary African Studies* 29(2):181–92. https://doi.org/10.1080/02589001.2011.555193.

Kragelund, Peter. 2010. "The Price of 'Openness': Towards Chinese Economic Control in Zambia." Pp. 208–17 in *The Rise of China and India in Africa*, edited by F. Cheru and C. Obi. London: Zed Books.

Kragelund, Peter. 2017. "The Making of Local Content Policies in Zambia's Copper Sector: Institutional Impediments to Resource-Led Development." *Resources Policy* 51(March):57–66. https://doi.org/10.1016/j.resourpol.2016.11.008.

Krueger, Anne O. 1974. "The Political Economy of the Rent-Seeking Society." *The American Economic Review* 64(3):291–303.

Kvale, Steinar. 2007. *Doing Interviews*. London: Sage Publications.

Kynge, James, Kathrin Hille, Benjamin Parkin, and Jonathan Wheatley. 2022. "China Reckons with Its First Overseas Debt Crisis." *Financial Times*. Retrieved July 16, 2023 (https://www.ft.com/content/ccbe2b80-0c3e-4d58-a182-8728b443df9a).

Lampert, Ben, and Giles Mohan. 2015. "Making Space for African Agency in China-Africa Engagements: Ghanaian and Nigerian Patrons Shaping Chinese Enterprise." Pp. 109–26 in *Africa and China: How Africans and Their Governments are Shaping Relations with China*, edited by A. W. Gadzala. Lanham: Rowman & Littlefield.

Landry, David. 2018. "The Risks and Rewards of Resource-for-Infrastructure Deals: Lessons from the Congo's Sicomines Agreement." *Resources Policy* 58(October):165–74. https://doi.org/10.1016/j.resourpol.2018.04.014.

Lange, Siri, and Abel Kinyondo. 2016. "Resource Nationalism and Local Content in Tanzania: Experiences from Mining and Consequences for the Petroleum Sector." *Extractive Industries and Society* 3(4):1095–104. https://doi.org/10.1016/j.exis.2016.09.006.

Large, Daniel. 2021. *China and Africa: The New Era*. Cambridge: Policy Press.

Larmer, Miles. 2005. "Reaction & Resistance to Neo-Liberalism in Zambia." *Review of African Political Economy* 32(103):29–45. https://doi.org/10.1080/03056240500120992.

Larmer, Miles. 2011. *Rethinking African Politics: A History of Opposition in Zambia*. Surrey: Ashgate.

Lee, Ching Kwan. 2014. "The Spectre of Global China." *New Left Review* September(89):29–66.

Lee, Ching Kwan. 2017. *The Specter of Global China: Politics, Labor, and Foreign Investment in Africa*. Chicago: University of Chicago Press.

Leslie, Agnes Ngoma. 2016. "Zambia and China: Workers' Protest, Civil Society and the Role of Opposition Politics in Elevating State Engagement." *African Studies Quarterly* 16(3–4):89–106.

Lesutis, Gediminas. 2021. "Infrastructure as Techno-Politics of Differentiation: Socio-Political Effects of Mega-Infrastructures in Kenya." *Transactions of the Institute of British Geographers* (April 2020):1–13. https://doi.org/10.1111/tran.12474.

Lesutis, Gediminas. 2022. "Disquieting Ambivalence of Mega-Infrastructures: Kenya's Standard Gauge Railway as Spectacle and Ruination." *Environment and Planning D: Society and Space* 026377582211254.https://doi.org/10.1177/02637758221125475

Levien, Michael. 2018. *Dispossession without Development: Land Grabs in Neoliberal India*. Oxford: Oxford University Press.

Lewis, Paul A. 2002. "Agency, Structure and Causality in Political Science: A Comment on Sibeon." *Politics* 22(1):17–23. https://doi.org/10.1111/1467-9256.00154.

Lewis, Peter M. 1994. "Economic Statism, Private Capital, and the Dilemmas of Accumulation in Nigeria." *World Development* 22(3):437–51.

Li, Xing. 2016. "Conceptualising the Dialectics of China's Presence in Africa." Pp. 77–106 in *Emerging Powers in Africa: A New Wave in the Relationship?*, edited by J. Van der Merwe, I. Taylor, and A. Arkhangelskaya. Basingstoke: Palgrave Macmillan.

Li, Xing, ed. 2019. *Mapping China's "One Belt One Road" Initiative*. Cham: Palgrave Macmillan.

Li, Xing, and Abdulkadir Osman Farah, eds. 2013. *China-Africa Relations in an Era of Great Transformations*. Farnham: Ashgate.

Lim, Kean Fan. 2010. "On China's Growing Geo-Economic Influence and the Evolution of Variegated Capitalism." *Geoforum* 41(5):677–88. https://doi.org/10.1016/j.geoforum.2010.04.003.

Links, Stacey. 2021. "Ascertaining Agency Africa and the Belt and Road Initiative." Pp. 113–39 in *Global Perspectives on China's Belt and Road Initiative: Asserting Agency through Regional Connectivity*, edited by F. Schneider. Amsterdam: Amsterdam University Press.

Lippolis, Nicolas, and Harry Verhoeven. 2022. "Politics by Default: China and the Global Governance of African Debt." *Survival* 64(3):153–78. https://doi.org/10.1080/00396338.2022.2078054.

Lisinge, Robert Tama. 2020. "The Belt and Road Initiative and Africa's Regional Infrastructure Development: Implications and Lessons." *Transnational Corporations Review* 12(4):425–38. https://doi.org/10.1080/19186444.2020.1795527.

Liu, Haifang. 2024. "The Freedom Railway Now and Then: The Enduring Relevance of the 'TAZARA Spirit' for South-South Cooperation." Pp. 68–88 in

Africa's Railway Renaissance: The Role and Impact of China, edited by T. Zajontz, P. Carmody, M. Bagwandeen, and A. Leysens. Abingdon: Routledge.

Liu, Haifang, and Jamie Monson. 2011. "Railway Time: Technology Transfer and the Role of Chinese Experts in the History of TAZARA." Pp. 226–51 in *African Engagements: Africa Negotiating an Emerging Multipolar World*, edited by T. Dietz, K. Havnevik, M. Kaag, and T. Oestigaard. Leiden: Brill.

Liu, Weidong, and Michael Dunford. 2016. "Inclusive Globalization: Unpacking China's Belt and Road Initiative." *Area Development and Policy* 1(3):323–40. https://doi.org/10.1080/23792949.2016.1232598.

Liu, Weidong, Michael Dunford, and Boyang Gao. 2018. "A Discursive Construction of the Belt and Road Initiative: From Neo-Liberal to Inclusive Globalization." *Journal of Geographical Sciences* 28:1199–1214.

Lopes, Carlos. 2016. "Reinserting African Agency into Sino-Africa Relations." *Strategic Review for Southern Africa* 38(1):50–68.

Lu, Zhiyao. 2017. "China's Excess Capacity in Steel: A Fresh Look." *Peterson Institute for International Economics*. Retrieved February 26, 2022 (https://www.piie.com/blogs/china-economic-watch/chinas-excess-capacity-steel-fresh-look).

Lumumba-Kasongo, Tukumbi. 2011. "China-Africa Relations: A Neo-Imperialism or a Neo-Colonialism? A Reflection." *African and Asian Studies* 10(2):234–66. https://doi.org/10.1163/156921011X587040.

Lupupa, Frank. 2017. "Kambwili Tells Lungu to Resign over 'Corrupt' Lusaka-Ndola Road Project." *The Mast*. Retrieved October 26, 2019 (https://www.themastonline.com/2017/09/13/kambwili-tells-lungu-to-resign-over-corrupt-lusaka-ndola-road-project/).

Lusaka Times. 2016. "Government Signs a $2.3 Billion Deal with a Chinese Firm to Construct a Chipata-Serenje Railway Line." *Lusaka Times*. Retrieved July 25, 2019 (https://www.lusakatimes.com/2016/11/03/government-signs-a-2-3-billion-deal-with-a-chinese-firm-to-construct-a-chipata-serenje-railway-line/).

Lusaka Times. 2017. "Construction of the $1.2 Billion Ndola-Lusaka Dual Carriageway Is a Scandal-GBM." *Lusaka Times*. Retrieved May 5, 2019 (https://www.lusakatimes.com/2017/09/16/construction-1-2-billion-ndola-lusaka-dual-carriageway-road-contract-scandal-gbm/).

Lusaka Times. 2018a. "Foreign Contractors Disobeying Presidential Directive to Employ Local Contractors." *Lusaka Times*. Retrieved July 5, 2019 (https://www.lusakatimes.com/2018/07/09/foreign-contractors-disobeying-presidential-directive-to-employ-local-contractors/).

Lusaka Times. 2018b. "Government Directs All Foreign Contractors to Adhere to the 20% Subcontracting Policy." *Lusaka Times*. Retrieved May 20, 2019 (https://www.lusakatimes.com/2018/05/23/government-directs-all-foreign-contractors-to-adhere-to-the-20-sub-contracting-policy/).

Lusaka Times. 2018c. "Kenneth Kaunda International Airport Will Not Be Surrendered to China-Dora Siliza." *Lusaka Times*. Retrieved July 25, 2019 (https://www.lusakatimes.com/2018/09/10/kenneth-kaunda-international-airport-will-not-be-surrendered-to-china-dora-siliya/).

Lusaka Times. 2018d. "Kitwe-Ndola Dual Carriageway Is Funded by the Zambian Government." *Lusaka Times*. Retrieved May 31, 2019 (https://www.lusakatimes.com/2018/06/24/kitwe-ndola-dual-carriageway-project-is-funded-by-the-zambian-government/).

Lusaka Times. 2018e. "On-Going Works on the Ndola-Kitwe Dual Carriageway Are a Serious Diplomatic Scandal-Sinkamba." *Lusaka Times*. Retrieved May 13, 2019 (https://www.lusakatimes.com/2018/06/21/on-going-works-on-the-ndola-kitwe-dual-carriageway-are-a-serious-diplomatic-scandal-sinkamba/).

Lusaka Times. 2019a. "ACC Arrests, Charges Minister Chitotela with 9 More Counts of Corruption." *Lusaka Times*. Retrieved July 17, 2019 (https://www.lusakatimes.com/2019/05/24/acc-arrests-charges-minister-chitotela-with-9-more-counts-of-corruption/).

Lusaka Times. 2019b. "Lusaka Magistrate Court Clears Chitotela, He Has No Case to Answer." *Lusaka Times*. Retrieved July 12, 2019 (https://www.lusakatimes.com/2019/07/11/lusaka-magistrate-court-clears-chitotela-he-has-no-case-to-answer/?fbclid=IwAR0BDdcsfsAXrUPZz-UvwCuccTBDB58MvSEzHYG_KRoRlEPQFWXLkWDCaBQ).

Lusaka Times. 2019c. "President Lungu Warns Ministers and PF Officials Abusing the 20% Meant for Local Contractors." *Lusaka Times*. Retrieved September 30, 2019 (https://www.lusakatimes.com/2019/09/30/president-lungu-warns-ministers-and-pf-officials-abusing-the-20-meant-for-local-contractors/?fbclid=IwAR2lBO2rmJA1c2KI2fU-10pHJT-YR1bSQgGt8RtrLHTjtzvr-PHyUMJAbWc).

Lusaka Times. 2019d. "Tanzania Orders Probe into $6.7 Million Funds for TAZARA." *Lusaka Times*. Retrieved August 19, 2019 (https://www.lusakatimes.com/2019/07/29/tanzania-orders-probe-into-6-7-million-funds-for-tazara/).

Lusaka Times. 2019e. "Zambia's Debt Continues Pilling up as First Half Growth Shrinks." *Lusaka Times*. Retrieved July 17, 2019 (https://www.lusakatimes.com/2019/07/17/zambias-debt-continues-pilling-up-as-first-half-growth-shrinks/).

Lusaka Times. 2020a. "Government Signs a Railway MOU with Railnet International." *Lusaka Times*. Retrieved March 8, 2020 (https://www.lusakatimes.com/2020/03/07/government-signs-a-railway-mou-with/?fbclid=IwAR24TP-8QAIsW-MWERYfg3uGm0qnFxQ2Hi1OTnU9XrOQX-tLGit4YmiWVl4).

Lusaka Times. 2020b. "National Road Fund Agency Collects K1.2 Billion in Toll Fees in 2019." *Lusaka Times*. Retrieved February 9, 2020 (https://www.lusakatimes.com/2020/02/08/262747/?fbclid=IwAR2s8S5I6KC5W1ldPdH27C_W7fQbPH9VTgznGsrtT810Wz_ImHXsOQyveio).

Lusaka Times. 2020c. "Zambia Signs over $824 Million Deal with China Railway for Line Upgrades." *Lusaka Times*. Retrieved March 8, 2020 (https://www.lusakatimes.com/2020/03/06/265085/?fbclid=IwAR3VebAqXdWL8o6SRXaGwT2xqeHGE16zUo0X8Eymy6UOzk5fLyfDZzjaPUw).

Lusaka Times. 2022. "Chingola-Kasumbalesa PPP Concession Agreement Inked." *Lusaka Times*. Retrieved July 11, 2023 (https://www.lusakatimes.com/2022/11/01/chingola-kasumbalesa-ppp-concession-agreement-inked/).

Luxemburg, Rosa. 2003 [1913]. *The Accumulation of Capital*. London: Routledge.

MacKinnon, Danny, Jon Shaw, and Iain Docherty. 2008. *Diverging Mobilities? Devolution, Transport and Policy Innovation*. Amsterdam: Elsevier.

Magufuli, John Joseph Pombe. 2017. "Foreword." Pp. viii–ix in *Tanzania's Industrialisation Journey, 2016–2056: From Agrarian to a Modern Industrialised State in Forty Years*, edited by A. A. Mufuruki, R. Mawji, M. Marwa, and G. Kasiga. Nairobi: Moran Publishers.

Makundi, Hezron, Huib Huyse, and Patrick Develtere. 2017. "Negotiating the Technological Capacity in Chinese Engagements: Is the Tanzanian Government in the Driving Seat?" *South African Journal of International Affairs* 24(3):331–53. https://doi.org/10.1080/10220461.2017.1391116.

Malanga, Alex. 2017. "China, Tanzania in Fresh Talks on Tazara Revitalisation Plan." *The Citizen*. Retrieved August 4, 2019 (https://www.thecitizen.co.tz/News/China--Tanzania-in-fresh-talks-on--Tazara-revitalisation-plan/1840340-4173116-e6pcnbz/index.html).

Mann, Michael. 1984. "The Autonomous Power of the State: Its Origins, Mechanisms and Results." *European Journal of Sociology* 25(2):185–213.

Mapapayi, Jackson. 2021. "US$250 Millian Road Deal Sealed." *Daily Nation*. Retrieved July 11, 2023 (https://dailynationzambia.com/2021/06/us250-million-road-deal-sealed/).

Marx, Karl. 1967. *Capital: A Critique of Political Economy*. 3 Volumes. New York: International Publishers.

Marx, Karl. 1971. *Capital: A Critique of Political Economy*. 3 Volumes. Moscow: Progress.

Marx, Karl. 1973 [1939]. *Grundrisse*. New York: Random House.

Marx, Karl. 2013. *Capital: A Critical Analysis of Capitalist Production*. Volumes 1 and 2, edited by M. G. Spencer. Ware: Wordsworth Editions.

Masabo, Conrad John. 2021. "Tanzania in China's MSRI: The 'Chinese Dream' Awaits Alignment with the African One." Pp. 137–64 in *China's Maritime*

Silk Road Initiative, Africa, and the Middle East: Feats, Freezes, and Failures, edited by J.-M. F. Blanchard. Singapore: Palgrave Macmillan.
Mayer, Maximilian, and Xin Zhang. 2021. "Theorizing China-World Integration: Sociospatial Reconfigurations and the Modern Silk Roads." *Review of International Political Economy* 28(4):974–1003. https://doi.org/10.1080/09692290.2020.1741424.
Mbewe, Zondiwe. 2018. "Govt Refutes TAZARA Concession Claims." *News Diggers*. Retrieved March 24, 2020 (https://diggers.news/?p=30394 Accessed on: 28.02.2019).
Mboya, Cliff. 2021. "The Maritime Silk Road Initiative: Connecting Africa." Pp. 53–80 in *China's Maritime Silk Road Initiative, Africa, and the Middle East Feats, Freezes, and Failures*, edited by J.-M. F. Blanchard. Singapore: Palgrave Macmillan.
Mbulo, Edwin. 2019. "It's Crazy for a Country to Get in Debt without Capability to Repay, Says Kikwete." *The Mast*. Retrieved August 10, 2019 (https://www.themastonline.com/2019/07/28/its-crazy-for-a-country-to-get-in-debt-without-capability-to-repay-says-kikwete/?fbclid=IwAR0sCaZIReAuUCbhjGd85Tm4Kn2tE5e2cL_U11flFkiVL8UuB0iSjUpiWUw).
McNally, Christopher A. 2012. "Sino-Capitalism: China's Reemergence and the International Political Economy." *World Politics* 64(4):741–76. https://doi.org/10.1017/s0043887112000202.
Médard, Jean François. 1982. "The Underdeveloped State in Africa: Political Clientelism or Neo-Patrimonialism?" Pp. 162–89 in *Private Patronage and Public Power: Political Clientelism and the Modern State*, edited by C. Clapham. London: Frances Pinter.
Médard, Jean François. 1991. "L'État Néo-Patrimonial En Afrique Noire." Pp. 323–53 in *États d'Afrique Noire. Formations, Mécanismes et Crise*, edited by J. F. Médard. Paris: Karthala.
Meuleman, Louis. 2008. *Public Management and the Metagovernance of Hierarchies, Networks and Markets*. Heidelberg: Springer.
Mhagama, Hilda. 2022. "Strategic Projects: Samia Goes for Healthy Borrowing." *Daily News*. Retrieved July 15, 2023 (https://dailynews.co.tz/strategic-projects-samia-goes-for-healthy-borrowing/).
Middell, Matthias. 2019. "Category of Spatial Formats: To What End?" Pp. 15–47 in *Spatial Formats under the Global Condition: Dialectics of the Global*. 1, edited by M. Middell. Berlin: De Gruyter.
Migdal, Joel S. 1994. "Introduction: Developing a State-in-Society Perspective." Pp. 1–4 in *State Power and Social Forces: Domination and Transformation in the Third World*, edited by J. S. Migdal, A. Kohli, and V. Shue. Cambridge: Cambridge University Press.
Minde, Nicodemus. 2023. "Samia Suluhu Hassan Is Reforming Tanzania—It's Winning Her Fans but Boosting the Opposition." *The Conversation*. Retrieved

July 17, 2023 (https://theconversation.com/samia-suluhu-hassan-is-reforming-tanzania-its-winning-her-fans-but-boosting-the-opposition-198793).

Ministry of Finance. 2018. *Annual Economic Report 2017*. Lusaka: Ministry of Finance.

Ministry of Finance. 2019a. *Annual Economic Report 2018*. Lusaka: Ministry of Finance.

Ministry of Finance. 2019b. *Highlights on the Performance of the Economy in 2018*. Lusaka: Ministry of Finance.

Ministry of Finance. 2019c. "Increase In China-Zambia Trade Projected." *Ministry of Finance*. Retrieved January 16, 2020 (https://www.mof.gov.zm/6114-2/).

Mitimingi, Taonga Clifford, and Matthew Hill. 2020. "Zambia Wants to Forgo $5 Billion in Contracted External Debt." *Bloomberg*. Retrieved March 1, 2020 (https://www.bloomberg.com/news/articles/2020-02-12/zambia-plans-to-cut-undisbursed-external-debt-by-5-billion).

Mittelman, James H. 2014. "A Global Perspective on International Regulation and Governance in Africa." *Global Change, Peace & Security* 26(1):113–20. https://doi.org/10.1080/14781158.2013.814628.

Mkandawire, Thandika. 2015. "Neopatrimonialism and the Political Economy of Economic Performance in Africa: Critical Reflections." *World Politics* 67(3):563–612. https://doi.org/10.1017/s004388711500009x.

Mofya, Mwenya. 2022. "Lusaka-Ndola Highway Was Never Signed as a Contract, It Never Existed—Ng'andu." *News Diggers*. Retrieved July 12, 2023 (https://diggers.news/local/2022/08/08/lusaka-ndola-highway-was-never-signed-as-a-contract-it-never-existed-ngandu/).

Mohan, Giles. 2013. "Beyond the Enclave: Towards a Critical Political Economy of China and Africa." *Development and Change* 44(6):1255–72. https://doi.org/10.1111/dech.12061.

Mohan, Giles, and Ben Lampert. 2013. "Negotiating China: Reinserting African Agency into China-Africa Relations." *African Affairs* 112(446):92–110. https://doi.org/10.1093/afraf/ads065.

Mohan, Giles, and May Tan-Mullins. 2019. "The Geopolitics of South–South Infrastructure Development: Chinese-Financed Energy Projects in the Global South." *Urban Studies* 56(7):1368–85. https://doi.org/10.1177/0042098018794351.

Momba, Jotham C. 2007. "The Intersection between Politics and Corruption in Zambia." *South African Journal of International Affairs* 14(1):115–25. https://doi.org/10.1080/10220460709545486.

Monson, Jamie. 2006. "Defending the People's Railway in the Era of Liberalization: Tazara in Southern Tanzania." *Africa: Journal of the International African Institute* 76(1):113–30.

Monson, Jamie. 2009. *Africa's Freedom Railway: How a Chinese Development Project Changed Lives and Livelihoods in Tanzania*. Bloomington: Indiana University Press.

Monson, Jamie. 2013. "Remembering Work on the Tazara Railway in Africa and China, 1965–2011: When 'New Men' Grow Old." *African Studies Review* 56(1):45–64. https://doi.org/10.1017/asr.2013.5.

Mosley, Paul. 2017. *Fiscal Policy and the Natural Resources Curse: How to Escape from the Poverty Trap*. Abingdon: Routledge.

MTC. n.d. *Request for Expressions of Interest for Public-Private Partnerships for the Financing, Construction, Operation and Maintenance of the Nseluka to Mpulungu Railway Spur in Zambia*. Lusaka: Ministry of Transport and Communications.

Mthembu, Philani. 2020. "China's Belt & Road Initiative: How Can Africa Advance Its Strategic Priorities?" Pp. 134–158 in *Africa and the World: Navigating Shifting Geopolitics*, edited by F. Kornegay and P. Mthembu. Johannesburg: Mapungubwe Institute for Strategic Reflection and Jacana Publishers.

Muneku, Austin. 2009. "Chinese Investments in Zambia." Pp. 199–254 in *Chinese Investments in Africa: A Labour Perspective*, edited by A. Y. Baah and H. Jauch. Harare: African Labour Research Network.

Musa, Jonathan. 2019. "Why Talks on Port Stalled—Video." *The Citizen*. Retrieved July 27, 2019 (https://www.thecitizen.co.tz/news/1840340-5124384-8pdm7b/index.html).

Mustapha, Abdul Raufu. 2002. "States, Predation and Violence: Reconceptualizing Political Action and Political Community in Africa." Paper presented at the 10th General Assembly of CODESIRA, Kampala, Uganda, 8–12 December. Kampala.

Muswala, Tamara. 2023. "HH Demands Quality on Chingola-Kasumbalesa Road." *ZNBC*. Retrieved July 11, 2023 (https://www.znbc.co.zm/news/hh-demands-quality-on-chingola-kasumbalesa-road/).

Mutati, Felix. 2017. "2018 Budget Address: 'Accelerating Fiscal Fitness for Sustained Inclusive Growth, Without Leaving Anyone Behind.'" *National Assembly of Zambia*. Retrieved March 25, 2020 (http://www.parliament.gov.zm/sites/default/files/images/publication_docs/2018Budget.pdf).

Mutesa, Fredrick. 2010. "China and Zambia: Between Development and Politics." Pp. 67–78 in *The Rise of China and India in Africa*, edited by F. Cheru and C. Obi. London: Zed Books.

Mwamba, Gilbert K. 2017. "Public Procurement in Zambia: A Commentary on the Law and Practice." *IJRDO Journal of Business Management* 3(9):24–44.

Mwase, Ngila. 1987. "Zambia, the TAZARA and the Alternative Outlets to the Sea." *Transport Reviews* 7(3):191–206. https://doi.org/10.1080/01441648708716655.

Mwase, Ngila. 2003. "The Liberalisation, De-Regulation and Privatisation of the Transport Sector in Sub-Saharan Africa: Experiences, Challenges and Opportunities." *Journal of African Economies* 12(Supplement 2):ii153–92. https://doi.org/10.1093/jae/12.suppl_2.ii153.

Mwenda, Joseph. 2019a. "Chitotela Probe Implicates Chinese, Lawyers, Fellow MP, Ministers and Others." *News Diggers*. Retrieved July 17, 2019 (https://diggers.news/local/2019/02/07/investigation-reveals-millions-linked-to-chitotela/).

Mwenda, Joseph. 2019b. "Lungu Fires Mawere, Transfers Chitotela, Luo." *News Diggers*. Retrieved July 19, 2019 (https://diggers.news/local/2019/07/19/lungu-fires-mawere-transfers-chitotela-luo/).

Nabudere, Dan. 1981. *Imperialism in East Africa Volume 1: Imperialism and Exploitation*. London: Zed Press.

National Assembly of Zambia. 2015. "Ministerial Statement on the Procurement of The Copperbelt 400 (C400) Road Rehabilitation Project in United States Dollars Currency." *National Assembly of Zambia*. Retrieved May 15, 2019 (http://www.parliament.gov.zm/sites/default/files/images/publication_docs/Works/and/Supply/Statement.pdf).

National Assembly of Zambia. 2017a. "Ministerial Statement on the Lusaka/Ndola/Dual Carriageway Project Given by the Hon. Minister of Housing and Infrastructure Development, Mr. Chitotela, MP." *National Assembly of Zambia*. Retrieved May 19, 2019 (http://www.parliament.gov.zm/sites/default/files/images/publication_docs/MINISTERIAL/STATEMENT/BY/THE/HON.MINISTER/OF/HOUSING/AND/INFRA.DEV.pdf).

National Assembly of Zambia. 2017b. "Ministerial Statements: Railway Transport System in Zambia." *National Assembly of Zambia*. Retrieved May 19, 2019 (http://www.parliament.gov.zm/sites/default/files/images/publication_docs/MINISTERIAL/STATEMENT/ON/THE/STATE/OF/RAILWAY/TRANSPORT/BY/HON/MUSHIMBA.pdf).

NCC. 2019. "List of Contractors." *National Council for Construction*. Retrieved June 22, 2019 (http://www.ncc.org.zm/classified/contractors/).

Ncube, Sipilisiwe. 2018. "Lusaka-Ndola Road Project Riddled with Corruption, Insists Simumba." *News Diggers*. Retrieved October 26, 2019 (https://diggers.news/local/2018/07/17/lusaka-ndola-road-project-riddled-with-corruption-insists-simumba/).

Negi, Rohit. 2008. "Beyond the 'Chinese Scramble': The Political Economy of Anti-China Sentiment in Zambia." *African Geographical Review* 27(1):41–693. https://doi.org/10.1080/19376812.2008.9756209.

Ngoma, Sydney, Muya Mundia, and Chabota Kaliba. 2014. "Benefits, Constraints and Risks in Infrastructure Development via Public-Private Partnerships in Zambia." *Journal of Construction in Developing Countries* 19(1):15–33.

Niemann, Michael. 2000. *A Spatial Approach to Regionalisms in the Global Economy*. Basingstoke: Macmillan Press.

Nkrumah, Kwame. 1965. *Neo-Colonialism: The Last Stage of Imperialism*. Edinburgh: Thomas Nelson and Sons.

Nölke, Andreas. 2014. "Introduction: Toward State Capitalism 3.0." Pp. 1–14 in *Multinational Corporations from Emerging Markets: State Capitalism 3.0*, edited by A. Nölke. Basingstoke: Palgrave Macmillan.

Nölke, Andreas, Tobias ten Brink, Christian May, and Simone Claar. 2020. *State-Permeated Capitalism in Large Emerging Economies*. Abingdon: Routledge.

NRFA. n.d.-a. *National Road Fund Agency: Annual Report 2017*. Lusaka: National Road Fund Agency.

NRFA. n.d.-b. "NRTP (PHASE II)." *National Road Fund Agency*. Retrieved July 12, 2023 (https://nrfa.org.zm/nrtp-phase-ii/).

Nugent, Paul. 2018. "Africa's Re-Enchantment with Big Infrastructure: White Elephants Dancing in Virtuous Circles?" Pp. 22–40 in *Extractive Industries and Changing State Dynamics in Africa*, edited by J. Schubert, U. Engel, and M. Elisio. Abingdon: Routledge.

Nwapi, Chilenye, and Nathan Andrews. 2017. "A 'New' Developmental State in Africa? Evaluating Recent State Interventions Vis-a-Vis Resource Extraction in Kenya, Tanzania, and Rwanda." *Journal of Sustainable Development* 13(2):223–67.

Nyabiage, Jevans. 2021. "China cancels Democratic Republic of Congo loans as it joins Belt and Road." *South China Morning Post*. Retrieved February 22, 2022 (https://www.scmp.com/news/china/diplomacy/article/3116837/china-cancels-democratic-republic-congo-loans-itjoins-belt).

Nyabiage, Jevans. 2023. "Chinese Consortium to Build US$650 Million Toll Road in Cash-Strapped Zambia, but Will It Pay Off?" *South China Morning Post*. Retrieved July 12, 2023 (https://www.scmp.com/news/china/diplomacy/article/3213048/chinese-consortium-build-us650-million-toll-road-cash-strapped-zambia-will-it-pay).

Nyerere, Julius. 2015. "Speech at the Official Handover of the Tanzania Zambia Railway to Tanzania and Zambia, Kapiri Mposhi, Zambia, 14 July 1976." Pp. 64–71 in *Julius Nyerere: Asante sana, Thank You, Mwalimu*. Dar es Salaam: Mkuki na Nyota.

OECD. 2012. *OECD Investment Policy Reviews: Zambia*. Paris: Organisation for Economic Cooperation and Development Publishing.

OECD and ACET. 2020. *Quality Infrastructure in 21st Century Africa: Prioritising, Accelerating and Scaling Up in the Context of PIDA (2021–30)*. Paris: Organisation for Economic Cooperation and Development, African Center for Economic Transformation.

Ofstad, Arve, and Elling Tjønneland. 2019. *Zambia's Looming Debt Crisis—Is China to Blame?* CMI Insight No. 1. Bergen: Chr. Michelsen Institute.

Oirere, Shem. 2015. "Court Declares Tazara Staff Strike Illegal." *International Railway Journal*. Retrieved March 4, 2020 (https://www.railjournal.com/africa/court-declares-tazara-staff-strike-illegal/).

Olingo, Allan. 2017. "Tanzania's Turn to Turkey for SGR Funds Leaves China in Limbo." *The East African*. Retrieved August 2, 2019 (https://www.theeastafrican.co.ke/business/Tanzania-SGR-funds-/2560-3793116-m75574/index.html).

Olukoshi, Adebayo O. 1998. *The Elusive Prince of Denmark. Structural Adjustment and the Crisis of Governance in Africa*. Research Report No. 104. Uppsala: Nordiska Afrikainstitutet.

O'Mahoney, Joe, and Steve Vincent. 2014. "Critical Realism as an Empirical Project: A Beginner's Guide." Pp. 1–20 in *Studying Organizations Using Critical Realism: A Practical Guide*, edited by P. K. Edwards, J. O'Mahoney, and S. Vincent. Oxford: Oxford University Press.

Onuf, Nicholas Greenwood. 1998. *The Republican Legacy in International Thought*. Cambridge: Cambridge University Press.

Onyango, Emmanuel. 2019a. "Blow to Northern Corridor as Tanzania Signs Deal to Link SGR to Burundi, DRC." *The East African*. Retrieved March 10, 2020 (https://www.theeastafrican.co.ke/business/Tanzania-signs-mega-sgr-deal-with-burundi-drc/2560-5377324-75ujpd/index.html?fbclid=IwAR172nOaD4742dRHckKA0Yr3XbfD-8ZqpUoEuRckpK2EIMYSk9CKF-mGhnA).

Onyango, Emmanuel. 2019b. "China Could Finance Part of Tanzania's SGR Project." *The East African*. Retrieved August 2, 2019 (https://www.theeastafrican.co.ke/business/China-could-finance-part-of-tanzania-sgr-project/2560-5185404-1e7c77/index.html).

Osei-Kyei, Robert, and Albert P. C. Chan. 2016. "Developing Transport Infrastructure in Sub-Saharan Africa through Public–Private Partnerships: Policy Practice and Implications." *Transport Reviews* 36(2):170–86. https://doi.org/10.1080/01441647.2015.1077288.

Otele, Oscar M. 2020. "China, Region-Centric Infrastructure Drives and Regionalism in Africa." *South African Journal of International Affairs* 27(4):511–32. doi: https://doi.org/10.1080/10220461.2020.1856179.

Otiso, Kefa M., and Pádraig Carmody. 2024. "Powering African Transport or Transporting Chinese Power? The Spatial Political Economy of Chinese Railways in Africa." Pp. 49–67 in *Africa's Railway Renaissance: The Role and Impact of China*, edited by T. Zajontz, P. Carmody, M. Bagwandeen, and A. Leysens. Abingdon: Routledge.

Ovadia, Jesse Salah. 2013. "Accumulation with or without Dispossession? A 'both/and' Approach to China in Africa with Reference to Angola." *Review of African Political Economy* 40(136):233–50. https://doi.org/10.1080/03056244.2013.794724.

Paget, Dan. 2021. "Tanzania: The Authoritarian Landslide." *Journal of Democracy* 32(2):61–76. https://doi.org/10.1353/jod.2021.0019.

Patomäki, Heikki, and Colin Wight. 2000. "After Postpositivism? The Promises of Critical Realism." *International Studies Quarterly* 44(2):213–37. https://doi.org/10.1111/0020-8833.00156.

Patriotic Front. 2011. *2011–2016 Manifesto*. Lusaka: Patriotic Front.

Pawson, Ray. 1996. "Theorizing the Interview." *The British Journal of Sociology* 47(2):295. https://doi.org/10.2307/591728.

Pearson, Margaret, Meg Rithmire, and Kellee S. Tsai. 2021. "Party-State Capitalism in China." *Current History* 120(827):207–13.

Peiffer, Caryn, and Pierre Englebert. 2012. "Extraversion, Vulnerability to Donors, and Political Liberalization in Africa." *African Affairs* 111(444):355–78. https://doi.org/10.1093/afraf/ads029.

Perelman, Michael. 2000. *The Invention of Capitalism: Classical Political Economy and the Secret History of Primitive Accumulation*. Durham, NC: Duke University Press.

Phiri, Chris. 2019. "AVIC Partially Resumes Kitwe Road Works." *Zambia Reports*. Retrieved May 31, 2019 (https://zambiareports.com/2019/05/06/avic-partially-resumes-kitwe-road-works/).

Phiri, Tobias. 2018. "African Govts Weak in Negotiations with China Because They Go Crawling to Beg—Mutati." *The Mast*. Retrieved July 17, 2019 (https://www.themastonline.com/2018/11/24/african-govts-weak-in-negotiations-with-china-because-they-go-crawling-to-beg-mutati/?fbclid=IwAR2mK4aUaTowwAMEhP0fpm071kiMFAZe-Rg6UaHyKRZiokZaaaUVhMD-nPg).

Pitcher, Anne, Mary H. Moran, and Michael Johnston. 2009. "Rethinking Patrimonialism and Neopatrimonialism in Africa." *African Studies Review* 52(1):125–56. https://doi.org/10.1353/arw.0.0163.

Polus, Andrzej, and Wojciech Tycholiz. 2018. "Gold, Gas and Lies: Extractive Sector in a Sub-Saharan Functional State. The Case of Natural Resource Sector in Tanzania." *Politeja* 15(56):151–68. https://doi.org/10.12797/politeja.15.2018.56.09.

Polus, Andrzej, and Wojciech Tycholiz. 2019. "David versus Goliath: Tanzania's Efforts to Stand up to Foreign Gas Corporations." *Africa Spectrum* 54(1):61–72. https://doi.org/10.1177/0002039719848507.

Poulantzas, Nicos. 1978. *State, Power, Socialism*. London: Verso.

Power, Marcus, Giles Mohan, and May Tan-Mullins. 2012. *China's Resource Diplomacy in Africa: Powering Development?* Basingstoke: Palgrave Macmillan.

Pratap, Kumar V., and Rajesh Chakrabarti. 2017. *Public-Private Partnerships in Infrastructure: Managing the Challenges*. Singapore: Springer Nature.

PwC. 2016. "Budget 2016: PwC Insight and Analysis." *PricewaterhouseCoopers Tanzania*. Retrieved February 29, 2020 (https://www.pwc.co.tz/assets/pdf/budget-2016-presentations.pdf).

PwC. 2017. "Budget 2017: PwC Insight and Analysis." *PricewaterhouseCoopers Tanzania*. Retrieved February 29, 2020 (https://www.pwc.co.tz/assets/pdf/budget-2017-presentation.pdf).

PwC. 2018. "Reimagine the Possible: Budget 2018/2019." *PricewaterhouseCoopers Tanzania*. Retrieved February 29, 2020 (https://www.pwc.co.tz/assets/pdf/2018-19-budget.pdf).

PwC. 2019. "Sustaining the Momentum National Budget Bulletin 2019/20." *PricewaterhouseCoopers Tanzania*. Retrieved February 29, 2020 (https://www.pwc.co.tz/assets/pdf/2019-2020-budget.pdf).

Raballand, Gaël, Kate Bridges, Monica Beuran, and Audrey Sacks. 2013. *Does the Semi-Autonomous Agency Model Function in a Low-Governance Environment? The Case of the Road Development Agency in Zambia*. Word Bank Policy Research Working Paper 6585. https://doi.org/10.1596/1813-9450-6585.

Railway Gazette. 2018. "TRC Returns as Vertical Separation Ends." *Railway Gazette*. Retrieved March 25, 2020 (https://www.railwaygazette.com/news/policy/single-view/view/trc-returns-as-vertical-separation-ends.html).

RDA. 2015a. "20 Percent Mandatory Sub-Contracting Guidelines." *Road Development Agency*. Retrieved March 25, 2020 (http://www.rda.org.zm/jdownloads/Publications/RDA/20/PERCENT/MANDATORY/SUB-CONTRACTING/GUIDELINES.pdf).

RDA. 2015b. *Request for Expression of Interest for Public-Private Partnerships for the Financing, Design, Construction to Dual Carriageway, Operation, Maintenance and Tolling of Selected Roads in Zambia*. Lusaka: Road Development Agency.

RDA. 2016a. *Request for Proposals (RFP) for Public Private Partnerships for the Financing, Design, Construction to Dual Carriageway, Operation, Maintenance and Tolling of Selected Roads in Zambia*. Lusaka: Road Development Agency.

RDA. 2016b. *Roads: January–March 2016*. Lusaka: Road Development Agency.

RDA. 2017. *Road Development Agency 2016: Annual Report*. Lusaka: Road Development Agency.

RDA. n.d.-a. "2016 Road Sector Annual Work Plan." *Road Development Agency*. Retrieved March 25, 2020 (http://www.rda.org.zm/jdownloads/Programmes/RSAWP/2016/final/Dec/31.pdf).

RDA. n.d.-b. *Link Zambia 8000: "Transforming Zambia into a Truly Landlinked Country."* Lusaka: Road Development Agency.

Resnick, Danielle E. 2017. "Populism in Africa." Pp. 101–20 in *The Oxford Handbook of Populism*, edited by C. Rovira Kaltwasser, P. Taggart, P. Choa Espejo, and P. Ostiguy. Oxford: Oxford University Press.

Rettman, Rosalyn J. 1973. "The TANZAM Rail Link: China's 'loss-Leader' in Africa." *World Affairs* 136(3):232–58.

Reuters. 2015. "Tanzania Awards $9 Bln Rail Projects to Chinese Companies." *Reuters*. Retrieved August 4, 2019 (https://www.reuters.com/article/tanzania-railways/tanzania-awards-9-bln-rail-projects-to-chinese-companies-idUSL5N0YM09H20150531).

Reuters. 2017. "Zambia Awards Chinese Firm $1.2 Billion Road Expansion Project." *Reuters*. Retrieved May 15, 2019 (https://www.reuters.com/article/us-zambia-road/zambia-awards-chinese-firm-1-2-billion-road-expansion-project-idUSKCN1BJ1OT).

Reuters. 2018. "Zambia Denies White House Claim China Taking over Power Utility." *Reuters*. Retrieved July 25, 2019 (https://www.reuters.com/article/us-zambia-economy/zambia-denies-white-house-claim-china-taking-over-power-utility-idUSKBN1OE0LD).

Reuters. 2019a. "Barrick Gold Reaches Deal with Tanzania over Acacia Mining." *Reuters*. Retrieved February 18, 2020 (https://www.reuters.com/article/us-barrick-gold-tanzania/barrick-gold-reaches-deal-with-tanzania-over-acacia-mining-idUSKBN1WZ0DL).

Reuters. 2019b. "Tanzania's China-Backed $10 Billion Port Plan Stalls over Terms: Official." *Reuters*. Retrieved July 26, 2019 (https://www.reuters.com/article/us-tanzania-port/tanzanias-china-backed-10-billion-port-plan-stalls-over-terms-official-idUSKCN1ST084).

Reuters. 2019c. "Zambia Infrastructure Minister Arrested on Corruption Charge." *Reuters*. Retrieved May 15, 2019 (https://www.reuters.com/article/us-zambia-corruption/zambia-infrastructure-minister-arrested-on-corruption-charge-idUSKCN1PU20G).

Reuters. 2020. "Zambia Signs over $824 Million Deal with China Railway for Line Upgrades." *Reuters*. Retrieved March 8, 2020 (https://uk.reuters.com/article/zambia-railways-idAFJ8N2AI007).

Roder, Kai. 2019. "'Bulldozer Politics', State-Making and (Neo-)Extractive Industries in Tanzania's Gold Mining Sector." *Extractive Industries and Society* 6(2):407–12. https://doi.org/10.1016/j.exis.2018.10.012.

Rosenberg, Justin. 2013. "The 'Philosophical Premises' of Uneven and Combined Development." *Review of International Studies* 39(3):569–97. https://doi.org/10.1017/S0260210512000381.

Saasa, Oliver S. 2018. *Pro-Growth Road Infrastructure Development in Zambia: Challenges, Opportunities and Policy Options*. Lusaka: Premier Consult Limited.

Sachs, Jeffrey D., John W. Mcarthur, Guido Schmidt-Traub, Margaret Kruk, Chandrika Bahadur, Michael Faye, and Gordon McCord. 2004. "Ending Africa's Poverty Trap." *Brookings Papers on Economic Activity* (1):117–240. https://doi.org/10.1353/eca.2004.0018.

Sandbrook, Richard, and Jay Oelbaum. 1997. "Reforming Dysfunctional Institutions through Democratisation? Reflections on Ghana." *Journal of Modern African* 35(4):603–46.

Sautman, Barry, and Yan Hairong. 2015. "Bashing 'the Chinese': Contextualizing Zambia's Collum Coal Mine Shooting." Pp. 138–57 in *China in Africa: Strategic Motives and Economic Interests*, edited by S. Zhao. Abingdon: Routledge.

Sayer, Andrew. 1992. *Method in Social Science: A Realist Approach*. London: Routledge.

Schindler, Seth, Ilias Alami, and Nicholas Jepson. 2023. "Goodbye Washington Confusion, Hello Wall Street Consensus: Contemporary State Capitalism and the Spatialisation of Industrial Strategy." *New Political Economy* 28(2):223–40. https://doi.org/10.1080/13563467.2022.2091534.

Schindler, Seth, and Jessica DiCarlo, eds. 2022. *The Rise of the Infrastructure State: How US–China Rivalry Shapes Politics and Place Worldwide*. Bristol: Bristol University Press.

Schindler, Seth, Jessica DiCarlo, and Dinesh Paudel. 2022. "The New Cold War and the Rise of the 21st-Century Infrastructure State." *Transactions of the Institute of British Geographers* 47(2):331–46. https://doi.org/10.1111/tran.12480.

Schindler, Seth, and J. Miguel Kanai. 2021. "Getting the Territory Right: Infrastructure-Led Development and the Re-Emergence of Spatial Planning Strategies." *Regional Studies* 55(1):40–51. https://doi.org/10.1080/00343404.2019.1661984.

Schlimmer, Sina. 2018. "Talking 'land Grabs' Is Talking Politics: Land as Politicised Rhetoric during Tanzania's 2015 Elections." *Journal of Eastern African Studies* 12(1):83–101. https://doi.org/10.1080/17531055.2017.1410757.

Schoenberger, Erica. 2004. "The Spatial Fix Revisited." *Antipode* 36(3):427–33. https://doi.org/10.1111/j.1467-8330.2004.00422.x.

Scholvin, Sören. 2016. *The Geopolitics of Regional Power: Geography, Economics and Politics in Southern Africa*. Abingdon: Routledge.

Schoneveld, George, Laura German, and Davison Gumbo. 2014. *The Developmental Implications of Sino-African Economic and Political Relations: A Preliminary Assessment for the Case of Zambia*. CIFOR Working Paper 133. Bogor: Center for International Forestry Research.

Schumpeter, Joseph A. 1943. *Capitalism, Socialism and Democracy*. London: George Allen & Unwin.

Scott, Guy. 2019. *Adventures in Zambian Politics: A Story in Black and White*. Boulder: Lynne Rienner.

Shangwe, Muhidin J. 2017. "China's Soft Power in Tanzania: Opportunities and Challenges." *China Quarterly of International Strategic Studies* 3(1):79–100. https://doi.org/10.1142/S2377740017500026.

Shaw, Timothy M. 1985. *Towards a Political Economy for Africa: The Dialectics of Dependence*. London: Macmillan Press.

Shendy, Riham, Zachary Kaplan, and Peter Mousley. 2011. *Toward Better Infrastructure: Conditions, Constraints, and Opportunities in Financing Public-Private Partnerships in Select African Countries*. Washington: World Bank.

Sheppard, Eric. 2004. "The Spatiality of the Limits to Capital." *Antipode* 36(3):470–79. https://doi.org/10.1111/j.1467-8330.2004.00426.x.

Sheppard, Eric. 2006. "David Harvey and Dialectical Space-Time." Pp. 121–41 in *David Harvey: A Critical Reader*, edited by N. Castree and D. Gregory. Malden: Blackwell Publishing.

Shivji, Issa G. 2009. *Accumulation in an African Periphery: A Theoretical Framework*. Dar es Salaam: Mkuki na Nyota Publishers.

Shivji, Issa G. 2017. "The Concept of 'Working People.'" *Agrarian South: Journal of Political Economy* 6(1):1–13. https://doi.org/10.1177/2277976017721318.

Shlyk, Alexander. 2009. *Performance of the Contractual Arrangements of Public-Private Partnerships: Case of Railway Concession in Tanzania*. Master thesis, Lund University.

Sigalla, Huruma Luhuvilo. 2014. "Changing Trends in the Tanzania–China Relationship: A Sociological Inquiry into the Mixed Perceptions of the Tanzania–China Relationship on the Eve of Globalization." *Osterreichische Zeitschrift Für Soziologie* 39(1):61–78. https://doi.org/10.1007/s11614-014-0118-6.

Simpson, John A., and Edmund S. C. Weiner, eds. 1989. *The Oxford English Dictionary*. 2nd edition. Oxford: Oxford University Press.

Simumba, Trevor. 2018. *He Who Pays The Piper: Zambia's Growing China Debt Crisis*. Lusaka: Centre for Trade Policy and Development.

Simutanyi, Neo. 1996. "The Politics of Structural Adjustment in Zambia." *Third World Quarterly* 17(4):825–39.

Sinyangwe, Chiwoyu. 2022. "Zambia Cancels $1.2bn Chinese Road Project Linking Lusaka and Ndola." *The Africa Report*. Retrieved June 29, 2023 (https://www.theafricareport.com/185538/zambia-cancels-1-2bn-chinese-road-project-linking-lusaka-and-ndola/).

Sishuwa, Sishuwa. 2019. "The Real Reasons Why Lungu Won't Fire Chitotela." *Lusaka Times*. Retrieved July 4, 2019 (https://www.lusakatimes.com/2019/02/12/the-real-reasons-why-lungu-wont-fire-chitotela/).

Sklar, Richard L. 1974. "Zambia's Response to the Rhodesian Unilateral Declaration of Independence." Pp. 320–62 in *Politics in Zambia*, edited by W. Tordoff. Berkeley: University of California Press.

Smith, Chris, and Tony Elger. 2014. "Critical Realism and Interviewing Subjects." Pp. 109–31 in *Studying Organizations Using Critical Realism: A Practical Guide*, edited by P. K. Edwards, J. O'Mahoney, and S. Vincent. Oxford: Oxford University Press.

Söderbaum, Fredrik. 2002. *The Political Economy of Regionalism in Southern Africa*. Göteborg: Department of Peace and Development Research Göteborg University.
Söderbaum, Fredrik. 2016. *Rethinking Regionalism*. London: Palgrave.
Soulé, Folashadé. 2020. "'Africa+1' Summit Diplomacy and the 'New Scramble' Narrative: Recentering African Agency." *African Affairs* 119(477):633–46. https://doi.org/10.1093/afraf/adaa015.
Soulé-Kohndou, Folashadé. 2019. "Bureaucratic Agency and Power Asymmetry in Benin-China Relations." Pp. 189–204 in *New Directions in Africa-China Studies*. Abingdon: Routledge.
State Council. 2021. "China and Africa in the New Era: A Partnership of Equals." *Ministry of Foreign Affairs of the People's Republic of China*. Retrieved March 2, 2022 (https://www.fmprc.gov.cn/mfa_eng/wjdt_665385/2649_665393/202111/t20211126_10453904.html).
Sum, Ngai-Ling. 2019. "The Intertwined Geopolitics and Geoeconomics of Hopes/ Fears: China's Triple Economic Bubbles and the 'One Belt One Road' Imaginary." *Territory, Politics, Governance* 7(4):528–52. https://doi.org/10.1080/21622671.2018.1523746.
Sum, Ngai-Ling, and Bob Jessop. 2013. *Towards a Cultural Political Economy: Putting Culture in Its Place*. Cheltenham: Edward Elgar.
Summers, Tim. 2016. "China's 'New Silk Roads': Sub-National Regions and Networks of Global Political Economy." *Third World Quarterly* 37(9):1628–43. https://doi.org/10.1080/01436597.2016.1153415.
Sun, Irene Yuan, Kartik Jayaram, and Omid Kassiri. 2017. *Dance of the Lions and Dragons: How Are Africa and China Engaging, and How Will the Partnership Evolve?* New York: McKinsey and Company.
Swanborn, Peter G. 2010. *Case Study Research: What, Why and How?* London: Sage Publications.
Szeftel, Morris. 1982. "Political Graft and the Spoils System in Zambia: The State as a Resource in Itself." *Review of African Political Economy* 9(24):4–21.
Szeftel, Morris. 2000. "'Eat with Us': Managing Corruption and Patronage under Zambia's Three Republics, 1964-99." *Journal of Contemporary African Studies* 18(2):207–24. https://doi.org/10.1080/713675624.
Tangri, Roger. 1998. "Politics, Capital and the State in Sub-Saharan Africa." *Commonwealth & Comparative Politics* 36(2):108–22.
Tanzania Invest. 2023. "SGR: Tanzania Standard Gauge Railway." *Tanzania Invest*. Retrieved July 14, 2023 (https://www.tanzaniainvest.com/sgr).
Taylor, Ian. 2006a. *China and Africa: Engagement and Compromise*. Abingdon: Routledge.
Taylor, Ian. 2006b. "China's Oil Diplomacy in Africa." *International Affairs* 82(5):937–59. https://doi.org/10.1111/j.1468-2346.2006.00579.x.

Taylor, Ian. 2007. "Governance in Africa and Sino-African Relations: Contradictions or Confluence?" *Politics* 27(3):139–46. https://doi.org/10.1111/j.1467-9256.2007.00293.x.

Taylor, Ian. 2009. *China's New Role in Africa*. Boulder: Lynne Rienner Publishers.

Taylor, Ian. 2010. *The International Relations of Sub-Saharan Africa*. New York: Continuum International.

Taylor, Ian. 2014. *Africa Rising? BRICS—Diversifying Dependency*. Woodbridge: James Currey.

Taylor, Ian. 2015. "The Good, the Bad, and the Ugly: Agency-as-Corruption and the Sino-Nigerian Relationship." Pp. 27–44 in *Africa and China: How Africans and their Governments are Shaping Relations with China*, edited by A. W. Gadzala. Lanham: Rowman & Littlefield.

Taylor, Ian. 2017. "Transnationalizing Capitalist Hegemony: A Poulantzian Reading." *Alternatives: Global, Local, Political* 42(1):26–40. https://doi.org/10.1177/0304375417732849.

Taylor, Ian. 2020. "Kenya's New Lunatic Express: The Standard Gauge Railway." *African Studies Quarterly* 19(3–4):29–52.

Taylor, Ian, and Paul D. Williams. 2008. "Political Culture, State Elites and Regional Security in West Africa." *Journal of Contemporary African Studies* 26(2):137–49. https://doi.org/10.1080/02589000802124797.

Taylor, Ian, and Tim Zajontz. 2020. "In a Fix: Africa's Place in the Belt and Road Initiative and the Reproduction of Dependency." *South African Journal of International Affairs* 27(3):277–295. https://doi.org/10.1080/10220461.2020.1830165.

Taylor, Scott D. 2006. "Divergent Politico-Legal Responses to Past Presidential Corruption in Zambia and Kenya: Catching the 'Big Fish', or Letting Him off the Hook?" *Third World Quarterly* 27(2):281–301. https://doi.org/10.1080/01436590500432325.

TAZARA. 2018. "Annual Report Confirms a Rebound, Upward Trend Continues." *TAZARA Newsletter* (April–June):6–7.

Tembo, Yohane. 2015. *A Look at Zambia's Road Financing Strategies: The Impact of Incongruent Policies and Budgets*. Hamburg: Anchor Academic Publishing.

The Citizen. 2016. "China to Take over Tazara in New Plan." *The Citizen*. Retrieved September 20, 2019 (https://www.thecitizen.co.tz/news/China-to-take-over-Tazara-in-new-plan/1840340-3205138-an93ljz/index.html).

The Citizen. 2017. "TZ-China Relations 'Not on a Free Fall.'" *The Citizen*. Retrieved August 7, 2019 (https://www.thecitizen.co.tz/magazine/politicalreforms/TZ-China-relations--not-on-a-free-fall-/1843776-3823236-iu13m1z/index.html).

The Citizen. 2019. "How the Dream for a Port in Bagamoyo Became Elusive." *The Citizen*. Retrieved July 26, 2019 (https://www.thecitizen.co.tz/news/1840340-5124384-8pdm7b/index.html).
The Mast. 2019. "TAZARA Workers down Tools over Salaries." *The Mast*. Retrieved March 25, 2020 (https://www.themastonline.com/2019/04/03/tazara-workers-down-tools-over-salaries/).
The Zambian Observer. 2017. "Mutati Throws the $1.2billion Lusaka-Ndola Dual Carriage Way into Funding Confusion." *The Zambian Observer*. Retrieved May 15, 2019 (https://www.zambianobserver.com/mutati-throws-the-1-2billion-lusaka-ndola-dual-carriage-way-into-funding-confusion/).
The Zambian Observer. 2018. "Cadreism a Source of Construction Sector Corruption in Zambia—TIZ." *The Zambian Observer*. Retrieved May 20, 2019 (https://www.zambianobserver.com/cadreism-a-source-of-construction-sector-corruption-in-zambia-tiz/).
The Zambian Observer. 2019. "Scope For Lusaka-Ndola Dual Carriage Was Irregularly Changed—Public Protector." *The Zambian Observer*. Retrieved June 29, 2019 (https://www.zambianobserver.com/scope-for-lusaka-ndola-dual-carriage-was-irregularly-changed-public-protector/).
Theobald, Robin. 1982. "Patrimonialism." *World Politics* 34(4):548–59.
Transparency International. n.d. "Corruption Perceptions Index." *Transparency International*. Retrieved February 20, 2020 (https://www.transparency.org/research/cpi/overview).
TSDI. 2016. *Renovation Project of Tanzania-Zambia Railway: Feasibility Study*. Tianjin: Third Railway Survey and Design Institute Group Corporation.
Tsubura, Machiko. 2018. "'Umoja Ni Ushindi (Unity Is Victory)': Management of Factionalism in the Presidential Nomination of Tanzania's Dominant Party in 2015." *Journal of Eastern African Studies* 12(1):63–82. https://doi.org/10.1080/17531055.2017.1410758.
UNDP. 1976. *A Profile of the Zambian Economy*. Lusaka: United Nations Development Program.
UNICEF and WHO. 2019. *Progress on Household Drinking Water, Sanitation and Hygiene: 2000–2017*. New York: nited Nations Children's Fund and World Health Organization.
van der Merwe, Justin. 2016. "Theorising Emerging Powers in Africa within the Western-Led System of Accumulation." Pp. 17–38 in *Emerging Powers in Africa: A New Wave in the Relationship?*, edited by J. Van der Merwe, I. Taylor, and A. Arkhangelskaya. Basingstoke: Palgrave Macmillan.
van der Merwe, Justin. 2019. "The One Belt One Road Initiative: Reintegrating Africa and the Middle East into China's System of Accumulation." Pp. 197–217 in *Mapping China's "One Belt One Road" Initiative*, edited by X. Li. Cham: Palgrave Macmillan.

Vhumbunu, Clayton Hazvinei. 2016. "Enabling African Regional Infrastructure Renaissance through the China-Africa Partnership: A Trans-Continental Appraisal." *International Journal of China Studies* 7(3):271–300.

Wagner, Maren. 2016. *Social Emergence in International Relations*. Palgrave Macmillan.

Wai, Zubairu. 2012. "Neo-Patrimonialism and the Discourse of State Failure in Africa." *Review of African Political Economy* 39(131):27–43. https://doi.org/10.1080/03056244.2012.658719.

Wambura, Bethsheba. 2022. "Private-Public Partnership Has Not Been Realized as Envisioned by Mkapa, Says Samia." *The Citizen*. Retrieved July 15, 2023 (https://www.thecitizen.co.tz/tanzania/news/national/private-public-partnership-has-not-been-realized-as-envisioned-by-mkapa-says-samia-3880726).

Wang, Lily. 2018. "Making the Chinese Standard Shine in Africa." *China's Foreign Trade* (5):32.

Wang, Yuan. 2022. "Executive Agency and State Capacity in Development: Comparing Sino-African Railways in Kenya and Ethiopia." *Comparative Politics* 54(2):349–73. https://doi.org/10.5129/001041522x16225661565091.

Wang, Yuan, and Uwe Wissenbach. 2019. "Clientelism at Work? A Case Study of Kenyan Standard Gauge Railway Project." *Economic History of Developing Regions* 34(3):280–99. https://doi.org/10.1080/20780389.2019.1678026.

Wanjala, Peter. 2022. "Chingola-Kasumbalesa Road Concession Agreement Signed, Zambia." *Construction Review*. Retrieved July 11, 2023 (https://constructionreviewonline.com/news/chingola-kasumbalesa-road-concession-agreement-signed-zambia/).

Watson, Matthew. 2005. *Foundations of International Political Economy*. Basingstoke: Palgrave Macmillan.

Weber, Max. 1978 [1922]. *Economy and Society: An Outline of Interpretative Sociology*, edited by G. Roth and C. Wittich. Berkley: University of California Press.

Weinland, Don. 2019. "China to Tackle Corruption in Belt and Road Projects." *Financial Times*. Retrieved March 14, 2020 (https://www.ft.com/content/a5815e66-a91b-11e9-984c-fac8325aaa04).

Wethal, Ulrikke. 2019. "Building Africa's Infrastructure: Reinstating History in Infrastructure Debates." *Forum for Development Studies* 46(3):473–99. https://doi.org/10.1080/08039410.2019.1616609.

Wheatley, Jonathan, and James Kynge. 2020. "China Curtails Overseas Lending in Face of Geopolitical Backlash." *Financial Times*. Retrieved December 18, 2020 (https://www.ft.com/edinburgh?ft-content-uuid=1cb3e33b-e2c2-4743-ae41-d3fffffa4259).

White House. 2023. "Remarks by President Biden and Prime Minister Rishi Sunak of the United Kingdom in Joint Press Conference." *The White House*.

Retrieved July 16, 2023 (https://www.whitehouse.gov/briefing-room/speeches-remarks/2023/06/08/remarks-by-president-biden-and-prime-minister-rishi-sunak-of-the-united-kingdom-in-joint-press-conference/).

van Wieringen, Kjeld, and Tim Zajontz. 2023. "From Loan-Financed to Privatised Infrastructure? Tracing China's Turn towards Public-Private Partnerships in Africa." *Journal of Current Chinese Affairs*, online first. https://doi.org/10.1177/18681026231188140.

Wight, Colin. 1999. "They Shoot Dead Horses Don't They? Locating Agency in the Agent-Structure Problematique." *European Journal of International Relations* 5(1):109–42. https://doi.org/10.1177/1354066199005001004 .

Wight, Colin. 2004a. "State Agency: Social Action without Human Activity?" *Review of International Studies* 30(2):269–80. https://doi.org/10.1017/S0260210504006060.

Wight, Colin. 2004b. "Theorizing the Mechanisms of Conceptual and Semiotic Space." *Philosophy of the Social Sciences* 34(2):283–99.

Wight, Colin. 2006. *Agents, Structures and International Relations: Politics as Ontology*. 2nd edition. Cambridge: Cambridge University Press.

Wight, Colin, and Jonathan Joseph. 2010. "Scientific Realism and International Relations." Pp. 1–30 in *Scientific Realism and International Relations*, edited by J. Joseph and C. Wight. Basingstoke: Palgrave Macmillan.

World Bank. 2000. *Report No. PID9176: Zambia-Railway Restructuring Project*. Washington: World Bank.

World Bank. 2005. *United Republic of Tanzania: Privatization Impact Assessment: Report No: 69628*. Washington: World Bank.

World Bank. 2010. *Implementation Completion and Results Report (IDA-33040 & IDA-3304A; P0498838): Report No: ICR00001459*. Washington: World Bank.

World Bank. 2013. *Opening the Gates: How the Port of Dar Es Salaam Can Transform Tanzania*. Tanzania Economic Update. Dar es Salaam: World Bank.

World Bank. 2014. *International Development Association: Project Appraisal Document on a Proposed Credit: Report No: 78925-TZ*. Washington: World Bank.

World Bank. 2020. "Concessions, Build-Operate-Transfer (BOT) and Design-Build-Operate (DBO) Projects." *Public-Private Partnership Legal Resource Center*. Retrieved June 17, 2021 (https://ppp.worldbank.org/public-private-partnership/agreements/concessions-bots-dbos).

World Bank. n.d.-a. "Access to Electricity (% of Population)." Retrieved July 15, 2023 (https://data.worldbank.org/indicator/EG.ELC.ACCS.ZS).

World Bank. n.d.-b. "PPP Contract Types and Terminology." *PPP Knowledge Lab*. Retrieved September 15, 2019 (https://pppknowledgelab.org/guide/sections/6-ppp-contract-types-and-terminology#table-3).

World Bank. n.d.-c. "Tanzania." *World Bank Public Documents*. Retrieved February 21, 2020 (https://pubdocs.worldbank.org/en/278341492207296350/data-tza.pdf).

World Bank. n.d.-d. "Zambia." *World Bank Public Documents*. Retrieved February 21, 2020 (https://pubdocs.worldbank.org/en/359911492207299026/data-zmb.pdf).

Wylde, Christopher. 2017. *Emerging Markets and the State: Developmentalism in the 21st Century*. London: Palgrave Macmillan.

Xinhua. 2020. "Standard Chartered Bank, Tanzania Sign Facility Agreement for SGR Project." *XinhuaNet*. Retrieved February 26, 2020 (http://www.xinhuanet.com/english/2020-02/14/c_138781409.htm).

Yalvaç, Faruk. 2010. "Critical Realism, International Relations Theory and Marxism." Pp. 167–185 in *Scientific Realism and International Relations*, edited by J. Joseph and C. Wight. Basingstoke: Palgrave Macmillan.

Yan, Karl. 2021. "The Railroad Economic Belt: Grand Strategy, Economic Statecraft, and a New Type of International Relations." *British Journal of Politics and International Relations* 23(2):262–79. https://doi.org/10.1177/1369148120940938.

Yescombe, E. R. 2007. *Public-Private Partnerships: Principles of Policy and Finance*. Oxford: Butterworth-Heinemann.

Yescombe, E. R., and Edward Farquharson. 2018. *Public-Private Partnerships for Infrastructure: Principles of Policy and Finance*. 2nd edition. Oxford: Butterworth-Heinemann.

Yeung, Henry Wai-chung. 2010. "Critical Realism and Realist Research in Human Geography: A Method or a Philosophy in Search of a Method?" Pp. 325–54 in *Realist Methodology Volume I: Practical Realist Ontology*, edited by W. Olsen. London: Sage Publications.

Yu, George T. 1971. "Working on the Railroad: China and the Tanzania-Zambia Railway." *Asian Survey* 11(11):1101–17.

Zajontz, Tim. 2021. "Infrastructure." Pp. 127–47 in *Yearbook on the African Union*. Vol. 1, edited by U. Engel. Leiden: Brill.

Zajontz, Tim. 2022a. "Debt, Distress, Dispossession: Towards a Critical Political Economy of Africa's Financial Dependency." *Review of African Political Economy* 49(171):173–83. https://doi.org/10.1080/03056244.2021.1950669.

Zajontz, Tim. 2022b. "Infrastructure." Pp. 120–38 in *Yearbook on the African Union*. Vol. 2. Leiden: Brill.

Zajontz, Tim. 2022c. "Railway Imperialisms in East Africa: Laying the Tracks for Exploitation." Pp. 515–34 in *Oxford Handbook of Economic Imperialism*, edited by Z. Cope and I. Ness. Oxford: Oxford University Press.

Zajontz, Tim. 2022d. "Tanzania and Zambia Want to Upgrade the 'Uhuru Railway'—But Can They?" *The Conversation*. Retrieved June

22, 2023 (https://theconversation.com/tanzania-and-zambia-want-to-upgrade-the-uhuru-railway-but-can-they-190659).
Zajontz, Tim. 2022e. "The Chinese Infrastructural Fix in Africa: Lessons from the Sino-Zambian 'Road Bonanza.'" *Oxford Development Studies* 50(1):14–29. https://doi.org/10.1080/13600818.2020.1861230.
Zajontz, Tim. 2022f. "'Win-Win' Contested: Negotiating the Privatisation of Africa's Freedom Railway with the 'Chinese of Today.'" *Journal of Modern African Studies* 60(1):111–34. https://doi.org/10.1017/S0022278X21000446.
Zajontz, Tim. 2024a. "Chinese Globalism, African Regionalisms and State Spatial Strategies: The Intricacies of Regionalising Africa's Railway Renaissance." Pp. 112–36 in *Africa's Railway Renaissance: The role and impact of China*, edited by T. Zajontz, P. Carmody, M. Bagwandeen, and A. Leysens. Abingdon: Routledge.
Zajontz, Tim. 2024b. "The Political Economy of China's Globalising Railways – And their Arrival in Africa." Pp. 26–48 in *Africa's Railway Renaissance: The role and impact of China*, edited by T. Zajontz, P. Carmody, M. Bagwandeen, and A. Leysens. Abingdon: Routledge.
Zajontz, Tim, and Mandira Bagwandeen. 2023. "Infrastructure." Pp. 134–58 in *Yearbook on the African Union*. Vol. 3, edited by U. Engel. Leiden: Brill.
Zajontz, Tim, Pádraig Carmody, Mandira Bagwandeen, and Anthony Leysens. 2024. "Introduction: China's Role in Africa's Railway Renaissance." Pp. 1–25 in *Africa's Railway Renaissance: The Role and Impact of China*, edited by T. Zajontz, P. Carmody, M. Bagwandeen, and A. Leysens. Abingdon: Routledge.
Zajontz, Tim, and Ian Taylor. 2021. "Capitalism and Africa's (Infra)Structural Dependency: A Story of Spatial Fixes and Accumulation by Dispossession." Pp. 190–213 in *Africa and the Global System of Capital Accumulation*, edited by A. D. Cooper and E. Oritsejafor. Abingdon: Routledge.
ZDA. 2014. "Public-Private-Partnerships in Infrastructure Development in Zambia." *Zambia Development Agency*. Retrieved March 25, 2020 (http://www.zda.org.zm/?q=download/file/fid/60www.zda.org.zm/?q=content/zambia-triple-power-generation-two-years-solar).
Zhang, Hong. 2023. *From Contractors to Investors? Evolving Engagement of Chinese State Capital in Global Infrastructure Development and the Case of Lekki Port in Nigeria*. China Africa Research Initiative Working Paper No. 53. Washington: Johns Hopkins University.
Zhang, Xin. 2017. "Chinese Capitalism and the Maritime Silk Road: A World-Systems Perspective." *Geopolitics* 22(2):310–31. https://doi.org/10.1080/14650045.2017.1289371.
Zhao, Suisheng. 2011. "China's African Relations and the Balance with Western Powers." Pp. 61–80 in *China and the European Union in Africa*, edited by J. Men and B. Barton. Farnham: Ashgate.

Zhuawu, Collin. 2012a. *Engaging Africa in a Changing International Political Economy: Mauritius' Activism and Co-Operation in the World Trade Organisation (WTO)*. PhD dissertation, University of Birmingham.
Zhuawu, Collin. 2012b. "Reconceptualising the African State in the Strategic Relational Approach: A Case of Mauritius State and Trade Policy-Making." *African Journal of Political Science and International Relations* 6(7):130–41. https://doi.org/10.5897/ajpsir11.134.
Zhuawu, Collin. 2013. *Applying the Strategic Relational Approach to African States: A Case of Mauritius and Trade Policymaking*. South African Institute of International Affairs Occasional Paper No. 147.
ZIPAR. 2019. *Nurturing the Seeds of Humanity: Analysis of the 2020 National Budget*. Lusaka: Zambia Institute for Policy Analysis and Research.
Ziso, Edson. 2018. *A Post State-Centric Analysis of China-Africa Relations: Internationalisation of Chinese Capital and State-Society Relations in Ethiopia*. Cham: Palgrave Macmillan.
ZNBC. 2023. "Chingola-Mutanda Dual Carriage Road Works on Cards." *ZNBC News*. Retrieved July 11, 2023 (https://www.znbc.co.zm/news/139507-2/).

Index

A
abduction, 20–22
abstraction, 15, 18–21, 25, 28, 44, 45, 61, 78, 93, 267
accumulation by dispossession, 16, 28, 44, 50, 51, 53, 54, 63, 64, 80, 82, 84, 97, 100, 132, 141, 180, 196, 212, 223, 271, 272
Africa-China studies, 12, 13, 76, 82, 85
African Development Bank (AfDB), 2, 116, 122, 132, 134, 135, 139, 167
African Union (AU), 3, 275
agency
  African agency, 4, 11–16, 23, 74, 85, 95, 98, 269, 276
  'African agency turn', 12, 13, 74, 95
  elite agency, 9, 28, 72, 74, 75, 89, 269
  state agency, 4, 9, 13–16, 28, 62, 72, 89, 112, 161, 166, 177, 185, 221, 222, 268, 270, 273
  structure-agency, 15, 16, 21, 85–88, 113
  voluntarist conceptions of agency, 85
'all-weather friendship', 111, 119
Arrighi, Giovanni, 45, 46, 51, 53, 55, 60
  Adam Smith in Beijing, 55
  The Long Twentieth Century, 60
Arusha Declaration, 167
Asian Infrastructure Investment Bank, 57
authoritarianism, 75, 164, 169, 237, 270
autocratic, 138, 153, 160, 165, 171, 185, 186, 269, 270
Aviation Industry Corporation of China (AVIC), 202, 203, 216, 217, 240, 251, 253

T. Zajontz, *The Political Economy of China's Infrastructure Development in Africa*, International Political Economy Series,
https://doi.org/10.1007/978-3-031-44449-4

B

Bagamoyo, 15, 20, 153, 178, 180, 185, 270
Belt and Road Initiative (BRI), 1–4, 7–9, 52, 56, 57, 59, 71, 97, 125, 141, 156, 169, 178, 205, 207, 213, 222, 271, 273–275
Bhaskar, Roy, 17, 18, 93
bidding
  competitive bidding, 201, 203, 240, 252
  non-competitive bidding, 246, 249
Biden, Joe, 4, 5, 271, 273
Blinken, Antony, 273
Brautigam, Deborah, 5, 23, 52, 96, 97, 131, 198, 204, 207, 214, 215, 222, 238, 272
Breslin, Shaun, 2, 4
BRICS grouping, 275
  BRICS New Development Bank, 57
Build-Operate-Transfer (BOT), 133, 179, 212, 214, 254, 255, 272
bureaucratic, 14, 28, 72, 76–78, 82, 84, 91, 185, 203, 235, 236, 241, 249, 254, 257, 269

C

Calabash Freight, 131, 175
capital
  capital accumulation, 17, 28, 43, 44, 46–48, 50, 51, 53, 64, 72, 80–85, 90, 101, 239, 271
  capitalist class, 81, 84
  Chinese capital, 4, 7, 8, 11, 14, 16, 23, 29, 43, 45, 58, 75, 81, 94, 97, 99, 100, 112, 125, 141, 212, 215, 221, 239, 241, 242, 246, 257–259, 267–269, 274
  surplus capital, 5, 8, 43, 47, 49, 50, 53, 54, 56, 61, 63, 64, 124, 132, 197, 269
Carmody, Pádraig, 12, 73–75, 81, 85, 95, 96, 98
Central Corridor, 181
Chama cha Demokrasia na Maendeleo (CHADEMA), 162
Chama cha Mapinduzi (CCM), 161–163, 165, 178, 185
China Civil Engineering Construction Corporation (CCECC), 120, 127, 128, 140, 151, 158, 181, 182, 184
China Development Bank, 8, 59, 203, 207
China Exim Bank, 8, 59, 182, 206, 217
China Henan Corporation, 203
China Jiangxi Corporation for International Economic and Technical Cooperation (CJIC), 217, 250, 252, 254–256
China Merchants Holdings International (CMHI), 178–180
China Railway, 128
China Railway Construction Corporation (CRCC), 119, 128, 184
China Railway Engineering Corporation (CREC), 119
China Railway Expert Team (CRET), 120, 173, 174
China Railway Rolling Stock Corporation (CRRC), 128
China Railway Seventh Group, 215, 217, 251
Chinese Communist Party, 2, 7
Chinese policy banks, 4, 8, 155
Chinese State Council, 1
Chitotela, Ronald Kaoma, 247, 252–255
class
  capitalist class, 81, 84
  class structure, 61, 81, 236

political class, 235
rentier class, 81, 237, 239
clientelism, 79, 81, 235, 237
clientelistic networks, 122, 161, 162, 165, 177, 178, 185, 241, 246, 258, 268
colonialism, 2, 3, 10, 23, 27, 51, 63, 100, 113, 115, 117, 235, 271
colonial state, 10
commodification, 10, 23, 29, 51, 53, 54, 63, 97, 217, 219, 223, 268, 271
Common Framework, 6, 97, 223
comprador class, 82
concession
concession-based PPP, 153, 159, 172, 184, 214, 259
railway concession, 113, 132, 133
tax concession, 129, 132
connectivity, 1, 2, 4, 8, 9, 56, 197, 273
contractor facilitated initiative (CFI), 213, 214, 255, 256
copper
Copper Belt, 114, 195, 202, 214, 215
Zambia Consolidated Copper Mines (ZCCM), 122, 209
corridor
Beira corridor, 140, 215
Central corridor, 181
Dar es Salaam corridor, 120, 122
Lobito corridor, 115
Nacala corridor, 158
Northern corridor, 275
Southern corridor, 139
TAZARA corridor, 24, 141
corruption, 12, 72, 76, 79, 81, 100, 157, 162, 236, 239, 253, 274
anti-corruption, 73, 161–163, 178, 181, 269, 274
Anti-corruption Commission, 253
critical realism, 17

D

Dar es Salaam, 24, 28, 113, 115, 122, 123, 166, 176–178, 182, 249
debt
Chinese-owned debt, 5, 273
commercial debt, 207
concessional debt, 208
debt crisis, 132, 196, 204, 206, 215
debt dependency, 6, 12, 96, 97
debt distress, 54, 183, 274
debt finance, 50, 59, 222, 258, 268
debt-for-equity swap, 5
debt sustainability, 9, 16, 59, 131, 214, 222, 250, 274, 275
'debt trap', 4, 5, 207, 213, 271
loan-debt investment, 8, 57, 58, 180, 182, 207, 221, 257, 272
sovereign debt, 4, 6, 52–54, 59, 96, 121, 131, 140, 142, 152, 157, 185, 212, 215, 221–223
Democratic Republic of Congo (DRC), 4, 5, 24, 139, 141, 158, 214, 216, 275
dependency, 75, 84, 88, 96, 98, 99, 140, 157, 182
debt dependency, 6, 12, 96, 97
devaluation, 29, 52, 53, 112, 120, 121, 123, 141, 161, 177, 186, 222, 276
developmentalism, 2, 130, 161, 163, 165, 169, 180, 184, 210, 218
autocratic developmentalism, 160, 171, 186, 270
developmental state, 140, 165, 166
autocratic developmental state, 138, 153, 160, 270
developmentalist state model, 165
'development-through-infrastructure', 29, 152, 196, 204, 211, 215, 222, 241, 268

Djibouti, 52, 59

E
East Africa, 8, 58
economic liberalisation, 236, 237
economic nationalism, 53, 138, 153, 160, 164, 166, 171, 185, 186
Engel, Ulf, 77–79, 91
Engineering-Procurement-Construction (EPC), 2, 131, 212, 271
 Engineering-Procurement-Construction+Finance (EPC+F), 158, 213, 251, 252, 254–257, 272
Erdmann, Gero, 77–79, 91
Ethiopia, 48, 59, 75, 81, 99, 119, 181
Eurobond, 206–208
expanded reproduction, 50, 51, 63, 64, 80, 84, 97, 180, 223, 271
extraversion, 75, 239

F
feasibility, 16, 126, 127, 129, 131, 136, 140, 170, 203, 221, 274
finance capital, 51
Forum on China-Africa Cooperation (FOCAC), 1, 2, 271, 274, 275
Freedom Railway, 54, 112, 113, 117, 169, 186

G
geoeconomics, 113, 114, 273
geopolitics, 5, 8, 113, 273
global financial crisis, 11, 52, 55, 56, 125, 205, 210
Global Gateway, 273
Global South, 4–6, 197, 273
'going out' policy, 7, 238
governance
 financial governance, 9, 29, 59, 131, 141, 157, 196, 208, 213, 217, 222, 250, 259, 272
 financial governance of the Belt and Road Initiative (BRI), 9, 59, 141, 213, 222
 geogovernance, 73
 multi-scalar governance, 97
 neopatrimonial governance, 73, 75, 78, 80, 81, 83, 84, 99, 140, 152, 234, 244, 254
Group of 7 (G7), 273
Group of 20 (G20), 6

H
Harvey, David, 8, 16, 17, 20, 21, 28, 43–54, 58–63, 65, 71, 84, 85, 96, 97, 123, 125, 132, 141, 157, 186, 202, 212, 221, 223, 267, 268, 271, 274
 The Limits to Capital, 44, 45
 The New Imperialism, 45, 50, 63
Hassan, Samia Suluhu, 131, 132, 185, 186, 270
Hay, Colin, 15, 16, 86–91, 94, 142, 234
He, Yafei, 56, 57
Hichilema, Hakainde, 131, 142, 185, 216

I
imperialism, 16, 50, 51, 60–64, 84, 117, 118, 180
independence, 10, 100, 111, 113, 114, 116, 118, 167, 235
information and communication technology (ICT), 2, 3, 58, 273
infrastructural fix, 17, 21, 23, 28, 29, 44, 54, 58, 62, 64, 65, 71, 95–100, 112, 120, 126, 131,

132, 134, 141, 166, 169, 184–186, 196, 201, 212, 222, 223, 233, 234, 241, 242, 257, 259, 268, 269, 271, 272, 274–276

infrastructure
- infrastructure bilateralism, 275
- infrastructure boom, 6, 43, 99, 241, 267
- infrastructure-led development, 4, 11, 52, 197, 205
- infrastructure nationalism, 161, 169, 175
- privatisation of infrastructure, 10, 82, 208, 217, 254
- public infrastructure, 71, 97, 121, 165, 209, 212, 216
- road infrastructure, 115, 171, 195, 208, 211, 217, 258
- transport infrastructure, 3, 54, 113, 116, 130, 152, 195, 197, 250, 256

infrastructure funding gap, 2, 58, 210, 218

infrastructure state, 7, 9–11, 21, 71, 93–95, 99
- nationalist infrastructure state, 29, 142, 166, 169, 171, 180, 184, 185, 270
- neopatrimonial infrastructure state, 234, 239, 244, 249, 257

international financial institutions (IFIs), 3, 11, 51, 134, 244

International Monetary Fund (IMF), 6, 97, 121, 142, 167, 204, 208, 222, 223, 272

International Political Economy (IPE), 13, 89

International Relations (IR), 13, 16, 75, 89

investment
- equity investment, 9, 57, 125, 141, 160, 186, 212, 215, 217, 222, 259, 272
- foreign direct investment (FDI), 54, 81, 163, 166, 209
- loan-debt investment, 8, 57, 58, 180, 182, 207, 221, 257, 272

J

Jessop, Bob, 15–19, 21, 28, 43, 46–49, 51, 52, 61, 62, 65, 81, 83, 86–100, 112, 113, 132, 142, 233, 234, 268, 270, 274, 275

K

Kakubo, Stanley Kasongo, 219, 220

Kaunda, Kenneth, 111, 113, 116

Kenya, 5, 48, 59, 181, 273, 275

Kijazi, John, 127, 171

Kikwete, Jakaya, 161–163, 165, 167, 168, 171, 176–178

Kragelund, Peter, 12, 74, 85, 95, 96, 98

L

Li, Keqiang, 55

Link Zambia 8000 programme, 196, 237

loans
- Chinese loan financing, 4, 29, 58, 59, 98, 196, 200, 201, 221, 239, 240, 259, 268
- commercial loans, 57, 203, 207
- concessional loans, 23, 198, 201–203
- export credit offer, 202
- loan-debt investment, 8, 57, 58, 180, 182, 207, 221, 257, 272
- loan finance, 4, 29, 53, 57–59, 158, 167, 272

Lobito corridor, 115
local content, 29, 174, 241, 242, 244, 245, 248, 249, 268
Lungu, Edgar Chagwa, 15, 153, 201, 205, 215, 221, 234, 236–238, 246–248, 253
Lusaka, 24, 52, 132, 140, 142, 152, 157, 195, 197, 211, 214, 215, 238
  Lusaka 400 programme, 199, 202, 240
Lusaka-Ndola dual carriageway, 15, 20, 23, 29, 201, 216, 234, 240, 249–251, 253–258, 269, 272
Lusinde, Job, 111, 122, 130, 171, 175
Luxemburg, Rosa, 50, 51, 85
Lu, Youqing, 55, 125

M
Macro Ocean Investment, 216, 251, 257
Magufuli, John Pombe, 15, 28, 29, 53, 73, 113, 130, 135–138, 142, 153, 154, 158, 160–167, 169–186, 269, 270
Mao, Zedong, 111
Marx, Karl, 18, 19, 43–46, 50, 51
  Grundrisse, 43
minying qiye, 247
Mkandawire, Thandika, 76, 81, 84, 85
Monson, Jamie, 23, 115–118, 121, 125, 130
Movement for Multi-Party Democracy (MMD), 196, 204, 206, 236
'moving out' strategy, 5, 56, 58, 125, 197, 258, 275
Msiska, Roland, 127
Mushimba, Brian, 140, 155–158
Mutati, Felix, 200, 201, 206, 253, 255
Mwanakatwe, Margaret, 206, 208, 211
Mwanawasa, Levy, 200, 204, 236

N
neoliberalism, 7, 10, 11, 53, 83, 209–211, 271
neopatrimonialism, 28, 72, 74–79, 81, 83–85, 89, 160, 270
  neopatrimonial governance, 73, 75, 78, 80, 81, 84, 152, 244, 254
  neopatrimonial mode of governance, 83, 99, 140, 234
  neopatrimonial state, 29, 76, 78, 83, 84, 91, 99, 100, 235, 236, 238, 268, 269
Ng'andu, Bwalya, 206, 208, 251
'not so public' procurement, 29, 233, 235, 238–241, 248, 249, 251, 253, 257–259, 268, 269, 274
Nyerere, Julius, 111, 116, 117, 119

O
ontology, 4, 11, 15, 17, 19, 24, 72, 89
overaccumulation, 7, 16, 44–47, 49, 54, 55, 58, 60, 62, 64, 94, 98, 182, 197, 242, 267

P
Paris Club creditors, 6
Partnership for Global Infrastructure and Investment (PGII), 273
party cadres, 235, 245, 249
path dependency, 92
patrimonialism, 28, 72, 73, 75, 77–80, 82–84, 91, 100, 178, 233, 235, 236, 244, 248, 249, 257–259, 269

Patriotic Front (PF), 156, 196, 204, 207, 210, 216, 237, 238, 259
PF cadres, 248
PF-led government, 197, 205, 207, 211, 218, 222, 223, 237, 244, 249, 251
patronage, 72, 76, 79, 81, 100, 235–237
port
Bagamoyo port, 15, 153, 178, 180, 185, 270
Dar es Salaam port, 122, 123, 177
mega-port, 20, 178
post-colonial, 10, 63, 83, 116
Poulantzas, Nicos, 90
primitive accumulation, 50, 84
privatisation, 6, 10, 16, 20, 23, 29, 51, 53, 54, 71, 80, 82, 97, 112, 121, 125, 129, 131–134, 137–139, 142, 151–153, 157, 160, 171, 184, 196, 208–211, 217, 222, 223, 237, 254, 259, 268–272, 274
procurement, 23, 29, 80, 100, 136, 161, 167, 174, 183, 196, 202, 203, 221, 234, 237, 240, 242, 244, 274, 275
'not so public' procurement, 29, 233, 235, 238–241, 248, 249, 251, 253, 257–259, 268, 269, 274
public procurement, 166, 167, 181, 185, 201, 240, 244–246, 248, 257, 269
project finance, 29, 59, 196, 208, 209, 211–215, 217, 222, 234, 250, 254–258, 268, 269, 271, 272
public-private partnership (PPP), 16, 127, 132, 134, 136, 138, 140–142, 153, 158–160, 208–211, 215, 216, 240, 251, 255–257, 269, 271
PPP Act, 209–211

R

Rail India Technical and Economic Services (RITES), 132, 134, 135
railway
Benguela Railway, 115
Freedom Railway, 54, 112, 113, 117, 169, 186
railway concession, 113, 132, 133
railway privatisation, 10, 29, 132, 133, 138, 142, 151, 157, 184, 269
Standard Gauge Railway, 15, 20, 48, 181, 183
Tanzania-Zambia Railway, 10, 111, 126, 129, 140
Railway Systems of Zambia (RSZ), 138, 139, 153, 157
reductionism, 11, 13, 15–17, 72, 74, 76, 77, 85, 88, 89, 160
regional economic community (REC), 9, 275, 276
Rehabilitate-Operate-Transfer (ROT), 127, 128, 131–133, 141, 153, 269
reification, 65, 81, 89
Reli Assets Holding Company (RAHCO), 134, 135
rent-seeking, 72, 73, 79, 80, 100, 239, 245, 246, 248
resource nationalism, 163
retroduction, 20, 21
Rhodesia, 113–116
unilateral declaration of independence (UDI) of Rhodesia, 115
road
Chingola-Kasumbalesa road, 216
Chingola-Solwezi road, 199, 215

Lusaka-Ndola road, 251, 253, 256
road development, 196–198, 203, 205, 214, 217, 220, 222, 234, 255, 259
Road Development Agency (RDA), 197
Road Development Agency (RDA), 196, 203, 213–216, 218, 220, 221, 244–246, 251–253, 256
road infrastructure, 115, 171, 195, 208, 211, 217, 258
road toll(ing), 196, 217, 218, 222, 255
trunk road, 23, 115, 214, 217, 221, 249, 268, 271

S

Sata, Michael, 139, 176, 178, 196, 205, 210, 218, 221, 237, 238, 244, 253
Scott, Guy, 117, 122, 178, 201
Second Cold War, 273
Shivji, Issa, 50, 64, 80, 82–85, 130, 180, 212, 236
South Africa, 113, 116, 138, 139
Southern Africa, 58, 100, 111, 113, 114
sovereign debt, 4, 54, 59, 96, 121, 131, 140, 142, 152, 157, 185, 215, 221, 223
sovereign debt crisis, 6, 52, 53, 215, 222
spatio-temporal fix, 16, 17, 20–23, 26, 28, 29, 43–54, 57, 60–65, 71, 72, 93–97, 100, 125, 141, 157, 195, 212, 221, 233, 241, 242, 249, 267, 268, 275
infrastructural fix, 17, 21, 23, 28, 29, 44, 54, 58, 62, 64, 65, 71, 95–100, 112, 120, 126, 131, 132, 134, 141, 166, 169, 184–186, 196, 201, 212, 222, 223, 233, 234, 241, 242, 257, 259, 268, 269, 271, 272, 274–276
spatial fix, 8, 44, 49, 51, 52, 202
Special Economic Zone (SEZ), 178, 185
Bagamoyo SEZ, 178
Special purpose vehicle (SPV), 215, 217
Spoornet, 138, 139
Standard Gauge Railway (SGR), 15, 119, 135, 178, 182, 184–186, 270, 275
in Kenya, 275
in Tanzania, 153, 179, 181–183
state agency, 4, 9, 13–16, 28, 62, 72, 89, 112, 161, 166, 177, 185, 221, 222, 268, 270, 273
state capital, 170
statehood, 72, 78, 88
state-owned bank (SOB), 23, 52, 58, 202
state-owned enterprise (SOE), 2, 23, 122, 135, 215, 237, 258
state power, 14, 51, 64, 89–93, 98, 178, 215, 233, 235, 237, 268
state theory, 17, 21, 28, 44, 65, 71, 83, 88, 89, 99
neo-Marxian state theory, 81, 90
stimulus package, 55, 57, 125
strategic-relational approach (SRA), 15, 16, 21, 28, 29, 72, 85–96, 98, 101, 152, 178, 268
strategy, 43, 57, 86–88, 91, 125, 135, 136, 138, 140, 153, 160, 165, 168, 171, 186, 196, 208, 211, 215, 221, 222, 241, 257, 259, 268, 270
strategic learning, 113, 134, 142, 184, 269
strategic selectivity, 86, 87, 91, 92, 95, 97, 99, 134, 159, 244, 270

structural adjustment programme, 10, 121, 209
structuralism, 14, 16, 85
structure-agency, 15, 16, 21, 87, 88
structure-agency dialectics, 16, 85, 113
structure-agency dualism, 86
subcontracting, 244–249, 258
20 per cent subcontracting policy, 233, 241, 248
supply chain, 56, 241, 242
surplus capital, 5, 8, 43, 47, 49, 50, 53, 54, 56, 58, 63, 64, 94, 112, 125, 132, 141, 197, 212, 215, 259, 269

T
Tanzania China Friendship Promotion Association (TCFPA), 170, 171
Tanzania Ports Authority (TPA), 179, 180
Tanzania Railways Corporation (TRC), 134, 135, 137
Tanzania Railways Limited (TRL), 134, 135, 137, 171
Tanzania-Zambia Railway, 10, 111, 126, 129, 140
Tanzania-Zambia Railway Authority (TAZARA), 15, 20, 21, 23, 24, 29, 97, 100, 112, 113, 116–131, 133, 137, 139–142, 151, 152, 157, 160, 169, 170, 172, 174, 179, 267, 269, 270
TAZARA corridor, 24, 141
'TAZARA spirit', 112, 140
Taylor, Ian, 6, 7, 10, 23, 48, 55, 56, 58, 71–73, 79, 125, 238, 242, 275
Third Railway Survey and Design Institute Group Corporation (TSDI), 126–129, 170
tolling, 159, 196, 214, 217–222, 251, 252, 254–256, 271
Transnet, 132, 138
transparency, 2, 209, 219, 254

U
United Party for National Development (UPND), 216, 219, 223, 251, 257

V
value chain, 11, 197, 241, 243, 258, 273

W
Wang, Yi, 5, 10, 119, 238, 275
Weber, Max, 77, 78
'win-win' cooperation, 2, 3, 100, 169, 186, 249
World Bank, 2, 3, 116, 121, 122, 127, 134, 135, 138, 157, 167, 201, 203, 204, 206, 209, 210, 252
International Finance Corporation, 134

X
Xi, Jinping, 55, 178, 238

Y
Yapı Merkezi, 182

Z
Zambia Consolidated Copper Mines (ZCCM), 122, 209
Zambia Development Agency (ZDA), 209–211, 214

Zambia Railways Limited (ZRL), 134, 138–140, 152, 153, 155
Zhenjiang Communications Construction Group, 217, 251
Zhou, Enlai, 118
Ziso, Edson, 14, 74, 75, 81, 99

Milton Keynes UK
Ingram Content Group UK Ltd.
UKHW022359041223
433798UK00006B/293

9 783031 444487